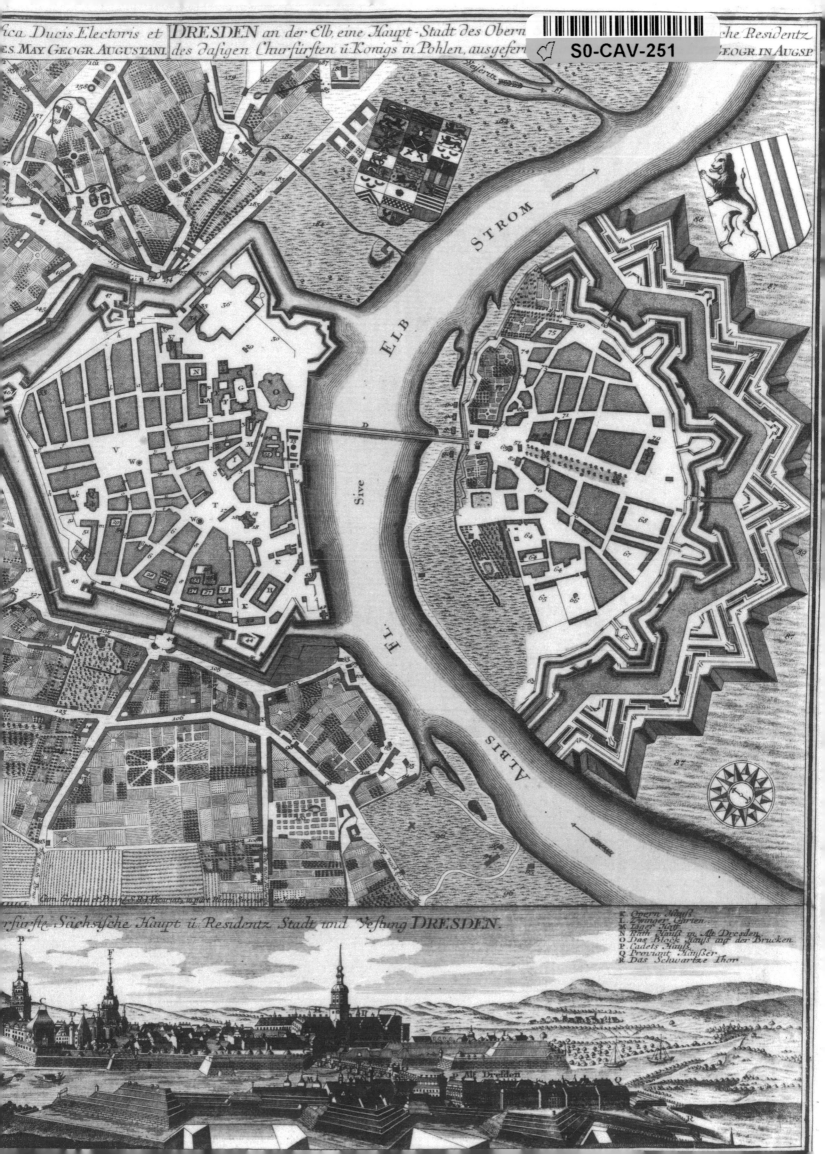

...ica Ducis Electoris et DRESDEN an der Elb, eine Haupt-Stadt des Ober... ...che Residentz
...S. MAY. GEOGR. AUGUSTANI. des dasigen Churfürsten u. Königs in Pohlen, ausgefer... ...GEOGR. IN AUGSP.

ELB

STROM

Sive

FL.

ALBIS

...rfürstl. Sächsische Haupt u. Residentz Stadt und Vestung DRESDEN.

K. Opern Haus.
L. Zwinger Garten.
M. Jäger Hoff.
N. Rath Haus in Alt Dresden.
O. Das Block Haus auf der Brucken.
P. Cadets Haus.
Q. Proviant Häuser.
R. Das Schwartze Thor.

Alt Dresden

The Glory of
Baroque ♔ Dresden

The Glory of Baroque Dresden

The State Art Collections Dresden

Presented by
The Mississippi Commission for
International Cultural Exchange, Inc.

Mississippi Arts Pavilion
March 1—September 6, 2004
Jackson, Mississippi

SPONSORS

OFFICIAL SPONSOR
BellSouth

TITLE SPONSORS
AmSouth Bank
Trustmark National Bank

PRINCIPAL SPONSOR
BancorpSouth

MAJOR SPONSORS
AmSouth Foundation
The Clarion-Ledger
Entergy
Gertrude C. Ford Foundation

SPONSORS
EastGroup/Parkway Foundation
Mr. and Mrs. Stuart C. Irby, Jr.

PATRONS
Adams and Reese LLP
Kane and Betsy Ditto Pass-Through Fund of the
    Community Foundation of Greater Jackson
Feild Co-Operative Association, Inc.
Gil Ford Photography, Inc.
Liquid Creative, Inc.
McGlinchey Stafford, PLLC
Quail Ridge Press, Inc.
Mr. and Mrs. E. B. Robinson, Jr.

CONTRIBUTORS
Albriton's Jewelry
Central Mississippi Medical Center in memory of
    Dr. Robert R. Smith
Chisholm Foundation
Delta Industries
Eaton Foundation
Hilton Jackson
Mr. and Mrs. Charles L. Irby
Mr. Stuart M. Irby
Mr. and Mrs. William D. Mounger
Pruet Companies
St. Dominic Health Services, Inc.

GUARANTORS
J. Kane Ditto
William D. Mounger
E. B. Robinson, Jr.
Leland Speed
Stuart C. Irby, Co.

This project has been partially funded through grants
provided by the State of Mississippi, Mississippi Development Authority, Mississippi Division of Tourism
Development; City of Jackson; and the Jackson Convention & Visitors Bureau.

HONORARY ORGANIZING COMMITTEE

Honorable Daniel R. Coats
Ambassador of the United States
of America

His Excellency Wolfgang Ischinger
Ambassador of the Federal
Republic of Germany

Honorable Thad Cochran
United States Senator

Hans-Ulrich Klose
Vice Chairman of the Committee on Foreign
Affairs of the German Bundestag and
Chairman of the German–American
Parliamentarians' Group

Honorable Haley Barbour
Governor of the State of Mississippi

His Excellency Georg Milbradt
Minister President of the Free State of Saxony

The State Art collections Dresden

The Mississippi Commission for International Cultural Exchange, Inc.

This catalog is dedicated to the memory of MCICE Board Member Robert R. Smith, M.D.
(1933–2003).

Contents

Opening Words

It is an event of great magnitude to envision the splendor and the abundance of the Dresden State Art Collections and Moritzburg Castle exhibited in the Mississippi Arts Pavilion in Jackson. The Baroque idea of gloriously combining art with a claim to power lends a special aura to the collections, rendering them incomparable. The concentration and the density of the materials selected for this special show is both unprecedented and hardly repeatable. It is especially made possible by the re-establishment of the Saxon rulers' Treasury Museum, the Green Vault, in its original space, the Residential Palace, which starts in September 2004. This authentic location will then be the unique place where such a wealth of works of art is on display.

Now, the question arises why this exhibition takes place in Jackson/Mississippi. There is a precedent of numerous successful exhibitions which were organized by The Mississippi Commission for International Cultural Exchange, Inc. (MCICE) which gave rise to our decision to make "The Glory of Baroque Dresden" part of this worthy series. Beneath this lies our desire to present the Saxon Art Collections as a mirror of world culture in the South of the United States and thereby to further deepen the traditional ties between Germany and the United States of America. After all, culture is a significant pillar of Germany's foreign policy.

The Dresden Art Collections did exhibit selections of their holdings in New York, Washington, and San Francisco even before German unification. In Jackson, however, the splendor of this exhibition as a singular event with unequalled educational and installation-related ambitions will be even more intense than in other places. It was a great joy for my colleagues and for myself to witness the tremendous preparation which went into all aspects of the exhibition. With regard to education and programs for students, Jackson is simply the leader. It only remains to be hoped that such an international venue may lead to the creation of a permanent museum for Jackson and for Mississippi. We in Dresden are more than prepared to contribute our share towards this goal.

Such an exhibition could not have been realized without the involvement of many individuals. My special thanks go to the directors of the Dresden museums who contributed by carefully selecting highest-caliber works of art and thus made this exhibition their own in order to do justice to Dresden's claim to being as one of the crown jewels of European culture. Without the leadership and the intense preparatory work undertaken by Dr. Ulrich Pietsch and Dr. Sabine Siebel of the State Art Collections this exhibition could not have been realized. Likewise, "The Glory of Baroque Dresden" depended heavily on the support of politicians and diplomats who recognized its national significance. They endorsed the idea of having this unique treasure from the heart of Europe visit our American friends. In this context my special thanks go to the German Ambassador to the United States His Excellency Wolfgang Ischinger and the former German Consul General in Atlanta and current German Ambassador to Libya His Excellency Heinrich-Peter Rothmann, as well as to the members of the Honorary Organizing Committee of the exhibition. The involvement of uncounted friends and supporters remains a crucial addition to this endeavor. For lack of space I will only mention E. B. Robinson and J. Kane Ditto, Chairman and Vice Chairman of the Board of Directors of the MCICE . My heartiest thanks are reserved, however, for our colleague, friend, and partner Mr. Jack L. Kyle—a true patron of the art and untiring ambassador for Dresden.

Professor Dr. MARTIN ROTH
Director General
State Art Collections Dresden

Foreword

The Glory of Baroque Dresden is the fourth international exhibition organized by The Mississippi Commission for International Cultural Exchange, Inc. To mark the tenth anniversary of the Commission's establishment, the State Art Collections Dresden (Staatliche Kunstsammlungen Dresden) have joined hands with the Commission to present the first monumental exhibition from Dresden in North America in twenty-five years. This exhibition is a landmark event in German-American cultural relations, not only in Mississippi and the American South, but for the entire United States.

Dresden, a name synonymous with art, architecture, and music, reached its cultural zenith during the Baroque period. This high achievement and earned stature which placed Dresden on the world cultural stage are due in large measure to two historical figures, namely, Augustus the Strong (1670-1733) and his son and successor Augustus III (1696-1763), both of whom were Elector of Saxony and King of Poland. The creation of the magnificent art collections of Dresden, known the world over, is due to the enlightment and connoisseurship of these two historical figures. The Dresden Collections and The Glory of Baroque Dresden exhibition reflect the uniquely private connoisseurship of this princely collection.

While the authors of the various essays in this scholarly representation of The Glory of Baroque Dresden exhibition will illuminate the magnificence of the Dresden Collections and exquisite tastes of the two historical figures who were its creators, it goes without saying that every person who comes in contact with this city is struck by the high quality, scope, and wealth of the city's art collections, architecture, and music. This impact fell heavily upon me, as with visitors over the centuries who have walked its streets and experienced the exhilarating and breathtaking images which evoke the history, beauty, and greatness of this special city.

While no experience can supplant a personal visit to Dresden to be immersed in its charm as expressed in the view of the Dresden Residential Palace from the opposite side of the Elbe River similarly depicted centuries ago by Bernardo Bellotto, and to be swept away in thought of centuries past by a stroll in the courtyard of that most magnificent of Baroque architectural ensembles—the Zwinger, The Glory of Baroque Dresden will evoke in countless visitors who come into contact with the exhibition the grandeur and timeless beauty of this city, a monument to mankind's creative genius and the soaring aspirations and artistic expressions of the human spirit.

Toward this end, a debt of gratitude is expressed to Dr. Martin Roth, director general of the Staatliche Kunstsammlungen Dresden, who so graciously received me on a stark and cold December day in his then-office in the Albertinum and extended a thoughtful and welcome ear to loaning some of the greatest artistic expressions of mankind to a small city in the American South then unknown to him. To Dr. Ulrich Pietsch, director of the world-renown Porcelain Collection of the Zwinger who became the project director for The Glory of Baroque Dresden exhibition and who inspired his colleagues to unite in purpose to organize in Jackson, Mississippi, for all of America this rare showing of masterpieces from the Dresden Collections, I express my warmest appreciation.

This marvelous gesture of cultural exchange and international cooperation is an example of the goodwill and mutual admiration not only of our two cultural organizations, but as importantly of the admiration and respect in which Germans and Americans and all people of goodwill hold for each other. Art unites and brings all people closer together.

While all of the works of art in The Glory of Baroque Dresden exhibition are deserving of special recognition, of particular note is the magnanimous gesture on the part of the State Art Collections Dresden in offering and making available the loan of "The Procuress" by Jan Vermeer. To Dr. Harald Marx, director of the famed Old Masters Picture Gallery, and Ms. Marlies Giebe, director of the Restoration Workshop for Paintings who undertook the historic restoration of this work of art, I extend my deepest appreciation. In addition, to Dr. Dirk Syndram, director of the Green Vault, whose gracious permission to include the rare Dresden Green Diamond, one of Dresden's greatest and most famous cultural treasures, will long be remembered in the minds and imaginations of the countless visitors who will experience this rare cultural opportunity in America, I extend my appreciation.

No accomplishment of this magnitude and significance can be achieved without the passion, commitment, and dedication of a legion of supporters. The Glory of Baroque Dresden exhibition is no exception. However, I would be remiss in not calling attention to several special individuals whose personal involvement has contributed immeasurably to the realization of this cultural endeavor which has created an atmosphere of enlightment, enjoyment, and international understanding. These individuals include: German Ambassador to the United States His Excellency Wolfgang Ischinger, German Ambassador to Libya His Excellency Heinrich-Peter Rothmann, United States Ambassador to the Federal Republic of Germany Daniel R. Coats, German Consul General Hans-Jörg Brunner, United States Consul General Fletcher M. Burton, Cultural Counselor of the German Embassy Thomas Wriessnig, and Head of the Press Section of the German Embassy Martina Nibbeling-Wriessnig. My special appreciation is also extended to Dr. Sabine Siebel of the State Art Collections Dresden whose assistance throughout the project has been of tremendous value and made my work such a pleasure.

For support without which projects such as The Glory of Baroque Dresden exhibition would not be possible, I wish to thank John M. McCullouch, President of BellSouth/Mississippi, for his support and that of BellSouth to serve as the "Official Sponsor" of the exhibition. To all officials of the State of Mississippi, City of Jackson, and Jackson Convention and Visitors Bureau, I express gratitude for your financial commitment which made this exhibition possible for the benefit of all Mississippians. Special appreciation is extended to the many corporate sponsors, foundations, and individuals whose financial and in-kind support have made the exhibition possible.

Finally, my personal gratitude is expressed to the members of the Board of Directors of The Mississippi Commission for International Cultural Exchange, Inc. under the leadership of Chairman E.B. Robinson, Jr. and Vice Chairman J. Kane Ditto for their unwavering commitment to making this exhibition possible and to a passionate and dedicated staff and corps of volunteers without whom we could never fulfill our dreams of bringing personal joy and meaningful experiences to countless human beings.

JACK L. KYLE

Executive Director
The Mississippi Commission for International
Cultural Exchange, Inc.

Zwinger, Rampart Pavillon, Zwinger built in 1709–28 by M. D. Pöppelmann and B. Permoser

Revolution and Reciprocity

Transatlantic Relations during the Baroque Era

Andrew I. Port

Den Vereinigten Staaten
Amerika, du hast es besser
Als unser Kontinent, das alte,
Hast keine verfallene Schlösser
Und keine Basalte.
Dich stört nicht im Innern
Zu lebendiger Zeit
Unnützes Erinnern
Und vergeblicher Streit.

To the United States
America, you're better off
Than our continent, the old.
You've no decaying castles
Nor basalt to behold.
Within, nothing daunts you
In times rife with life,
No memory haunts you
Nor vain, idle strife.

Though composed a half century after the American Revolution, Johann Wolfgang von Goethe's 1827 paean to the new republic—and the New World—still contained echoes of the positive chord that the colonists' earlier struggle had struck in the German-speaking lands. In fact, news of the revolt was met with great interest and enthusiasm throughout much of Europe, where America came to be seen by many as a haven of liberty and equality, as a society without the stifling political and socio-economic strictures characteristic of the "Old World." Paid mercenaries from Goethe's native Hesse may have supported the British militarily, and many Europeans may have become less enamored of "revolution" following the bloody excesses that marked the French experience less than two decades later, but at the time, the events in the colonies appeared to herald the dawn of a new and more promising era.

The high hopes and positive associations that America evoked in Europe had, of course, long preceded the War of Inde-

J. F. Eberlein, P. Reinicke, and J. J. Kaendler,
"America", Meissen, model 1745, copy ca. 1775–80,
porcelain, H. 9 3/4 in., Porcelain Collection

pendence. Beginning in the early 17th century, large numbers of Protestant dissidents from England and the Netherlands migrated to the newly established colonies in search of religious refuge and greater economic opportunity. The last flowering of the Baroque era in Europe witnessed a new flow of emigrants, primarily from Germany, Ireland, and Scotland, and by the time the first official census was taken in the United States in 1790, those of either German birth or descent made up approximately one-tenth of the population.

Like those who had arrived earlier, the new settlers from the German-speaking lands of the Holy Roman Empire were motivated above all by the desire to escape religious oppression, economic misery, and political upheaval at home. Persecution by Catholic princes and the ravages of religious warfare prompted the first major wave of immigrants in the 1680s, when Protestants from the upper Rhine Valley in southwest Germany eagerly accepted refuge in a new colony recently founded by the Quaker William Penn in the Delaware Valley. The so-called Pennsylvania Dutch (or Deutsch) were largely Pietists and Mennonites from the Rhenish Palatinate, and would comprise no less than one-third of the colony's population the year the Declaration of Independence was signed in 1776. The attractive prospects of religious toleration, cheap and abundant

land, as well as relatively high wages soon brought others in their wake: the high point of German migration to the colonies took place during the waning years of the Baroque period, when severe agricultural crisis and continued persecution led tens of thousands to leave for America between 1749 and 1754 alone.

As a rule, the newcomers tended to remain together in isolated rural settlements, where they endeavored to maintain their customs, culture, and language by establishing local schools and newspapers. Stringent citizenship laws made it difficult for them to become naturalized British subjects, however, resulting in various forms of discrimination and even victimization—despite the initial promise and allure of a fresh and more propitious start in the New World. Alienated from the British government and often hostile to local authorities, many consequently settled in the hinterlands far away from the colonial capitals, where they usually earned a living by working the land or by manufacturing paper and textiles.

The foregoing should not suggest that the German immigrants had little or no impact on the shaping of political, social, and cultural life in colonial America. One of the first major declarations condemning the institution of slavery was issued by German settlers in 1688, for example. But despite the large influx of this and other new ethnic groups during the 18th century, the dominant influence from abroad nevertheless remained that of the earliest settlers, the English. This was true above all in the realm of ideas as well as culture—in the broadest sense of the term. As one historian has observed, "The key figures in the American colonies had been products of the European [and specifically English] world. In America they had been isolated physically but not psychologically, intellectually, or spiritually."

The initial transfer of European culture and traditions to the New World was further reinforced by the continued preservation of strong ties to the homeland—not least through regular correspondence and the movement of individuals back and forth between the two continents. Scholars generally agree, nevertheless, that by the close of the 17th century, a distinct American culture had emerged in the colonies, largely in response to the practical demands and exigencies of a new physical environment. Yet a provincial sense of cultural inferiority often resulted in deliberate and often self-conscious forms of borrowing from abroad. In other words, the colonists continued to look to the Old World for inspiration and guidance, especially when it came to higher forms of culture. Europe set the standard, and its fashions in thought, behavior, and artistic expression were vigilantly emulated overseas.

These broad claims deserve some qualification. The period that witnessed the founding and flourishing of the American colonies coincided with the Baroque age in Europe, an era whose artistic style was characterized in painting, architecture, sculpture, music, home furnishings, and even dress by a strong emotional appeal to the senses. Sensuousness, exaggeration, and extravagant ornamentation were its primary hallmarks—in stark contrast to the highly disciplined, vigorously self-controlled, and severely simple aesthetic tastes and values of the Calvinists and other Protestant sects living in New England. Some have even suggested that Puritanism was, at least in part, a severe reaction against the new artistic movement most closely associated with the religious Counter-Reformation in Europe and, later, with the political Restoration in England.

That should not imply that America was left completely untouched by Baroque influences. Increasing wealth in the colonies led to the rise of a new commercial and agricultural elite that characteristically looked to Europe to help satisfy its developing taste for the so-called refinements of life. The English painters and architects who traveled to America in the early 18th century, for example, were enthusiastically welcomed by members of the emerging American "aristocracy", who eagerly commissioned works redolent of Baroque refinery; this was especially true in the southern colonies. Stimulated by what they had seen in the New World, these and other transitory visitors from Europe returned home, where they would often adorn their new artistic creations with the strange and exotic peoples, plants, animals, and other wonders they had seen for the first time while abroad.

As this suggests, cultural influences between the Old and New Worlds were often reciprocal, with each side of the Atlantic having a significant and discernible impact on the other. This was also clearly the case in the realm of politics and ideas. In a classic study, R. R. Palmer aptly characterized the latter half of the 18th century as the "Age of the Democratic Revolution," which arguably began with the revolt of the North American colonies in the 1770s. But the ideational and ideological underpinnings of their bid for independence emanated from abroad—and, not least, from the very country against which their struggle was directed. It would be difficult, of course, to deny the important influence and impact of Enlightenment thought on the colonial cosmology: Thomas Jefferson and Benjamin Franklin—to name only two of the new republic's major intellectual luminaries—were clearly children of the "Age of Reason" that first flowered on the European continent. Yet as one preeminent historian of the colonial world has convincingly demonstrated, there was another, equally important intellectual tradition "transmitted most directly to the colonists by a group of early 18th century radical publicists and opposition politicians in England", whose "peculiar strain of anti-authoritarianism" had originated during the English Civil War of the mid-17th century. The "fear of a comprehensive conspiracy against liberty throughout the English-speaking world," Bernard Bailyn concludes, "lay at the heart of the Revolutionary movement."

It is tempting to draw an analogy between the Atlantic trade routes of the early modern era and the concomitant traffic in ideas: just as raw materials flowed from America to Europe, where they were then crafted into manufactured products later purchased by the colonists, it could be argued that the raw ideological materials that flowed from Europe to North America were, in turn, later fashioned into revolutionary products that were then exported back to the Old World. The connection between the two seminal upheavals of the period—the end of British rule in the colonies and the demise of the ancien régime in France—was obviously much more complex than that. But few would dispute the important way in which the events in America contributed—at least in part, and in the words of R. R. Palmer—to the "democratic and revolutionary spirit in Europe, to the desire, that is, for a reconstitution of government and society" along socially more equitable and politically less exclusionary lines. This interconnectedness between the Old and New Worlds suggests that the substance behind the idea of globalization—the new buzzword of the 21st century—is much older than the term itself and was already in evidence long before.

Whatever the origins and ultimate effects of the American War of Independence may have been, the event was clearly part and parcel of a *single* revolutionary movement that gripped both halves of the occidental world at the time, from the western shores of the Atlantic to the Polish lands formerly ruled by the German prince electors of Saxony during the waning years of that glorious artistic era known as the Baroque.

Selected bibliography: Bailyn 1967.—Bailyn et al. 1992.—Dippel 1977.—Kraus 1949.—Liss 1983.—Palmer 1959.—Savelle 1948.—Trommler/McVeigh 1985.

J. F. Eberlein, "Europe", Meissen, model 1746–47, copy ca. 1775–80, porcelain, H. 10 in., Porcelain Collection

Baroque in Dresden: History — Architecture — Collections

Gerald Heres

There are three different terms that refer to the history and art of Saxony in the first half of the 18th century and essentially describe the same phenomenon: the Saxon-Polish Union, Augustinian Dresden, and Dresden Baroque. Under Prince Elector Frederick Augustus I, who was also called Augustus II as king of Poland, and under Frederick Augustus II (Augustus III) the electorate of Saxony and the Polish kingdom formed a personal union. One of the major achievements of this era was the transformation of the Saxon capital, Dresden, into a Baroque residence which—as a city of the arts—was comparable to Vienna and Munich.

History

After the untimely death of his elder brother, Johann Georg IV, in 1694, Frederick Augustus I assumed the rulership of Saxony. The highly talented prince had received a comprehensive education and had become familiar with a number of different European courts and countries. His extraordinary physical strength contributed to his later nickname, "the Strong" (*der Starke*). Although the new responsibilities came as a surprise to him, the 24-year-old mastered them elegantly.

Saxony was one of the largest and most affluent territories which comprised the Holy Roman Empire of the German

Zwinger, Crown Gate, Zwinger erected in 1709–28 by M. D. Pöppelmann and B. Permoser

Nation. After more than half a century, the aftermath of the Thirty Years War (1618–48) was overcome and economy and trade flourished. Since medieval times, the so-called *Landstände*, groups of people comprised of aristocracy, clergy, and urban burghers, had exerted considerable influence on the country's politics. Their most noticeable means of intervention was their right to grant taxes. In his endeavor to create a modern, centralist administration, the prince elector was repeatedly forced to diminish their rights. However, in contrast to neighboring Brandenburg, the Saxon rulers were never able to completely eliminate the power of the *Stände*.

After the death of the Polish king, Jan Sobieski, Frederick Augustus applied for the crown of the elective kingdom. Thanks to his substantial financial investments he was crowned in Kraków on September 15, 1697. A prerequisite was his conversion to Catholicism, the consequences of which were far-reaching: Saxony lost its role as leader of the Protestant *Reichsstände* within the empire to Brandenburg. The Wettin's marriage policies were no longer oriented towards the Protestant north but to the Catholic south. The king had to sign an affidavit concerning assurance of religion, a so-called *Religionsversicherungsdekret*. The document stated that his personal conversion would not affect his people or his country's church. With reference to the Poles, he was obliged to assure that he would recover Livonia, pay for his own personal bodyguards, and that he would only employ domestic civil servants in Poland.

As a personal union, the Saxon-Polish Union lasted from 1697 until 1763. The courts as well as administrative and military structures remained separate. A territorial connection never materialized because of an approximately thirty-mile-wide corridor that belonged to Prussia and Austria. Polish and German historians' evaluation of the Union has been highly controversial to this day. Only in more recent times have the

more positive sides been emphasized: the creation of a supranational European power with economic, cultural, and political advantages.

By forming alliances with Denmark and Russia, Augustus the Strong wanted to undermine Sweden's position of supremacy in the north. As a consequence, the Nordic War began in 1700 which ended with a catastrophic defeat of the allied forces. The Swedes, under Charles XII, occupied Saxony, and Augustus was forced to give up the Polish crown, but was entitled to continue carrying the title of king. Despite the enormous burdens, the administrative reforms pressed forward. In 1706, Augustus created, as the highest central administrative office, the Privy Cabinet (*Geheimes Kabinett*) with departments of the Interior, Foreign, and Military. In the following year, he managed to introduce—against the violent protest of the *Landstände*—a tax comparable to today's VAT. Likewise, for the first time anywhere in Germany a financial control body was created.

Beside the struggle for the Polish crown, the king's activities were redirected towards the politics of the *Reich*. Following the death of Emperor Joseph I in 1711, Augustus the Strong served as Imperial Curate (*Reichsvikar*), a post to which the Saxon prince electors were entitled. Following the prince elector's conversion in 1712, future marriage policies were determined. After the victory of Czar Peter I over Charles XII in 1709, and subsequent to further battles, Augustus regained the Polish crown, and on the Imperial Diet (*Reichstag*) of Warsaw in 1717 was reconfirmed as Polish king.

In 1719, the electoral prince—whose conversion to Catholicism had not been made public until 1717—married Archduchess Maria Josepha, a daughter of Emperor Joseph I. Tied to this wedding was the hope for securing the Hapsburg throne and hence the rank of emperor for a Saxon prince elector. The preparations for the wedding were proportional to Augustus's aspirations: all of Dresden was filled with numerous weeks of splendid festivities (see pp. 31ff.).

With the peace treaty of Nystadt in 1721, Sweden accepted Augustus as Polish king. Yet Livonia did not fall to Poland but to Russia instead, and the much-desired land bridge between Poland and Saxony did not materialize. The remaining decade until the king's death was filled with peace as well as multilayered political and cultural activities. The military reform, begun in 1722, culminated in the so-called *Zeithainer Lager*, a magnificent public demonstration of military power and achievements of the newly organized Saxon army in 1730. A new compilation of laws, the "Codex Augusteus," was published in 1724.

On January 10, 1733, despite his inferior health, Augustus left Dresden for the opening of the Imperial Diet in Warsaw. He reportedly replied to warnings: "I feel the approaching danger but I am obligated to pay more attention to the well-being of my peoples than to my own person." On February 1, 1733, the king died in Warsaw. His body was buried in the cathedral of Kraków Castle, the Wawel, and his heart was entombed in Dresden's Court Church (*Hofkirche*). To sum up his time in office, state reformer Thomas von Fritsch's words of 1763 may be quoted: "During the last ten years of Augustus the Strong's reign, Saxony was in a better state than ever before. And in his untiring work, this great king strove to advance Saxony even further. The finances were in best shape [...]. All ministries were well staffed, every single one led by a distinguished head [...]. Owing to Saxony's excellent interior condition, it was also held in highest esteem inside and outside the Holy Roman Empire of the German Nation [...]."

Augustus the Strong's son succeeded his father as Prince Elector Frederick Augustus II of Saxony. Initially, the Union was endangered: Both France's candidate of choice, Stanisław Leszczyński, and the Saxon prince elector were elected king by their supporters. It was not until after the war of succession that Frederick Augustus II could be crowned as Augustus III. For matters of domestic and foreign politics, the king initially relied on Cabinet Minister and Head Chamberlain Count Sulkowski who was succeeded in 1738 by Count Heinrich von Brühl. Already equipped with abundant power as chamber president, Brühl was made a count in 1737 and promoted to cabinet minister in 1746. This

heretofore unprecedented accumulation of offices made him the most powerful and—owing to his unscrupulous finance politics—most hated man in Saxony. His neglect of the army and his failed attempt to find fit allies contributed considerably to Saxony's defeat in her conflicts with Prussia and ultimately led to the Union's failure.

The political situation for Saxony had become a difficult one. After the death of

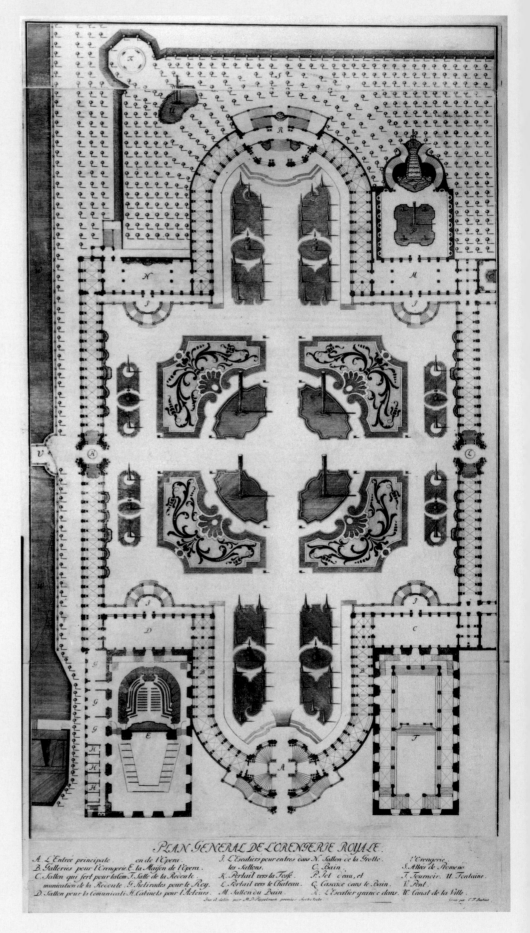

PLAN GENERAL DE L'ORENGERIE ROYALE.

1 M. D. Pöppelmann and C. F. Boetius, "General Map of the Royal Orangerie", 1729, copperplate engraving, 35 1/2 x 19 1/4 in., CDPP

2 Dresden Residential Palace, western part of the Large Courtyard; the Residential Palace developed from a castle, first mentioned in 1287, into one of the most splendid Renaissance palaces in Europe

Emperor Charles VI in 1740, Augustus served as Imperial Curate until the Bavarian prince elector, Charles Albrecht, was made Emperor Charles VII in 1742. In his "Pragmatic Sanction," dated 1713, Charles VI had tried to secure female succession for the Hapsburg territories. Because of her own claims, Saxony did not accept this. After King Frederick II of Prussia invaded Silesia in 1740, the Austrian war of succession broke out and lasted until 1748 when the "Pragmatic Sanction" and Maria Theresa's government were internationally approved. In 1745 Frederick II had occupied Dresden and pressed charges for a contribution amounting to a million thalers. As a consequence of the various conflicts, Saxony had neither been able to gain the much desired land bridge to Poland nor had it been possible to achieve moderation on the part of Prussia.

In August 1756 Frederick II attacked Saxony. After the capitulation of the Saxon army, Augustus III and Brühl were granted safe conduct to Warsaw. When they returned to their residential city, Dresden, their entire lives had been altered by the war. Both men died in the year of their return, 1763. The country's debt had risen to 45 million thalers. As early as 1762 a restoration commission had started work. The political, economic, and cultural restructuring of Saxony after the Seven Years War was an achievement already much admired by contemporaries. Yet the Union with Poland and the Augustinian Era had come to an end.

Architecture

In a description of Dresden, Augustus the Strong is praised as the one who found a small city made primarily of wood but left behind one that was large and made of stone. Despite all the impressive achievements during Augustinian times, this statement is inaccurate.

In 1547 Duke Moritz gained the title of Saxon prince elector for the Albertinian branch of the House of Wettin. During a long phase of peace under his brother Augustus (1526/53–1586) and his successors, Christian I (1560/86–1591) and Christian II (1583/1601–1611) Dresden was remodeled into an electoral residence. Apart from the Residential Palace, numer-

ous court buildings were created which also continued to serve their function during Augustinian times. Some of them have survived to this day—albeit in heavily modified forms: among them are the Arsenal (*Zeughaus*), the Stable Court (*Stallhof*) and Stables Building (*Stallgebäude*, its upper floors once housed the Armory), and, on the right bank of the Elbe, the spacious hunting castle, *Jägerhof*.

The recently recreated Chancellery Building (*Kanzleihaus*) was the first administrative building in the city. Beside the court buildings rose the stately houses of the bourgeoisie. The fortification ring was continuously expanded and modernized. Although Dresden was spared major destruction during the Thirty Years War, its aftermath, including country-wide devastation, was omnipresent. The country only started a slow recovery following the peace treaty of Kötzschenbroda near Dresden which Prince Elector Johann Georg I negotiated in 1645. It was not until the reign of Johann Georg II, 1656–80, that art and building activities were once again contemplated and then realized. The officer and architect Wolf Caspar von Klengel was made Chief Building Master (*Oberlandbaumeister*) in 1656. His were the buildings which introduced Baroque to Dresden; yet most of them were later sacrificed to alterations. The sole witness to Klengel's noble style is the chapel in Moritzburg Castle. With the creation of the Large Garden (*Großer Garten*) just outside the city gates and with the erection of the palace in its center (see fig. p.129), Johann Georg Starcke and Johann Friedrich Karcher were responsible for the first Baroque sites in Dresden, starting in 1683.

When Augustus the Strong succeeded his brother, in 1694, the architect Matthäus Daniel Pöppelmann, the sculptor Balthasar Permoser, and the goldsmith Johann Melchior Dinglinger were already active in Dresden. This trio determined Dresden's image at the beginning of the new century. Valued as a versatile "Ordonneur du Cabinet," the architect Raymond Leplat came to Dresden in 1698. A building owner and an art aficionado himself, Count Augustus Christoph Wackerbarth—since 1696 head of civil and military building activities—was formative and influential as well. In 1718, the Executive Building Administration (*Oberbauamt*) was founded with Pöppelmann, Zacharias Longuelune (active in Dresden since 1713), and, starting in 1719, Johann Christoph Knöffel working together. Jean de Bodt—previously active in Berlin—succeeded Wackerbarth in 1728. Indicative of the way in which these architects worked was their collaborative planning of many buildings; as a consequence it is often almost impossible to unequivocally assign their individual contributions.

Plans for a new Residential Palace remained unrealized; instead the king determined to extend the old palace. One of the reasons for this decision was the immense time pressure of the anticipated marriage between the electoral prince and Archduchess Maria Josepha, planned for 1719. Spaces that were destroyed during a fire in 1701 were recreated, and in the west wing a suite of sumptuous parade rooms was created.

In 1710 Pöppelmann began construction of the *Orangerie* near the fortification wall: provisionally completed for the festival year, the *Zwinger* is one of the most breathtaking buildings from the European High Baroque era. Despite the various damage and destruction caused over the course of the centuries, the lighthearted building—embellished with splendid sculptures contributed by Permoser and

3 *Pillnitz Castle, Water Palace, built since 1720
after plans by M. D. Pöppelmann*

his collaborators—has retained its magic
to this day. Its original condition was documented by Pöppelmann in the large engravings of a volume published in 1729
(see fig. 3, p. 29). Even then, the majority
of the gallery and pavilions were predominantly used for museum purposes.

In 1717 the Dutch Palace (*Holländisches
Palais*) was acquired. Remodeled into a
four-winged structure since 1728 and re-
named Japanese Palace (*Japanisches Palais*)
(see fig. p. 181), its primary use was to
accommodate the extensive porcelain
collection. Though the interior design remained incomplete, starting in the late
18th century, the noble structure—architects involved in reshaping it included
Pöppelmann, Longuelune, and de Bodt—
contained the Collection of Antiquities,
the Coin Cabinet, and the Library. Based
on Pöppelmann's plans, the old bridge
across the Elbe was reerected as *Augustus-
brücke* between 1727 and 1731; in the early
20th century it was modified for modern
navigation.

One of the impressive documents of
Dresden's civic pride and Protestant faith
is the famous *Frauenkirche*, based on plans
supplied by Municipal Building Master
(*Stadtbaumeister*) George Bähr starting in
1726. Ruined during World War II, the
church ist expected to be reconstructed by
2006 for the celebration of Dresden's 800th
anniversary. The dignified private houses
in the Old City (*Altstadt*) and new dwellings
in the New Royal City (*Neue Königsstadt*)—
the latter erected on the right river bank
following a fire—were largely responsible
for Dresden's reputation as a Baroque

city. A decree from 1720 specified facade
designs as well as the height of the buildings and even mandated stone steps in the
interiors as a fire prevention measure.

The residence was surrounded by a
number of hunting and pleasure palaces,
although neither were all plans realized
nor did all structures reach the envisioned
dimensions. The Elbe played a major role
as a means of transport; and roads and
strictly planned axes were to connect all
palaces. Beginning in 1720, a Water Palace
(*Wasserpalais*) was begun beside the Old
Castle (*Altes Schloß*) in Pillnitz. The former
was complemented by a Mountain Palace
(*Bergpalais*), conceived as its mirror image.
In northwestern Dresden, Eosander von
Göthe built a palace for Count Flemming
starting in 1724. Purchased by the king in
1726, he then included it in his plans (today
ruined). In 1723 the king acquired the park
at Großsedlitz from Count Wackerbarth: in

it, the festivities for the Polish Order of the
White Eagle were scheduled to take place.
Plans for a new city castle did not materialize. With its sweeping staircases, the
orangeries and the abundantly rich sculpture decoration, Großsedlitz became the
most beautiful French garden in Saxony. It
has been reconstructed according to the
strictest landmark specifications and
attracts countless visitors again.

In the year 1723 Pöppelmann was put
in charge of modifying the Hunting Castle
Moritzburg (*Jagdschloß Moritzburg*) into
the so-called Castle of Diana (*Dianenburg*).
Erected between 1542 and 1546 for Duke
Moritz, the transformations led to a massive building dominated by four corner
towers and a well-proportioned facade set
within a landscape of forests and lakes.

In the decades following the death of
Augustus the Strong (1733) the splendor
and the originality of his time were never
reached again. The reserved buildings by
Knöffel, influenced by Longuelune's Classicism, anticipate the rococo idiom. The
great challenge under the reign of Augustus
III (1696/1733–63) is the Catholic court
church for which a model was furnished by
Gaetano Chiaveri in 1738. Begun secretly,
the building, rising on a striking spot beside
the Dresden Residential Palace, was not
finished until 1755. Beside the *Zwinger*, it is
one of the most significant landmarks of
Baroque Dresden. Upon the king's command, the Stables Building—modified into
visitors quarters with festival spaces between 1729 and 1732—was transformed by
Knöffel into a Picture Gallery, starting in
1745. The resulting four-winged structure
contained no fewer than seven Long Galleries (*Langgalerien*), in which the Royal
Collection of Paintings was exhibited until

4 *Pillnitz Castle, Mountain Palace, built in 1723–24
after plans by M. D. Pöppelmann*

its move into the so-called *Semperbau* in 1855 (see fig. p. 43).

However, the greatest challenge with which Knöffel was confronted was the realization of the palace and garden ensemble belonging to Count Brühl and located on the fortification walls facing the Elbe, the so-called *Brühlsche Garten*. Beginning in 1740, the palace, a library, a gallery building, a belvedere, as well as pavilions and fountains were created. Owing to later building campaigns (*Ständehaus*, Art Academy, *Albertinum*) and war destruction (*Belvedere*), scarcely anything remains of the original layout. What prevails is the *Brühlsche Terrasse*, accessible, since the early 19th century, from the *Schloßplatz* via an outside staircase.

Collections

When Prince Elector Frederick Augustus I came to power, he found a rich museum tradition in Dresden. The continuation and completion of the collections was to be one of his life's goals—and it was perhaps the one task that he completed to perfection.

During the 17th century the *Kunstkammer*, founded by Prince Elector Augustus in 1560, had become one of the leading institutions of its kind in Europe. Apart from holdings of minerals, animals, and plants, it contained important works made of ivory, gold, silver, and precious stones, as well as valuable pieces of furniture, an impressive number of sculptures, and paintings. It was also renowned for its wealth of mechanical tools and instruments. The earliest inventories date to 1587, and the first printed guide of Art Chamberlain Tobias Beutel dates to 1671. This publication also covers the Anatomy Chamber (*Anatomiekammer*), established in 1620, as well as the Armory (*Rüstkammer*). The collections were open to the public with certain restrictions; for 1684 some 800 visitors are documented.

On his Grand Tour, between 1687 and 1689, Prince Frederick Augustus had the opportunity to familiarize himself with numerous European art centers. The visit

to the Uffizi in Florence and the adjacent workshops left lasting impressions, as did his sojourns in Vienna. Because of the political and the military situation, the museum-related activities of the elector king were mostly focused on the last two decades of his life.

In the years around 1700 numerous German princes began to assemble important art collections. The concept of the Baroque *Kunstkammer* with its universal cosmological ideas was considered obsolete. Galleries and cabinets, united into autonomous museum complexes, started to present pictures and sculptures under aesthetic and historic aspects. Initially, Augustus the Strong's passion as a collector extended to jewels and porcelain. His love for precious stones not only resulted in a flourishing of the art of goldsmiths and jewelers in Dresden, it was also instrumental in the creation of the Treasury Museum (*Schatzkammermuseum*). Augustus's enthusiasm for East Asian porcelain led to the foundation of Europe's first porcelain manufactory and to the creation of Dresden's porcelain collection, which to this day remains unsurpassed in the world.

In 1716 Augustus ordered a service and individual pieces to be purchased in

Holland. Acquisitions from the porcelain cabinets of the Prussian castles of Charlottenburg and Oranienburg count among the most spectacular successes; in return for the porcelain Augustus sacrificed 600 of his cavalry to Prussian military service in 1717. The king's acquisition of the Dutch Palace falls into the same year. Its two lower floors were furnished with porcelain arrangements, and the remaining inventory of the *Kunstkammer*, dissolved in 1710, was moved to the attic. A request of Cardinal Annibale Albani for drawings of the arrangements indicates how famous this magnificent presentation of the porcelain was in Europe at the time. The Dutch Palace contained elements indicative of a museum, although the collection was not presented in that manner. It served primarily as living quarters and location for official functions. Even after it was remodeled, since 1728, and transformed into the Japanese Palace, it retained, as its primary function, that of palace, although the exhibition of the East Asian porcelain, in particular, was enhanced.

At the beginning of Augustus the Strong's concepts for a museum stands a sketch that was presumably executed in 1718. The connection of a massive central

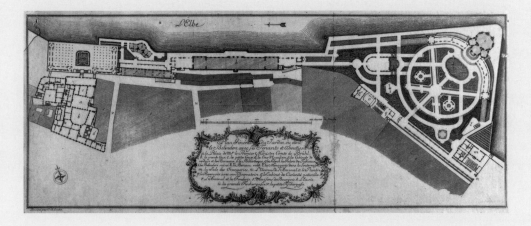

7   Zwinger, Crown Gate with Long Gallery, Mathematisch-Physikalischer Salon, and Rampart Pavilion, Zwinger built in 1709–28 by M. D. Pöppelmann and B. Permoser

building with a narrow gallery wing is unconvincing. It must be assumed that this is a forecast of the space required, and not, in fact, the basis for a concrete project. A total of 32 spaces are evenly distributed over two floors. The ground floor foresees the Hall of Antiquities, the Coin Cabinet, the Model Chamber, a Cabinet of Natural Products, and a "laboratory." The Collection of Drawings, Prints, and Photographs is located in a part of the building which ultimately leads to the Gallery Wing. This quarter also contains the Collections of Maps and Plans and the holdings of Decorative Arts. The upper floor is supposed to house the library, which is to take up most of the space. The Gallery Wing itself is anticipated as the worthiest place to present the paintings and the sculptures.

When the sketch was made, the king had already begun to extract individual segments from the *Kunstkammer* and to transform them into separate collections. In accordance with Saxon mining traditions, the Collection of Minerals stood at the beginning. Then the remaining scientific areas followed. Among them was also the Collection of Drawings, Prints, and Photographs because of its function as a center for documentation. The king appointed his personal physician, Johann Heinrich Heucher, to be the head of the museum organization. When Heucher was able to present a first result, in 1720, he had erected the so-called *Collection-Gebäude* in a dwelling complex and, as a reward for his achievements, was knighted. At the same time, the king appointed one of his ministers, Count Manteuffel, "directeur général" of the

8   J. A. Corvinus (1683–1738), "View of the Royal or Dutch Palace and Garden, as seen from the Bank of the Elbe River", CDPP

collections. Starting in 1728, their administration was handled by the *Oberkammerherrenamt* and was thus firmly tied to the court.

Meanwhile, Heucher demanded that the collections be moved into an official, illustrious building. From 1727 onward the king dedicated much of his time and effort to museum projects. Since the realization of a new building proved impossible, he decided to use the *Zwinger* to accommodate the collections in the summer of 1728. Since time was of the essence, the creation of elaborate furnishings was inconceivable. This was particularly true since all efforts were then focused on the Green Vault.

The pavilions and galleries of the *Zwinger* contained the library, the Collection of Drawings, Prints, and Photographs and the Science Collections consisting of:

Minerals and Fossils Gallery, Vegetables and Animals Gallery, Anatomy Chamber, and the *Mathematisch-Physikalische Salon*. The Coin Cabinet was kept separately, in the Residential Palace. Competent inspectors were appointed for all collections. Because of high admission fees, public access was quite limited.

In the early sketch and in later plans by the king, the scientific collections and the holdings of applied arts played an outstanding role. In the years 1721–23 three rooms were inaugurated in the vaults of the Privy Custody (*Geheime Verwahrung*). They were earmarked exclusively for the presentation of goldsmiths' and stone cutters' works. Starting in 1727, the king had the entire tract of seven spaces remodeled into a unique museum for decorative arts and a treasury museum. Subsequently, this place became known as the Green Vault.

Vue du Palais Roiale . ou de Hollande , et du Jardin , prise du côté de la rivière de l'Elbe .

One further focus to emerge was ancient sculpture. The marble sculptures, predominantly portrait busts, which had been brought from Berlin to Dresden in 1717, were exhibited—along with sculptures from the Renaissance and the Baroque eras—in the Picture Gallery. After long negotiations, the king managed to acquire more than 200 sculptures from the Chigi and Albani collections in Rome in 1728. Longuelune designed a noble museum of antiquities to appropriately exhibit the material. It was supposed to conclude the *Zwinger* towards the Elbe River. Unfortunately, those grand plans remained unbuilt, and the antiquities were mounted in the *Palais* in the Large Garden (see fig. p. 129).

Although Augustus the Strong acquired an impressive number of important paintings, it appears that he related more strongly to sculpture. When the Picture Gallery was furnished in the Residential Palace in 1718, the king was absent, leaving the task of hanging the paintings to Count Wackerbarth. Already in 1726 the Gallery was rededicated again into living quarters. The inventory of paintings and sculptures found a temporary home in the Giant Hall (*Riesensaal*), which had undergone provisional restoration, and in the following suite of rooms leading to the princely living quarters.

In relatively short time, Augustus had organized—with the support of a very few helpers who were for the most part inexperienced with museum issues—a surprisingly effective and modern association of museums. Ultimately, his activities encompassed all museum aspects ranging from the amateurish love of art, dedication to collecting, and connoisseurship to organization, presentation, and publishing. At the same time, he was acutely aware of the lacunae: until his death he was involved in further plans which focused on the completion of the *Zwinger* with galleries and pavilions on the Elbe side. It was his intention to better accommodate, beside the library, paintings and sculptures as well.

A brief period of stagnation immediately followed Augustus the Strong's death: Augustus III had neither his father's impetus nor his universal regard. The focus of his interest in art was painting. When Count Brühl was appointed head of the royal collections, in 1738, the period of grandiose picture purchases began. The Stables Building on the *Neumarkt* was refurbished into a Picture Gallery by Knöffel in 1745. Under inspector Johann Gottfried Riedel, the holdings grew continuously.

In 1730 the *Kunstkammer* holdings were once again exhibited in the Residential Palace and then moved again, in 1733, into the gallery space of the Anatomy Chamber which had been dissolved. Since 1747—that is approximately twenty years after its inception—fundamental renovation and partial new design of the exhibition spaces in the *Zwinger* commenced. The *Mathematisch-Physikalische Salon* moved into the space it keeps to this day, and the library was able to use a space that is known today as the *Glockenspielpavillon*.

With the outbreak of the Seven Years War, in 1756, the museum activities came to an end. Two-thirds of the sculptures in the Large Garden were destroyed. The remaining collections were opened again after the end of the war, once some of the damage to the buildings had been repaired and a partial reinstallation had taken place.

Selected bibliography: Löffler 1981.—Exh.-cat. Essen 1986.—Milde 1990.—Heres 1991.—Saxonia 1995.—Dresdner Hefte 1995.—Exh.-cat. Dresden 1997b.—Saxonia 1998.—Reeckmann 2000.—Groß 2001.—Der Große Garten 2001.—Richter-Nickel 2002, p. 57–100.

10   H. A. Williard (1832–1867), "The Large Avenue in the Royal Large Garden", lithograph, 7 1/4 x 9 3/8 in., Stadtmuseum Dresden

Augustus the Strong as the Sun God Apollo

Jutta Bäumel

By attaining the Polish crown, Augustus the Strong advanced to the primary league of European rulers. While his position as prince elector of Saxony was already influential, his rank as sovereign of the Polish kingdom enabled him to act independently, beyond German borders. Augustus sought the comparison with King Louis XIV of France whose fame and absolute power he attempted to emulate. Like Louis, he staged himself as Roman emperor, Hercules, and as the sun god Apollo. The fame and the glory of his French idol's and rival's government remained unattainable to the elected king of a divided knights' republic. If the Hercules motifs dominate in Augustus's self-representation, this indicates the massive resistance he faced within the Saxon-Polish Union. Thus, the one is remembered as "Sun King" whereas the other is memorialized as "The Strong" and as "Hercules saxonicus".

The dominant symbol of Louis XIV's glorification is the sun, through which the king and the ancient mythological sun god Apollo are merged. This union meant universal rule and divine light. Thus, Louis's sun symbol went far beyond the otherwise common poetry of praise in which the ruler was commonly addressed as the "country's sun." For the appropriate portrayal of himself, Louis XIV maintained a huge apparatus in which the nation's intellectual elite participated. His motto, *L'état c'est moi*, implied state access to all resources and each indivudual comment. The king himself enacted and celebrated this principle, which did not even stop

*B. Permoser, "Apollo" (detail), 1715,
see cat. no. 3.8, p. 134*

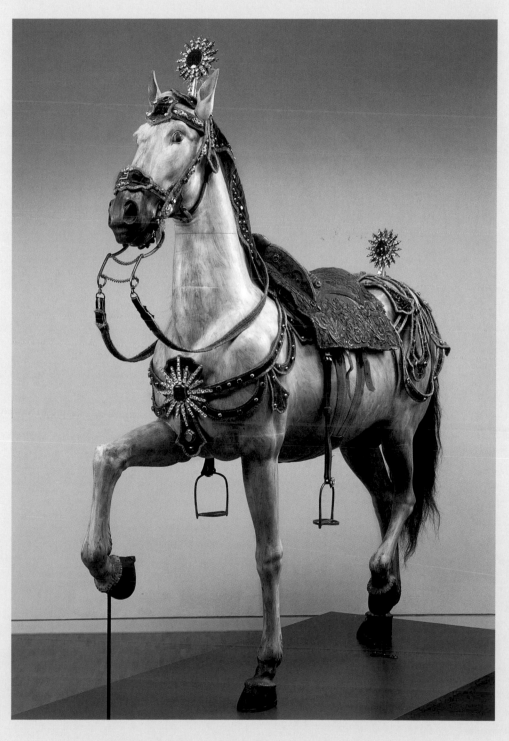

1   *Parade Riding Equipment, 1694, see cat. no. 7.10, p. 243*

2   J. M. Dinglinger, Invention Mask – Sun Mask
with the Likeness of Augustus the Strong, 1709,
see cat. no. 7.21, p. 247

matic gimmick intended to single out the king once more as sun god.

Equipped with a wooden amphitheater for this event, the garden of the *Zwinger* was earmarked to house an extensive, newly erected complex of palace structures. The Imperial Curate (*Reichsvikariat*) of 1711 initiated the building activities with an orangery made of stone which also contained pavilions, galleries, water games, and a gathering place. The *Zwinger*—ultimately the most famous building created under Augustus the Strong (the anticipated palace remained unbuilt)—housed a Grotto Hall (*Grottensaal*) (fig. 3), begun in 1714 and located in the southwestern Corner Pavilion (*Eckpavillon*). The meaning is derived from Louis XIV's Versailles grotto dedicated to Thetis: Apollo, alias the king, ventures into Neptune's realm in order to repose from his notable deeds and to take care of the arts.[1] Since it was demolished in 1684 to make room for extensions in Versailles, Augustus did not see the grotto of Thetis—comprehensively published by Félibien—during his visits there. Yet the ruler visited the "Bosquet des Bains d'Apollon," where the marble sculpture of the Thetis grotto had been translocated. Of its main group, "Apollo with Nymphs," Augustus acquired a small bronze version by François Girardon through court architect Raymond Leplat in Paris.[2] Apart from Leplat, the king also sent the *Zwinger* creator, Matthäus Daniel Pöppelmann, to Paris for study purposes in 1715. The Grotto Hall with its intricate water spectacles received a ceiling painting with Neptune and Amphitrite. In a sequence of niches two figures created by Court Sculptor Balthasar Permoser and executed in "Saxon marble" were installed: "Apollo" (cat. no. 3.8), and "Minerva" (1716), representing the wise state art, bore idealized portraits of Augustus and of the queen.

Simultaneous with the creation of the *Zwinger* the Residential Palace was also remodeled. On the third floor two parallel ceremonial enfilades were created, each of which had two antechambers that led to the Audience Chamber (*Audienzzimmer*) and the Parade Bed Chamber (*Parade-schlafzimmer*), respectively. For the paintings Augustus invited Louis de Silvestre, student of the Sun King's "premier peintre" Charles LeBrun, to Dresden. While still in Paris, in 1715, Silvestre created the ceiling painting on canvas for the Parade Bed Chamber equipped in the French style: Dawn is hailed by Aurora who

short of the bedroom. For Augustus the Strong a concrete reference to the buildings and spaces, the gardens and monuments, pictures, ceremonies, and court festivities of Louis was feasible owing to his own personal experiences and meetings with the king on the occasion of his extended visits to Paris, Versailles, and Fontainebleau in 1687/88. In a carefully designed plan, Augustus brought French artists to his court and obtained the publications of Louis's leading artists and historiographers including Claude Perrault, Charles LeBrun, and André Félibien. The text printed for *Ballet royal de la nuit* (1653)—the only event in which Louis XIV ever appeared as the sun god Apollo—was also acquired for Dresden. This apotheosis of the sovereign was carefully staged and further developed in other media and for different roles.

To speak of Augustus the Strong in the role of the sun god Apollo, means the depiction of the zenith of his reign, and it implies writing his—incoherent—success story. "NASCOSCO APARISCE"/"The concealed one appears" is the motto Augustus utilized when introducing himself as future prince elector on the occasion of an equestrian contest. The tournament shield preserved in the Dresden Armory is decorated with the sun piercing through

the clouds and surrounded by the coats-of-arms of Saxon provinces.

Following the cumbersome accession to the Polish throne in 1697 was the Nordic War in which August was defeated in 1706 and temporarily lost the crown. Tsar Peter the Great's victory over Emperor Charles XII in 1709 prepared the path for Augustus's regaining the crown. He visualized this triumph symbolically on June 22, 1709, when he appeared as the sun god Apollo in a procession of the gods. He conceded the role of Mars, god of war, to his visitor and important ally, King Frederick IV of Denmark. Augustus had his personal horse equipped with the same parade riding equipment it had worn on the occasion of his coronation in Kraków, adding golden signs of the sun which were clearly visible from the far distance (fig. 1). The king's sun mask—created as a lasting souvenir by court jeweler Johann Melchior Dinglinger—was made of gleaming gold (fig. 2; cf. cat. no. 7.21). Like the Armory's wax mask of Augustus's "statua" with his coronation outfit, the sun mask bears the king's facial features. During the procession through town, the Apollo-King—accompanied by poets and musicians—was preceded by an Aurora carriage. The continuation of the equestrian tournament as a nocturnal running at the ring was a dra-

announces Apollo's dynamic emergence through the clouds and on sun beams, riding on a white horse.[3] Apollo motifs also dominated the quarters of Louis XIV.

The increased turn toward France occurred before the background of improved diplomatic relations with Louis XIV and culminated in a treaty of friendship. In 1714–15 the Saxon electoral prince visited the royal French court. Augustus was only slowly able to solidify his position in Poland. In 1717 he had a medal struck to commemorate his final return to the Polish throne for which a contract had been ratified. On it, he is depicted as Apollo riding over the clouds in a quadriga. Apollo in the quadriga as an apotheosis of Louis XIV may be observed in the "Bassin d'Apollon" on Versailles's Allée Royale where it was rendered as a monumental gilt figure group in 1671.

In order to successfully secure his son's aspirations for the imperial crown, Augustus worked hard to arrange a wedding with a daughter of the emperor. Apart from numerous building activities that accompanied the preparations for the wedding, he also purchased the Japanese Palace (*Japanisches Palais*) on the right bank of the Elbe which he furnished with porcelain and lacquer cabinets in the chinoiserie style. He had a platform installed into the Mirror Cabinet (*Spiegelkabinett*) in the southwestern corner room containing the history of Phoebus Apollo.[4] The beginning of the festivities of the planets took place in the Dutch Palace with the Apollo feast opening the wedding ceremonies of the

electoral prince with the emperor's daughter Maria Josepha in 1719. The fireworks on the Elbe depicted the conquest of the Golden Fleece with the electoral prince playing the role of Jason. For the Carousel of the Four Elements, Augustus the Strong appeared as the "chief of the fire"—a variation of the sun god theme. Once again, he utilized the riding equipment of his coronation and the Apollo costume of 1709. However, this time he mounted even large, fire-red suns. During the horse ballet and the tournament in the *Zwinger* it was easy to identify the king, who equaled the sun. On the occasion of the Saturn festivity's ultimate scene—which also concluded the festivals of the planets—the symbols of the planets were demonstrated. Attached to a rock, the installation culminated with the symbols of the sun, which was brightly illuminated. At the foot of the rock a temple had been erected in which the sun shone over the king's crowned initials. In 1721 Augustus named the bastions of the Dresden fortification after the planets. He entitled the bastion located on *Feuerwerksplatz*, across from the Dutch Palace (*Holländisches Palais*) , "Sol."

In the newly created Festival Hall (*Festsaal*) of the Hunting Castle Moritzburg, which Augustus remodeled between 1727 and 1730, he installed two of four ceramic stoves with the sun prominently displayed (fig. 4). At the royal residence of Warsaw Augustus had started in 1709 to try to purchase and then to remodel the nearby palace of Wilanow, owned by the former king, Jan III Sobieski. Through sale

4   Stove, ca. 1727–33, Moritzburg Castle, see also p. 269

and inheritance the palace had changed hands and was owned by Duchess Dönhoff who offered it to Augustus in exchange but stipulated that no changes could be made. Apart from its architectural charm, Wilanow bore particular symbolic powers: Still extant and mounted at the attica over the main portal near the inner courtyard was a golden sphere of the sun. It was flanked by reliefs depicting Sobieski's victorious battles during the Turkish Wars. Finally, the platform in the king's bedroom showed Apollo on the sun chariot, an allegory of summer.

Notes

1 Petzet 2000, pp. 503–530.
2 Syndram 1999, p. 176.
3 Marx 1975, pp. 14–16.
4 Schwarm-Thomisch 2002, p. 57.

GROTE QVI EST, DANS UN SALLON A L'ORANGERIE ROYALE.

3   M. D. Pöppelmann, "The Zwinger Copperplate Works", sketch for the Grotto Hall in the Mathematisch-Physikalischer Salon, 1729, copperplate engraving by A. Zucchi, 17 1/8 × 25 1/8 in., CDPP

Contest of the Gods in Dresden

The Festivities of the Planets during the Prince Elector's Wedding in 1719

Claudia Schnitzer

The 1719 wedding of Saxon Prince Elector Frederick Augustus (II) to Maria Josepha, daughter of the emperor, was an event of the greatest political and dynastic significance for the Wettins (fig. 1).[1] Prince Elector Frederick Augustus of Saxony, called Augustus the Strong (*August der Starke*), was already king in Poland. His grand aspirations for his son were personified by this promising bond between the two dynasties: he hoped that his son might thus obtain the imperial crown.[2]

The wedding festivities, scheduled for September, were intended to be without parallel and unsurpassed. The elector king himself emerged as stage director and chief program designer. For the duration of one entire month, he arranged one new attraction per day to take place either in Dresden or its surroundings (fig. 2).[3] The theme of the lavish events was the seven planets. The topic of the planetary gods as well as the individual event types were firmly rooted in Dresden court traditions. In preparing the festivities, Augustus was therefore able to fall back on elements known, well tried, and tested.[4] However, the innovative aspect was the coordination of the different festivities in unprecedented programmatic, chronological, spatial, and technical matters. The wedding celebrations were one of the highlights and culminating events in the Saxon festival culture which had been famous since the 16th century. The nuptials of 1719 achieved renown as "Augustus the Strong's festivities of the planets."

C. H. J. Fehling, The Great Illumination at the Miners' Festivity in the Plauensche Grund on September 26, 1719 (detail), see fig. 3 on p. 32

1   J. F. Wentzel, Sketch for a Title Page with Portraits of Bride and Groom Frederick August (II) of Saxony and Archduchess Maria Josepha, pen and brush in gray and watercolors, 24³/₈ x 35³/₄ in., CDPP

The king's high aim manifested itself not only in the illustrious festivities themselves, but also in the extensive illustrated report he ordered, which was to be executed in a large and luscious format. The tome was supposed to proclaim the marriage across regional borders and portray the Saxon prince electors in glowing colors for future generations.[5] Had the ambitious publication been completed, it would have been the most elaborate festival account of all time. Yet, because of its immense dimensions and the exorbitant costs involved, it failed. An entire team of artists spent years preparing the illustrations for the planned publication. After the death of his father in 1733, Frederick Augustus II discontinued the commissions for work on the wedding report and sent the preparatory drawings and engravings to the Collection of Drawings, Prints, and Photo-graphs (*Kupferstich-Kabinett*)[6] for safekeeping. Even in their incomplete state, these holdings offer a fantastic insight into the festivities of 1719.

The Dresden wedding celebrations commenced with the ceremonial escort of the bride. On Saturday, September 2, Maria Josepha traveled down the Elbe, in a parade gondola, from the city of Pirna to the village of Blasewitz just outside the Dresden city gates (fig. 2). Here, the king received the young electoral princess in a specially constructed camp and invited her to dine. After this refreshment the bride's journey to the residence continued with a stately parade on land. Led through triumphal arches, the procession terminated in the Dresden Residential Palace, where, after a brief recreation, Maria Josepha was greeted and escorted to the audience.

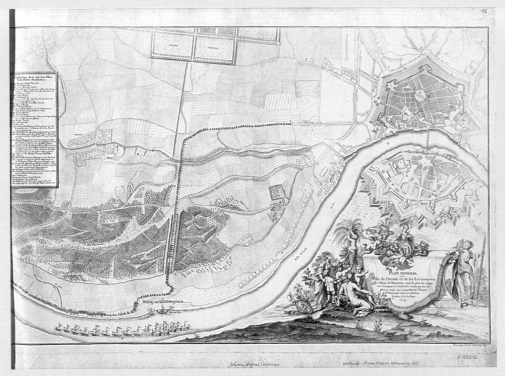

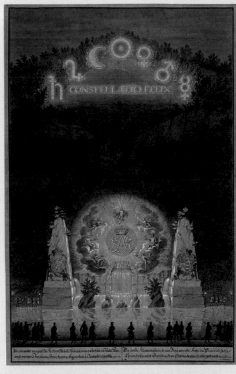

2 J. A. Corvinus after Major General Grawert (plan) and A. M. Werner (cartouche), General Map of Dresden with Surroundings, Camp and Parade Route on September 2, 1719, etching, 23 x 35³/₈ in., CDPP

3 C. H. J. Fehling, The Great Illumination at the Miners' Festivity in the Plauensche Grund on September 26, 1719, pen and brush in gray, heightened with white, on blue paper, 34³/₈ x 21⁷/₈ in., CDPP

The long journey was tiring for the bride. Therefore, the first week of ceremonies involved less fatiguing festivities such as banquets, performances of operas and comedies, balls, animal baiting, as well as a running at the ring in the Stable Court (*Stallhof*). These activities were supposed to whet the guests' thirst for the real festival cycle of the seven planets. On Sunday afternoon, September 10, the festivities of the planets were ceremoniously inaugurated in the garden of the Dutch Palace (*Holländisches Palais*), today called the Japanese Palace (*Japanisches Palais*) (fig. 4).

For this occasion, Johann David Heinichen composed an inaugural serenade entitled "La gara degli dei." Italian singers personified the planet gods in order to greet the bride and groom and to convey their good wishes.[7] They told the audience that each god would organize a party to honor the newlyweds and that all present were invited. The serenade therefore offered the guests a programmatic overview of the festivities; at the same time, their expectations were raised.

Apollo (Sol) announced that a fireworks drama would occur that evening.

Scheduled to take place on the Elbe and the other riverbank, the myth of the Argonauts would be performed (fig. 5). Special attractions included a sea battle of the parade gondolas, the temple of fireworks, and the fire-spitting dragon. The conquest of the Golden Fleece by Jason alluded to the prince elector's conquering the daughter of the emperor.

On the following Tuesday the festival of Mars began on the Market Place (*Altmarkt*). This was a tilt and foot tournament "across the barrier," in which the god of war appeared in a chariot (fig. 6). The sen-

4 J. A. Corvinus after A. M. Werner, Opening Ceremony of the Festivities of the Planets in the Garden of the Dutch Palace on September 10, 1719, etching and copperplate engraving, 14³/₈ x 21¹/₂ in., CDPP

5 J. A. Corvinus after M. D. Pöppelmann, Fireworks on the Elbe behind the Dutch Palace on September 10, 1719, etching, 24³/₄ x 33¹/₄ in., CDPP

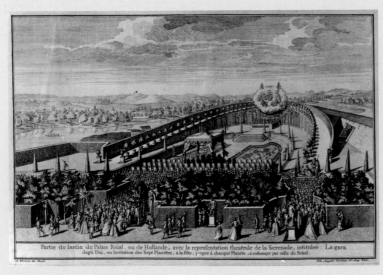

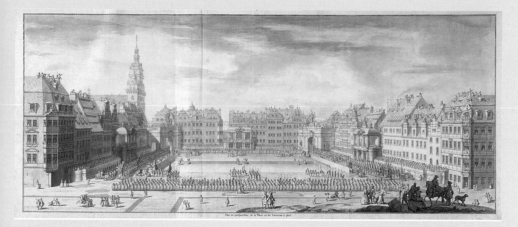

6   B. Reynard (?), Foot Tournament on the Market Place on September 12, 1719, pen and brush in gray, 24³/₈ x 56 in., CDPP

tant elements were the riders' agility with their horses and their aptitude with regards to the use of different weapons.

The event began in front of the royal box with a musical presentation honoring Jupiter. Godfather resided in Chaos, which was created by a complicated theater machine that stirred up the elements fire, water, earth, and air. In the depiction of the quadrille elements' entry into the

sational aspect of this event was that historic, rather dangerous, and literally "martial" tournament types were performed. Prerequisites for a lance tournament on horseback—as well as combat on foot with spear and sword—included the use of protective armor. A number of historic suits of armor from the Armory (*Rüstkammer*) were utilized once again. Augustus the Strong and his son did not actively participate in these risky contests. Instead, they watched as spectators from a special box of honor along with the princess and the queen.

The godfather Jupiter was the patron of the Carousel of the Four Elements, which premiered in the *Zwinger* on Friday, September 15 (fig. 7). With a total of 637 people and 429 horses participating in the procession, it was among the largest and the most lavish of all Baroque equestrian games.[8] In terms of its scope and its design this carousel was comparable to the Viennese horse ballet that occurred for Emperor Leopold I's wedding in 1667, the central theme of that was also the contest of the elements. By continuing the tradition of the famous equestrian game, Augustus the Strong paid homage to the Hapsburg bride. One further unmistakable ingredient of this gesture was his attempt to continue and ultimately to surpass the

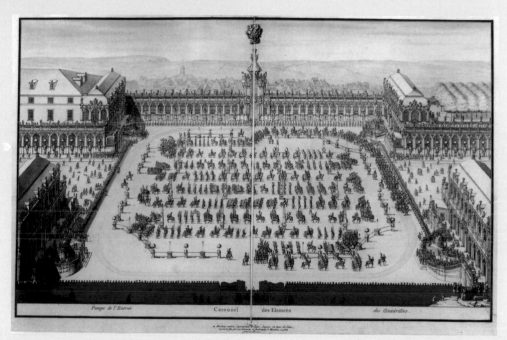

7   C. H. J. Fehling, Entry of the Quadrilles for the Carrousel of the Four Elements into the Zwinger on September 15, 1719, pen and brush in gray, 22³/₄ x 35³/₈ in., CDPP

imperial festival tradition: His hope was to obtain, thanks to this advantageous marriage, imperial status for his own dynasty. In contrast to the tournament on the Market Place, this modern carrousel was an equestrian game in which the most impor-

Zwinger, the appearance and the disappearance of this chaos machine is made comprehensible thanks to a small moveable drawing which is adhered to a strip of parchment. In the ensuing contest, the participants were commanded to reach for

8   C. H. J. Fehling (?), Arrival of Diana on the Elbe on September 18, 1719, pen and brush in gray, 22 x67⁵/₈ in., CDPP

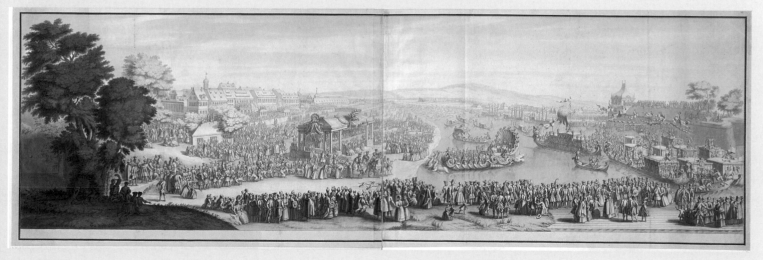

Vûes de la Plaçe inferieure du Iardin Roïal de l'Orangerie, avec les differenfes Comparfes et Amufémens de la Mercerie.

9 J. A. Corvinus after C. H. J. Fehling, "Mercerie" in the Zwinger on September 20, 1719, etching and copperplate engraving, 21 1/2 x 33 3/8 in., CDPP

the ring with their lances, to hit two discs with their javelins, and to push a ball made of papier-mâché off its pedestal with their small swords. Augustus the Strong appeared in the most exquisite of all carrousel garments as "chief of the fire." His robe was embellished with diamond-studded crossed straps which were decorated on the back and on the front with the star of the Polish White Eagle Order (cat. no. 4.35). The queen and the electoral princess distributed the sumptuous prizes to the contest winners. Afterwards, another contest on horseback took place with shields and clay balls, a so-called "carisel." The conclusion of the Jupiter festival consisted of a horse ballet which was lead by Augustus the Strong as rider.

Diana (Luna) was the patroness of the waterfowl shooting on the river Elbe on Monday, September 18 (fig. 8).[9] It took place above the only Elbe bridge then in existence: the area between what is today the *Brühlsche Terrasse* and the hunting lodge (*Jägerhof*) on the right river bank, which is where the royal tent had been erected. At circa 2 p. m., Diana's stately ship, which was pulled by two (wooden) deers, entered the waters of the hunting grounds. The goddess of the hunt and her mates were accompanied by the court orchestra and the choir when they performed the cantata "Diana su l'Elba." Then a total of some 400 stags, deers, and boars were driven into the Elbe. The animals were forced to swim down river, past the royal tent. In a five-hour-long hunt, they were slaughtered by the aristocratic participants. The courtiers found repose from this massacre in a French comedy, which ended the day.

On Wednesday, September 20, mes-

10 C. H. J. Fehling, Ladies' Running at the Ring in Front of the Palace in the Large Garden on September 23, 1719, pen and brush in gray, over graphite, 22 1/2 x 31 1/8 in., CDPP

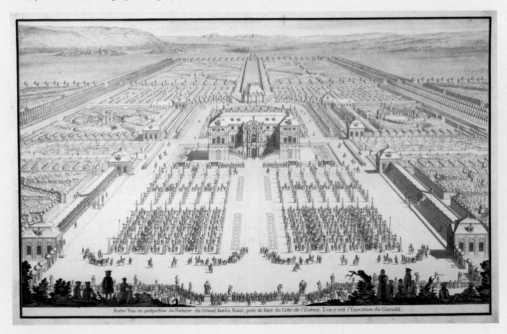

Autre Vûe en perfpective du Parterre du Grand Iardin Roïal, prife de Face du Côté de l'Entrée. L'on y voit l'Execution du Carousel.

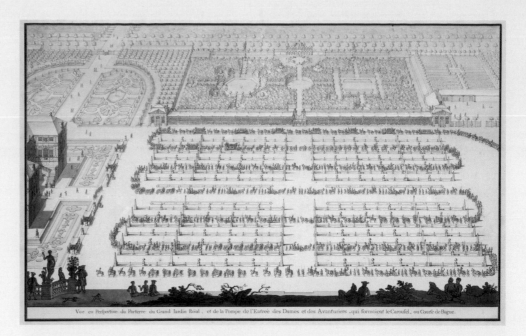

senger of the gods and god of trade, Mercury, initiated a so-called "mercerie," i. e. a fair with a national tavern in the *Zwinger* (fig. 9). This masquerade required the royal couple, disguised as tavern keepers, to receive the courtiers who appeared in costumes of different nations. The prince electoral couple was the first in the group of Persians. The congregation of the nations consisted of approximately 376 people who strolled across the fairground, which offered a total of 60 booths as well as numerous performances by acrobats and actors. After a festive banquet, the group returned to the fairground, where the ladies received their lottery prizes, which comprised valuable watches, miniatures, embroidered French shoes, and many other fancy goods donated by the king. Their combined value amounted to more than 60,000 thalers. The masked party danced until late into the night in the Marble Hall (*Marmorsaal*).

The festival for the ladies was dedicated to Venus, the goddess of love. It occurred on Saturday, September 23. Among the seven festivals of the planets it was particularly appropriate for the glorification of the prince electoral wedding as a "fruitful" marriage of love. All of these divertissements embodied the themes of courtly love, gallantry, beauty, and fertility (fig. 10–18). The participants left the castle at 11 a.m. on a long procession to the place of the festival, the cultivated nature of the Large Garden (*Großer Garten*), situated outside the city (fig. 10 and 11). Apart from the organizers, the referees, the near

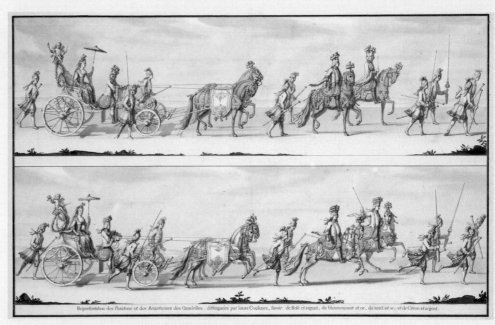

12 C. H. J. Fehling, Carriages for the Ladies' Running at the Ring, pen and brush in gray, over graphite, 22¹/₂ x 34¹/₂ in., CDPP

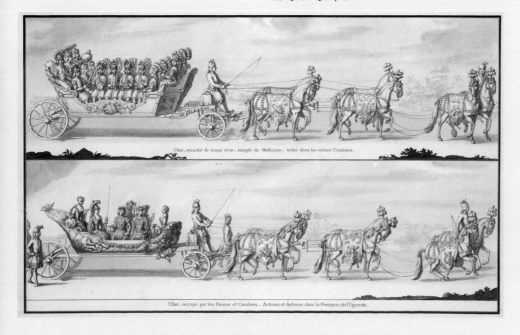

horses, and the footmen, the procession included the carriages and the riders of the four quadrilles for ladies' running at the ring (fig. 12). In addition, there were four carriages with 18 nymphs each, one carriage with musicians, one with the singers of the opera ballet (fig. 13), as well as four carriages with six court ladies and six gentlemen each carrying the disguises for the gardeners, the cutters, the winemakers, and the "north landers" who personified the four seasons in the ballet interludes. Three so-called "sausage carriages" carrying French and Italian comedians were at the tail end of the procession.

13 C. H. J. Fehling, Carriages of the Musicians and Singers, pen and brush in gray, over graphite, 22⁵/₈ x 34¹/₈ in., CDPP

Baroque Dresden **35**

14 C. H. J. Fehling, *The Natural Theater in the Large Garden*, pen and brush in gray, 22 x 34¹/₈ in., CDPP

exquisite robes, led each quadrille. As in 1709, also in 1719 the ladies were accompanied by two cavaliers on horseback who attempted to pierce the ring with their lances on separate race courses.

The pink quadrille carried the color of Venus and was led by the bride, Maria Josepha, as the principal (fig. 12). *Oberhofmarschall* Graf von Dietrichstein was the driver of the carriage. The groom and Augustus the Strong, the father in law, served as "runners." The group of principals of the pink-colored quadrille was the most sumptuously dressed of all teams.

The four groups of principals opened the ladies' running at the ring. Upon finishing their twelve courses they watched their quadrilles in the tournament. First,

The ladies' running at the ring was the main attraction of the morning (fig. 10). Once they arrived in front of the palace, the participants moved through the race-courses where the tournament subsequently took place (fig. 11). During this chivalrous game, a lady in a carriage aimed to pierce a ring with her lance, while a courtier led the carriage.[10] Augustus the Strong had organized a ladies' running at the ring once before during the 1709 visit of King Frederick IV of Denmark. While the festival of 1719 referred to its predecessor, its chronology, scope, and choreography were further enhanced and most definitely improved. The creation of twelve racecourses—in 1709 there were but three—enabled a simultaneous race of the four quadrilles and the running at the ring. The effect of this performance was thus magnified. At the same time, it proved more challenging to coordinate the show. 34 ladies participated, ten more than in 1709. The costumes, carriages, decorations, and the piercing lances of the four quadrilles had the following color combinations: pink and silver, blue and silver, green and gold, yellow and gold. The structuring into quadrilles was not just a reference to the Carousel of the Four Elements. More importantly, it referred to the "Four Seasons" which was supposed to be performed as a ballet in the natural theater of the Large Garden after the running at the ring. A group of principals, dressed in

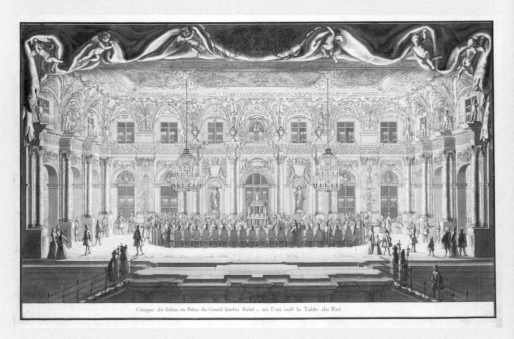

15 C. H. J. Fehling, *The Palace in the Large Garden, with a View of the Halls*, pen and brush in gray, 22⁵/₈ x 34³/₈ in., CDPP

16 C. H. J. Fehling, *Festival Hall in the Palace in the Large Garden*, pen and brush in gray, 22¹/₂ x 34¹/₄ in., CDPP

17   C.H.J. Fehling, View of the Large Garden with
Nocturnal Illumination, pen and brush in gray,
heightened with white, on blue paper, 23¹/₄ x 34³/₈ in.,
CDPP

each cavalier's score was added up for the
respective lady; then the sum of the whole
quadrille was credited to the patroness.
The grand prize was awarded to Maria
Josepha. It was a hairpin in the shape of a
sizeable, flat, and crowned heart, studded
with brillant-cut diamonds.

After the awarding of prizes the courtly
society convened at the nature theater for
the opera-ballet "Les quatre saisons" by
Johann Christoph Schmidt (fig. 12).[11]
According to the libretto, the subject, plan,
and cast of the French divertissement were
conceived by the king. The presentations
of the songs and the dances were performed by courtiers.

After the performance, the company of
courtiers went to the palace where tables
were set up for guests and participants
(fig. 15 and 16). Carl Heinrich Jacob Fehling documented the banquet with three
drawings. The first offers the spectator
views of the different spaces within the
palace. The second illustrates the laid table
in the upper floor from a bird's eye perspective.[12] The third sheet captures the
grand hall with a table festively set for 50
people. The table was decorated with a
centerpiece in the shape of a temple of
Venus. Between the columns of the temple
the head of Augustus the Strong may be
seen.

Meanwhile the garden was illuminated
with hundreds of lamps and large wax
torches (fig. 17). After the meal the nobility
proceeded to their gondolas and went
across the lake to the temple of Venus located on the other side. There, they danced

until the wee hours of the morning. An
audience had gathered on ascending trib-
unes outside the temple and watched the
courtly divertissement (fig. 18).

The festivities of the planets culminated in the gorgeous Miners' Festivity
(*Bergwerksfest*) under the patronage of Saturn which took place on Tuesday, Septem
ber 26 (fig. 19, 20, and frontispiece).[13]
Saturn's reputation was one of ill-humor.
His special position vis-à-vis the other
planets had already been indicated in the
opening serenade. In order not to "obscure
the otherwise happy constellation of the
heavens above through a hostile aspect,"[14]
Saturn had to think of something special.
This was not an easy task. Excluded from
the "planetary pleasure heaven," Saturn
had no choice but to encourage the
miners—who dwell under rocks—to continue their old trades and to demonstrate

all the splendor and glory hidden in the
subterranean.[15]

Augustus the Strong's intention here
was to emphasize the strength of the Saxon
mining works and related industries and to
thereby demonstrate the economic vigor of
his country. The merriment took place in
the *Plauensche Grund* southwest of Dresden
and was opened in the early afternoon with
a hunt. It was followed by an Italian comedy on an open-air stage. At 7 p.m. the
participants gathered in a festival building
which had been expressly erected for this
function. Designed as an illuminated
mountain or a temple of Saturn, a sumptuous meal was served inside. The royal family was seated under the cupola where their
tables were arranged in the shape of the
letter A, in reverence to the king's name.
The table decoration consisted of sugar
mountains and sugar sceneries relating to
mining (fig. 20).[16] This miniature presentation was repeated in life-size by roughly
1,600 men who had gathered on the square
in front of the festival building (fig. 19):
This parade depicted the most important
processes of mining and metal manufacture. At the same time raw materials and
related products such as coins were also
exhibited. Illuminated rocks across the way
served as the background for the two-hour
performance. As a result, the scenery was
reflected in the river Weißeritz and in the
mirror decorations of the festival hall on
the other side (fig. frontispiece). The program of the illumination—beautifully
complemented by the decoration of the
temple of Saturn—did not just pay homage to the planet gods alone. More than

18   C.H.J. Fehling, Temple of Venus in the Large
Garden, pen and brush in gray, over graphite,
22¹/₄ x 33⁵/₈ in., CDPP

19　A. Zucchi after C. H. J. Fehling, *The Miners' Festivity in the Plauensche Grund on September 26, 1719*, etching, 23¹/₄ × 32⁵/₈ in., CDPP

toral Saxon coats of arms complemented the illumination.

The gods had gathered for the opening serenade in order to announce their contest in honor of the bride and groom. At the end of the festivities they met again in order to reach a conclusion from their endeavors. The divine competition for the highest honor had given place for harmony. The planets assembled around the "terrestrial god," Augustus the Strong, and his dynasty. Not only was he admitted into their midst, but the planets seemed to circle around him like satellites. The message of the festivities could not have been made more clearly. Everyone was supposed to recognize that prosperous times lay ahead for Augustus the Strong and his country. The king and the marriage of the prince electoral couple did not occur under only *one happy star*, but under *seven*!

Notes

1 See Weber 1985; Schlechte 1990a; Schlechte 1993.
2 See Weber 1985, pp. 15–17.
3 See the contemporary report "Das Königliche Denckmahl [..]" (1719); Jöchner 1997; Jöchner 2001, pp. 135–149.
4 About the Dresden planet inventions, see Schlechte 1990a, vol. 1, pp. 114–118; Schlechte 1993, pp. 119–121; Exh.-cat. Dresden 2000a, pp. 132f., 265–267. See also Watanabe-O'Kelly 1992, especially pp. 111–138.
5 See Schlechte 1993, p. 125.
6 Inv. no. Ca 200–204 (some volumes dissolved), also *Mappe Festlichkeiten 1719*.
7 See Schlechte 1990a, pp. 131–134.—The Collection of Drawings, Prints, and Photographs preserves figurines for the costumes of the planetary gods. Exh.-cat. Dresden 2000a, pp. 269–272.
8 See Weber 1985, p. 57.
9 See Exh.-cat. Dresden 1978, pp. 164f.
10 See Schnitzer 1998.
11 See Schlechte 1990a, source no. 34.
12 Inv. no. C 6723.
13 See Schlechte 1990b; Günther et al. 1998.
14 "Denckmahl" 1719, p. 104.
15 Ibid., pp. 107f.
16 See Schlechte 1990c, pp. 56–61.

anything else it was a glorification of the ruler.

Illuminating the top of the temple were seven metal attributes of the gods which were arranged in a semicircle around the motto "CONSTELLATIO FELIX." The signs and letters were illuminated in such a way that they appeared to be pieced together of stars. The arrangement of the planets did not follow the rules of astronomy but the order of contemporary metallurgy: Sol/gold in the highest position, to the right Luna/silver, to the left across from them Venus/copper,

to the right Jupiter/tin and Saturn/lead, to the left again Mars/iron and Mercury/mercury. Personifications of the gods appeared on clouds below. Wearing a star on their heads, they held corresponding metal signs and enclosed the crowned monogram of the king (AR, Augustus Rex) in an aura of light. The latter was surrounded by rays of light which made it appear to be a majestic star. Thanks to their arrangement and the presentation of the metals, the gods of the planets appeared to be worshipping the royal name. Cascades of water and flanking obelisks with the royal Polish and the Elec-

20　C. H. J. Fehling, *Royal Table with Mines' Decoration at the Miners' Festivity*, pen and brush in gray, heightened in white, on blue paper, 22 × 34¹/₈ cm, CDPP

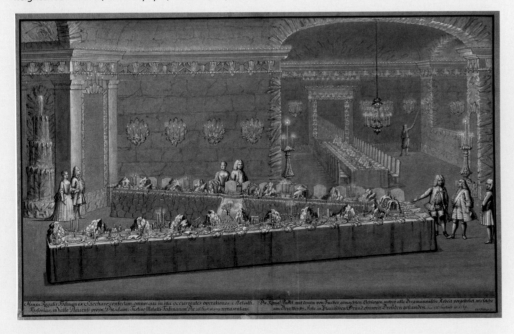

Introductions
to the Collections and
Catalogue
of Exhibited Works

Remarks and Thoughts about the History of Dresden's Old Masters Picture Gallery

Harald Marx

The Prince Electoral *Kunstkammer* as the Basis for the Later Collections

The beginnings of Dresden's world famous Old Masters Picture Gallery (*Gemäldegalerie Alte Meister*) date back to the 16th century, but in the prince electoral *Kunstkammer* paintings played only a secondary role.[1] A completely new phase regarding the arts and collecting began during the reign of Prince Elector Frederick Augustus I (1670–1733). In 1697 he also became king of Poland and went by the name King Augustus II.[2] He followed the example of other German princes when he began to acquire paintings and other works of art on a large scale. However, he soon outdid his models because he commissioned purchases—ranging from the acquisition of individual works to entire collections—to be made on his behalf in Italy and especially in the Netherlands and in Flanders.[3]

There was no space for all these purchases in the *Kunstkammer*, and the paintings were also not intended to be placed there. Instead, they were soon given an exhibition space in the Parade Rooms (*Paraderäume*) of the Dresden Residential Palace. Between 1722 and 1728 the king ordered Privy Chamberlain (*Geheimer Cämmerier*) Adam Friedrich Steinhäuser to compile a separate paintings inventory. In it he listed the complete holdings of paintings in the Residential Palace, in the palaces Pillnitz and Moritzburg, as well as in other places. Soon afterwards, the paintings were transferred

K. L. Preusser, "In the Dresden Picture Gallery" (detail), 1881, see p. 42

into the specially modified Giant Hall (*Riesensaal*), which ultimately remained provisional.

Augustus the Strong (*August der Starke*) was fully aware of the gallery's provisional character: In his museum plans dating after 1730, he anticipated a future picture gallery behind the *Zwinger*.[4] However, a new era regarding collecting and exhibiting paintings did not start until the reign of King Augustus III.

The Picture Gallery as a Creation of King Augustus III

The death of Augustus the Strong, in 1733, and the subsequent succession of his son did not immediately mean a completely new start for the arts and for collecting art in Dresden. Yet, as time went by, a change in taste became noticeable, and the focus of acquisitions was altered. Like his father, the new king was deeply infatuated by art and was a true connoisseur in various fields.

In order to become Polish king, Augustus the Strong was required to convert to Catholicism, which he did in 1697. In this, his son followed him.[5] Thereby, a Catholic tendency in Dresden increased, which was not inconsequential with regard to collecting. It was only during the rule of King Augustus III that the glory days of Dresden's picture collection commenced. He really started what we admire today as the Old Masters Picture Gallery. The purchases lasted until 1756, the beginning of the Seven Years War—and they were never continued with the same magnitude after this point. The Dresden Gallery was essentially created in a matter of one half century. It represents the most distinguished courtly taste of its time, resulting in certain strengths and weaknesses, leading to the collection's specific character. It encompasses masterworks

1   B. Bellotto, called Canaletto (1721–1780), "Dresden's New Market Place, as seen from the Jüdenhof", 1749, etching, 21⁵/₈ x 33 in., CDPP

from the High Renaissance and from the Italian Baroque eras, and 17th-century Dutch paintings. The exquisite group of Leiden Fine Painters[6] and the plethora of highest-quality pictures by so-called minor masters warrant special mention. Furthermore, it was also possible to purchase 17th-century French master-works by such painters as Nicolas Poussin and Claude Lorrain. Dürer, Cranach, and Holbein were collected, or they were already represented in the inventory of the *Kunstkammer*, as leading representatives of German art.

All prior acquisitions for the royal gallery were greatly surpassed, when, in 1745, the 100 best paintings from the collection of Francesco III, Duke of Modena,[7] were purchased. These were major Italian Renaissance works that no other collector north of the Alps had owned until this time. Among them were four large altar-pieces by Correggio,[8] Titian's "Trib-ute Money," and the four largest can-vases by Veronese. Also included were superb works by Garofalo, Dosso, Battista Dossi, and Gerolamo

2   K. L. Preusser, "In the Dresden Picture Gallery", 1881, oil on canvas, 26³/₄ x 34¹/₄ in., Modern Masters Gallery

da Carpi.[9] Also among the works were Andrea del Sarto's "Sacrifice of Abraham" and paintings that anticipated the 17th century or already belonged to the Baroque, by artists such as Annibale Carracci, Guido Reni, and Guercino; paintings by Velàzquez, Rubens, and Holbein[10] were also represented.

It was with one sudden stroke that the Dresden Gallery had advanced from a beautiful and remarkable princely German collection to one of European rank. But the acquisitions continued. The zenith of this entire epoch was reached with the purchase of Raphael's "Sistine Madonna" in 1754. Until then, the picture had been kept in the monastery church S. Sisto in Piacenza; the purchase price was 20,000 ducats. One of Augustus's long-standing desires had finally been fulfilled: the acquisition of one of Raphael's undisputed masterworks.

Owing to all these additions, a fundamental change regarding the paintings' accommodation was mandatory. As stated before, until this date the paintings were kept in the palace. But in 1745 it was decided to use the electoral Stables Building (*Stallgebäude*) for the picture gallery and to redesign it fundamentally. The festive impression emanating from the Picture Gallery in those days was recorded by Johann Wolfgang von Goethe upon his first visit in 1768 (*Dichtung und Wahrheit*, vol. 8): "My amazement was greater than can be expressed. This astonishing hall—apparently in utter harmony with itself—was dominated by magnificence and immaculateness in which the greatest silence prevailed. The gleaming frames, all of them only fairly recently gilt, the polished floors, and the fact that most of those using the space were spectators rather than laborers—all of this added to a notion of solemnity. This uniqueness was reinforced by sensations comparable to those we have when stepping into a house of God: much of the adornment originated from temples, yet the subject of an adoration appeared to be installed here once again only for the holy purpose of art appreciation."

In the second half of the 18th century the collection's fame and splendor increased continuously, playing a dominant role in the life of many artists and poets of the Classical and Romantic eras. As evidenced by contemporary sources and by evaluations from our time, it is clear that the Picture Gallery was among the most significant cultural achievements in Saxony during the Augustian era. Carl Heinrich von Heineken

3 The Old Masters Picture Gallery, before 1945, as seen from the Zwinger courtyard

wrote: "Nothing is more worthy of a ruler than to choose his pleasures in such a manner that the public may profit from it in pleasurable ways. [...] If someone wants to call a Picture Gallery a public school (*école publique*), he is right in as far as this is a place where you can learn in one view what otherwise takes plenty of books to research."[11]

The Picture Gallery in the 19th Century

It was not until the 19th century that slow changes as well as significant caesuras were brought about. Decisions concerning the Gallery increasingly became public issues. The establishment of the "Gallery Commission" in 1836, was a step in this direction, and the necessity for a new gallery building was one of the results. After long discussions, the New Royal Museum (*Das Neue Königliche Museum*) was erected near the *Zwinger*.

In the middle of the century, acquisitions began to increase once again. Although most of the pictures purchased were from the 19th century (one of the side effects was the creation of the Modern Masters Gallery/*Galerie Neue Meister*), some new accents were established for the Old Masters as well. The new arrivals in Dresden included, in 1853, fifteen 17th-century Spanish paintings from the estate of the French "king of the people," Louis Philippe. At this time Spanish art was very little known in Germany; subsequently a Spanish department was founded within the gallery.[12] Even in the 1870s and 1880s, a number of exquisite paintings by Italian and Dutch masters could still be added to the holdings.

The Picture Gallery in the 20th Century

While the Dresden Gallery was never entirely untouched by the country's political and economic developments, it appears that the 20th century brought about a national catastrophe and the Gallery's temporary demise. The time of the National Socialist dictatorship caused severe losses for the Modern Department: In 1937 so-called "degenerate art" was singled out. And finally, the Dresden Gallery experienced the greatest threats in its entire history during World War II.[13]

The Gallery was closed in 1938/39. When the war with its horrors began to be fought on German soil, and when bomb attacks increased in 1942, the paintings were moved away. Therefore, when the city was destroyed, on February 13, 1945, the paintings were not in Dresden. The museum building and the *Zwinger*, however, were badly damaged. Upon marching into the city, the Russian "Trophy Commissions" were placed in charge of the works in the Dresden collections and were to determine what was to remain in Germany and what was to be taken away. The central collecting point was the Pillnitz castle, which had not been destroyed. The convoys were assembled here—containing what was then considered the collections' most valuable items—and then moved the holdings to Moscow and Kiev. It appeared that all of this material would be eternally lost to Dresden.[14]

However, after ten years an event that no one had dared to hope for occurred: On August 25, 1955, a delegation of the German Democratic Republic's government was handed over the Dresden paintings in Moscow. They reappeared in public, emerging from their decade-long secret custody where they had all but disappeared, and it was illegal even to mention them. Although the majority of the Gallery's inventory safely made it through the war, the losses incurred are painful. In 1963 the Dresden Art Collections published a catalog, listing the war losses. It contains the definitively lost paintings by Old and Modern Masters. At the same time, this publication forms the basis for any search related to missing works. The catalog mentions 206 destroyed and 507 missing paintings, of which only 50 have been retrieved to date.[15]

After 32 years, in February 1988, a fundamental restoration commenced. With the new political and economic possibilities arising from the German unification, it was possible to address some of the central issues. The point of departure for the renovation of the years 1988–92 were technical requirements. The question of such a gallery's intention and its function today called for an answer. In Dresden, the losses of historic building substance—due to war and the postwar decades—are frighteningly extensive. Perhaps it is exactly because the sense of history is so much alive that a solution was sought which would be bound by the best of museum traditions and would thereby be appropriate for the present. The Old Master Paintings fascinate us because in them the fates and hopes, the experiences and dreams of entire eras resonate. When Louis Aragon and Jean Cocteau talked about the return of the paintings from the Dresden Gallery, in Paris, in 1956, Aragon remarked that the pictures are "reflections of humankind."[16]

Notes

1 See Holzhausen 1927; Menzhausen 1985; Watanabe-O'Kelly 2002; Vötsch 2002.
2 See Haake 1927; Czok 1989.
3 See Exh.-cat. Munich 1990.
4 See Heres 1980 (1983).
5 See Staszewski 1996.
6 See Exh.-cat. Leiden 2001.
7 See Winkler 1989.
8 See Exh.-cat. Dresden 2000b.
9 See Exh.-cat. Ferrara 2002.
10 See Marx 1999.
11 Heineken 1753/57; Marx 1999.
12 See Marx 2000a; Weniger 2002.
13 See Seydewitz/Seydewitz 1957; Petropoulos 1999.
14 See Akinscha/Koslow 1995.
15 See Exh.-cat. Dresden 1998a.
16 Aragon/Cocteau 1975, p. 9.

"A Piece with Four Life-Size Persons…"

An Early Keywork of Johannes Vermeer in Dresden's Old Masters Picture Gallery

Marlies Giebe/Uta Neidhardt

Vermeer's 1656 painting "The Procuress" (cat. no. 1.18) is significant for several reasons, not only because it is the first dated work in the surviving œuvre of the Delft painter. Executed after his two early history paintings, this is at the same time an astonishing and unexpected work whose singular position becomes increasingly apparent. While this is Vermeer's first preserved genre scene, it also breaks away from its predecessors with regard to a number of components related to content and style. Whereas "The Procuress" denotes an early turning point in Vermeer's creativity, it also represents the crucial link to the contemplative, small genre scenes that were to occupy him until the end of his life.

The large, unusually dimensioned picture shows four life-size figures—partly obscured by a carpet over a balcony—who are communicating with one another and before the viewer. The thematic content of the scene remains partly opaque, allowing for the proposal of different theories. The meeting between the girl in the yellow jacket and the young suitor, elegantly dressed in red, speaks a rather obvious language. He has put his hand on her chest while he drops a coin into her open right hand. If one follows this interpretation, which identifies the dark, smiling features of the elderly woman slightly in the background as the procuress, then one can confirm that the painting depicts a prostitution scene.

The male figure near the left edge wears a 16th-century costume and holds a glass and a lute in his hands. He is the only individual who makes eye contact with the spectator. A totally different explication of this painting occurs if one focuses on the central position of the latter figure within the arrangement and if one pursues the notion that it bears traces of a self-portrait. The scene could then be conceived as the Prodigal Son with the prostitutes. Since it is well known that Vermeer frequently referred—both thematically and stylistically—to works of the Utrecht Caravaggisti, with whom he was intimately familiar, contemporary viewers might have derived one further meaning from it: the figure group is reminiscent of renderings of the five senses as seen in Christiaen van Couwenbergh's work. His figure scenes also portray the personified senses meeting one another in an "easygoing" ambiance. The reduction of the composition to only four figures would then just be one further variant in the plethora of unconventional, sometimes surprising decisions Vermeer made during the process of creating this painting.

The work is full of contradictions and surprises with regard to its composition and painting technique. The exact location of the protagonists—apparently placed on a slightly elevated balcony—remains unresolved. A small table with a glass and a Delft pitcher placed rather daringly near its edge is visible in one corner of the balcony and appears to obstruct the seated girl's body. In a later step, Vermeer applied two layers of paint over the heavy, precious carpet and painted in a black coat. In doing so, he deliberately toned down the coloration of the left portion of the painting in order to guide the viewer's attention more directly towards the young couple and their interaction. The palette of pure yellow, white, and red in conjunction with the blue of the clay pitcher is repeated in the pattern of the carpet in the picture's lower half. With the help of numerous similar formal tricks, Vermeer sought to create a meaningful and balanced composition. This process entailed a deliberate deviation from the realistic rendering of things: for instance, Vermeer changed the outer contour of objects such as the Delft pitcher in order to achieve greater overall clarity and equilibrium of the painting. Additionally, he undertook various modifications, some of them drastic, during the painting process. Thanks to X-rays, it has been possible to bring these changes to light, which include the long-haired beau's hat and the direction in which the girl looks; she now gazes toward the coin above her right hand, which was originally closed.

The ultimate goal of the conservation treatment for "The Procuress" was to find answers to crucial questions regarding the creative process and the technical construction of the painting. Initial observations revealed that the painting is a true experiment. The canvas is Vermeer's second largest after his early work "Christ with the Virgin and Martha" in Edinburgh. A horizontal seam runs along the lower quarter of the canvas which is primed with two foundation layers: While a white layer contains chalk and lead white as a filling compound, a second one consists of reddish ocher and lead white. Vermeer applied the ground directly with a broad brush and oil paint, utilizing pigments customary at the time: lead white, lead-tin yellow, vermilion, red varnish, smelts, and earth colors, as well as ultramarine for the Delft pitcher. His painting technique is very unrestrained, executed with broad brushes and developed with free brush strokes. He frequently applied the deepest color values at the end of the painting process. Consequently, the brush's bristles sometimes became stuck in the drying paint. Vermeer painted the girl's lit face and the white bonnet with accomplished sensitivity and artistic certainty resulting in a quasi-Impressionist idiom. Except for the rendering of the outline of the pitcher, which is incised, he did not concentrate on contours in this picture.

The conservation treatment entailed removing old varnish, reworking an older relining, filling and retouching numerous—sometimes minute—damages to the paint layers, and the subsequent filling of numerous minor losses. After conservation the painting appears distinctly more colorful and more differentiated in its contrasts. The newly applied varnish gives the effect of depth, resulting in the picture's reinstated illusion of space. Consequently, the scene regained its

J. Vermeer, "The Procuress" (detail), 1656, see cat. no. 1.18, p. 65

liveliness, appearing, once again, as though it was happening on a stage.

During conservation, the creative process of "The Procuress" was made more transparent, adding significantly to its status as a key painting within Vermeer's oeuvre. The painting was considered a work of Gerard van Honthorst when Prince Elector Frederick Augustus II acquired it in 1741. Catalogued as such, the 1737 register of Count Waldenstein's collection in Dux/Bohemia calls it "A Piece with Four Life-Size Persons ..." In the ensuing years it was attributed to Jan Vermeer II van Haarlem, among others, and, until 1862, to Jacob van der Meer van Utrecht, partly because only a few years after his demise, the true creator's identity had sunk into oblivion. When Thoré-Bürger, the commendable rediscoverer of Vermeer, searched European collections for works by the unknown Delft master, "The Procuress" was one of the first he could securely attribute to the master in 1858.

ANDREA MANTEGNA
(1431–1506)

The Holy Family
CA. 1495–1500
TEMPERA ON CANVAS
$29^{1}/_{2} \times 24^{1}/_{4}$ IN.
GAL. NO. 51

Provenance: *Acquired in 1876 from the Estate of Charles Eastlake, London.*

Mantegna, court painter of the Gonzaga in Mantua since 1459, made a significant contribution to Italian Renaissance art. This painting's austere composition bears clear similarities to antique reliefs. The heads of Joseph and Elizabeth in the background look like realistic Roman portrait busts, whereas the graceful charm of the Virgin and Child are related to Florentine reliefs from the early Renaissance. The little St. John in the lower right corner points to Christ with the inscription "Ecce Agnus Dei" ("See the Lamb of God"). The cruciform-shaped twig with foliage which St. John sports may be interpreted as a reference to Christ's later death on the cross. For the past three years the painting's sensitively applied and differentiated colors have been appreciated once again. This is a result of its recent conservation treatment at the J. Paul Getty Museum in Los Angeles which revealed that the composition was originally conceived much narrower on the left and right sides, comparable, for instance, to the very similar painting in the Museo di Castelvecchio, Verona.

Lit.: *Exh.-cat. Mantua 1961, p. 50 (no. 31).—Bellonci/Garavaglia 1967, p. 116 (no. 84).— Camesasca 1992, pp. 68 f.*
GW

CAT. NO. 1.2

JACOPO ROBUSTI, called
Tintoretto *(1518/19–1594)*

Portrait of a Lady in Mourning

CA. 1550–55
OIL ON CANVAS, 41 × 34¼ IN.
GAL. NO. 265A

Provenance: *Purchased in
1746 from the Galleria Estense,
Modena.*

The viewer beholds a
noble lady dressed in
mourning who leans
to the left while her head is
turned to the right. It may be
deduced—from the figure's
pose—that this portrait was
not intended as a pair (as is
usually the case with married
couples) and that Tintoretto
conceived the widow as an
independent portrait. Attributed to Titian when it was
acquired in 1746, the painting
was purchased together with
other similarly sized female
portraits by the artist, all of
which were exhibited in a row
(cat. no. 1.3). The depiction
of the mourning lady definitely
reflects the great influence
Titian exerted on the young
Tintoretto, who distinguished
himself in Venice primarily
with his monumental religious
paintings. Among them were
works for the Doge's Palace,
numerous churches, and the
Scuola Grande di San Marco
and San Rocco. Tintoretto's
Dresden "Portrait of a Lady in
Mourning" shows him as a
master of restraint, of concise
composition, and of subdued
colors. All this culminates in a
stupendous characterization of
the sitter.

Lit.: *Rossi 1973, pp. 103f.—
Exh.-cat. Washington/New York/
San Francisco 1978/79, p. 211
(no. 518).—Exh.-cat. Venice
1994, p. 98 (no. 12).*

GW

TIZIANO VECELLIO,
called Titian *(1476 or ca.
1485/1490–1576)*

Titian's Daughter Lavinia

CA. 1560–65
OIL ON CANVAS, 40½ × 34 IN.
MARKED UPPER RIGHT:
LAVINIA TIT. V. F. AB. EO. P.
GAL. NO. 171

Provenance: *Purchased in
1746 from the Galleria Estense,
Modena.*

The Latin inscription
identifies the sitter
Lavinia and states that
the portrait was painted by
her father. Born around 1530,
she married in 1555 and died
during the birth of her sixth
child, in 1561. Based on stylistic arguments, some scholars
date the picture to this time,
whereas others suggest a slightly later date of circa 1565. If
this was the case, Titian would
have painted Lavinia posthu-
mously. He depicts her in precious clothes, and the image
derives its rhythm largely from
the figure's slight turn and the
placement of the hands. In her
right hand Lavinia sports a fan
made of ostrich feathers while
her left hand holds the cloth of
her garment. Thus, the impression of a slight movement to
the left is created. Titian's contribution to the development of
portrait painting cannot be
overestimated: Many successful
patterns can be traced back to
him, influencing, in ensuing
centuries, such artists as
Rubens, van Dyck, and others
and helping them to accom-
plish their multifaceted challenges.

Lit.: *Wethey 1971, p. 116
(no. 61).—Exh.-cat. Modena
1998, pp. 326f. (no. 101).*

GW

after three days (Matthew 27:57-28:7). In the background Veronese shows a later scene: three women came to the sepulcher in the morning to anoint Christ's body, but an angel related the miracle of his resurrection to them. Veronese's model was an altar painting by Titian of 1522 (St. Nazaro e Celso, Brescia) from which he derived the basic asymmetrical composition. But compared to his prototype, he increased the elegance and the compositional density by the multiple overlapping layers of space and figures. Together with the brilliance of the colors, Veronese created a true little masterpiece.

Lit.: *Pignatti 1976, pp. 137f. (no. 184).—Exh.-cat. London 1983, no. 143.—Exh.-cat. Essen 1986, pp. 345f. (no. 460).*

GW

CAT. NO. 1.5

ANNIBALE CARRACCI (1560–1609)

St. Sebastian
CA. 1583/84
OIL ON CANVAS, 74³/₈ × 42¹/₈ IN.
GAL. NO. 194 B

Provenance: *Purchased in 1746 from the Galleria Estense, Modena.*

When this painting was acquired as part of the one hundred most important works from the Galleria Estense, it was thought to be by Domenico Fetti. In Dresden it remained catalogued as a picture by an anonymous Venetian master until Benati identified it as a major work by the young Carracci in 1996. Thanks to the power of his academy, Carracci had the utmost influence on art—both in Bologna and

CAT. NO. 1.4

PAOLO CALIARI, called Veronese *(1528–1588)*

The Resurrection of Christ
CA. 1570–75
OIL ON CANVAS, 53³/₄ × 41 IN.
GAL. NO. 235

Provenance: *Purchased by Riedel in Vienna in 1741.*

The solemn art of Veronese received renewed popularity after the year 1700 with Venetian artists such as Sebastiano Ricci and Giambattista Tiepolo who emulated his style more than a century and a half after his career. It is thus hardly surprising that Augustus III purchased a considerable number of Veronese's paintings, among them four large works in 1746 and, in the year 1741, the relatively small picture exhibited here. Entombed after the Crucifixion, Christ rose

Rome—later in his career. The painting shows the faithful Sebastian, pierced by arrows, yet alive. The way Carracci composed this martyrdom is particularly unusual: The saint, suffering excruciating pain, leans forward and holds onto a column that throws a shadow on his upper body. His demanding gaze fixates on the spectator, thereby directly addressing him. In doing so, Carracci deliberately deviates from the customary iconography, which demanded that the saint be depicted with his eyes lifted upward to indicate his imminent salvation.

Lit.: *Benati 1996.—Exh.-cat. Modena 1998, pp. 382 f. (no. 124).*

GW

CAT. NO. 1.6

GUIDO RENI (*1575–1642*)

Ecce Homo
CA. 1639–40
OIL ON CANVAS, 31 1/8 × 25 5/8 IN.
GAL. NO. 330

Provenance: *First mentioned in the Inventory 1754.*

Reni is the painter who made this image of Christ popular, but many of his innumerable followers diluted its high artistic quality. Reni's original intention is made visible in the most convincing way. After the flagellation, the torturers dressed Christ in a purple robe, placed a crown of thorns on his head, and gave him a stick as his scepter. They mocked him with the words "Hail Thee, King of the Jews!" (Matthew 27:28 f.). Pilate spoke "Ecce Homo"—"Look at this man," when he presented Christ to the people (John 19:5). Reni focuses the narrative on the pain-filled suffering of the mocked Christ. Based on ancient teachings in rhetoric and poetics, the artist elicits the viewers' empathy, which is supposed to be transferred to the image when he sees the suffering Christ. In his treaty *Della pittura*, Leon Battista Alberti stated that the moral formation of the faithful could be best achieved through a particularly affective rendering of the scenes in question.

Lit.: *Pepper 1988, p. 284 (no. 152).—Exh.-cat. Dresden 1998a, p. 198 (no. 41).—Exh.-cat. Dresden 1998b, pp. 45 f. (no. 14).*

GW

CAT. NO. 1.7

CARLO MARATTA
(1625–1713)

Holy Night
AFTER 1652
OIL ON CANVAS, 39 × 29½ IN.
GAL. NO. 436

Provenance: *Purchased in
1743 by Le Leu and Rigaud from
the Collection Carignan, Paris.*

Maratta painted this "Holy Night" as a slightly altered spatial repetition of a lunette fresco that he created in approximately 1652 for the Capella Alaleona in San Isidoro, Rome. The picture's great calm and intimacy are largely determined by the composition of the light. A supernatural glow emanates from the child, carving a cave of safety out of the night's blackness. The miracle of the son of God's birth is thereby made visible. Metaphorically speaking, this is how the light of Christianity penetrates the world's darkness. The source for the image is Correggio's famous altarpiece from San Prospero in Reggio Emilia which was part of the Galleria Estense until it was purchased by Augustus III. During the second half of the 17th century, Maratta became the leading painter of religious topics in Rome—he had the support of seven consecutive popes. Based on such models as Raphael, the Carracci, and Correggio, Maratta perfected his late Baroque style.

Lit.: *Voss 1924, p. 595, 600.—
Posse 1931, p. 47.—Exh.-cat.
Dresden 2000b, pp. 75f.
(cat. no. 17).*

GW

CAT. NO. 1.8

FRANCESCO TREVISANI
(1656–1745)

**The Virgin and Child
with St. John**
OIL ON CANVAS, 39⅛ × 29⅛ IN.
MARKED IN THE BOOK ON THE
LEFT: F. T. 1708
GAL. NO. 448

Provenance: *Purchased in
1743 by Le Leu and Rigaud
from the Collection of Cardinal
Polignac, Paris.*

At the beginning of the 18th century small cabinet paintings became particularly popular in Rome. Far removed from the pathos of Baroque rhetoric, these works were intended primarily for private collectors. Although Maratta prepared the ground for this kind of art, his successors perfected it. Trevisani shows the Virgin lifting up the cloth covering the Christ child so that St. John may worship him. The roses and white lilies, allusions to the Virgin's purity, are Marian symbols. The utmost finesse and smoothness of the painting technique inspired numerous other artists' repetitions. While Maratta's influence may be sensed almost universally, it is also true that he and Trevisani were still under the spell of Correggio whose fascinatingly graceful figures were subsequently copied with some frequency. Therefore, it is not surprising

that Augustus III—who purchased four large altarpieces by Correggio dating to 1514–30 in 1746—also collected the images of the Virgin by Maratta and Trevisani.

Lit.: *DiFederico 1977, p. 48 (no. 35).—Exh.-cat. Philadelphia/Houston 2000, p. 445 (no. 293).—Exh.-cat. Dijon 2001, p. 228 (no. 69).*

GW

CAT. NO. 1.9

ANTONIO CANAL, called Canaletto *(1697–1768)*

The Square of San Giacomo di Rialto in Venice

CA. 1725/26
OIL ON CANVAS, 37⁵/₈ × 46¹/₈ IN.
GAL. NO. 583

Provenance: *First mentioned in the Inventory 1754.*

Virtually unchanged since the 12th century, the small square in front of the little church was the center for money and commerce in Venice. The continuation of the shops on the left opens up the vista of the Rialto, the large main bridge across the Canal Grande. In his balanced composition, Canaletto combines the accurate rendering of the square with his artistic principles to represent the light in and the life of Venice. With paintings such as this one, Canaletto lay the foundations for his famous views. This is one of a group of seven paintings which Canaletto created in the 1720s, presumably commissioned by Colloredo, the imperial minister in Venice. The paintings came to Dresden in conjunction with a large work by Luca Carlevarijs which shows the duke's entry into the Doges' Palace in 1726. Two of the works, among them the counterpart of the exhibited painting with a view of St. Mark's Square, were later removed from the Dresden collection.

Lit.: *Constable 1962, II, no. 297.—Exh.-cat. New York 1989, no. 7.—Kowalczyk 2001, pp. 136f. (no. 58).*

GW

CAT. NO. I.IO

BERNARDO BELLOTTO,
called *Canaletto (1722–1780)*

The Ruins of Dresden's Former *Kreuzkirche*

1765
OIL ON CANVAS, 31¹/₂ × 43¹/₄ IN.
MARKED AT THE LOWER CENTER:
BERNAR: BELOTO DE
CANALETTO. FEC. A.
MDCCLXV
GAL. NO. 638

Provenance: *Delivered by
the artist himself via the Art
Academy in 1765.*

In July 1760, in the middle
of the Seven Years War,
Prussia attacked Dresden.
The *Kreuzkirche*'s tower was hit,
and the ensuing fire destroyed
the nave. During the process of
integrating the ruin into the
new building, the tower's east
wall caved in on June 22, 1765.
Thanks to the aid of a ladder
with only one bar, it was possible to pull down the tower. All
this can be deduced from Bellotto's painting which thereby
becomes an impressive document of the war's destruction,
the church ruin, its demolition,
and its re-erection. With an
effective light composition, Bellotto manages to stage the wide
open architecture. The heap
of rubble is hence transformed
into the base of the tower ruin
which reaches up even higher as
a consequence. Similarities to
other paintings of the Tower
of Babel have repeatedly been
pointed out. In 1765 Bellotto
worked at the Dresden Art
Academy as an instructor for
perspective. Although he was
obliged to deliver paintings—
free of charge—to the academy,
he was paid the sum of 200
thalers for this painting—"out
of pity." Soon afterward, he
obtained a more lucrative position as court painter in Warsaw.

Lit.: *Kozakiewicz 1972, vol. 1,
pp. 136f.; vol. 2, pp. 238, 241.—
Rizzi 1996, p. 144 (no. 116).—
Exh.-cat. Columbus 1999,
pp. 69ff. (no. 7).*

GW

CAT. NO. I.II

PETER PAUL RUBENS
(1577–1640)

Diana's Return from the Hunt

CA. 1616
OIL ON CANVAS, 53¹/₂ × 72¹/₂ IN.
GAL. NO. 962 A

Provenance: *Purchased
through de Witt from Antwerp in
1709; first mentioned in the
Inventory 1722/28.*

After his return to Ant-
werp, Ruben's interest
in themes derived from
Greek and Roman mythology
continued. The figure of the
goddess Diana was particularly
important for him in the years

around 1615: It enabled him to combine Diana with one of his favorite themes, the hunt. The Dresden version accentuates the character of the powerful, beautiful, sensible female and does not emphasize the element of extreme movement, typical of many other images of the hunt. Diana—also goddess of chastity—and her female companions face a group of satyrs who belong to the contrasting, bacchic domain in Rubens's oeuvre. Their bearing and the loot surrounding them demonstrate that the Satyrs epitomize lust; they are diametrical opposites to Diana. Rubens underscores this by painting contrasting colors and

textures between the fur and the light garment, the heavy-robust and the sensuous-elegant bodies. The still lifes and the dogs were rendered by Frans Snyders who worked in Rubens's studio at the time.

Lit.: *Exh.-cat. Antwerp 1977, p. 103 (no. 40 with fig.).—Exh.-cat. Boston/Toledo 1993/94, pp. 30f. (fig. 22).—Exh.-cat. Berlin 2002a, pp. 126f. (no. 47 with fig.).*

UN

Cat. no. 1.12

DANIEL SEGHERS
(1590–1661)

Stone Relief of the Holy Virgin with Child Surrounded by Flowers

Ca. 1655/60
Oil on canvas, 55½ × 44⅛ in.
Signed lower left:
Pater Daniel Segers
Gal. no. 1204

Provenance: *Purchased through Rechenberg in 1728; first mentioned in the Inventory 1722/28.*

Seghers was a clergyman. One of this Jesuit's preferred motifs for his paintings were stone cartouches with figural reliefs surrounded by flower garlands or symmetrically arranged bouquets. He did not paint such images for the open market, but as gifts for the decoration of church interiors or for honorable individuals from the secular or spiritual realms. This monochromatic relief in trompe l'oeil technique comes from Erasmus II Quellinus, with whom Seghers collaborated particularly closely during the 1650s and 1660s. The stone relief forms the center of a richly ornamented

stone cartouche that is decorated by five slightly overlapping flower arrangements, organized in an oval shape and rendered mostly in white and red tonalities. Developed from flower wreaths by his teacher, Jan Brueghel the Elder, Seghers's picture type was further advanced by other painters, among them Joris van Son and Nicolaes van Veerendael.

Lit.: *Hairs 1985, p. 42.—De Bruyn 1988, pp. 239f. (no. 199 with fig.).*

UN

ANTON VAN DYCK
(1599–1641)

**Portrait of a Gentleman
in Black Dress in Front
of a Column**

**Portrait of a Lady in
Black Dress in Front of
Red Drapes**
CA. 1628/30
OIL ON CANVAS
50 × 36¼ IN., 49⅝ × 36¼ IN.
GAL. NOS. 1027, 1028

Provenance: *Purchased through
Heineken in Hamburg, 1741.*

In 1627 van Dyck returned
from Italy to his native
Antwerp where he im-
mediately received multiple
lucrative commissions. Particularly prestigious were assign-
ments for portraits by the
Antwerp bourgeoisy, aristocratic circles, and the Dutch
court. These half-length portraits, intended as a pair, are
depictions of an unidentified
couple. Apparently ordered by
a well-to-do Antwerp family
who insisted on appropriately
representative renderings,
they are comparable to the
portraits of the Antwerp art
dealer Pieter Stevens and his
wife from 1627/28. Van Dyck
emphasized the couple's rank
through adequate surroundings, facial expressions, and
gestures and by having them
pose in front of red drapes.
Thanks to his masterful
painterly subtleties, all details
of the exquisite garments are
represented. The solemn
brushstrokes develop the
three-dimensional qualities of
the painting through the use
of impasto, typical of his
painterly approach during his
second Antwerp period.

Lit.: *Larsen 1988, pp. 229f.
(no. 568f.).*

UN

CAT. NO. 1.14

ADRIAEN VAN UTRECHT
(1599–1652/53)

**Still Life with a Hare
and Birds on a Ring**
1645–49
OIL ON CANVAS, $33^{7/8} \times 46^{1/8}$ IN.
TRACES OF A SIGNATURE IN
LOWER CENTER OF THE TABLE
EDGE (ILLEGIBLE)
GAL. NO. 1215 A

Provenance: *First mentioned in
the Inventory 1754.*

The work of van
Utrecht is distin-
guished by a multitude
of marvelous hunting still lifes.
The exact, almost fine-
painterly manner in which he
renders the plumage of a dead
bird or the fur of a dead hare
speaks for his particular com-
prehension of the subject matter and suggests to the viewer a
direct observation of death.
The Dresden still life belongs
to a group of paintings—begun in the early 1640s—executed under the influence of
small hunting still lifes by Jan
Fyts. The chosen motifs un-
derscore the artist's intimate
knowledge of his subjects: in
this case they are exclusively
derived from the lower echelons of the common hunt—the
dead animals are game.

Lit.: *Greindl 1956, p. 192.—
Gemäldegalerie Dresden 1992,
p. 390 (with fig.).—Exh.-cat.
Vienna/Essen 2002, pp. 210f.
(with fig.).*

UN

REMBRANDT
HARMENSZ. VAN RIJN
(1606–1669)

**Samson, Propounding
a Riddle at the Wedding
Banquet**

1638
Oil on canvas, 49⁵/₈ × 68⁷/₈ in.
Signed center bottom:
Rembrandt.f.1638.
Gal. no. 1560

Provenance: *First mentioned in
the Inventory 1722/28.*

Painted only a few years before his "Nightwatch," this pivotal history painting is one of the highlights in Rembrandt's early work. For his rendering of the biblical Samson story (Judges 14:10–18), Rembrandt chose the scene in which the long-haired hero propounds a riddle to the participants in the wedding banquet. During the course of events, his bride, a Philistine, gives away the solution to her compatriots. As a consequence, the enraged Samson kills thirty Philistines and abandons his bride. The prominent position of the statuesque, immobile female at the center of the composition refers to her fateful significance within the story. The painting left a deep impression on Rembrandt's countrymen, even at the time of its creation. The painter Philips Angels, for instance, praised the work in a speech entitled "Lof der schilder-konst" which he delivered at Leiden's St. Luke's Guild in 1641, calling it prototypical of a well-conceived, faithful, and historically accurate rendering of a historic scene.

Lit.: *De Bruyn et al. 1982–89,
vol. III, pp. 248ff. (no. A 123
with fig.).—Gemäldegalerie
Dresden 1992, p. 313 (with
fig.).—Exh.-cat. Amsterdam
2000, pp. 86f. (cat. no. 54 with
fig.).*

UN

GOVAERT FLINCK
(1615–1660)

**Portrait of Rembrandt
in Red Coat**

Ca. 1640
Oil on oak panel
21¹/₈ × 18¹/₈ in.
Gal. no. 1573

Provenance: *First mentioned
in the Guarienti Inventory
(after 1747).*

This work is strongly influenced by Flinck's second teacher, Rembrandt, whose studio in Amsterdam became his artistic inspiration in the years 1633–36. As a consequence, Flinck created a number of single figures in fantastic costumes that are equally typical of his early work as are large history paintings. Flinck's identification with the style of Rembrandt reached its climax in the late 1630s and is epitomized by this picture. Long considered a Rembrandt self-portrait—the sitter is shown in a historic costume with beret and fur coat—the work can be dated between 1630 and 1640. Toward the end of the 1630s Rembrandt portrayed himself in clothes from Cranach's time, as illustrated by one of his small chalk drawings, "Self-Portrait with Beret" (National Gallery of Art, Washington). This self-portrait obviously served as Flinck's model: He copied it—albeit as a mirror image—down to the details of the outfit and extended its format to a half-length portrait.

Lit.: *Exh.-cat. Cleves 1965,*
p. 31 (no. 30).—Moltke 1965,
p. 111 (no. 221 with fig.).—
Gemäldegalerie Dresden 1992,
p. 201 (no. 1573 with fig.).
                    UN

JOHANNES VERMEER
(1632–1675)

The Procuress
1656
OIL ON CANVAS, 56¹/₄ × 51¹/₈ IN.
MARKED IN THE LOWER RIGHT:
JVMEER.1656
GAL. NO. 1335

Provenance: *Purchased
from the Collection Wallenstein,
Dux/Bohemia, in 1741.*

Vermeer's first large-scale genre scene occupies a key position within his oeuvre because it marks an early turning point in his career. It also constitutes a link between the early, large history paintings and a long series of quiet genre scenes, indicative of his later work. While Vermeer undertook various changes during the painting process, his interest shifted in certain instances from a realistic rendering to the creation of a compelling composition. The content of this multilayered scene permits numerous interpretations: the depiction of a brothel, a reduced rendering of the five senses, or—if one interprets the figure near the left edge as a self-portrait of the artist—a scene from the parable of the Prodigal Son. When the painting was purchased for Dresden, it was considered a work of Gerard van Honthorst; only in 1858 did Thoré-Bürger identify Vermeer of Delft as its creator.

Lit.: *Gemäldegalerie Dresden
1992, p. 396 (no. 1335 with
fig.).—Exh.-cat. New York/
London 2001, pp. 365–368
(cat. no. 66 with fig.).*

UN

JACOB ISAACKSZ.
VAN RUISDAEL
(1628 or 1629–1682)

**The Waterfall in Front
of the Castle Mountain**
CA. 1665/70
OIL ON CANVAS, 39 × 33¹/₂ IN.
SIGNED LOWER LEFT:
J V RUISDAEL (JvR IN LIGATURE)
GAL. NO. 1495

Provenance: *First mentioned
in the Steinhäuser Inventory
(before 1740).*

Paintings of landscapes with waterfalls or violent rivers comprise the largest group within the painterly oeuvre of Ruisdael, amounting to more than 150 works. Inspired by the motif of the "Nordic landscape" by the Scandinavian pictures of Allart van Everdingen, such subject matters played a major role in Rusidael's creative process beginning in the late 1650s. As opposed to his student and painter-colleague, he found inspiration for his impressive, often dramatic landscape scenarios from other works of art and not from nature itself. In contrast to his paintings, Ruisdael's collected drawings only include a single sheet with this topic: a preparatory study for his group of landscapes with waterfalls. "The Waterfall in Front of the Castle Mountain" is clearly connected to this drawing, which anticipates major elements of the composition such as the waterfall, the farmhouse surrounded by conifers in the middle ground, and the mountain to the right.

Lit.: *Slive 2001, p. 189
(no. 181 with fig.).*

UN

DIEGO RODRÍGUEZ
DE SILVA VELÁZQUEZ
(1599–1660)

Portrait of Juan Mateos
SHORTLY BEFORE 1634
OIL ON CANVAS, 43 × 35⅝ IN.
GAL. NO. 697

Provenance: *First quoted in
the Inventory 1722; brought by
Baron Schacht.*

Authentic works by
Velázquez are very rare
outside Spain, and
with three paintings Dresden
possesses the largest group in
Germany. The present one
is not only artistically the most
important of these three, it is
one of the very few portraits
depicting neither members of
the royal family nor their
dwarfs and fools where the sitter could be identified. In all
probability, it represents the
Master of the Hunt to King
Philip IV, Juan Mateos, who
died in 1643. The three portraits arrived in Dresden in
1746, as part of the hundred
best paintings from Modena.
Velázquez was so little known
at that period that the present
picture was offered as a Rubens
and remained as such for a
hundred years, with the inter-
lude of an attribution to Titian
in the catalogues from 1817 to
1838. Unfamiliar with the
extraordinarily economic
brushwork of the master, the
painting was long considered
to be a mere sketch.

Lit.: *Justi 1888, vol. I, p. 395.—
Brown 1986, pp. 144–146.—
López-Rey 1996, no. 58.—
Exh.-cat. Madrid 1999, no. 22.*
MWE

JUSEPE DE RIBERA
(1591–1652)

Diogenes
DATED 1637
OIL ON CANVAS, 29⅞ × 24 IN.
GAL. NO. 682

Provenance: *First quoted in
the Inventory 1722; brought by
Baron Schacht.*

As acknowledged by his
contemporaries, the
virtuosity of Ribera's
brushwork even surpassed that
of the great founder of the
tenebrist movement, Caravaggio. His works were in great
demand in his lifetime and his
popularity has never truly
faded away. It goes without
saying that Augustus II and
Augustus III desired as large a
group of his work as possible.
The old catalogues link more
than ten paintings to his name.
No less than seven of them
were considered worthy
enough for inclusion among
the hundred pictures of the
Galerie reproduced in two volumes of prints (1753, 1757).
The present work is the first
of these to have arrived in
Dresden (before 1722) and the
best preserved among those
still considered to be by
Ribera. Its subject, the cynic
philosopher Diogenes, who
said he needed a lantern to find
humans among a crowd of
people, was much in favor during the period.

Lit.: *Heineken 1753/57,
no. 31.—Pérez Sánchez/Spinosa
1978, no. 110.—Exh.-cat. New
York 1992, no. 43.*
MWE

was hit by bullets, the impacts of which are still visible. The painting belongs to a small group of "Virgins" of superb quality Murillo painted in the very last years of his life, and the paint is applied with supreme subtlety.

Lit.: *Íñiguez 1981, no. 147.*
MWe

CAT. NO. 1.22

LUCAS CRANACH THE YOUNGER *(1515–1586)*

Adam and Eve
AFTER 1537
OIL ON LINDEN WOOD
EACH $67^{3}/_{8} \times 24^{3}/_{4}$ IN.
GAL-NOS. 1916 A, 1916 AA

Provenance: *First mentioned in the Inventory 1722/28.*

Cranach the Younger's depiction of the first human couple is characteristic of the Cranach workshop tradition that lasted for decades. Cranach the Elder developed a multitude of compositional variants after 1509. Apart from small renderings on individual panels, life-size pairs of pictures were executed, and Dresden's Old Masters Picture Gallery owns this set plus another one by Cranach the Elder and dated 1531. It can be assumed that Dürer's first Adam and Eve images, originating from between 1504 and 1507, stimulated Cranach's contemplation of the subject. In contrast to Dürer, however, Cranach was less interested in antiquity and classical proportions, instead remaining within the northern tradition where anatomic minutiae were less important than an elegant overall impression.

Lit.: *Schuchardt 1851, vol. II, p. 42, no. 228f.—Exh.-cat. Berlin*

CAT. NO. 1.21

BARTOLOMÉ ESTEBAN MURILLO *(1618–1682)*

Virgin with Child
OIL ON CANVAS, $65^{3}/_{8} \times 45^{1}/_{4}$ IN.
GAL. NO. 705

Provenance: *Bought at the Pasquier sale, Paris, March 1755.*

This is for already 250 years the best-loved Spanish painting in Dresden. Given that works by Velázquez (cat. no. 1.20) and others went disguised for more than a century under misattributions, it was also among the first to be presented to the visitors as a truly Spanish piece. Beside Ribera, Murillo was the only Spanish Baroque painter whose fame crossed the Pyrenees during his lifetime. Since then, Murillo's works have been on the international market, which is why the "Virgin" was purchased in 1755 at an auction in Paris. In the revolutionary disturbances of May 1849, it shared the fate of other pictures in the Spanish room: it

Cat. no. 1.23

Cat. no. 1.23

1983, p. 301.—Friedländer/ Rosenberg 1989 p. 141, no. 357. —Schoen 2001, p. 204.

KK

CAT. NO. 1.23

LOUIS DE SILVESTRE
(1675–1760)

Alliance Portraits of King Augustus II of Poland and the Prussian King Frederick William I

BEFORE 1730
OIL ON CANVAS,
110⁵/₈ × 79¹/₂ IN.
GAL. NO. 770

Provenance: *First mentioned in the Dresden Picture Inventory "before 1741" (Steinhäuser Octav-Inventar); according to this, delivered by Silvestre in 1730.*

This painting is a replica by the artist of a picture that was presumably made in 1728. Kept in the Hall of Bronzes in Potsdam's City Castle until 1945, it was subsequently lost in the war. The Potsdam version was reportedly made on the occasion of a visit of Augustus the Strong to Berlin and engraved by Lorenzo Zucchi in 1728. The two kings stand in a space whose simple architectural shapes are partly disguised by heavy and precious draperies. Near the left edge is a table upon which the crown and scepter are displayed resting on a red velvet cushion. Rendered on the shield of a coat of arms is a pyramidal composition displaying, closely intertwined, the scepter and electoral sword. Superimposed over this and flying from the left to the right side, are both the Polish

and the Prussian eagles. Both rulers are dressed in a cuirass. Augustus is wearing the orders of the Knights of the Golden Fleece and of the Polish White Eagle with the appropriate star. Frederick William I sports the order of the Prussian Black Eagle and its star. The double portrait is one of an alliance and of an event at the same time. It visualizes a symbolic handshake and a pact between two states, simultaneously documenting a personal friendship and a political event.

Lit.: *Sponsel 1906, no. 138.— Marx 1976/77, p. 76.—Exh.- cat. Dresden 1997b, no. 327.— Marx, in: Exh.-cat. Berlin 2002a, no. 38.*

HM

CAT. NO. 1.24

LOUIS DE SILVESTRE
(1675–1760)

King Augustus II of Poland

1718
OIL ON CANVAS, 99⁵/₈ × 60¹/₄ IN.
INSCRIBED ON VERSO: PORTRAIT DE SA MAJESTÉ LE ROI DE POLOGNE ET ELECTEUR DE SAXE, PEINT A DRESDE PAR SILVESTRE 1718
GAL. NO. 3943

Provenance: *First mentioned in the Dresden Picture Inventory 1722/28.*

In the life-size "portrait d'apparat" the king may be seen standing between the throne and a table with the Saxon electoral sword and the royal Polish insignia. Dressed in a demi-suit of armor and ermine cloak with red velvet, he holds the scepter in his right hand and his left hand rests on his hip. While the

ruler wears the decoration of the Polish Order of the White Eagle on a blue ribbon, the star of this order is embroidered onto the coat. To his left lie burgonet and gauntlets. With this gala portrait, Silvestre created an "official" image whose importance is not only emphasized by the unusually extensive signature but also by its original location in the parade rooms of the Residential Palace. The numerous variations, copies, and repetitions are further proof of the picture's preeminence.

Lit.: *Sponsel 1906, mentioned under no. 134.—Marx 1975, no. 113.—Marx 1999, no. 40.*

HM

CAT. NO. 1.25

LOUIS DE SILVESTRE
(1675–1760)

King Augustus III of Poland in Polish Dress

CA. 1737
OIL ON CANVAS, 20⁷/₈ × 70¹/₂ IN.
GAL. NO. 3951

Provenance: *Painted for the Banquet Hall in the Brühlsches Palais on Dresden's Augustusstraße. After the Brühlsches Palais was demolished, the portrait was transferred to the Dresden Residential Palace in 1899.*

This portrait and three others in the same format form a group: one is of Augustus III's wife, Maria

Josepha, while the other two show his parents, Augustus the Strong and Christiane Eberhardine. In this full-figure portrait in Polish dress, Augustus III poses in front of the throne with his ermine cloak to the left and a table displaying the Polish crown insignia and the Saxon electoral hat to the right. Augustus wears the Polish Order of the White Eagle and the Hapsburg Order of the Golden Fleece. Warsaw Castle is visible between the two columns. The painting can be dated by the year 1737, visible in the reproduction of a copperplate engraving by Jean

Daullé in the companion portrait of Queen Maria Josepha. The monumental porcelain figure of Augustus III which Johann Joachim Kaendler and Johann Friedrich Eberlein produced in 1741 (Porcelain Collection, inv. no. PE 470) is based on this painting.

Lit.: *Sponsel 1906, no. 137.—Marx 1975, no. 29.—Exh.-cat. Dresden 1997b, no. 527.*

HM

CAT. NO. 1.26

LOUIS DE SILVESTRE
(1675–1760)

Venus and Adonis
BEFORE 1722
OIL ON CANVAS
41 3/8 (48) × 59 5/8 IN.
GAL. NO. 3940

Provenance: *First mentioned in the Dresden Picture Inventory 1722/28; according to this, delivered by Silvestre.*

Originally painted as a supraport for the Throne Room of Augustus the Strong, the content of this scene is based on Ovid's *Metamorphoses* (10.529–559, 708–739). Adonis was the son of Venus and the brother of Myrrha, who—transformed into a myrrh tree—miraculously gave birth to him: "The tree bark begins to crackle and it emerges through it a living creature—a whimpering boy." His overwhelming beauty, present from birth, almost rendered Venus incapable of resisting his attraction: "He is the one she adores, the only

one whom she follows […] wandering with him through forests and mountains, over thorny cliffs." But she also warns the courageous hunter to beware of lions and wild boars. In our painting, Amour intends to prevent the boy from hunting; however, he already points into the direction of the woods, while Venus points the opposite way, toward the open landscape. Evidently, the model of this work was a composition by Peter Paul Rubens whose picture on the same topic is kept at the Metropolitan Museum of Art (New York).

Lit.: *Weigert 1932, no. 82.— Marx 1975, no. 6.—Marx 1999, no. 41.*

HM

CAT. NO. I.27

LOUIS DE SILVESTRE (1675–1760)

Vertumnus and Pomona

BEFORE 1722
OIL ON CANVAS
41 3/8 (48) × 59 5/8 IN.
GAL. NO. 3745

Provenance: *First mentioned in the Dresden Picture Inventory 1722/28; according to this, delivered by Silvestre.*

The content of this supraport from the Throne Room of Augustus the Strong is based on Ovid's *Metamorphoses* (14.623–771). Depicted on the left is Vertumnus, god of the seasons and transformations, who has just seduced Pomona, goddess of fruits and gardens, into love. Previously disguised as an old woman, he now removes the mask from his face and reveals himself.

Lit.: *Weigert 1932, no. 86.— Marx 1975, no. 7.—Marx 2000b, pp. 198, 202.*

HM

CAT. NO. 1.28

LOUIS DE SILVESTRE
(1675–1760)

**Rinaldo in Armida's
Magic Garden**

BEFORE 1722
OIL ON CANVAS
41³⁄₈ (48) × 59⁵⁄₈ IN.
GAL. NO. 3941

Provenance: *First mentioned
in the Dresden Picture Inventory
1722/28; according to this,
delivered by Silvestre.*

This work was painted
as a supraport for
the Throne Room
of Augustus the Strong in the
Dresden Residential Palace.
The content is based on the
poem *Jerusalem Liberated* by
Torquato Tasso (XVI, 17 ff.).
The sorceress Armida kid-
napped and beguiled the
knight Rinaldo, thereby pre-
venting him from participating
in the crusade to Jerusalem.
His comrades, Carlo and
Ubaldo, do find him in the end
and ultimately free him. In the
painting, the two lovers rest on
a turf bench located in an
untamed, shadowy landscape.

Putti bring flowers and garlands. Rinaldo holds a mirror
in which Armida looks at herself. The spectator sees a fountain to the left, in the center
background an indication of a
palace facade, and to the side
Carlo and Ubaldo, eavesdrop-
ping on the two. In this supraport, the artist returned to an
idea he had executed in the
past: The same composition
was engraved as early as 1708
when Nicolas Château and
Jean Audran fabricated a print
after a work by Silvestre.

Lit.: *Weigert 1932, no. 81.—
Marx 1975, no. 8.—Marx
2000b, pp. 197f.*

HM

The Picture Gallery of Augustus III— an Artwork in Itself

Gregor J. M. Weber

The Picture Gallery has been considered one of Dresden's special attractions for centuries. It is indeed justified to include it among the world's leading collections of its kind: in terms of the quality and the quantity of occidental art history's masterworks kept here, the Dresden Gallery can only be compared with the world's other great galleries. At the same time, in light of its special characteristics, the Dresden Gallery is quite different: until this day, it reflects precisely the taste of its most significant founders, who lived during the first half of the 18th century.

While Augustus the Strong (*August der Starke*) inherited an impressive picture inventory from his ancestors, he continued to enlarge the holdings by adding fabulous pieces. It was also upon his command that the first inventory dedicated exclusively to paintings was created in 1722. This year is therefore generally considered the beginning of the Dresden "picture collection as gallery." In reality, the inventory is only a compilation on paper; the location of the 3,574 paintings listed ranges from Poland to Dresden, hunting and pleasure castles, the residence, and the king's royal offices.

It was, however, Augustus III—who succeeded his father Augustus the Strong as prince elector of Saxony and king of Poland in 1733—who formed a truly royal picture gallery by combining the material with a plethora of new acquisitions until the Seven Years' War broke out in 1756. Each year, hundreds of paintings came to Dresden: in 1741–42 alone 715 works were acquired. Agents searched the European art centers looking for appropriate paintings and even entire collections. The most significant acquisition occurred in 1746, when one hundred of the best paintings from the famed Galleria Estense in Modena were purchased; among them four large altarpieces by Correggio, two works by Annibale Carracci, and four large oil paintings by Paolo Veronese. It was apparent that this number of objects required adequate accommodations. Augustus III took the opportunity to erect a gallery whose type had not previously existed anywhere in Europe—and, one might add, he created a gallery that would be inconceivable today.

Initially, the former Stables Building (*Stallgebäude*) near the *Jüdenhof* in Dresden was remodeled. By merging two stories, one single floor was created with a ceiling height of more than 35 feet. By constructing an imposing wall in a room located near an inner courtyard, it was possible to hang pictures on either side resulting in one "inner" and an "outer gallery." The length of this wall was approximately 100 feet while the lateral walls measured circa 90 feet long. Added to this were the wall spaces between the windows, the so-called pilasters. The complex picture arrangement covered all the walls and was modified three times between 1747 and 1754. One aspect of this design entailed the uniform framing of all paintings, most of which retain their frames to this day. Under the guidance of the sculptors Matthäus Kugler and Franz Deibel fabulous, rocaille embellished gold frames were created which sported a central AR (Augustus Rex) monogram at the bottom, while the top was crowned with Augustus III's coats of arms. This facilitated an optically homogenous grouping of different paintings while simultaneously staging them adequately for representational royal requirements.

The most perfect solution for hanging the paintings, kept intact until the 19th century, happened in 1754: the long wall segments were subdivided into rectangular arrangements of picture groups that were organized without interruption. Later, the so-called departments or divisions were given continuous num-

Giovanni Ghisolfi (1623–1683), The Ruins of Carthage (detail), see cat. no. 1.36. p. 86

bers, facilitating easy identification. Correggio's "Holy Night" was installed in a central spot of the "inner gallery," to signal its uniqueness and its major importance. The altarpiece was flanked by paintings arranged in pairs, among them two images of the Virgin by Giulio Romano and Giulio Cesare Procaccini of identical height. Mounted above this group was the large, almost fifteen-foot-wide painting "The Alms of St. Roch" by Annibale Carracci. Its width it filled the entire division. It was logical to place small paintings in the lowest row—in this case even below the "Holy Night"—and to arrange them in the established symmetrical order.

To the left and the right sides of the division, more groups of paintings were symmetrically arranged: on the top hung same-format altarpieces by Guido Reni, below paintings by Deferrari and Titian with religious subject matter corresponding to each other. Beneath this was a pair of pictures—also in this present exhibition—by Benedetto Castiglione, as well as additional symmetrically arranged small works. The divisions following on the left and on the right sides continued this system by always placing a large Veronese painting of the same size at the top and other groups of pictures below. Upon closer scrutiny, the arrangement reveals itself as a complex, symmetrically arranged system of picture groups that established a broader sense of symmetry over the long distances of the gallery. The outcome was a decorative spatial pattern that subordinated all paintings under one common installation principle that was repeated on all walls. From the profusion of frames, one unique nucleus per wall was singled out, including "Holy Night," which was juxtaposed to "The Flight into Egypt" by Francesco Trevisani on the opposite side. Finally, on the shortest wall of the "inner gallery" Garofalo's "Triumph of Bacchus" was installed. It was by virtue of the hanging alone that the major works were indicated.

A creation such as this far surpassed all other collections in existence. To name but a few: The small Galleria Estense in Modena contained individual exhibition spaces whose height did not even measure half of Dresden's. The Galleria Doria Pamphili, later created in Rome, was much smaller, the galleries in Potsdam, Düsseldorf, or St. Petersburg unsuccessfully attempted to copy the Dresden prototype but attained neither equal quality nor comparable quantities of paintings, and they lacked Dresden's special space configuration. It was only in depictions of fictitious picture galleries that similarly complex hanging arrangements were illustrated. Augustus III remained the only monarch to realize such a fantastic gallery.

The hanging arrangements not only mirror the king's aristocratic splendor, but are also content-based. Carl Heinrich von Heineken, the excellent connoisseur who was among those responsible for gallery purchases and design, describes the intentions in the first volume of engravings concerning the Royal Gallery, published in 1753: The paintings, assembled with great care, knowledge, and good judgment were ultimately arranged in the appropriate order ("avec simmetrie et avec intelligence"). He continues, stating that such an infinite abundance would not fail to enhance the spectator's imagination and lift his spirits—indeed, the effect would be his yearning to gain further insights.

This concept was most definitely understood: Johann Wolfgang von Goethe, Friedrich Schlegel, Wilhelm von Humboldt, and many others describe their impressions of the gallery, which did not simply evoke sheer amazement. Inspired by the installation, they comprehended the paintings' inherent idiosyncrasies, or they were motivated to make comparisons, establish connections between different schools, or to pursue specific subjects. One of the proofs for these types of effects may be seen in Augustus Wilhelm Schlegel's *Galeriegespräch* (1799).

Augustus III was justifiably proud of this particularly rich and unique gallery. The second tome of the corpus of engravings (1757) shows a new type of allegory on its title vignette: The "genius of painting" has completed its work in front of an easel and now orders the paintings' hanging. In this print, the installation of the gallery is attributed the same artistic importance as the art of painting—the gallery assumed the status of a work of art.

The former installation cannot be recreated in the gallery building used today, located near the *Zwinger* and inaugurated in 1855. There is an enfilade of rooms, the ceilings are considerably lower, and a number of paintings burned in 1945. However, many combinations of paintings can still be realized by copying the 18th-century symmetrical arrangement, thus evoking the general character of Augustus III's gallery.

In the installation for the exhibition in Jackson, Mississippi, a late Baroque impression will be recreated by arranging one entire wall in symmetrical order. Additional paintings by Netherlandish and Italian masters will be symmetrically grouped around the imposing Luca Giordano with its vertical format. According to the principles of the old gallery, the large-scale paintings will occupy the upper positions, while others will hang at eye level. The establishment of thematic references across different schools was attempted. Such juxtapositions include depictions of harbor scenes or shepherds with their flocks. Perhaps the visitor can thus imagine the sensation caused by this installation method on an endless forty-foot-high wall in 1754!

Selected bibliography: Weber 1999.

CAT. NO. 1.29

GUIDO RENI (*1575–1642*),
workshop

St. Jerome
CA. 1636–37
OIL ON CANVAS, 31 1/8 × 25 3/8 IN.
GAL. NO. 331

Provenance: *Transferred from
the Royal Chambers in 1740.*

St. Jerome is deeply vener-
ated as one of the four
Church Fathers. He is
the first translator of the Bible
into Latin. In this painting he
is shown as a repentant hermit
who may be identified by his
formulaic physiognomy and his
red cardinal's cloak. Reni
created a similar composition
in circa 1624–25 that is today
in the National Gallery in
London. There, the saint
is rendered in almost identical
posture and surroundings,
except that his hand, in which

he holds a cross, rests on a
skull. This very detail is
painted rather crudely in the
Dresden example, showing
how assistants and students
copy or vary their master's
work; yet without the same
quality of Reni's own hand.

Lit.: *Pepper 1984, p. 274
(no. 160).*

GW

CAT. NO. 1.30

GUIDO RENI (*1575–1642*)

**Christ with the Crown
of Thorns**
CA. 1636–37
OIL ON COPPER, 29 7/8 × 23 5/8 IN.
GAL. NO. 329

Provenance: *Purchased in
1749 from the Imperial Gallery,
Prague.*

This work—executed
on an unusually large
copper plate—only
recently underwent conservation treatment that revealed,
under old layers of overpaint-
ing in the lower left corner, the
collector's mark of Emperor
Leopold. The picture came to
Dresden during the reign of
his successor, Emperor Charles
VI, from the latter's gallery.
The Dresden Old Masters
Picture Gallery owns a total
of three depictions by Reni
showing Christ with the crown
of thorns. Another one, also
included in this exhibition,
depicts Christ with eyes wide
open, his pathos-filled expres-

sion staring upward. In contrast to it, this variant shows
Christ with an inward, almost
meditative gaze. The effect on
the spectator is certainly carefully calculated in all instances.
In this case, the viewer's empathy is elicited by Christ's silent
and devoted suffering. The
intention is made manifest in
the subdued colors of this
particularly elegant painting,
the ash-colored garment, and
Christ's gray skin color. The
scene is also in accordance with
the biblical narrative that
relates the cruel mocking of
Christ (Matthew 27:28f.).

Lit.: *Pepper 1984, pp. 274f.
(no. 162).—Spear 1997, pp. 199,
365.*

GW

JOHANN ANTON EISMANN *(1604–1698)*

A Harbor

OIL ON CANVAS, 46¹/₈ × 65³/₄ IN.
GAL. NO. 472

Provenance: *Purchased in 1744 from the Casa Grimani Calergi, Venice.*

This picture was acquired along with Ghisolfis' "Ruins of Carthage", which has identical measurements. Based on this evidence, the paintings were always considered to be pendants, and thus "A Harbor" was attributed to Ghisolfi. Only in 1976 did Safarik publish the painting with the correct authorship. The Mediterranean harbor as a picture type evolved in Netherlandish painting: distant harbors, foreigners in picturesque outfits, and ruins as witnesses to a great past are frequently recurring motifs, all of which satisfied the need to visualize distant countries. With his harbor views and his seascapes, Eismann fully fits the description of the picture type. While many of his motifs are reminiscent of works by Lingelbach, Asselijn, and others, the style is particularly close to Hans de Jode. Eismann anticipates the later Venetian landscape paintings by such masters as Carlevarijs and Canaletto.

Lit.: *Posse 1929, p. 207.— Safarik 1976, p. 71.—Zanzotto 1996, p. 282.*

GW

GIOVANNI BENEDETTO CASTIGLIONE *(1609–1664)*

Outside Noah's Ark

CA. 1650
OIL ON CANVAS, 57¹/₈ × 76⁵/₈ IN.
GAL. NO. 659

Jacob's Return Home

CA. 1630/40
OIL ON CANVAS, 56³/₄ × 78 IN.
GAL. NO. 660

Provenance: *Both purchased by DeBrais in Paris in 1742.*

Castiglione had contact with Flemish artists whose realistic painting style inspired him to render his own images of animals and still lifes. Distinguished by his powerful yet carefully thought out coloration, Castiglione applies the oil paint thickly, resulting in an almost three-dimensional effect and emphasizing the color contrasts in dense clusters. Jacob was Isaac's chosen son and was supposed to find a wife abroad. After considerable hardship, he finally returned home to the land of his fathers with Rachel. At this time he was a wealthy man who owned uncounted cattle, male and female servants, camels, and donkeys (Genesis 30:43; 31:17–21). In two zones, Castiglione depicts Jacob's procession, showing neither its beginning nor its end, in this way suggesting a vast crowd.

The other painting leads back to even more distant events. Before the flood God had charged Noah with building an ark and with the rescue of one pair of each animal species (Genesis 7:1–9). Once again, Castiglione skillfully manages to portray only a segment of the event with the consequence that the vessel's immense size and the abundance of animals are merely suggested to the viewer. Cas-

tiglione painted the subject of Noah's ark numerous times. The versions executed between 1645 and 1655 are the closest to the Dresden painting. Among them is a composition in Nantes, Musée des Beaux-Arts, as well as one dated 1654 and kept in a private collection in Genoa. These two examples also give an indication as to the date of the Dresden work. It remains undecided whether Castiglione conceived both pictures as a pair: their compositions are not symmetrical, and "Noah's Ark" has a greater color intensity. Based on stylistic grounds, "Jacob's Return Home" is dated earlier.

Lit.: *Delogu 1928, p. 24—Exh.-cat. Genoa 1990, p. 133.*
GW

CAT. NO. 1.33

SIMONE CANTARINI
(1612–1648)

Joseph and Potiphar's Wife

OIL ON CANVAS, 54³/₈ × 70¹/₂ IN.
GAL. NO. 382
Provenance: *First mentioned in the Inventory 1754.*

This painting was made for Senator Melara of Bologna and remained in the family's collection until 1750. The Abbott Giovanni Battista Bianconi negotiated a deal with Gallery Inspector Pietro Guarienti, whereupon the work came to Dresden. An identical copy is kept in Bologna's Galleria Nazionale. The popular Old Testament story may be found in Genesis 39. The pharaoh's wife tried to seduce Joseph, who resisted her and managed to flee. However, Potiphar's wife was able to hold on to his cloak, which she later produced as evidence that Joseph had tried to seduce her. Cantarini depicts both protagonists as life-size half-length figures in the fore-ground. Together with the light configuration, this type of rendering is reminiscent of the art of Caravaggio and his successors. The narrative is made impressively tangible.

Lit.: *Mancigotti 1975, p. 156.*
GW

CAT. NO. 1.34

BARTOLOMEO
MANFREDI *(1582–1622)*
school of

The Card Players

OIL ON CANVAS, 48³/₈ × 68¹/₈ IN.
GAL. NO. 414

Provenance: *Purchased in
1746 from the Galleria Estense,
Modena.*

Caravaggio's revolution
in painting around
1600 in Rome initiated
an international movement
entitled *Caravaggism,* a term
obviously not used at the time.
In 1675 the German painter
and historian Joachim von
Sandrart had already described
the new style as "Manfrediana
methodus," connecting it
primarily with Caravaggio's
most prolific pupil, Manfredi.
Indeed, many painters referred
to the latter's paintings and

not to the oeuvre of the real
initiator. Indicators of "Manfredi's Method" include the use
of raking light, dark backgrounds, half-length figures
moved to the painting's edge,
and the depiction of predominantly working-class people.
All these features may be found
in this painting, which was
acquired together with its
counterpart, "St. Peter's Be-
trayal." Both works have recently been attributed to
Manfredi's student, Nicolas
Tournier.

Lit.: *Nicolson 1979, p. 72.—
Exh.-cat. Modena 1998, p. 396.*
GW

CAT. NO. 1.35

LUCA GIORDANO
(1632–1705)

Bacchus and Ariadne

CA. 1682

OIL ON CANVAS, 103¹/₂ × 70⁷/₈ IN.
GAL. NO. 484

Provenance: *Purchased in
1741 from the Wallenstein
Collection, Dux/Bohemia.*

It was thanks to Ariadne's
thread that Theseus man-
aged to escape from the
Minotaur's labyrinth on the
island of Crete. Although she
fled with him, Theseus aban-
doned her on the island of
Naxos, where Bacchus found
her and made her his wife. In
the end, Jupiter removed her
crown and threw it into the
heavens, where it turned into
stars. In his complex composition, Giordano depicts this
subject—particularly popular

on stage—showing the
mourning Ariadne with her
thread. While Bacchus is
accompanied by the personification of peace in the middle
ground, the heavenly realm
is occupied by the assembly of
the gods, who are gathered
around Ariadne's wreath of
stars. Numerous figures from
Bacchus's entourage may be
identified; among them, to the
left, Amor, god of love, pushes
the antagonists of peace into
the abyss. Giordano's decorative paintings of this type had
considerable influence on the
art of painting both in Italy
and southern Germany.

Lit.: *Ferrari/Scavizzi 1966,
vol. 1, p. 97, 100; vol. 2, p. 111.*
GW

CAT. NO. 1.36

GIOVANNI GHISOLFI
(1623–1683)

The Ruins of Carthage
OIL ON CANVAS, 46¹⁄₈ × 65³⁄₄ IN.
MARKED ON THE LEFT IN
THE FOREGROUND:
HIC. CARTHAGO. FUIT
GAL. NO. 471

Provenance: *Purchased in
1744 from the Casa Grimani
Calergi, Venice.*

Ghisolfi specialized in
the depiction of land-
scapes with ancient
ruins which were only partially
based on reality. Instead, he
created his own compositions,
which he based on diverse vari-
able elements. The entire

height of the picture's right
side is occupied by palatial
ruins, including an Ionic order
vestibule and fragments of a
relief on the ground. Ghisolfi
placed a ruin with vaulted
ceilings in the left middle
ground. Although this conjures
up associations of the Roman
Forum, Ghisolfi added a Latin
inscription on a block of
stone which claims: "Here was
Carthage." The artist thereby
stimulates the viewer to con-
template the lost grandeur and
the tragic fate of the Mediterranean capital. It was Salvator
Rosa, a friend of Ghisolfi's,
who in his history paintings
repeatedly evoked the heroic
greatness of antiquity. This
is exactly what Ghisolfi does
in this landscape, in which the
surroundings as well as the

soldiers in ancient outfits
bear strong resemblance to
antiquity.

Lit.: *Posse 1929, p. 207.—
Zanzotto 1996, p. 282.*

GW

CAT. NO. 1.37

ANTONIO BELLUCCI
(1654–1726)

Virgin and Child
OIL ON CANVAS, 28 × 22¹⁄₄ IN.
GAL. NO. 546

Provenance: *First mentioned in
the Inventory 1754.*

Bellucci belongs to the
most successful painters
around the year 1700.
He is documented in Venice in
1684 as a member of the
"Fraglia dei pittori" where he
was—along with Ricci and
Pellegrini—the leading artist
before Tiepolo. His activities
in territories north of the Alps
included commissions at the
Palais Liechtenstein in Vienna,

the Düsseldorf court, the prince bishops of Schloss Pommersfelden (Franconia), and ultimately even the English court. In this intimate work, Bellucci clearly deviates from the customary rhetoric of his often large-format decorative cycles and his virtuoso ceiling paintings. The "Virgin and Child" is closely tied to the religious art of Maratta, Trevisani, and Luti. The observer sees the Virgin busy fixing the child's diapers, a motif frequently encountered in older paintings in order to demonstrate to the faithful a private and yet familiar episode related to the mother of God. The choice of a rather narrow format, which moves the subjects close to the viewer, serves the same purpose.

Lit.: *Posse 1929, p. 241.*

GW

Cat. no. 1.38

BENEDETTO LUTI (*1666–1724*)

The Blessing Christ

Oil on canvas, 28⁷/₈ × 23⁵/₈ in.
Marked on the verso: Eques Benedictu
Luti Romae faciebat 1723 A
Gal. no. 513

Provenance: *Purchased in 1742 in Prague.*

This painting was purchased together with its identically sized counterpart which Luti himself dated 1722. The latter work—belonging to the war losses of Dresden's Old Masters Picture Gallery—was a depiction of the mourning Virgin with her hands on her breast. The work of the blessing Christ, too, is typical of Luti's religious sensitivity in his late years, during which period he returned to a simple yet superior "ars sacra." The concentration on an individual religious figure was a feature Reni practiced some one hundred years earlier. It was also typical of later artists such as Dolci or Maratta. Luti's refined style, use of deliberately pale colors, and the almost feminine beauty of his introverted Christ figure, who gazes to the ground, are refinements of his predecessors' styles. Dated one year before his death, his successful work in Rome—center of the Catholic church—satisfied Luti who had become a member of the Academy of St. Luke's in 1694.

Lit.: *Posse 1929, p. 225.— Bowron 1979, pp. 183f., 259f.*

CAT. NO. 1.39

PIETER BODDING VAN LAER (1599–1642 ?)

Near the Wine Barrel beneath the City Walls

OIL ON CANVAS ON OAK PANEL 14^{1}/$_{2}$ × 18^{7}/$_{8}$ IN. GAL. NO. 1364

Provenance: *First mentioned in the Inventory 1754.*

When van Laer was young he was influenced by the landscape paintings produced in his native Haarlem. Belonging to the second generation of Dutch travelers to Italy, the so-called Italianites, van Laer invented a special type of Italianite genre painting. His nickname, *bamboccio*, Italian for a big, awkwardly shaped child, refers to his misshapen figure. It was given to him by the Bentveughel—a Netherlandish artists' colony in Rome—and became the technical term for the type of genre scene he painted. Van Laer was the most important representative of this kind of painting, which concentrated on densely populated street scenes of the ordinary Roman population. The group of men playing cards and the simple wine bar near the city walls in this example offered an insight into the *vita populare*, the common life, which must have been particularly appealing and interesting for van Laer's patrons.

Lit.: *Posse 1930, p. 116 (no. 1364).*

UN

CAT. NO. 1.40

PIETER BODDING VAN LAER (1599–1642 ?)

Paying the Wages

OIL ON CANVAS, 15^{3}/$_{4}$ × 18^{7}/$_{8}$ IN. GAL. NO. 1367

Provenance: *First mentioned in the Inventory 1754.*

From approximately 1625 until 1637 van Laer lived in Rome, where he was a leading member of the Netherlandish artists' colony Bentveughel. He became famous because of his *bambocciads*, a type of genre painting he developed that derives its scenes from the everyday life of common Italians. The slightly stout and rough figures so typical of van Laer may be seen in this painting where they are represented in their very own surroundings. Such renderings were of vast interest in Rome during the first half the 17th century. As a result, van Laer not only painted his *bambocciads* for the free market but was also commissioned by noble patrons such as Cardinal Brancaccio and Ferdinando de Riberas, the vice king of Naples.

Lit.: *Posse 1930, p. 116 (no. 1367).*

UN

CAT. NO. 1.41

JAN MIEL *(1599–1664)*

Peasants Playing Boccia

Ca. 1650/55
Oil on canvas, 19 1/2 × 25 3/8 in.
Gal. no. 1365

Provenance: *First mentioned in the Guarienti Inventory 1750.*

The ultimate attribution of this painting to Jan Miel—since its acquisition for Frederick Augustus II ascribed to van Laer—only occurred when Kren published his Miel monograph in 1980. The work of the Flemish painter who spent most of his life in Rome and Turin, has only recently been more thoroughly scrutinized as a major contribution to the painting of the Netherlandish *bamboccanti*. While Miel specialized in abundantly figured everyday scenes of Italian country people, he was far less interested in the surrounding architecture and the landscapes, a clear deviation from his model van Laer. One of Miel's favorite subjects was the boccia game, which was particularly popular in Italy. Various versions of this topic were created of which the Dresden painting is considered the last and the most virtuosic.

Lit.: *Kren 1980, vol. 1, pp. 98f., 40f., fig. 23.—Exh.-cat. Cologne/ Utrecht 1991/92, pp. 242f. (no. 24.2 with fig.).*

UN

CAT. NO. 1.42

JACQUES DES ROUSSEAUX(?) *(ca. 1600–1638)*

Old Woman with Spectacles in Her Hand

Oil on canvas, 24 × 29 1/8 in.
Gal. no. 1254

Provenance: *Purchased from Leipzig in 1740; first mentioned in the Steinhäuser Inventory (before 1741).*

This picture, largely ignored in Dresden until recently, was included by Nicolson in his Terbrugghen catalogue, assigning it to an "anonymous artist influenced by Terbrugghen." The impasto technique of the fur and the treatment of the headdress are particularly striking and suggest a stylistic proximity to Terbrugghen's oeuvre. As of late, the Rembrandt follower Jacques des Rousseaux has been suggested

certain picturesque motifs such as the velvet coat and the feather beret from the latter. The Dresden painting combines associations of Backer's later painting style—distinguished by clear lines and contours—with the motif of the study head in Rembrandtesque masquerade. The careful painterly rendering in contrast to a more open approach as evidenced in his Dresden work "Old Bald-Headed Man" (cat. no. 1.45) suggests that this is more a portrait rather than a study. The sitter, equipped with a sword and an earring, bears indications of a self-portrait. In his other self-portraits, Backer customarily depicted himself as a shepherd with wreath and flute.

Lit.: *Bauch 1926, p. 84.— Sumowski 1983, p. 199 (no. 45), 248 with fig.*

ER

as the creator of this work. This attribution was further substantiated when a privately owned "Allegory of Meanness" by the artist surfaced on the art market. The Dresden painting, a character study of an old woman, is similar to the latter both stylistically and thematically. A comparable version of this work may be found in the Collection of the Earl of Lonsdale in Askham.

Lit.: *Nicolson 1958, no. E 103, fig. 109b.—Nicolson 1979, vol. 1, cat. no. 1193; vol. 3, fig. 1193.— Exh.-cat. Dresden 1996a, p. 30 (no. 21).*

UN

Cat. no. 1.43

JACOB ADRIAENSZ. BACKER (1608–1651)

Young Man with Red Coat and Dark Feather Hat

Ca. 1645/50
Oil on oak panel
$28^{3}/_8 \times 21^{5}/_8$ in.
Gal. no. 1587

Provenance: *First mentioned in the Matthäi Catalogue, Dresden 1835.*

This half-length portrait—a depiction in fantasy outfit—is a late work of Backer's in which he excels as a virtuoso. It was after 1640 that Backer opted for the new classic style. With the *tronies* of his late work he developed once again a greater proximity to Rembrandt. It can be argued that Backer adapted

Cat. no. 1.44

JACOB ADRIAENSZ. BACKER (1608–1651)

Old Man with Beret and Fur

Ca. 1635
Oil on canvas, $25^{3}/_4 \times 21^{1}/_4$ in.
Marked on the right in the center: JAB. (in ligature)
Gal. no. 1583

Provenance: *First mentioned in the Matthäi Catalogue, Dresden 1835.*

The half-length portrait of an old man in picturesque costume is one of Backer's early works which he painted immediately following his move from Leeuwarden to Amsterdam in the mid-1730s. His study heads with allegorical undertones, based on interesting, albeit anonymous models—so-called *tronies*—were influenced by

Rembrandt's paintings. The depiction of a repeatedly recurring character type in varying costumes and poses was much favored by Backer since it enabled him to demonstrate his highly distinguished skills as colorist and virtuoso painter of diverse textures. The Dresden picture belongs to a group of images of old men for which he obviously used the same model.

Lit.: *Sumowski 1983, pp. 197 (no. 30), 233 with fig.—Exh.-cat. Brunswick 1993, p. 158.—Exh.-cat. Dresden 1996a, p. 18 (no. 1 with fig.).*

ER

CAT. NO. 1.45

JACOB ADRIAENSZ. BACKER *(1608–1651)*

Old Bald-Headed Man
CA. 1633/35
OIL ON CANVAS, 25 × 20⅞ IN.
GAL. NO. 1585

Provenance: *First mentioned in the Inventory 1722/28.*

This portrait, painted in Amsterdam, is a partial repetition of a work executed in 1630, entitled "Hippocrates Visits Democritus in Abdera," belonging to the Collection Bader in Milwaukee. The latter work's date confirms that portrait studies for the head of the old man as Hippocrates still date to Backer's Leeuwarden time. Another drawing of the same head was formerly kept in the Collection Gruner, Munich. The model's idiosyncratic features, including his protruding nose and the remarkably wrinkled face, neck, and throat may be identified in numerous other *tronies* by Backer. They include two works in St. Petersburg's Hermitage entitled "St. Peter"

and "Old Man in Clerical Garments" as well as "Half-Length Portrait of an Old Man in Profile," kept in the Uffizi in Florence, and the especially allegorical depiction of an "Old Man with the Shard of a Mirror" in Berlin's Picture Gallery.

Lit.: *Bauch 1926, pp. 21, 30, 78 (no. 27, plate 19).—Sumowski 1983, pp. 195 (no. 18), 221 with fig.—Exh.-cat. Brunswick 1993, p. 158.*

ER

CAT. NO. 1.46

PHILIPS WOUWERMAN *(1619–1668)*

Rest outside the Shoeing Forge
OIL ON CANVAS, 21⅝ × 23⅝ IN.
MARKED IN THE LOWER LEFT: PHILS. W. AND PW
GAL. NO. 1420

Provenance: *Purchased from the Collection Crozat, Paris, 1751.*

Philips Wouwerman was a Haarlem painter with special preference for horses. This picture—which can be called a portrait of a white horse—speaks of his love for renderings of horses in different situations, poses, and light conditions. The procedure of shoeing integrates the animal into a genre scene with a rural smith's shop, a setting preferred by Wouwerman in the 1650s. The juxtaposition of the country people with the elegant group of waiting

Provenance: *First mentioned in the Inventory 1754.*

The business of selling fish was a welcome opportunity for Wouwerman to render a balanced group of figures of different ages and social backgrounds and to turn it into a charming genre scene. A group of fishermen take a rest on a narrow piece of beach with a low horizon line. Surrounded by women and children, they repose in the shade of a hut while another group is busy saddling a white horse. To the left, the actual vending scene may be spotted: An elegant couple with rider appears to be discussing business with ordinary fishermen. Juxtapositions such as this are frequent occurrences in Wouwerman's people adds a peculiar charm that results from the different social backgrounds of the individuals. Anecdotal genre scenes such as this one—taking place in a landscape with the spectator's gaze being led along city walls and thereby being guided into the picture's depth—were particularly popular with Wouwerman's well-to-do clients. In the rendering of this landscape, he proves to be an excellent colorist.

Lit.: *Bürger 2001, vol. 1, pp. 96f.; vol. 2, fig. 31.*

UN

CAT. NO. 1.47

PHILIPS WOUWERMAN
(1619–1668)

Fishermen near the Beach

OIL ON OAK PANEL
21⅝ × 23⅝ IN.
MARKED IN THE LOWER LEFT:
PHILS W.
GAL. NO. 1434

oeuvre. Fishermen scenes with travelers are part of the 17th-century standard repertoire of the Dutch Italianites whose paintings also strongly influenced Wouwerman.

Lit.: *Bürger 2001, vol. 1, pp. 111f.; vol. 2, fig. 40.—Müllenmeister 1981, p. 106 (no. 548).—Schumacher 1989, no. 35.*

UN

CAT. NO. 1.48

PHILIPS WOUWERMAN
(1619–1668)

The Trumpet Player in Front of the Vendor's Tent

OIL ON OAK PANEL
18³/₄ × 16¹/₂ IN.
MARKED IN THE LOWER LEFT:
PHILS W.
GAL. NO. 1433

Provenance: *First mentioned in the Inventory 1722/28.*

The topic of the encampment bears close proximity to the world of military scenes such as battles and riders' duels. It counts among Wouwerman's favorite subjects. Background to this great popularity in the 17th and 18th centuries was apparently the combination of military topic—particularly liked during the Thirty Years War—with genre scenes. This painting's storyline focuses on the carefree activities on the encampment's periphery and places special emphasis on the agreeable nature and the pleasant amenities of the soldier's life. In doing so, Wouwerman concentrated on numerous narrative details. They include the figure drinking wine, the rider giving a signal with his trumpet, the flirtatious soldier, and the

sutler-women who belong to the military's entourage. The kneeling beggar introduces an aspect of social criticism.

Lit.: *Bürger 2001, vol. 1, pp. 84f.; vol. 2, fig. 24.*

UN

PHILIPS WOUWERMAN
(1619–1668)

Rest during the Falcon Hunt

OIL ON OAK PANEL
18¹/₂ × 25³/₈ IN.
MARKED IN THE LOWER LEFT:
PILS. W.
GAL. NO. 1432

Provenance: *First mentioned in the Inventory 1722/28.*

Wouwerman repeatedly depicted the various different types and facets of the princely hunt. Following a particular demand of his clientele toward the end of his life, he turned to depictions of hunting activities that were largely restricted to aristocratic circles. In the foreground of this late painting, an elegant group—just returned from the falcon hunt—has gathered. Some of the hunters on horseback still carry their falcons, while others inspect

their prey. At the base of a stone sculpture which represents Pan, god of the shepherds and of the hunt, a couple reposes; another couple may be spotted near the right edge of the painting. Wouwerman painted an intentionally subtle confrontation of the humans with Pan, who, driven by his sexual urges, pursued the nymph Syrinx.

Lit.: *Balzer 1956, fig. 98.—Bürger 2001, vol. 1, p. 53; vol. 2, fig. 10.*

UN

CAT. NO. 1.50

PHILIPS WOUWERMAN
(*1619–1668*)

The Return from the Hunt

OIL ON OAK PANEL
$17^7/8 \times 25^3/8$ IN.
MARKED IN THE LOWER LEFT:
PHILS. W.
GAL. NO. 1439

Provenance: *Purchased after 1755 from the Estate of the Collection Pasquier, Paris.*

In his late work of the 1660s, Wouwerman predominantly painted hunting scenes, which were particularly popular with aristocratic collectors. Since the hunt was a privilege and the preferred pastime of the princely classes, aristocrats tended to identify with this topic, which Wouwerman depicted in more than 200 of his paintings. This painting—showing the return of a group of individuals from the hunt—was conceived as the pendant to "The Start of the Hunt," also belonging to Dresden's Old Masters Picture Gallery. The huntsmen arrive at the rural castle where servants greet them. One of the hunters presents a dead hare to some of the ladies who have gathered near the entrance. The action clearly bears erotic undertones easily understood by Wouwer-

man's contemporaries: the comparison of the hunter chasing the hare was commonly paralleled with the courtier pursuing the "she hare."

Lit.: *Schumacher 1989,* pp. 217f.—*Exh.-cat. Dijon 2001, no. 55.—Bürger 2001, vol. 1, pp. 62f.; vol. 2, fig. 15.*

UN

CAT. NO. 1.51

JOHANNES LINGELBACH
(*1622–1674*)

A Harbor with a Lighthouse

OIL ON CANVAS, $42^1/2 \times 35^1/4$ IN.
MARKED ON THE RIGHT:
I LINGELBACH FECIT
GAL. NO. 1627

Provenance: *First mentioned in the Guarienti Inventory 1750.*

Lingelbach belongs to the second generation of Dutch painters who traveled to Italy. Upon his return he utilized his impressions of the Italian landscape and people. Under the influence of the older van Laer—who was one of the key figures of Italianite painting—these younger artists painted Roman street scenes with genre figures, entitled *bambocciads*. Lingelbach was in Italy from 1644

until roughly 1650. Here, he painted a harbor immersed in southern light and framed by Romanizing architecture. The scene is framed by sailboats, an antique statue, and *bambocciant* figures. The same group of three men playing dice in the foreground may be found in his other paintings. The cap-riccio with anecdotal content which Lingelbach composed consists of numerous architec-tural elements, figure types, and the popular harbor motif. The southern atmosphere, emanating from all his pic-tures, is particularly realistic.

Lit.: *Posse 1930, p. 119 (no. 1627).*

ER

Cat. nos. 1.52A and 1.52B

PIETER VAN BLOEMEN
(1657–1720)

A Procession of Nomads
Oil on canvas, 28³/₈ × 39¹/₈ in.
Gal. no. 1121

Provenance: *First mentioned in the Inventory 1754.*

Cattle Market in the Ruins of Rome
Oil on canvas, 28³/₈ × 38 in.
Marked lower right:
P. V. B.1710.
Gal. no. 1117

Provenance: *Purchased from Prague in 1742 by Riedel.*

UN

The Entire World in Pictures

Dresden's *Kupferstich-Kabinett*

Wolfgang Holler

The Dresden Collection of Drawings, Prints, and Photographs (*Kupferstich-Kabinett*) comprises 500,000 works, which are kept in containers, volumes, illustrated books, and portfolios or frames. Its beginnings reach back to the year 1560, when the dukes of Saxony created a *Kunstkammer* that also integrated printed matter.

A fundamental reorganization of the collections occurred under Prince Elector Frederick Augustus I: The *Kunstkammer* was dissolved and divided into various specialty collections which were ambitiously enlarged. In 1720 the Collection of Drawings, Prints, and Photographs became an independent museum institution which was first accommodated in the so-called *Regimentshaus* near Dresden's New Market Place (*Neumarkt*), before moving to the *Zwinger*'s ground-floor location, called the "*Deutscher Pavillon.*"

The creation of a museum for works on paper was an extraordinarily progressive step. In Europe the few institutions similarly founded were Basel (1661), Florence (before 1675), and, most importantly, the Cabinet des Estampes (1667) as well as the Cabinet des Dessins (1671) in Paris. From the beginning Dresden never separated drawings from printed works—especially widespread in the United States where it remains popular in some places to this day. The Dresden model was conceived as universal, reaching from the beginning of an individual art form to the present and extending to all countries, even East Asia. The Dresden approach was prototypical, especially for the German-speaking world.

A. d'Enrico, called Tanzio da Varallo (1575–1635), "Man and Angel" (detail), before 1629, see cat. no. 2.13, p. 107

The creation of a systematic museum is largely owed to its first director, Johann Heinrich von Heucher (1677–1746). Apart from merging the printed works from the *Kunstkammer* with other electoral collections, he focused on new acquisitions. For example, Heucher bought works from Orlandi in Bologna and from Weidemann in Leipzig. Among the purchases were pivotal works by Rembrandt, Jordaens, Rubens, Bloemaert, Bruegel, Raphael, and Le Brun. In 1728 he acquired the collection of the Leipzig municipal city builder, Gottfried Wagner, which comprised more than 10,000 drawings. This array of high-caliber masterworks and the number of works by younger artists remains the backbone of Dresden's drawings collection to this day.

The inventory that Heucher created in 1738 gives a first overview of the holdings. Between 1739 and 1746 the annual acquisition funds amounted to 1,000 thalers, which facilitated strategically planned purchases. In 1743 Heucher accomplished one of the great purchases of the era: He secured the Rembrandt engravings from the estate of Prince Eugene of Savoy for Dresden. When Heucher died in 1746, the Collection of Drawings, Prints, and Photographs numbered 49,111 works.

In the year 1746 Carl Heinrich von Heineken (1706–1791) became the head of the "Kupffer-Stiche und Handtzeichnungen." By the time the Seven Years War began in 1756, he had added more than 80,000 sheets to the inventory. His main acquisition activities were focused on French, Netherlandish, and Italian prints and also on early German engravings predating Dürer's time, a segment largely ignored in those days. Heineken was closely connected with art dealers, agents, scholars, and collectors including the Parisian scholar Pierre-Jean Mariette and the Venetian art aficionado Antonio Maria Zanetti. These contacts also led to acquisitions of contemporary art: By 1756 the cabinet contained more than 800 graphic sheets by or after such praised Venetians as Canaletto, Piranesi, Piazzetta,

1 J. van Eyck, "Portrait of an Unknown Man (Cardinal Niccolò Albergati),"
1535–38, silverpoint, 8³/₈ x 7¹/₈ in., CDPP

collection of close to eight hundred portraits was
obtained.

The Collection of Drawings, Prints, and Photographs experienced another boom after moving to
the new museum building designed by Gottfried Semper near the *Zwinger* in 1856. A total of 72 master
drawings from the London art dealer Samuel Woodburn were acquired in 1860, among them works by
Luca Signorelli, Correggio, Fra Bartolommeo, Bronzino, and Holbein the Younger.

A second great blossoming took place between 1882 and 1914 when cataloguing and first systematic,
scholarly work were instigated by Max Lehrs (director 1896–1904, 1908–23). Among his many publications,
the nine- volume compendium *Geschichte und kritischer Katalog des deutschen, niederländischen und französischen
Kupferstichs im 15. Jahrhundert* (1908–34) is still considered a standard work. Lehrs acquired significant
works ranging from early unique woodcuts to master drawings by Grünewald, Dürer, Guardi, Tiepolo,
Rembrandt, and Goya. In 1908 a total of 1,200 drawings from the collection of Leipzig-based collector
Eduard Cichorius were secured. Specializing in the German Romantic artists, works by Friedrich, Fohr,
Koch, Schnorr von Carolsfeld, Olivier, Richter, and others were included.

In those years, Woldemar von Seidlitz (1850–1922) also played a major role: A high-ranking civil servant
and an art historian himself, this active collector and open-minded, generous donor contributed much to the
Collection of Drawings, Prints, and Photographs—including stimulation and suggestions—in the realm of
modern art. As early as 1895, for example, sixteen prints were purchased directly from the studio of James Ensor.
Starting in 1895, the collection of lithographs by Henri de Toulouse-Lautrec was begun which culminated with
the purchase of the famous "Elles" portfolio in 2003.

A special interest in the works of Edvard Munch, Käthe Kollwitz, James McNeill Whistler, Anders Zorn,
Mary Cassatt, Edouard Vuillard, and Pierre Bonnard may also be observed. Two further specialty divisions
were created under Lehrs, one of the most fortunate results of his tenure. One is a small section of high-
quality "Artistic Photography," while the other one is based on the study of *Japonisme* which led to a systematic gathering of Japanese color woodcuts numbering
more than 6,000 works today.

and the Tiepolo family. Heineken, often called "father of the art of engraving," put the collection into systematic order and further refined and rationalized the
arrangements initiated by Heucher; in 1771, he published his ideas in his fundamental treaty entitled *Idée
générale d'une collection complète d'estampes.*

Heineken's successor was the connoisseur, art collector, writer, and diplomat Christian Ludwig von Hagedorn (1712–1780). Appointed in 1763, he was soon
put in charge of the Picture Gallery and the Collection of Antiquities. He was also the head of the recently
founded Dresden Art Academy. Under his leadership, the growth of the cabinet was only moderate. Yet, in
1774, he managed to obtain the collection of the deceased court painter Christian W. E. Dietrichs, which
contained, among other priceless objects, Jan van Goyen's magnificent sketchbook of the years 1648–53.
In the following decades, noteworthy acquisitions included approximately 6,000 prints, primarily by English artists, plus sixty drawings originating from the
estate of the Swiss-born artist Adrian Zingg. In 1837 Francisco Goya's "Caprichos" were purchased, and in

However, it must be said that the curatorial staff was not open to the contemporary art movements of the new century: The magnificent contributions of Dresden art to the 20th century—as epitomized by the group known as *Die Brücke* (1905) with Kirchner, Heckel, Schmidt-Rottluff, and Bleyl—were completely ignored. It was not until Lehrs's successor, Kurt Zoege von Manteuffel (director 1923–42), that some of the gaps were filled. Unfortunately, 381 of the most important works by Klee, Kokoschka, Kirchner, and many others were confiscated and then sold in 1937 as part of the National Socialists' campaign denouncing it as "degenerate art."

Much more disastrous were the consequences of World War II, when the majority of the Collection of Drawings, Prints, and Photographs holdings were brought to the Soviet Union. The return of the masterpieces from the Dresden Collections that began in 1955 also entailed the re-creation of the Collection of Drawings, Prints, and Photographs in 1958. Currently, approximately 5,000 drawings and circa 45,000 prints are still missing—among them many masterworks by such artists as Dürer, Cranach, Rubens, Menzel, Leibl, and Kollwitz— which continue to surface on the black market but also with official art dealers.

Despite the difficult conditions in the German Democratic Republic, the collection thrived once again under Werner Schmidt (director 1958– 90). Among the notable donations of those years, Daniel Henry Kahnweiler's gift of Picasso prints warrants particular mention as does the fabulous bequest of the artist Otto Dix.

During this period, special segments dedicated to the art of the GDR, Czechoslovakia, Poland, Hungary, and the USSR were constituted. At the same time, it was possible to win the true avant-garde for the museum: Today, more than 40 drawings by A. R. Penck belong to the inventory as well as works by the much sought after Russian artists Bulatov and Kabakov.

Since 1990 an attempt to enlarge the inventory in a meaningful way and to create new areas of special emphasis has been made. While it is still the intention to obtain the best examples of contemporary Dresden and German art production, a distinguished attempt is also being made to further strengthen the collection's international profile. Concise efforts are underway to continue purchasing art from our eastern neighbors, but also from Japan. Innovative contemporary art is incorporated into the collection thanks to the particular discernment of the Department of Photography. An unusual recent purchase for the museum was some 10,000 sheets of graphic art originating from the famous collection of the Saxon King Frederick Augustus II and comprising all schools up to the year 1800.

2   A. Watteau, "Study with a Lady, Three Pilgrims, and Cupid,", ca. 1709, red chalk, 8 1/8 x 8 1/4 in., CDPP

Italian School

Series One

CAT. NO. 2.1

ANTONIO ALLEGRI, called
Correggio (1489/94–1534)

Madonna and Child with St. George

BRUSH AND BROWN INK,
HEIGHTENED WITH WHITE,
OVER PEN AND BROWN INK
9³/₈ × 7³/₈ IN.
INV. NO. C 367

Provenance: *Purchased in 1860 from the Estate of Woodburn, London.*

This is a composition design for the painting "Madonna with St. George" (1530–32) in Dresden's Old Masters Picture Gallery, which was originally created for the brotherhood of S. Pietro Martire in Modena. There are considerable differences between the painterly qualities of light and shadow, emphasized in the drawing and the painting. The center is dominated by the Virgin and Child seated under a rounded arch. They are flanked by two saints on each side. Of them, St. John in the left foreground and St. George on the right are more closely defined. The two angels, in the painting positioned in the center of the foreground, are not included here. The framing architecture, delineated in strict Tuscan order, also deviates significantly from the picture. Woermann argues that this is due to the drawing's function as a *modello*.

Lit.: *Woermann 1896–98, folder VI, p. 63 (no. 192), plate IV.—Popham 1975, p. 73.—Giampaolo 1990, no. 83.*
CM

CAT. NO. 2.2

SOFONISBA
ANGUISSOLA
(1530/40–1625)

Portrait of a Lady

LATE 16ᵀᴴ CENTURY
BLACK CHALK ON BLUE PAPER
9 × 6³/₈ IN.
INV. NO. C 1937—785

Provenance: *Acquired in 1937 from the Lahmann Bequest.*

This tenderly executed drawing bears the contemporary signature "di Sofonisba di Cremona." It is an important example of Anguissola's mature work. The individual facial features and the intense gaze directed at the spectator are convincingly captured, taking priority over details of dress and jewelry: the open collar represents a contrast to the austere Spanish collar in vogue at the same time and is only hinted at. The artist, invited to Philipp II's Madrilene court in 1559, remained in Spain until the 1580s when she returned to Italy. The sitter's dress is not a direct quotation of contemporary Spanish fashion; instead it reveals Lombardo-Venetian influences. Giulio Bora points out the extraordinarily sophisticated execution of line and the stupendous physiognomy which results from the skillfully modeled transitions between light and dark areas.

Lit.: *Exh.-cat. Cremona 1994, pp. 28off. (ill. 41).*
CM

BACCIO BRANDINI,
called Baccio Bandinelli
(1493–1560)

Two Male Nudes
Pen and brown ink
16¹/₈ × 11¹/₈ in.
Inv. no. C 1896—27

Provenance: *Collection Artaria, Vienna; Auction Artaria 1896.*

This sheet is signed Bandinelli by a later, unrelated hand in the lower left and belongs to a large group of similar studies which may be found in numerous drawings collections all over the world. Bandinelli drew his standing, gesticulating male nudes, who are frequently seen in rather agitated poses, almost exclusively in pen. Usually, the contours are rendered fluently and are clearly outlined while the inner areas are modeled with luscious cross and parallel hatchings. Often taking Michelangelo as his point of departure, Bandinelli pushes the former's formal language to Mannerist distortions, which is clearly evidenced in these elongated and contorted bodies. While Bandinelli's sculptural and painterly oeuvre was often criticized by his contemporaries, they admired his accomplished drawing skills.

Lit.: *Ward 1982, no. 34.—Exh.-cat. Saarbrücken 1997, pp. 78f. (fig. 7).*

WH

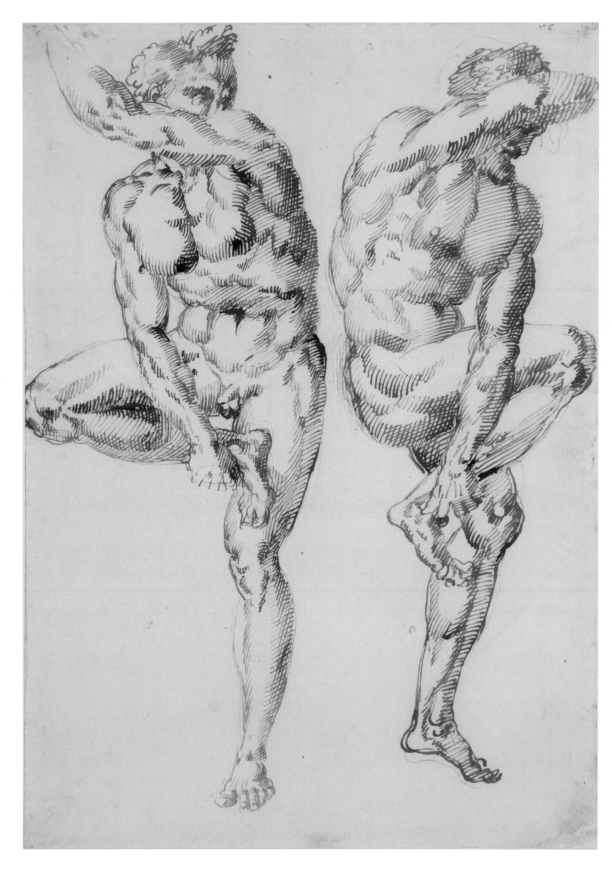

This magnificent draw-
ing by one of the
major masters of the
classicizing Florentine Mannerism is closely related—both
with regards to style and scenic
composition—to the sheet
"Armida and Rinaldo," kept in
a volume of the Gabinetto
Nazionale delle Stampe in
Rome. In his art Boscoli was
primarily influenced by his
teacher, Santi di Tito. However, he also absorbed Dutch
influences through the work of
such artists as Stradanus and
Peter Candid. Based on Ovid's
Metamorphoses, this drawing
recounts in five scenes the
unhappy love between
Salmacis, a nymph at a well
near Halicarnassos, and Hermaphrodite, the handsome
son of Hermes and Aphrodite.
When Hermaphrodite, who
does not reciprocate Salmaci's
affection, takes a bath in the
well, she is united with him—
at her own instigation—
forming a hermaphrodite.

Lit.: *Woermann 1896–98,
folder VI, p. 67 (no. 204).—Voss
1928, p. 393, fig. 154.*

WH

Initially attributed to
Andrea del Sarto, this
powerful drawing is a figure study for St. Zacharias in
the San Ruffillo altarpiece now
in the Santissima Annunziata,
Florence. The kneeling figure
holds a book or a plaque in
the left hand, and was copied
almost literally in the fresco.
On the one hand, the saint is
modeled through powerful
contour lines, while other areas
are deliberately kept blank and
a soft modeling of the drapery
passages in the arms and the
back lead to enhanced plasticity. Pentimenti, such as overlapping lines, allow the viewer
to comprehend the artist's
search for the ideal composition. The study was trimmed,
and the spear-bearing man on
the verso was identified by
Byam Shaw as a study for
St. Michael in the same fresco.

Lit.: *Woermann 1896–98,
folder VI, pp. 65f. (no. 200),
plate X.—Cox Rearick 1964,
p. 103 (no. 4).—Exh.-cat.
Vienna 1978, p. 40 (no. 17).*

CM

CAT. NO. 2.6

FRANCESCO MAZZOLA, called Parmigianino (*1503–1540*)

Study of a Female Nude
PEN AND WASH IN BROWN INK, HEIGHTENED WITH WHITE
9³/₄ × 5⁷/₈ IN.
INV. NO. C 1920—54

Provenance: *Gift of Vogtländer, Collection Winkler, 1920.*

This wonderful drawing on brown paper has an easy and gracious air about it. It shows a female nude in front of voluminous drapes. While her face is only lightly indicated, the body's contour lines remain partly unexecuted. The area of the body as well as vaguely outlined bulks of cloth, are height-ened with white with the addition of light blue accents. A calm balance and nobility emanate from the slender figure. Numerous preparatory drawings—many of which were reproduced during the 17ᵗʰ and 18ᵗʰ centuries—are known. They relate to Parmigianino's frescos and paintings in Parma, Milan, Rome, and Bologna, where this drawing was also made. In the 1530s a number of independent drawings and models for engravings were created. At the time, this technique was only infrequently applied. The exact function and the iconography of this drawing have not yet been closely scrutinized.

CM

CAT. NO. 2.7

JACOPO ROBUSTI, called Tintoretto (*1518–1594*)

Digging Man
CA. 1560
CHARCOAL, HEIGHTENED WITH WHITE, SQUARED FOR TRANSFER; GREY-BLUE PAPER
12 × 6⁵/₈ IN.
INV. NO. C 1968—356

Provenance: *Former Royal Collection, acquired before 1756.*

Today a number of Tintoretto's individual figure studies have been identified as preparatory drawings for paintings. No executed work has yet been identified for the Dresden drawing whose subject might be a gravedigger. Also, the concrete identification of the figure remains difficult, although a similar posture can be found in several of Tintoretto's dramatic paintings. The broken "nut-like" contours—rendering the bent posture of the digging man in a perspectively correct manner—are considered characteristic of Tintoretto's oeuvre. The balanced contrapposto of the man indicates that the study was using a live model, and it is dated to the 1560s.

Lit.: *Hadeln 1922, plate 53.—Exh.-cat. Vienna 1978, pp. 46f. (no. 25).—Tietze 1948, no. 1487.*
CM

Series Two

CAT. NO. 2.8

JACOPO BARBIERI, called
Guercino (1591–1666)

Sibyl

CA. 1660
RED CHALK
8¹/₈ × 5⁷/₈ IN.
INV. NO. C 527

Provenance: *Former Royal
Collection, acquired before 1756.*

Sibyl is one of the priest-
esses of ancient mythol-
ogy who—owing to her
prophetic powers and allusions—became meaningful to
Christianity in reference to the
advent of Christ. The young
woman's softly modeled face is
turned in the direction of the
spectator, who is met directly
by her gaze. Comparatively,
her headdress, clothing, and
hands are of minor impor-
tance. A soft light touches
upon her in a manner compa-

rable to a sheet dated 1635 and
kept in Vienna. Particularly
noteworthy are the subtle color
nuances and the sheet's graphic
qualities. According to Czére,
this, together with the figure's
countenance, is characteristic
of Guercino's classicizing phase
which followed initial drawings
done in a realistic vein. Guercino is considered a master
with red chalk, which enabled
him to achieve delicate shad-
ings. In his late work, red chalk
increasingly replaced the pen,
which he had preferred until
then.

Lit.: *Exh.-cat. Vienna 1978,
p. 56 (no. 38).—Exh.-cat. Rome
2002, p. 76 (no. 26).*

CM

BACCIO DEL BIANCO
(1604–1656)

Young Man in a Costume

PEN AND WASH IN BROWN INK
10³/₈ × 8¹/₈ IN.
INV. NO. C 117

Provenance: *Former Royal
Collection, acquired before 1756.*

This drawing stands in
the tradition of depic-
tions of festivities.
The young man wears a rich
costume to which belong a hat
with feather decoration in the
style of Louis XIII and a decorative lance with a large shield,
presumably used for tournaments. Possibly, this detailed
drawing served as a model for a
costume employed in one of
the many ballets, comedies, or

tournaments that del Bianco
staged at the Medici court in
the 1630s. Baldinucci lists a
number of drawings depicting
masquerade costumes and
theater machines del Bianco
staged at the court of Philipp
IV in Spain after 1650. There
he continued to furnish operas
and plays, sending selected
stage set designs and drawings
pertaining to his work to
Ferdinando II de' Medici in
Florence.

Lit.: *Gramaccini/Meier 2003,
pp. 156 (no. 166), 324 (ill.).*

CM

CAT. NO. 2.10

ANNIBALE CARRACCI
(1560–1609)

Allegory of the Night
PEN AND WASH AND BROWN INK,
TRACES OF RED CHALK
11 × 16¹/₂ IN.
INV. NO. C 464

Provenance: *Purchased in
1860 from the Estate of Woodburn, London.*

This drawing shows the
allegory of the night
floating across the
landscape from the left and
holding two sleeping children
in her arms, personifications of
sleep and death. The wide,
moonlit landscape lies under a
starry sky. Animals and humans

are asleep, the sails of the boats
in the background are down.
This sheet of Carracci's corresponds to his painting "The
Night in Flight" from the
Palazzo Farnese, Rome, today
in Chantilly. In the 18th century it was engraved by Francesco Bartolozzi. The painting
departs from the drawing in a
number of details and was part
of a series dedicated to the
times of the day. Together, this
series formed the ceiling decoration of one of the nine
camerini in the Palazzo Farnese. Albani (1578–1660), who
was a student of Carracci's, also
treated the topic various times
and copied the Carracci drawing with all its details. This
drawing, along with another
one kept in the Dresden Collection of Drawings, Prints,

and Photographs, comes from
the Collection of Mariette on
whose judgment today's attri-
butions are based.

Lit.: *Mahoney 1962.*

CM

CAT. NOS. 2.11A AND 2.11B

SEBASTIANO CONCA
(1695–1764)

Diana and Endymion
BLACK CHALK, HEIGHTENED
WITH WHITE
18¹⁄₈ × 12¹⁄₄ IN.
INV. NO. C 562

Provenance: *Former Royal
Collection, acquired before 1756,
possibly from the Woodburn
Collection.*

NICOLAS LE SUEUR
(1691–1764)

**Colored Woodcut after
the Drawing by Conca**
17³⁄₄ × 12³⁄₈ IN. (IMAGE)
18³⁄₄ × 12³⁄₄ IN. (PRINT
BLOCK/SHEET WITH TITLE)
INV. NO. A 106312

Provenance: *Former Royal
Collection, purchased before 1858,
in the Inventory 1858/60.*

This unusually large
and finely finished
drawing, rendered on
blue paper, is signed—probably by a later hand—in the
lower right. Conca was a student of Francesco Solimena
and is considered one of the
major classicizing masters
of Rome. The depiction is
based on the Greek myth of
the moon goddess Selene's
love. In the middle of the
night, she leaves her chariot
led by Amor, in order to look
at the handsome sleeping
shepherd Endymion. While
Amor illuminates her way with
his torch, he sends the dogs
and the herd into a deep sleep.
In the drawing, two putti light
the goddess's path. It appears
that the drawing was sent to
Paris, where Le Sueur trans-

formed it into a woodcut, a
reproduction technique newly
developed in the 16th century.
By this process, he attempted
to maintain the painterly
quality and to render precisely
the bright and dark passages
indicated in the drawing with
white heightening.

CM

CAT. NO. 2.12

GIOVANNI BENEDETTO
CASTIGLIONE (1609–1664)

Pastoral Scene
OIL ON PAPER, CHALK AND
PREPARATORY DRAWING IN PEN
AND BROWN INK
10⁵⁄₈ × 15⁵⁄₈ IN.
INV. NO. C 427

Provenance: *Purchased in
1860 from the Estate of Woodburn, London.*

Brush drawings, intended
as independent works
of art and not serving as
modelli for paintings, were
executed as early as the 1630s.
Since this sheet shows no
corrections, Castiglione considered it an autonomous
work. His oil sketches bear the
character of drawings. They
are mostly rendered in a few
subtly varying hues of yellow-
brown color with heightening.
The pastoral and lighthearted
subject, a moving herd with
dogs and children, combines
Flemish and Venetian influences: The love for details and
the depiction of landscapes

was brought to Genoa by Netherlandish painters. Castiglione's compositions were frequently engraved and copied, and their most notable influence initially occurred in Genovese painting. Artists influenced outside Genoa by this drawing style in the 18th century included Tiepolo, Fragonard, and Boucher.

Lit.: *Exh.-cat. Vienna 1978, p. 60 (no. 44).*

CM

CAT. NO. 2.13

ANTONIO D'ENRICO, called Tanzio da Varallo (*1575–1635*)

Man and Angel

BEFORE 1629
RED CHALK
$15^5/8 \times 11^3/8$ IN.
INV. NO. C 1937–840

Provenance: *Acquired in 1937 from the Lahmann Bequest.*

The figure group in this drawing corresponds to the 1629 ceiling frescos in the Nazari Chapel in San Gaudenzio in Novara. Andrews was able to demonstrate that this is one of the most complete preparatory drawings for Novara. This sheet—originally attributed to Morazzone—reveals that only a few variants or details were left open. In the frescos, the bent leg of the man led to heaven and the luscious drapery are executed more voluminously. Both figures are rendered fully three-dimensionally, exuding a remarkable elegance and ease customarily associated with the manner of Florentine artists. There are more comparable preparatory sketches in the cabinets of Dresden and Berlin.

Lit.: *Andrews 1967.—Exh.-cat. Vienna 1978, pp. 52f. (no. 33).— Exh.-cat. Milan 2000, p. 188 (no. 61).*

CM

GIOVANNI BATTISTA
PIRANESI *(1720–1778)*

Architectural Capriccio
AFTER 1740
PEN AND WASH AND BROWN INK,
RED CHALK
8³/₈ × 11¹/₈ IN.
INV. NO. C 1920–59

Provenance: *Gift of Vogtländer;
Collection Winkler, 1920.*

This drawing presents a juxtaposition of different architectural features: a large exterior staircase leads to a triumphal arch; in the background a round building may be spotted; to the right, in front of the corner of a temple, is a tomb embellished with trophies and weapons. The scene is framed by a kind of Coliseum building. Washes and perspectival foreshortening create spatial

CAT. NO. 2.14

FRANCESCO GUARDI
(1712–1793)

**View of the Dogana
in Venice**
PEN AND WASH AND BROWN INK,
BROWN PAPER, PREPARATORY
DRAWING IN BLACK CHALK
11 × 15³/₈ IN.
INV. NO. C 1896–29

Provenance: *Auction Artaria,
Vienna, 1896.*

The view includes the majestic Dogana (Customs Building) entrance and the Grand Canal. On the water numerous gondolas and sailboats may be spotted. The buildings on the Giudecca in the background appear closer than they are. Erected 1676–82 on the tip of land in front of S. Maria della Salute, the Dogana is depicted here only in part. The preparatory drawing in chalk and the more precise pen and ink drawing suggest that this is a study from nature. A drawing kept in Cologne and a painting in Milan reveal that Guardi executed this very view more than once. Based on comparisons with paintings,

the "Flagellation of Christ" on the verso was assigned to Guardi's early phase. It might, however, also be by his brother Gianantonio, with whom he collaborated and for whom figure studies were less unusual.

Lit.: *Robels 1967, p. 59.—Exh.-cat. Vienna 1978, p. 68 (no. 54).*
CM

depth and an atmosphere flooded with light. Possibly, this might be a design for a theater decoration; it could also simply be a fantastic assemblage of architecture. If it were the latter, this would be a sharp contrast to detailed views painted by Francesco Guardi or Bernardo Bellotto. The term *capriccio* appears to go back to a series of Callot prints that were produced for the Duke de' Medici in 1617. *Capriccio* series—such as the ones made by della Bella, Piranesi, and Goya—contain, apart from the title sheet, sketches or prints which delineate different subject matter filled with fantasy and humor.

CM

CAT. NOS. 2.16A AND 2.16B

FRANCESCO
BACCIARELLI *(1731–1818)*

Madonna delle Rose
1753–55
BLACK CHALK
14³/₄ × 11¹/₈ IN.
INV. NO. C 1970–17

Provenance: *Acquired in ca. 1755.*

CARL HEINRICH VON
HEINEKEN *(1706–1791)*

Recueil d'estampes d'après les plus célèbres tableaux de la Galerie royale de Dresde, vol. 2, no. 3

1758
29³/₄ × 21¹/₄ IN.
INV. NO. B 102,4

This drawing is a copy after a painting by Parmigianino in Dresden's Old Masters Picture Gallery. At the same time, it is a preparatory drawing for the engraving published by Heineken in his 1757 *Galeriewerk*, a tome issued in an edition of 600, accounting for and reproducing the Picture Gallery's masterworks. Incorporated into the *Galeriewerk*'s second volume were five copies of drawings by Bacciarelli who worked at the Warsaw court since 1756. There, he became court painter in 1766 and twenty years later was made director of the royal collections like his counterpart, Heineken, in Dresden. The drawing relates to the Dresden painting and shows the Virgin seated in front of black drapery. The Christ child on her lap rests his one hand on an orb while the other hand holds a rose, a symbol of carnal love. This makes the painting appear ambiguous, allowing an identification as Venus and

Amor, especially since the Virgin's halo remained unpainted. The engraving that Johann Christoph Teucher executed after Bacciarelli's drawing shows a mirror image of the painting. The print was made in a technique combining copperplate engraving and etching. At the bottom center of the impression, two coats of arms may be seen. The one on the right belongs to electoral Saxony. Both coats of arms are united under a crown. Despite the detailed drawing, deviations from the painting can be observed, including the less elongated proportions, the two figures' facial features, and the modeling of the transitions from light to dark areas.

Lit.: *Walther 1992, p. 293 (no. 161).—Wazbinski 2000.*

CM

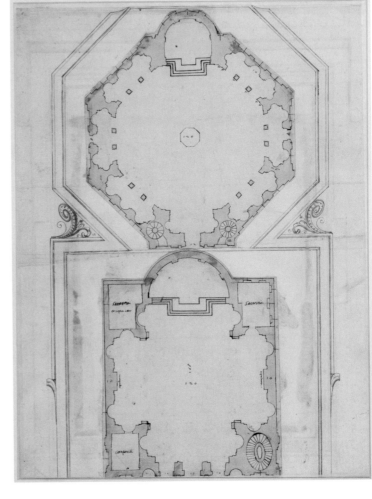

CAT. NO. 2.17

MICHELANGELO
BUONARROTI (1475–1564)

Sheet from the *Libro de' disegni* by Vasari

RECTO: VERTICAL ELEVATION OF
A MONUMENT
VERSO: TWO GROUND PLANS FOR
RELIGIOUS EDIFICES (CENTRALLY
PLANNED BUILDINGS)
PEN AND BROWN INK, WASH, RED
CHALK CORRECTIONS (RECTO)
PEN AND BROWN INK, GREEN
WASH (VERSO)
14¹/2 × 11 IN.
INV. NO. C 49

Provenance: *Purchased before 1865 from the Collection Giorgio Savari, Florence.*

Unfortunately, this large sheet from Giorgio Vasari's famous *Libro de' disegni* is only rarely given consideration, yet it could be of substantial interest for the art historical discourse concerning drawings attributed to Michelangelo. The work's execution with a ruler and a compass has heretofore made explicit evaluations difficult. Popp was the first to assign it to Michelangelo. There is no doubt that the parts rendered in free hand testify to an accomplished draftsperson. In addition, similar striations and the term *braccio* (which refers to the scale) may be found in many of Michelangelo's drawings. Furthermore, a comparison of the writing suggests that this is his handwriting. Based on the coat of arms, Popp and Tolnay argue that the drawing pertains to a 1524 design for a wall tomb that was developed in conjunction with the plans for tombs of the Medici popes Leo X and Clement VII in the New Sacristy of San Lorenzo in Florence. Other authors speak of a free-standing tomb or an altar design. The connection with the two sketches on the verso remains unclear: Neither the rendering nor the motifs indicate the authorship of either Michelangelo or his students.

Lit.: *Morrogh 1992, pp. 143–163.—Popp 1927, pp. 389–451.—Tolnay 1975–80, corpus 276.*

AZ

CAT. NO. 2.18

ALBRECHT DÜRER
(1471–1528)

Frolickers Surprised by Death

CA. 1500
BLACK CHALK, RED SPLASHES
DIAM. 10⁷/8 IN.
INV. NO. C 2210

Provenance: *Former Royal Collection.*

Depicted as a skeleton with a scythe over his shoulder and an hourglass in his hand, Death's appearance evokes a multitude of different reactions in the people, who are all in their prime. Their emotions range from horror, lament, and apprehension to protest, resistance, and the realization that

cations that Dürer altered his composition while working on it. Such corrections are referred to as pentimenti. The conspicuously grand scale of figure and shield might indicate that this was a design for a glass painting. Alternatively, it may have served as a sketch for a painting. Around the year 1500 Dürer repeated similar depictions of wild men as bearers of coats of arms—as seen in his painting of the Haller-Madonna (Washington, National Gallery of Art) or the wings of the portrait of Oswald Krell (Munich, Alte Pinakothek).

Lit.: *Winkler 1936, vol. 1, p. 115 (no. 168).—Exh.-cat. Dresden 1971, p. 134 (cat. no. 151).—Goldberg et al. 1998, p. 251 (fig. 3.19).*

CS

death is inevitable and can either be viewed with anxiety or tolerant anticipation. The composition underscores the drama: while the approaching Death is seen in front of a bright and open landscape, the apprehensive crowd appears to be literally squeezed to the drawing's edge and pressed into the darkness of the forest. This is a preparatory drawing for a stained-glass window. Until Winkler ascribed it to Dürer—an attribution which is not undisputed—it was considered the work of Dürer's student, Hans Baldung Grien.

Lit.: *Winkler 1936, vol. 1, pp. 151f. (no. 215).—Exh.-cat. Dresden 1963, p. 38 (cat. no. 92), plate 22.—Exh.-cat. Dresden 1971, pp. 134f. (cat. no. 153).*

CS

CAT. NO. 2.19

ALBRECHT DÜRER
(1471–1528)

Wild Man Holding a Coat of Arms

CA. 1500
PEN AND BROWN INK, CHARCOAL
11 5/8 × 7 1/2 IN.
INV. NO. C 2160

Provenance: *Former Royal Collection.*

A popular heraldic motif, the wild man appears most often holding or guarding a sign. Dürer rendered the wild gaze of the forest man in a thrilling manner: he stares suspiciously at the spectator from the corners of his eyes. Executed with a broad pen, the outlines of the figure and the coat of arms are rendered in expansive, sweeping lines. There are indi-

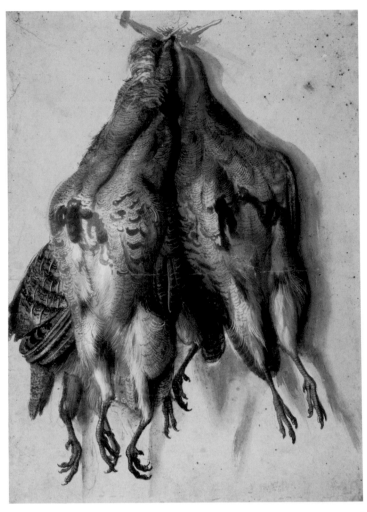

CAT. NO. 2.20

LUCAS CRANACH
THE ELDER *(1472–1553)*

**Wild Man Holding a
Coat of Arms and a Bell
beneath a Stone Portal**

CA. 1520/30
PEN AND BLACK INK, WATER-
COLOR, OVER CHARCOAL
12³/₈ × 8¹/₂ IN., ARCHED
INV. NO. C 2170

Provenance: *Former Royal
Collection.*

Beginning in 1505 Cra-
nach the Elder was
employed in Wittenberg
as versatile court painter of
Prince Elector Frederick the
Wise of Saxony and his two
successors. Cranach's sons
Hans and Lucas (the Younger),
whose work is often difficult
to distinguish from that of
their father and the workshop,
worked as his students and
assistants. Rosenberg assumes
this drawing might be the
work of a Cranach student who

used a preparatory sketch of
the master. Its cursory organization and the powerful coloration, however, do not rule
out the authorship of Cranach
the Elder since the artist was
striving for artistic simplicity.
Perhaps this sheet once
belonged to a heraldic book,
served as a design for a glass
painting, or was intended as a
model for another decorative
object. The meaning of the
coat of arms, showing a pike
head, as well as the bell in the
wild man's hand remains unan-
swered. The latter could have
been inspired by the iconography of Saint Anthony Abbot
who lived in the wilderness and
whose attribute is the bell.

Lit.: *Rosenberg 1960, p. 37, no.
A 13 with ill.—Exh.-cat. Dresden 1971, p. 111 (cat. no. 121).—
Exh.-cat. Basel 1974, vol. 2,
p. 595 (cat. no. 489).*

CS

CAT. NO. 2.21

LUCAS CRANACH
THE ELDER *(1472–1553)*

Four Dead Partridges

CA. 1530/32
WATERCOLOR AND OPAQUE
PAINT, HEIGHTENED WITH
WHITE OVER GRAY WASH
17⁵/₈ × 12⁵/₈ IN.
INV. NO. C 1193

Provenance: *Former Royal
Collection.*

Apart from this nature
study, the Dresden
Cabinet of Prints and
Drawings owns further drawings of birds and game originating from the Cranach workshop's extensive holdings of
very high quality patterns. The
topic is derived from the genre
of the hunting still life, a subject first introduced by Jacopo
de' Barbari. This Italian
painter and graphic artist is
documented as working for
Prince Elector Frederick the
Wise—employer of Cranach

since 1505—between 1503 and
1505. Cranach's motif of the
four dead partridges was later
used in two of his paintings
from 1532: "Hercules and
Omphale" (formerly Munich,
Kunsthandel Scheidwimmer)
and "The Payment" (Stock-
holm, National Museum). The
Physiologus—one of the major
medieval works on zoology—
ascribes to the partridge an
untamed libido; therefore, the
depiction of this animal in
images of courtship suggests a
symbolic reference to carnal
love.

Lit.: *Exh.-cat. Dresden 1971,
pp. 112f. (cat. no. 125).—Koreny
1985, pp. 50f. (cat. no. 8 with
ill.).—Exh.-cat. Kronach/Leipzig
1994, p. 360 (cat. no. 188b).*

CS

horizon line underscores the overall vastness of the background.

Lit.: *Exh.-cat. Dresden 1963, p. 53 (cat. no. 147).—Exh.-cat. Dresden 1971, p. 231 (cat. no. 417).—Winzinger 1979, vol. 1, pp. 97f. (no. 66), vol. 2, ill. 66.*

CS

CAT. NO. 2.22

WOLF HUBER
(ca. 1485–1553)

Hilly Landscape with Church

1536
PEN AND BLACK INK
5 1/8 × 8 1/4 IN., BORDER CUT
INV. NO. C 2260

Provenance: *Former Royal Collection.*

Along with Albrecht Altdorfer, Huber is one of the outstanding representatives of the *Donauschule* (School of the Danube River), a movement in German and Austrian art between 1490 and 1540. For the first time, landscapes were recognized as autonomous and worthy subjects. Huber's drawings contributed significantly to their new status. The dated landscape is by his own hand and belongs to the artist's late style. Winzinger presumes that this is a survey of nature which Huber finished in the fashion of a painting by adding, in heavy pen strokes, the fence and the shrubbery in the foreground as well as the cut foliage along the left edge. The effort required for the creation of the middle ground is remarkable: The landscape is characterized by a transparent and dynamic set of almost abstract, short pen strokes. This densely populated system of lines is juxtaposed to vast empty spaces which add to the sheet's peculiar rhythm.

Lit.: *Exh.-cat. Dresden 1971, p. 231 (cat. no. 418 with ill.).— Dresden 1978, p. 128 (cat. no. 133).—Winzinger 1979, vol. 1, pp. 110f. (no. 90), vol. 2, ill. 90.*

CS

CAT. NO. 2.23

WOLF HUBER
(ca. 1485–1553)

Church Path

CA. 1518/20
PEN AND BLACK INK
8 3/8 × 6 1/8 IN., BORDER CUT
INV. NO. C 2203

Provenance: *Former Royal Collection.*

This seemingly simple vista proves to be a fully developed composition with exquisitely refined tectonics. Huber guides the viewer's sight directly to the church, which is located slightly off center. The church choir and the spectator's viewpoint coincide. Thanks to the skillful arrangement of buildings and the surrounding framing devices consisting of shrubs, densely foliated deciduous trees, and high, delicate conifers, the artist creates considerable depth. The low

CAT. NO. 2.24

HANS SÜSS VON
KULMBACH *(ca. 1480–1522)*

Bust of a Bearded Man
DARK BLACK CHALK, ON THE
FOREHEAD A RED PAINT SPOT
$4^{1}/_{4} \times 3^{1}/_{8}$ IN.
INV. NO. C 6404

Provenance: *Former Royal
Collection.*

Around the year 1500,
Süß von Kulmbach
began to work in
Dürer's workshop, where the
master became incomparably
significant for the young
graphic artist and painter. The
Dresden Collection of Drawings, Prints, and Photographs
preserves 29 drawings by Süß
von Kulmbach, mostly designs

for stained glass. The head of
the old man is distinguished by
strongly modeled lines full of
contrast. The visual effect is
largely due to the dark black,
greasy medium. The wrinkles
on the forehead, on the other
hand, consist of the finest lines.
Winkler proposes that this
heavily cut down drawing was
originally part of the inventory
of a stained-glass workshop,
from whence various of Dresden's Kulmbach works originate. The small red spot of oil
paint over the man's left eye—
an accidental yet effective and
exciting accent of color—further suggests that the drawing
was used as a workshop model.

Lit.: *Winkler 1942, p. 63
(no. 48), 26.—Exh.-cat. Dresden
1963, pp. 54f. (cat. no. 154).*
CS

CAT. NO. 2.25

HANS SÜSS VON
KULMBACH *(ca. 1480–1522)*

Bust of a Girl
BLACK AND WHITE CHALK ON
RED TINTED PAPER
$5^{5}/_{8} \times 4$ IN., BORDER CUT
VERSO: BUST OF A BEARDED
MAN
INV. NO. C 2188

Provenance: *Former Royal
Collection.*

In contrast to "Bust of
Bearded Man" (cat.
no. 2.24), Süß von Kulm-
bach sketches the face of the
girl with only a few black chalk
lines. The three-dimensional-
ity is chiefly evoked by the
use of white highlights. The
paper's red tint diminishes the

contrast between the chalks,
thus enhancing the painterly
quality of the sheet. This could
conceivably be a study for a
painting.

Lit.: *Winkler 1942, p. 65
(no. 53), 27.—Exh.-cat. Dresden
1963, p. 55 (cat. no. 155).*
CS

CAT. NO. 2.26

HANS VON AACHEN
(1552–1615)

Judith with the Head of Holofernes

AFTER 1605
PEN AND BROWN INK, GRAY
AND BROWN WASH, HEIGHTENED
WITH WHITE, OVER BLACK
CHALK, BORDERLINE IN BROWN
INK
10¼ × 7½ IN., UPPER EDGES
CUT AND RESTORED
INV. NO. C 1941—44

Provenance: *Former Royal Collection.*

Von Aachen served as the court painter to Emperor Rudolph II in Prague beginning in 1596. Together with Bartholomäus Spranger and Joseph Heintz, he was one of the most important painters of the so-called Rudolphian Mannerism. Among the biblical stories, that of Judith and Holofernes is the most popular one in his oeuvre. Judith was determined to save her city from the Assyrians' assaults. Therefore, the beautiful and fearless heroine went with her servant to the enemy camp in order to kill their leader. After a bout of heavy drinking, she decapitated the drunken Holofernes with his own sword and hid his head in a bag. This sheet is a quickly rendered chalk sketch that von Aachen revised with pen and then applied wash for its details using a brush. The areas of white heightening together with the finely modulated washes in gray and brown result in rich light and shadow effects within the figures, lending them extraordinary plasticity.

Lit.: *Exh.-cat. Essen 1988, pp. 335f. (cat. no. 186 with ill.).—Jacoby 2000, pp. 85f.*

CS

CAT. NO. 2.27

JOSEPH HEINTZ
(1564–1609)

Allegory

CA. 1590/1595
PEN AND BROWN INK, WATER-
COLOR, OVER GRAPHITE, BORDER-
LINE IN DARK BROWN INK
8 × 6⅜ IN.
INV. NO. C 6383

Provenance: *Former Royal Collection.*

Heintz, a student of Hans von Aachen's, was made a chamber painter to Rudolph II even before his mentor was. This drawing is an example for the intense art theoretical discourse led by the artists belonging to the "Rudolphian" circle. Such works had the quality of manifestos and reflected the classification of painting as a liberal art as well as artistic self-definition. During the first half of Rudolph II's reign, painters were already privileged members of society. However, in 1595 the emperor renewed the guild privileges, at which time he declared that henceforth painters were no longer considered craftspeople, but artists instead. This artistic self-promotion visualizes the artist in the pose of the thinker, wearing a laurel wreath, while he draws before a painting which is held for him by Fame and Minerva. The inscription says: "All will end well if I pursue simple taste with a sense of truthfulness."

Lit.: *Zimmer 1988, p. 131, no. A 46, ill. 84.—Exh.-cat. Prague 1997, p. 429 (cat. no. 1.192 with ill.).*

CS

CAT. NO. 2.28

TOBIAS STIMMER
(1539–1584)

Christic and the Samaritan Woman at the Well

Christ and the Samaritan Woman at the Well

CA. 1567
PEN AND BLACK WITH BROWN
INK, BORDERLINE IN BLACK INK
16¹/₈ × 12⁵/₈ IN.
INV. NO. C 2275

Provenance: *Former Royal Collection.*

One fifth of the surviving drawings by this Swiss painter and graphic artist are preparatory drawings for glass paintings. A drawing by Stimmer with the same theme and dated 1567 is kept in the Basel Collection of Prints and Drawings. Because of stylistic similarities and nearly identical sizes, the sheets from Dresden and Basel—likely variants for the commission of a so-called *Kabinettscheibe* (the gift of a pane with a coat of arms)—were possibly made at nearly the same time. Usually the frame for a *Kabinettscheibe* consists of a richly decorated architectural structure which frequently depicts figural scenes of high moral character. In this instance only the right half of the composition was executed. Stimmer added two Old Testament scenes to the main motif of Christ asking the Samaritan woman for water and offering her in return living water which would quench her thirst for eternity. Seen in the spandrels are "Noah grows wine and drink" as well as "Noah's drunkenness and mocking."

Lit.: *Exh.-cat. Dresden 1978, p. 133 (cat. no. 141).—Exh.-cat. Basel 1984, p. 430 (cat. no. 268), 429 (ill. 275, the drawing from Basel).*

CS

CAT. NO. 2.29

JUSEPE RIBERA
(1590–1652)

Saint Sebastian

PEN AND BROWN INK AND
BROWN WASH
9 × 6¹/₂ IN.
INV. NO. C 353

Provenance: *Former Royal Collection, acquired before 1756.*

Ribera, born in Valencia, Spain, repeatedly treated the martyred human body in his drawings. More than 15 drawings dating from the 1620s and 1630s are dedicated to the motif of a martyr chained to a tree. The Dresden sheet shows St. Sebastian whose body is pierced by two arrows. According to legend, the officer of Emperor Diocletian's bodyguard was persecuted for his Christian faith and ultimately sentenced to death, but survived. Ribera refrains from any narrative details in relating the event. He focuses entirely on depicting the elongated body by drawing it in a few soft pen strokes. The washes form the shaded areas around the mighty tree trunk, offering an effective contrast. The diagonal drive of body and tree is this composition's defining force.

Lit.: *Exh.-cat. Madrid 1992, pp. 47off. (D 56).*

TK

CAT. NO. 2.30

GEORG PETEL
(ca. 1601/02–1634)

Neptune Standing

CA. 1627/30
RED CHALK, BORDER LINE IN
BROWN INK
16¹/₈ × 10 IN., BORDER CUT
INV. NO. C 1966—126

Provenance: *Former Royal Collection.*

Arndt identified this drawing as Petel's design for a Neptune figure cast in bronze. Originally belonging to a fountain, the figure is exhibited today in the *Königsbauhof* of the Munich Residence. Because its execution and its modeling are so delicate, this drawing is considered to be one of the artist's best. Corrections in the shoulders, the arms, and the right leg are indications that this is indeed an original design. When the drawing was cut at a later time, the trident was eliminated. A comparison between preparatory drawing and sculpture reveals distinct differences: casting reeds in bronze was deemed too difficult. Therefore Neptune was dressed in an ordinary loin cloth with distinct drapery. Floral ornaments in his hair were simply omitted. The dolphin was first rendered smaller and then placed differently. Finally, the trident, originally intended to offer support to the sea god, was shortened so drastically that the deity's posture is no longer convincing. The disadvantageous alterations together with a bill of sale dated to 1641 suggest that the sculpture was cast after Petel's death.

Lit.: *Arndt 1967, pp. 200–206 (fig. 20).—Feuchtmayr/Schädler 1973, pp. 131f. (no. 39, ill. 90, drawing), 110f. (no. 24, figs. 91–93, bronze figure).— Exh.-cat. Dresden 1978, p. 136 (cat. no. 145).*

CS

Netherlandish School and French School

Series One

CAT. NO. 2.31

PIETER BRUEGEL THE ELDER *(1525/30–1569)*

Gooseherd
PEN AND YELLOW-BROWN INK
9³/₄ × 5⁷/₈ IN.
INV. NO. C 2128

Provenance: *Acquired before 1764.*

The "Gooseherd" is not only considered one of Pieter Bruegel the Elder's most beautiful figure studies but is also one of the earliest full-figure studies of any Netherlandish artist based on a profane model. The large size of the sheet alone is quite impressive. Bruegel took note of the figure's outline with a pen; parallel lines with occasional crosshatchings indicate shadow. The bushy hair is only delicately hinted at. The title "Gooseherd" stems from a small painting showing the herder in the midst of a flock of geese with a village in the background. A little round panel plus four other paintings—today attributed to Pieter Bruegel the Younger— make up a series of proverbs. The one associated with the "Gooseherd" is "Wie weet waer omme de ganzen bervoets gaen?" ("Who knows why the geese go barefoot?"), meaning that there is a reason for everything, even for the seemingly inexplicable.

Lit.: *Mielke 1996, p. 63 (no. 57).*

TK

JEAN COUSIN THE YOUNGER (*ca. 1522–1594*)

The Liberation of Souls from Purgatory

Pen and brown ink and brown wash

$17^{1}/_{2} \times 15^{3}/_{4}$ in.

Inv. no. C 1976–350

Provenance: *Acquired from the Collection Gottfried Wagner, Leipzig, 1728.*

Cousin's drawing visualizes the Christian concept of salvation. The Virgin Mary is depicted as the intercessor for humankind. She kneels in humility in front of Christ, her risen son. With her left hand, she points to the terrestrial sphere: set within classical vaults, men and women eagerly seek forgiveness for their sins. The realm of Hell is depicted as a barren landscape with antique ruins populated by monsters. Even the elegantly dressed nobleman is kneeling. He is seeking the salvation of his soul while gazing into his open book of life and humbly looking upwards toward Christ. The delicate drawing style of Cousin's, his slightly elongated figures, and the complexity of his composition can be traced back to his famous father, Jean de Cousin the Elder, who was presumably his teacher.

Lit.: *Exh.-cat. Paris/New York 1995, pp. 166f.*

TK

JAN GOSSAERT (*ca. 1478–1532*)

Standing Warrior with a Halberd

Pen and brown ink

$11 \times 6^{1}/_{2}$ in.

Inv. no. C 790

Provenance: *From the Kunstkammer, 1720.*

Gossaert belonged to the first generation of Netherlandish artists who spent a considerable amount of time in Italy. His intense study of Italian Renaissance art and of antiquity can be dated to 1508/09. This sheet is a free design that demonstrates how the artist was able to absorb the antique canon of forms into his own oeuvre. Without developing a didactic approach or that of an antiquarian, he assimilates elements freely and with great ease. In fact, the arm set akimbo is quite far removed from its antique prototype, the "Farnese Hercules." But the ancient quotations such as the sandals and the shoulder clasps are all part of the abundance of decorative embellishments. In their omnipresence, the adornments populate the armor, turning the warrior into an ornamental figure.

Lit.: *Exh.-cat. Dresden 1997a, pp. 34f. (no. 8).*

TK

CAT. NO. 2.34

FRANS FLORIS
(*1519/20–1570*)

The Beheading of John the Baptist
PEN AND BROWN-BLACK INK
AND GRAY WASH
9¼ × 10⅛ IN.
INV. NO. C 842

Provenance: *Acquired in 1728 from the widow of Gottfried Wagner, Leipzig.*

Floris was the head of a large painting workshop in Antwerp. Like Gossaert, he spent a long time in Italy. Apart from numerous paintings he left behind an extensive oeuvre of drawings, among them this carefully executed compositional sheet. It was upon her mother's command that Salome asked her stepfather, Herod Antipes, for the head of St. John as a reward for her arousing dance. Looking through one of the palatial arches, the spectator sees Herod's table to the right. Salome approaches, triumphantly offering him the head (Matthew 14:1–11). The slender and slightly elongated figures with their barely accentuated faces are typical of Floris's drawing style.

Lit.: *Van de Velde 1975, no. 131.*
TK

CAT. NO. 2.35

PETER CANDID
(*ca. 1548–1628*)

The Archangel Michael
PEN AND BROWN AND GRAY
WASH, HEIGHTENED WITH
WHITE
16¼ × 9¼ IN.
INV. NO. C 885

Provenance: *Former Royal Collection, acquired before 1756.*

Like many of his colleagues, Candid was a polyglot artist. Born in Bruges, he moved to Florence in 1558 where he began to work for the Medici in 1575. William V appointed him court painter in Munich in 1586. This finely worked and richly modelled drawing recalls a sculpture that Hubert Gerhards made for the Jesuit church of St. Michael in Munich in 1588. In its delineation of the volumes of both of the bodies, Candid's study does full justice to the three-

dimensional prototype. This drawing served as the design for a copperplate engraving by Lucas Kilian. In order to transfer the composition the contours were incised with a sharp pencil.

Lit.: *Exh.-cat. Dresden 1997a, pp. 84f. (no. 33).*

TK

CAT. NOS. 2.36A AND 2.36B

NICOLAS LAGNEAU
(ca. 1590–after 1650)

Portrait of a Laughing Man

RED AND BLACK CHALK
16¹/₂ × 10³/₈ IN.
INV. NO. C 606

Provenance: *Acquired in 1723 from Count J. G. von Rechenberg.*

Portrait of an Old Woman with a Bonnet

RED, BLACK, AND BROWN CHALK
16 × 10 IN.
INV. NO. C 607

Provenance: *Former Royal Collection, acquired before 1756, Count J. G. von Rechenberg 1720.*

Lagneau is a mere speck on the map of art history. The first time he is mentioned is in 1672: the famous French collector Abbot Michel de Marolles refers to him in connection with a volume of portrait drawings. Marolles did not even give the first name of the artist, whose identity remains a mystery to this day. Today, a multitude of chalk portraits, mostly of elderly persons, is labeled with the name Lagneau. Customarily, they are distinguished by hyperrealistic faces which are sometimes supplemented

with caricatured features. The faces of the old woman and of the friskily laughing man do not conform to an aesthetic norm. Artists' fascination with images of elderly people began long before Leonardo. Their skill as draftspeople enables them to carefully investigate the traces life leaves in the wrinkles of the skin or in facial deformities.

Lit.: *Exh.-cat. Paris/New York 1995, pp. 294–297.*

TK

Series Two

JACQUES DE GHEYN II
(1565–1629)

Scene of Sorcery
PEN AND BROWN INK
15 × 11⅛ IN.
INV. NO. C 907

Provenance: *Acquired from
the Collection Gottfried Wagner,
Leipzig, 1728.*

This sheet is among the most mysterious renderings within the sizable oeuvre of drawings by de Gheyn. Of the Witches Sabbath alone, eight further versions by his hand are known. The motif has a long tradition within Netherlandish art. Artists such as Hieronymus Bosch and Pieter Bruegel the Elder have repeatedly turned to the fantastic world of ghosts and apparitions. The seemingly bizarre architecture of ruins anticipates the architectural world of Piranesi. De Gheyn found a specific drawing style for his fantasy world: While creating powerful lines with a repeatedly reapplied pen, he conceives multitudes of zigzag lines with dynamic crescendos. This ultimately offers vehement expression for his ideas. Instead of a signature a reflective figure may be seen in the lower right corner. In light of the world presented here the figure can only sink into melancholy.

Lit.: *Van Regteren Altena 1983,
vol. 2, p. 85 (no. 520), ill. 260.*
TK

CAT. NO. 2.38

JOACHIM ANTHONISZ. WTEWAEL (1566–1638)

The Golden Age
PEN AND BLACK AND BROWN INK
AND GREY WASH
9 × 11¾ IN.
INV. NO. C 1977—82

Provenance: *Acquired in 1723
from the Leipzig book dealer
Moritz G. Weidemann.*

In his *Metamorphoses* (1.113), Ovid describes the Golden Age as a "lawless" state. In it, the peoples of the earth would live without fear or sorrow, "in soft and quiet peace." Wtewael was working in Utrecht as a history painter. In this drawing he renders his vision of paradise. The same composition forms the basis for a small painting today in the Metropolitan Museum, New York. Presumably, it served as the model. Carel van Mander translated Ovid's *Metamorphoses* into Netherlandish in 1604, and this edition provided inspiration for many artists. Equally important was van Mander's interpretation of ancient myths. The Golden Age symbolized peaceful political circumstances under the auspices of a wise and fair ruler. Seen before the background of the protracted military conflicts of the Seven Northern Provinces of the Netherlands with the Spanish occupational forces, the contemporary viewer was offered an idyllic counter image to the reality which surrounded him.

Lit.: *Lowenthal 1997.*

TK

CAT. NO. 2.39

JAN MULLER (1571–1628)

Mars and Venus Surprised by Jupiter
PEN AND BLACK AND BROWN INK
AND BROWN WASH, HEIGHTENED
WITH WHITE
10⅞ × 8⅛ IN.
INV. NO. C 888

Provenance: *Former Royal
Collection, acquired before 1756.*

In his *Metamorphoses* (4.171–189), Ovid relates how Jupiter is the first

among the gods to discover that Venus, wife of Vulcan, had committed adultery with Mars. The ancient source focuses on the revenge of Vulcan who attempts to capture the surprised lovers with a net while the entire assembly of gods watches, falling over backwards with laughter. The Dresden drawing shows Jupiter alone intruding into the idyllic love scene. Muller has captured the outline of the overly long body with just a few energetic lines. The overall painterly impression of the composition results from the washes and the white heightening surrounding the radiance which emanates from Jupiter and accentuates the nude bodies. The draftsman and engraver Muller belonged to the small circle of the so-called "Haarlem Mannerists" who—thanks to their exagger-

ated figure proportions and their preference for erotic themes—were instrumental in influencing art around the year 1600.

Lit.: *Reznicek 1980, p. 130 (no. 7), fig. 2.*

TK

Cat. no. 2.40

JACOB ADRIAENSZ. MATHAM (*1571–1631*)

Unequal Lovers
Pen and brown ink and light brown wash
$7^{7}/_{8} \times 6^{1}/_{8}$ in.
Inv. no. C 1962 – 107

Provenance: *Former Royal Collection, acquired before 1756.*

While Matham attained great fame as an engraver, only a small number of his drawings are known. The theme of the "Unequal Lovers" is no less erotically charged than Muller's "Mars and Venus Surprised by Jupiter" (cat. no. 2.39). However, Matham does not allude to classical mythology. Instead he discloses the carnal lust of a lascivious elderly man impor-

tunately approaching a young girl. Her glance appears to be directed towards the jester behind her. The objects in the jester's hands characterize the unequal couple: the man's lasciviousness, symbolized by the phallus attached to the fool's staff, corresponds to the owl, a sign of blindness. Matham was in Italy between 1593 and 1597. A copy of a detail after Michelangelo's famous Moses sculpture on the verso of the sheet testifies to his investigations into the art of the Renaissance.

Lit.: *Exh.-cat. Dresden 1997a, pp. 106f. (no. 44).*

TK

PETER PAUL RUBENS
(*1577–1640*)

Study of a Female Nude
BRUSH AND BROWN INK OVER
BLACK CHALK, HEIGHTENED
WITH WHITE
9³/₄ × 5³/₈ IN.
INV. NO. C 964

Provenance: *Acquired in 1723
from the Leipzig book dealer
Moritz G. Weidemann.*

Before embarking on his career as court painter in Antwerp, Rubens spent a relatively long time in Italy. Renaissance works were as much artistic prototypes as they were objects of study. Apart from drawing copies after paintings by Leonardo, Raphael, or Titian, Rubens also reworked drawings by colleagues. There is a controversy among scholars regarding this study. On the one hand, it has been suggested that it is a drawing by Rubens's hand copying an unidentified model. On the other hand, it is assumed that Rubens may have reworked the drawing of another Italian artist (circle of Fra Bartolommeo). The suggestion is, further, that the subtle qualities of the surface and the contour lines were reworked. Also, the cloth for the garment was enhanced through light and by stressing the three-dimensional qualities of the drapery folds. Often, the Italian studies served Rubens as patterns for his huge history paintings.

Lit.: *Exh.-cat. Dresden 1997a,
pp. 150f. (no. 67).*

TK

CAT. NOS. 2.42A AND 2.42B

HERCULES SEGERS
(1598/90–1633)

**River Valley with
a Waterfall**

ETCHING, PRINTED IN BLACK ON
WHITE PAPER, LATER BROADLY
OVERPAINTED WITH DARK BLUE
WATERCOLOR
$6^{1}/8 \times 7^{5}/8$ IN.
INV. NO. A 49372

**River Valley with
a Waterfall**

ETCHING, PRINTED IN BROWN
ON WHITE PAPER
$6^{1}/4 \times 7^{5}/8$ IN.
INV. NO. A 49373

Provenance: *Both Former
Royal Collection; Jacob Hou-
braken, Amsterdam; acquired
between 1753 and 1756.*

The graphic work of
Segers belongs to the
aesthetic and techni-
cal peculiarities of 17th century
Netherlandish art. Only 183
prints from a total of 54 etched
copperplates with their unique
themes are known today, but
no drawings. As evidenced by
these two sheets, he either
printed the same motif on a
variety of colored paper or he
used diverse tones of color
while printing identical motifs.
Occasionally, Segers used
canvas for printing his proofs,
thereby rendering every sheet
a unique impression. But
Segers's etching technique,

too, was revolutionary. His
wide valley landscapes—influenced by Pieter Bruegel are
not defined by virtue of individual lines or crosshatchings.
Rather, they are layers of
etched color values which are
reduced to an overal tonality of
ocher or dark blue, lending the
landscapes their fantastic, sur-
real character. Humans only
play minor roles in Segers's
chapped mountainscapes.

Lit.: *Haverkamp-Begemann
1973, p. 78 (no. 22^{II}f, 22^{IV}l).*
TK

CAT. NO. 2.43

REMBRANDT VAN RIJN
(1606–1669)

Cottage

EARLY 1640S
PEN AND BROWN INK
$7^{1}/4 \times 12^{7}/8$ IN.
INV. NO. C 1332

Provenance: *Acquired
before 1764; Collection Gottfried
Wagner, Leipzig, 1728.*

Rembrandt was a great
admirer of Segers's
painted and etched
landscapes, and owned eight
paintings by the artist. Yet
the contrast between Segers's
worldscapes and Rembrandt's
drawings of polderscapes could
not be greater. With a few

rapidly carried out strokes of
his plume pen Rembrandt
records the cottage, which is
surrounded by trees, the
wooden fence, and the haystack
to the left. In a second step—
presumably in his studio—he
accentuated the foreground
with a broader reed pen. As a
result, the cottage is moved to
the middle ground. The signature in the upper left is not
authentic: it is a transcription
of an autograph from the verso.
The collector's mark in the
upper right refers to the provenance from the collection of
Nicolaes Flinck, son of the
famous Rembrandt disciple
Govaert Flinck.

Lit.: *Benesch 1954–57, vol. IV,
p. 212 (no. 801).*
TK

On the Role of Sculpture for the Saxon Prince Electors

Moritz Woelk

Today, the Sculpture Collection (*Skulpturensammlung*) can only reflect certain facets of the Saxon prince electors' and Polish kings' collecting activities regarding sculpture. They not only assembled works of art for the *Kunstkammer* and the specialty collections emerging from it, but they also collected in order to furnish their residences and commissioned sculptures for churches, castles, parks, and public monuments. This must be taken into account in order to grasp the significant role of sculpture in the transformation of Dresden into a representative residential city in the 16ᵗʰ century.

Italian sculpture and domestic sculpture influenced by Italian models play an important role in the period of Augustus the Strong and Augustus III. By this preference they followed a tradition of their predecessors. Works made in Italy and under Italian influence are among the highlights of the Dresden collection. They include bronzes by such masters as Filarete, Francesco di Giorgio Martini, Giambologna, and Adriaen de Vries. Among the Italianate works originating in Saxony, mention must be made of the House of Wettin's funerary chapel in Freiberg Cathedral.

In 1547 Duke Moritz (ruled 1541–53) gained the title of Saxon prince elector for the Albertinian branch of the House of Wettin. Moritz and his successors were Lutherans. Much later, Augustus the Strong converted to Catholicism in order to enable him to become king of Poland. While Moritz took up residence in Dresden, the Albertinian's funerary chapel was at St. Mary's Cathedral in his birthplace, Freiberg in the Erzgebirge.

Originally, a monumental, three-story-high tomb memorial, adorned by many allegorical statues, was erected for Moritz. Based on designs by the Italian artists Benedetto and Gabriele Thola, it was constructed by the Antwerp sculptor Antonius van Zerroen. It is crowned by a kneeling figure of the prince elector in eternal adoration in front of a crucifix. Starting in 1585, Prince Electors Augustus (ruled 1553–86) and Christian I (ruled 1586–91) transformed the church choir into a funerary chapel for the Wettins. They commissioned the Italian architect Giovanni Maria Nosseni and the sculptor Carlo di Cesare, whom Giambologna had recommended from Florence. Bronze figures of the prince electors and their wives were placed in wall niches and take up the theme of eternal adoration. It can be argued that the accord of sculpture and architecture in this chapel is the greatest late Renaissance achievement in Saxony.

During the reign of Augustus the Strong, 1694–1733, sculpture in Dresden blossomed in a way that overshadowed what had gone on before. While many visitors today find it easier to relate to paintings, it is fair to say that Augustus had a particular preference for three-dimensional objects. Apart from the bronze and stone sculptures he acquired, this is also reflected in the interaction between sculptural inventions and other media. In this context, porcelain is as related to sculpture as are the numerous ephemeral decorations for various festivities and the art of medal engraving. The Court Sculptor Balthasar Permoser, trained in Italy and hired by Augustus for Dresden in 1689, along with the architect Matthäus Daniel Pöppelmann, was responsible for the mutual inspiration of architecture and sculpture in the *Zwinger*. Permoser and Johann Melchior Dinglinger created a masterly synthesis of sculpture and the art of the goldsmith.

In his oeuvre Permoser combined stimuli derived from antiquity and Roman Baroque sculpture, especially the work of Gianlorenzo Bernini, with Floren-

1 Funerary chapel for the Wettins, Freiberg Cathedral, bronze of Prince Elector Christian I by C. de Cesare

tine experiences from his work in Giovanni Battista Foggini's studio. A plethora of sculptures in Dresden contain allegorical references to Augustus the Strong. They include such works as the Hercules figures in the Large Garden (*Großer Garten*), the "Hercules Saxonicus," expressly created for the *Zwinger*, as well as "Apollo and Minerva." One of Permoser's most striking qualities was his ability to disregard iconographic traditions and replace them with expressions of individuality, especially when dealing with the interpretation of classical themes in sculpture. He must also be singled out for his virtuoso handling of diverse materials ranging from ivory to colored marble. He knew—like no other—how to maximize the expressive potentials of his materials, optimizing their visual character.

At the beginning of Augustus the Strong's remarkable Sculpture Collection stood the gathering of the fabulous antiquities. He purchased various French bronzes based on ancient prototypes as early as 1699 and 1715 in Paris. Starting in 1717, he acquired approximately fifty antique sculptures from the Prussian King Frederick William I, among them certain works from the former Collection Bellori including such

exquisite Roman works as the portrait of Antoninus Pius. The most important acquisition was the Roman collection of antiques from Count Agostino Chigi and Cardinal Alessandro Albani in 1728, which comprised some 200 sculptures. Together with the precious objects from the Green Vault and the Porcelain Collection, the invaluable collection of antiquities was another element in the adequate representation of a ruler who had recently gained enormous prestige: By attaining the title of king of Poland, Augustus had risen significantly within the rank of European rulers. Thus, the impressive art inventories served loftier purposes than the idle study of ancient art and art appreciation alone. The representative role attributed by Augustus to the antiques is also reflected in Raymond Leplat's luxurious tome of copperplate engravings commissioned by Augustus and published in 1733. Apart from antiquities including sculptures, vases, bronzes, and terracottas, the two volumes also contained illustrations of the king's possessions of "modern" sculpture.

In the beginning, Augustus had planned an independent museum of antiquities—it remained unbuilt—as an extension of the *Zwinger* buildings. Therefore, the antiquities received their initial museum exhibition in Dresden's first Baroque palace, the Palace in the Large Garden, where they were surrounded by a multitude of Baroque sculptures. Prince Elector Johann Georg III, at the time still electoral prince, had begun construction of the Large Garden to

2 View of today's Hall of Antiquities in the Albertinum

the southeast of the city walls in 1676. In the center of the park stands a little palace, intended for festivities, constructed by the architect Johann Georg Starcke between 1678 and 1689. Decorated on the outside with sculptures adorning wall niches and tympana, four cross-shaped avenues originate from the building. The areas immediately surrounding the palace were created according to plans by Johann Friedrich Karcher; the features included pavilions, fountains, and obelisks that helped accentuate the different parterres and vistas of the layout.

3   Large Garden, palace and statue "Time Abducts Beauty" by P. Balestra

etween the years 1709 and 1722 Augustus the Strong ordered the garden's preliminary completion. Thanks to the creation of a large pond and four bosks it was reminiscent of Louis XIV's summer residence, Marly le Roi. All the pieces of ancient sculpture, erected in the palace in 1729, had been restored and completed by Baroque sculptors. These additions, later removed by 19th-century archaeologists, are preserved as independent works of art. Together with a total of circa 160 pieces of Baroque sculpture exhibited in the Large Garden, the antiques with Baroque additions—along with the creation of the *Zwinger*—were major components in the transformation of Dresden into a metropolis for Baroque art. Unfortunately, the majority of Baroque sculpture was destroyed by Prussian soldiers in 1760; therefore, today's visitor can only imagine the quantity of sculpture once exhibited in the Large Garden.

A further commission of Augustus's entailed the creation of the sculptural embellishments in the Japanese Palace (*Japanisches Palais*) in chinoiserie style under Johann Christian Kirchner and Johann Matthäus Oberschall, starting in 1730. One of Augustus's final projects was the preparation of the erection of his equestrian statue, the famous "Golden Rider," by Jean Josephe Vinache. Not completed until 1736, the sculptor had based his work on models supplied by various court artists, among them Paul Heermann.

The most significant sculpture commission during the reign of Augustus III (ruled 1733–63)—whose major focus was to further develop the Picture Gallery—was the Italian sculptor Lorenzo Mattielli's decoration for the Court Church (*Hofkirche*), begun by architect Gaetano Chiaveri in 1739. Augustus III further enlarged his father's famous Collection of Antiquities (*Antikensammlung*) by purchasing the famous statues of the "Herculanean Women" in 1736. Johann Joachim Winckelmann, founder of modern archaeology, wrote his *Gedanken über die Nachahmung der griechischen Werke in der Malerei und Bildhauerkunst* (Thoughts on Imitating Greek Works of Art in Painting and Sculpture) in Dresden in 1755. The interest in archaeology increasingly shaped the role of the Collection of Antiquities within Dresden as well as the establishment of its own Art Academy in 1764. As part of the continuing enthusiasm vis-à-vis ancient art the originals were supplemented by 833 plaster casts originating from the collection of the painter Anton Raphael Mengs in 1783. This group was soon exhibited in a museum context in immediate proximity to the Picture Gallery. From then on, the Collection of Antiquities became a favorite attraction among travelers. With their travel reports, people like Johann Wolfgang von Goethe helped to establish Dresden's reputation as a city of the arts. In the discriminating eyes of the others, Dresden's greatest quality was its art treasures.

Selected bibliography: Asche 1978.—Knoll et al. 1993.—Der Große Garten 2001.—Watanabe–O'Kelly 2002.

concentrated on the face and his vigorous gaze. Over his cuirass the king wears a coat and the Polish Order of the White Eagle, the star of which—affixed to the garment—bears the motto "PRO FIDE REGE ET LEGE" (for faith, king, law). Initially, Heermann worked as a sculptor on allegorical figures for Troja Castle in Prague. Beginning in 1705, he is documented in Dresden. As one of Permoser's colleagues, he was also involved in fabricating the sculptures for the *Zwinger* and produced additional works including the model for the golden equestrian statue of Augustus the Strong.

Lit.: *Seelig 1977, pp. 67ff.— Exh.-cat. Dresden 2001b, p. 78 (cat. no. 12) .—Exh.-cat. London 2002, p. 53 (cat. no. 12).*

MW

Cat. no. 3.2

FRANÇOIS COUDRAY
(1678–1727)

Electoral Prince Frederick Augustus of Saxony (1696–1763)

1715
Marble
H. with base 33¹/₄ in.,
W. 20¹/₈ in., D. 11³/₄ in.
Inv. no. H4 2/7

Provenance: *Brought from Paris by Raymond Leplat in 1716; first mentioned in the Sculpture Inventory 1726.*

Cat. no. 3.1

PAUL HEERMANN
(1673–1732)

Prince Elector Frederick Augustus I of Saxony, as Augustus II King of Poland, Called "The Strong"

1718 or earlier
Marble
H. with pedestal 36¹/₄ in.,
W. 26¹/₈ in., D. 10⁵/₈ in.
Signed under the right arm:
PHeermann. Sc.
Inv. no. H4 2/6

Provenance: *Purchased from the estate of Count Heinrich von Brühl in 1763.*

The gorgeous bust with its voluptuous air is a depiction of Augustus the Strong as an energetic and sensuous ruler. The striking anatomical shapes of his face are emphasized, and the volume of his face underscores his powerful readiness for action thanks to the dynamic turn of the pose. All attention is thus

The prince elector's portrait was most certainly modeled during his Grand Tour visit to Paris in 1714. One year later Coudray submitted this marble bust when he applied for the position of Dresden court sculptor. The portrait shows the 19-year-old prince elector with youthful and smooth yet reso-

nant facial features. He wears a conventional cuirass and an allonge wig, parted in the middle, whose voluminous curls reach way beyond the left shoulder, almost to the bust's lower edge. In its posture and its expression, this likeness of the prince elector corresponds to the one painted by Hyacinthe Rigaud (Paris 1714) that belongs to Dresden's Old Masters Picture Gallery. The choice of a remarkably narrow bust, as well as the slightly draped cloak in which the piece terminates stress the volume of Frederick Augustus's head. These stylistic choices reveal the influence of Antoine Coyzevox, in whose workshop Coudray worked in 1697.

Lit.: *Souchal 1977, p. 126 (no. 3).—Exh.-cat. Essen 1986, p. 55 (no. 9).—Exh.-cat. Dresden 2001b, p. 76 (cat. no. 11).*

AN

CAT. NO. 3.3

JEAN LOUIS LEMOYNE *(1665–1755)* attributed

Raymond Baron Leplat
CA. 1714
MARBLE, TWO PIECES
H. 29 IN., W. 28³/₈ IN.,
D. 11³/₄ IN.
INV. NO. ZV 3222

Provenance: *Purchased from the Monastery St. Marienstern in 1932, where the bust was kept in the cemetery chapel, mounted on Leplat's epitaph.*

Starting in 1697, Leplat (1664–1742) worked for Augustus the Strong as interior designer, art agent, and general director of the museums. A skilled negotiator, numerous important and extensive acquisitions are owed to him, including the significant expansion of the antiquity and bronze collection. In 1714 Leplat accompanied the prince elector on his Grand Tour. Based on its style, it may be assumed that this portrait was made by Lemoyne in Paris. Leplat is portrayed in a simple coat; a cloak is draped over his right shoulder and protrudes visibly below the section of his left arm. His head is proudly lifted slightly upward, and his gaze is directed into the far distance. It is surprising that the bust was created in two parts: the sculptor used a piece of marble of insufficient size and hence was forced to add the head as a second piece.

This solution illuminates Leplat's relatively inferior social rank since it would have been inconceivable to portray a member of the high aristocracy in a sculpture assembled from two pieces of marble. It is also unusual that the entire marble surface has not been polished to perfection; as a result the powerfully modeled facial features appear rather softer than they really are.

Lit.: *Exh.-cat. Dresden 1992, pp. 54f. (cat. no. 39).—Heckmann 1996, pp. 128–132.—Exh.-cat. St. Marienstern 1998, p. 299 (cat. no. 4.62).*

AN

FRANCESCO DI
GIORGIO MARTINI
(1439–1501/02) attributed

Hercules(?)

Ca. 1495
Bronze
H. without pedestal
44¼ in., W. 25⅜ in.,
D. 12¾ in.
Inv. no. H² 21/78

Provenance: *Purchased from
the estate of Count Heinrich von
Brühl in 1763.*

To date, there is no
undisputed inter-
pretation of this sculp-
ture: apart from Hercules,
Aesclepius, Neptune, and Lao-
coön have been suggested. The
concentrated facial expression
and the strained body illustrate
the fight between man and
beast, likely identifying the figure as Hercules. Although the
image is definitely not a literal
rendering of any deed of Hercules—this neither depicts
his strangling of the serpent
sent by Hera when he was
still a child nor his fight, as an
adult, with the multiheaded
Hydra—it is most likely intended as Hercules, the virtu-
ous hero. The attribution to di
Giorgio Martini, who also
worked as painter and architect, is based on the stylistic
proximity of the Dresden
bronze to candlestick angels he
executed for the high altar of
Siena Cathedral.

Lit.: *Toledano 1987, p. 150
(cat. no. 64).—Exh.-cat. Berlin
1995, pp. 157f. (cat. no. 13),
159 (fig.).—Exh.-cat. Berlin
2002b, fig. 7.*

AN

CAT. NO. 3.5

ANTOINE COYZEVOX
(1640–1720)

Madame de la Ravois

1704
MARBLE
H. WITH BASE 27 IN.,
W. 11⅝ IN., D. 11¾ IN.
INV. NO. ZV 3627

Provenance: *Former Royal
Collection; presumably purchased
by Raymond Leplat in Paris;
first mentioned in the Sculpture
Inventory 1726.*

Coyzevox—"sculpteur
du roi" since 1666
and director of the
Académie Royale since 1702—
is considered one of the most
important portrait sculptors
under the French king
Louis XIV. This is convincingly demonstrated in this
exquisite portrait of a lady
about whom we know only her
name. The coiffure design of
the otherwise austere bust is
derived from ancient depic-

tions of Venus or Diana.
The reduction of the bust to
the half-oval neckline—facilitating the omittance of offi-
cious robes—may be called
Coyzevox's invention. As a
consequence, all attention is
drawn to the head, to the eyes'
expression of alertness, and the
sharply observant gaze. The
only decorative accessory apart
from a slowly dissolving braid
is a relief on the front of the
profiled base showing an Amor
figure in quiet relaxation. Calm
ease emanates from this portrait, surrounding it like an
aura.

Lit.: *Müller 1927.—Souchal
1977, p. 212 (no. 84).—
Exh.-cat. Dresden 2001b, p. 72
(cat. no. 9).*

AN

CAT. NO. 3.6

ANTONIO CORRADINI
(1688–1752)

Bust of a Vestal

1724
MARBLE
H. 30½ IN., W. 26 IN.,
D. 10⅞ IN.
INV. NO. 1765, BL. 201,
NO. 229/38 B

Provenance: *Purchased
from Venice by Raymond Leplat
in 1724; first mentioned in
the Sculpture Inventory 1765.*

Corradini was among the
most popular and most
productive Venetian
sculptors of the 18th century.
Between 1719 and 1723 his
deliveries to Dresden included
nine groups and statues as
well as three decorative vases.
Among them was also a statue
of the vestal Tuccia (now lost).
As early as 1717 Corradini had
repeatedly turned his attention
to the veiled female whom he
varied in age from youthful

adolescent to mature, with the
Dresden Vestal belonging
to the latter type. The veil
symbolizes the virtues of
chastity and virginity to which
vestals—the servants of the
goddess Vesta—were bound.
The over life-size bust is dazzling because of the technical
bravura with which the marble
is treated, resulting in illusion-
ist effects. The artfully draped,
flowing veil covers the face,
although the contours of eyes,
nose, and mouth remain visible.

Lit.: *Lipsius 1798, p. 513.—
Riccoboni 1952, p. 161.—Cogo
1996, pp. 260f.*

AN

with Georg Treu's proposal dated May 1890 (after the Grotto Hall and the Custody at the Museum for Minerals had been dissolved).

Originally, this "Apollo" was part of an artfully arranged ensemble of water games in the *Zwinger*'s Grotto Hall (destroyed during the war in 1813) where it was exhibited together with "Minerva." One of the most engaging aspects of "Apollo" is his powerful, dynamic thrust forward, which has a formal parallel in Gianlorenzo Bernini's (1598–1680) famous "Apollo and Daphne" group (1622–25). All static notions are immediately replaced by a sense of pure movement and a floating weightlessness. As the god of law and peace, protector of the arts, and leader of the muses, Apollo rushes through the clouds restlessly and, in his capacity as god of light, banishes the darkness. In doing so he overcomes Hypnos, the god of sleep, who is depicted as a putto near his feet. "Apollo" bears the idealized facial features of Augustus the Strong and thus epitomizes the monarch, glorifying him as the keeper of law and peace and pointing out his function as protector of the arts. The extensive inscription refers to the sculptor's pride—he was already 64 years old when he made the piece—regarding the fact that he presumably chiseled the sculpture directly from the stone, without using a model (*ohne Muster*).

Lit.: *Asche 1966, p. 296 (cat. no. 58).—Asche 1978, pp. 87f., 170 (W. 73).—Exh.-cat. Dresden 2001a, p. 52 (cat. no. 13).*

AN

CAT. NO. 3.7

BALTHASAR PERMOSER
(1651–1732)

Crying Boy

CA. 1726
COLORED MARBLE
L. 26⁵/₈ IN., W. 14⁵/₈ IN.,
H. 9¹/₂ IN.
INV. NO. ZV 3955

Provenance: *Purchased from the Art Dealer's shop Patzig, Freital, in 1976.*

This impressive work elucidates once more Permoser's multifaceted artistic virtuosity (see cat. nos. 3.8 and 4.38). His exact observation of a child's physiognomy leads him to render an extreme posture: The unruly boy appears to have thrown himself on the floor, and is portrayed with his head thrown back, his mouth wide open, and his right hand covering the eyes. As he twists toward the right, the resulting curvature of his left side produces a flowing motion in his entire body. The use of dark marble adds to the expressive sense of drama. It is assumed that this work, together with a bust made of colored marble, entitled "Damnation" (1725, Museum der Bildenden Künste, Leipzig), was intended for a tomb or an epitaph that was never completed.

Lit.: *Exh.-cat. Dresden 1992, p. 51 (cat. no. 35), ill. p. 21.— Exh.-cat. Brühl 2000, pp. 76f. (cat. no. XVII.4).—Exh.-cat. Dresden 2001a, p. 26 (cat. no. 7).*
AN

CAT. NO. 3.8

BALTHASAR PERMOSER
(1651–1732)

Apollo

1715
THE ORIGINAL IS MADE OF
SAXON MARBLE
H. 85⁷/₈ IN.
SEMICIRCULAR INSCRIPTION ON
LOWER RIGHT IN PLINTH: FRI:
AUG: KÖNIG IN POH: UND
CHURF / IN SACHS: HAT AUS DEN
HIESIGEN LANDT MARMOR /
DIESE ERSTE FIGUR VERFERTIGEN
LASSEN DURCH /BALTASAR ·
PERMOSER ·VON / SALZPURG.
HATS GEMACHT OHNE / MVSTER.
IN SEINEN / 64. IGSTEN /
IAHR. 1715
INV. NO. ZV 1042

Provenance: *Transferred to the Sculpture Collection in accordance*

PAUL HEERMANN
(1673–1732)

Autumn
Winter

CA. 1720
MARBLE
AUTUMN: H. WITH BASE
28³/₄ IN., W. 20⁷/₈ IN.,
D. 11³/₈ IN.
WINTER: H. WITH BASE
29⁷/₈ IN., W. 20¹/₂ IN.,
D. 19⁵/₈ IN.
INV. NOS. 1765, BL. 203, NO.
W. 75 AND W. 76

Provenance: *Purchased from the estate of Count Heinrich von Brühl in 1763.*

Personifications of the seasons belong to the most popular allegories. Often interpreted as an expression of the transitory, appropriate deities derived from ancient mythology symbolized the individual seasons: Flora as the goddess of growth and fertility for spring; Ceres as goddess of agriculture for the summer; the god of wine, Bacchus, for autumn; and Vulcan as the god of fire for winter. Heermann's

seasons appear much more worldly, lacking any of the divine sublime that may be observed in Permoser's "Ceres" and "Vulcan" at the *Zwinger*'s Crown Gate. "Winter" appears as an elderly man. With his eyebrows drawn together and the pensive wrinkles over his nose, his introverted appearance is filled with seriousness and sorrow. "Autumn" is the exact opposite: A broad smile covers his face, laugh lines surround his eyes, and the particularly opulent wreath of vines and grapes underlines the generally gay, wine-filled atmos-

phere. Conceived as a pair, the two busts function as antidotes for two contrasting mental states of being.

Lit.: *Asche 1961, p. 134 (figs. 138 f.).—Exh.-cat. Stockholm 1979, p. 209 (nos. 615 f.)*
AN

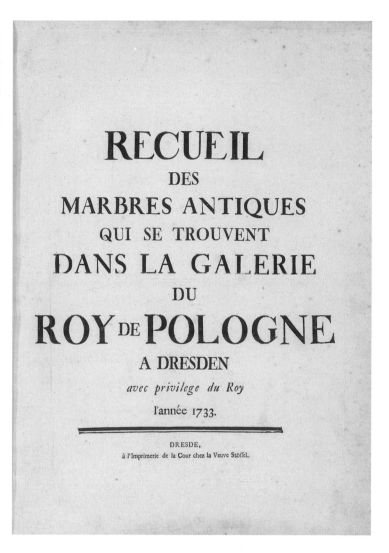

CAT. NO. 3.10

RAYMOND LEPLAT
(1664–1742)

Recueil des marbres antiques qui se trouvent dans la galerie du Roy de Pologne à Dresden [...]

DRESDEN, 1733
COPPERPLATE ENGRAVINGS
19⅝ × 15¾ IN. (WHEN CLOSED)

Provenance: *Former Royal Collection*

Augustus II commissioned this first comprehensive publication of the Dresden Collections. He planned this ornate compendium of engravings immediately following the acquisition of antique sculptures from the Roman collections Chigi and Albani, in 1728. With its 198 plates, it illustrates almost the entire inventory of antiquities kept in Dresden at the time. As a supplement, and with an extra title page, they are succeeded by 32 plates illustrating contemporary works of art. Baron Leplat was responsible for the execution of this work. He had negotiated the acquisition of the collections in Rome and had only recently been promoted to the post of director of all the Dresden collections. The engravings bear dates between the years 1729 and 1732. The draftspeople are documented thanks to their signatures. Of them, Anna Maria Werner, also creator of the title page, delivered by far the most designs. Among the eleven engravers the most frequently found signatures include Bernigeroth, Lindemann, Preisler, and Zucchi.

Lit.: *Heres 1983.*

KKn

group in Rome's Galleria Borghese, this Apollo is a new Baroque creation. An invoice for restoration work performed on ancient sculptures in the archives of the Chigi family in Ariccia identifies Buselli as restorer and sculptor of this group. After "Marsyas" had been recognized as a true antique statue of Pan, the group was separated sometime between 1839 and 1856. The archaeologist and Dresden museum director, Georg Treu, removed all remaining Baroque additions: part of the hair with the horn, the lower part of the beard, the right arm up to the shoulder, the lower part of the right leg, the left leg starting at midthigh, and the plinth's tree trunk. Thereby, a completely new sculpture was created: Pan's posture is reminiscent of a figure on the attack or standing in a bold contrapposto stance. The missing right arm was moved forward, while the left hand is kept resting on the back. It is assumed that the statue originally formed part of a group of Pan approaching Eros in a wrestling match, a scene known from Pompeiian painting. In 1995, the group's original configuration was recreated. This entailed bringing Apollo out of storage, fabricating a cast of the antique original, and reattaching all the Baroque additions.

Lit.: *Leplat 1733, plate 65.— Hase 1826, p. 42 (no. 159).— Montagu 1989, p. 163.—Exh.- cat. Munich 1995, pp. 152ff., cat. no. 6.*

KKɴ

CAT. NO. 3.11A AND 3.11B

ERCOLE BUSELLI
(1667 recorded)

Apollo and Marsyas
ROME, BEFORE 1667
MARBLE, GYPSUM
H. WITH PLINTH 53 IN.,
W. 44½ IN., D. 24⅜ IN.
INV. NO. HM 261

Pan
ROMAN COPY OF A
HELLENISTIC WORK
MARBLE
H. WITH BASE 36⅝ IN.,
W. 13⅜ IN., D. 17⅞ IN.
INV. NO. HM 261

Provenance: *Both purchased in 1728 from the Collection Chigi, Rome.*

As early as the 19th century, this group was recognized as a curious pastiche consisting of ancient and Baroque parts. The punishment of Marsyas by Apollo is depicted. Goat-footed "Marsyas," predominantly an ancient original, is tied to a tree trunk. Simulating Bernini's "Apollo and Daphne"

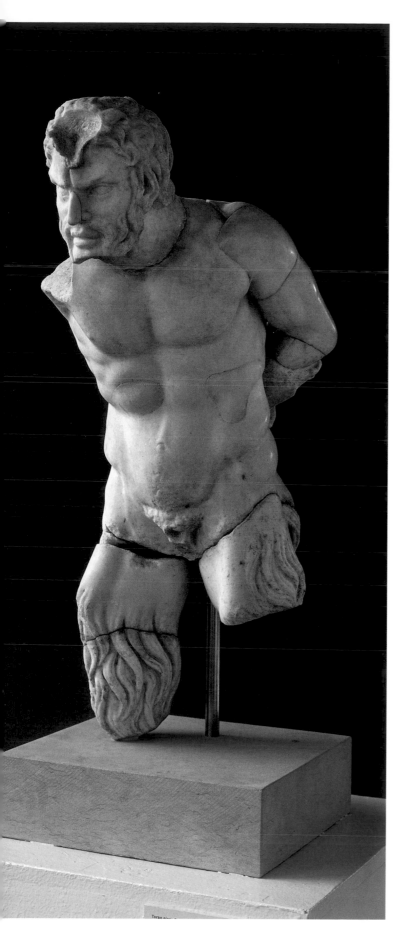

CAT. NO. 3.12

UNIDENTIFIED ROMAN ARTIST

Head of a Young Man

17ᵀᴴ TO EARLY 18ᵀᴴ CENTURY
MARBLE
H. WITH BASE 16⁷/₈ IN.,
W. 16¹/₄ IN., D. 8¹/₄ IN.
INV. NO. H⁴ 118/256

Provenance: *Purchased in 1728 from the Collection Chigi, Rome.*

This head belongs to the Baroque additions of a fragmentary antique sculpture preserved in the Sculpture Collection. Most of the antiquities which came to Dresden—first between 1723 and 1726 from the Berlin *Kunstkammer* and then in 1728 from the Roman collections Chigi and Albani—had been restored in Rome in the 17ᵗʰ and early 18ᵗʰ centuries. During the Renaissance and the Baroque, ancient sculptures were held in particularly high esteem by collectors and artists, although they preferred the pieces which surrounded them to be preserved fully intact. As a consequence, ancient fragments were frequently completed in contemporary style. It was not until 1893–98 that the then director of the Collection of Antiquities, Georg Treu, had the later additions removed and replaced either by removable gypsum additions or by casts of parts belonging to better preserved earlier examples.

Lit.: *Leplat 1733, plate 5.—Hettner 1881, p. 118 (no. 256).*
KKₙ

Cat. no. 3.13

UNIDENTIFIED
ROMAN ARTIST

Head of a Young Man
17ᵀᴴ TO EARLY 18ᵀᴴ CENTURY
MARBLE
H. WITH BASE 16³/4 IN.,
W. 9¹/2 IN., D. 8⁷/8 IN.
INV. NO. H4 53/2

Provenance: *Purchased in
1728 from the Collection Chigi,
Rome.*

This head, whose
long curls refer to
Apollo, was a Baroque
addition to the Sculpture Collection's ancient Apollo torso.
The artist who made the additions took as his point of departure the head of the "Apollo
Belvedere." This is testified to
by the head facing left, by the
way neck and shoulder are
composed, and by the fillet
over the forehead. The facial
relief, modeled sensitively and
dynamically, the materially
rendered, full hair, and the ten-
der air surrounding the face, all
point toward the identity of
the master as a distinguished
Italian Baroque sculptor.

Lit.: *Leplat 1733, plate 20.—
Hettner 1881, p. 53 (no. 2).*
                              KKN

Cat. no. 3.14

UNIDENTIFIED
ROMAN ARTIST

**Head of a Young Man
(Alexandro Magno)**
17ᵀᴴ TO EARLY 18ᵀᴴ CENTURY
MARBLE
H. WITH BASE 14³/8 IN.,
W. 9¹/4 IN., D. 8⁵/8 IN.
INV. NO. H4 118/254

Provenance: *Purchased in
1728 from the Collection Chigi,
Rome.*

This head belongs to
the Baroque additions
for an antique torso
in the Sculpture Collection.
Among the additions are the
head, the arms, the right leg,
and the left leg below the knee.
These elements turned the
nude youth into a statue of
Alexander the Great with his
capriciously elevated head resting on a lance. The additions
were removed in 1891. What
was gained, as a consequence,
is the torso of a winner statue
of the Westmacott type, a work
from the circle of Polyclitus.

Lit.: *Leplat 1733, plate 47.—
Hettner 1881, p. 118 (no. 254).*
                              KKN

Satyr Pouring a Libation
ROMAN COPY (PRESUMABLY
AFTER A WORK BY PRAXITELES),
CA. 370 BC
MARBLE
H. WITH PLINTH 63 IN.,
W. 20½ IN., D. 15¾ IN.
INV. NO. HM 102

Provenance: *Purchased in
1728 from the Collection Chigi,
Rome.*

The laurel wreath and the pointed ears identify this figure as a satyr. Working for Dionysus, he is on the verge of pouring wine into a bowl. A jug, not preserved but originally lifted over the head, can only be imagined by today's viewer. Satyrs belong to the wild, untamed entourage of Dionysus. The Dresden satyr appears rather civil and more reminiscent of classical winner statues created by artists such as Polyclitus. The smooth body with its gently twisted hips and the composition are typical features of the style dominant during the early 4th century BC. In addition, the soft shapes homogeneously lead into one another and underline the youth's attractiveness as well as his long and mannered gestures which have led scholars to suggest a particular closeness to works of Praxiteles.

Lit.: *Herrmann 1925, p. 32
(no. 102).—Exh.-cat. Rome
2000, vol. II, p. 452
(cat. no. 9).—Exh.-cat. Berlin
2002b, ill. 8.*

KKN

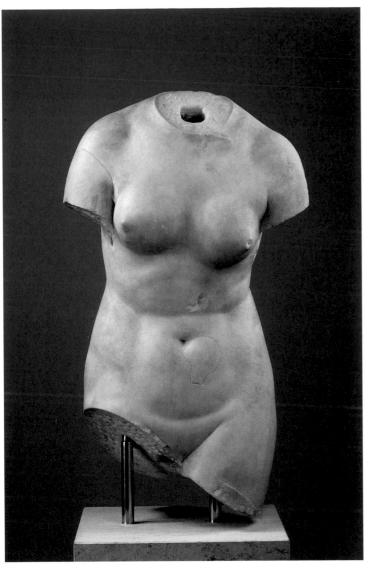

Cat. no. 3.16

Torso of a Statue of Aphrodite of the Capitoline Aphrodite Type

Roman copy after a Hellenistic work of the 2ND century BC
Marble
H. with base 38³/₈ in.,
W. 17⁷/₈ in., D. 13³/₈ in.
Inv. no. Hm 240

Provenance: *Presumably purchased in Rome in the late 18th century.*

This statue goes back to Praxiteles's "Cnidian Aphrodite," one of the most famous and most highly praised works in antiquity preserved in countless copies. There are two particularly well-known types of imitation: the Capitoline and the Medici Aphrodite. The Dresden torso,

with exquisite plasticity and sensitively sculpted surfaces shows the goddess in slightly tilted posture. Owing to a natural shyness she initially attempted to hide her nudity with a modest gesture, but she now displays the charm of her fully developed body in a naturalistic manner. Originally, her legs were covered by a garment of which only remnants can now be seen along the thighs.

Lit.: *Herrmann 1925, p. 63 (no. 240).—Exh.-cat. Dresden 2000c, p. 19 (cat. no. 12).*

KKn

Cat. no. 3.17

Eros and Psyche

Roman copy after a late-Hellenistic work of the 2ND to 1ST century BC, mid-3RD century AD
Marble
H. 28 in., W. 10 in.,
D. 11¹/₄ in.
Inv. no. Hm 211

Provenance: *Purchased in 1728 from the Collection Chigi, Rome.*

Eros was in love with Psyche whose beauty equaled that of Aphrodite. In order to spare her the jealousy of his mother Aphrodite, Eros ask Zephyrus, the west wind, to take her to his realm. There, Psyche surprised Eros who appeared in front of her in the darkness of the night—this was against the orders—whereupon he was

forced to abandon her. Only after plenty of detours and successfully mastered adventures did Zeus bring the two together again. This is how the writer Apuleius (born ca. 125 AD) relates the story in his tale *Amor and Psyche*. The Dresden couple belongs to the Capitoline type, named after the group kept in the Capitoline Museum in Rome. Many of the replicas go back to this group which appears to most closely resemble the late-Hellenistic original. The motif of the youthful couple is typical of a tendency within Hellenistic art which is sometimes referred to as "ancient Rococo" because of its preference for sweet and playful subjects.

Lit.: *Leplat 1733, plate 3.— Herrmann 1925, p. 58 (no. 211).—Aspris 1996, p. 13 (no. A13).*

KKn

Portrait of Emperor Septimius Severus (ruled 193–211 AD)

Roman, ca. 210 AD
Marble
H. 15³/4 in.
Inv.-no. Hm 393

Provenance: *Purchased between 1723 and 1726 from the Berlin Kunstkammer.*

This slightly over life-size head of the idealized and youthful emperor was originally part of a bust. The adopted son of Marcus Aurelius had himself portrayed in the tradition of the so-called emperor-philosopher portrait of which the hair, the beard treatment, and the slightly upward gaze into the distance are typical features.

Lit.: *Beger 1701, p. 343.—Leplat 1733, plate 157,4.—Herrmann 1925, p. 87 (no. 393).*

KKn

Portrait of Emperor Antoninus Pius (ruled 138–161 AD)

Roman, ca. 150 AD
Marble
H. with base 20¹/8 in.,
W. 10 in., D. 10⁵/8 in.
Inv. no. Hm 385

Provenance: *Purchased between 1723 and 1726 from the Berlin Kunstkammer; by 1698 Collection Bellori, Rome.*

Antoninus Pius was 52 years old when he succeeded Hadrian as Roman emperor. The portrait type inspired by this event takes his age into account. Typical features include the slightly limp and flabby cheeks, but also deep wrinkles originating from the nose and repeated as horizontal folds across the forehead. Heavy eyelids lend an air of fatigue to the face. The emperor was said to be pious, patient and temperate—character traits reflected in his serious and balanced expression. Heavily drilled, restless locks of hair frame the face. Presumably, this slightly over life-size head once belonged to a bust. Differences in the two halves of the face demonstrate that—like most portraits of this emperor—it originally faced slightly to the left. Considering the stylistic peculiarities, it can be dated to the middle of the emperor's reign.

Lit.: *Beger 1701, p. 344.—Leplat 1733, plate 158,4.—Wegner 1939, pp. 22, 127, 279.—Exh.-cat. Berlin 2002b, ill. 59.*

KKn

The Green Vault—
From National Vault
to Treasury Museum

Dirk Syndram

The name "Green Vault" (*Grünes Gewölbe*) was originally an architectural designation and did not refer to a treasury. During the course of its history, the Green Vault in the Dresden Residential Palace became synonymous with one of the most important European collections of precious objects from the Renaissance and the Baroque periods. Beginning in the late Renaissance, the enigmatic name referred to four galleries on the palace's ground floor and offered a convenient colloquial epithet. It stems from the green paint that was applied to architectural elements—such as capitals and bases—which supported the vault in this suite of rooms. The Saxon prince electors used this off-limits area of the palace as their national treasury.

The metamorphosis of the Green Vault from national vault to a publicly accessible treasury museum began in the summer of the year 1723. Prince Elector Augustus the Strong (*August der Starke*) was the true founder of the Green Vault as a public space. By 1723 he had already ruled the kingdom of Poland-Lithuania for a quarter of a century under the name Augustus II. It appears that the Green Vault is the oldest surviving museum in the modern sense of the word. During the first phase of its existence, in 1723–24, Augustus placed Matthäus Daniel Pöppelmann, superintendent of buildings, in charge of a new, festive interior decoration program. Experienced artists were consulted for the creation of the museum. Benjamin Thomae, Permoser's master student, was put in charge of the wooden sculpture. His assistants were Christian Kirchner and Johann Joachim Kaendler, who, after comple-

L. de Silvestre, "King August II of Poland", 1723, oil on canvas, 88 1/2 x 52 in., Old Masters Picture Gallery, detail

1   Copy after Count P. Rotari, "King Augustus III", ca. 1756, oil on canvas, 41 3/4 x 33 7/8 in., Old Masters Picture Gallery

tion of the Green Vault, emerged as the master of models for the Meissen Porcelain Manufactory. In Meissen he became the founder of European sculptural porcelain production. The suite of rooms obtained its Baroque coloration from the court artists Martin Schnell and Christian Reinow.

Green vanished behind newly carved consoles, colorfully varnished wall panels, and delicate mirrors. The space was transformed into a late-Baroque suite of galleries. However, the name "Green Vault" remained, and was now applied to the treasury museum and its collection. The little Tower Room (*Turmzimmer*) of

The Saxon court's infatuation with French fashion began shortly after 1670. Even as youngsters, Augustus the Strong and his older brother, Johann Georg (IV), were given representative diamond ornaments and jewels by their grandfather, the then reigning prince elector. In 1677, when Frederick Augustus was only seven years old, his Christmas gifts included six dozen golden buttons, each of which was embellished with a diamond. The next year, his brother and future prince elector received a pair of golden shirt buttons and the breast pin for a hunting suit which was adorned with a crown of diamonds. For his name day in 1679 he received diamond-studded shoe buckles.

Johann Georg (IV) preceded Augustus the Strong as prince elector for a little under four years, and was the first of the Saxon prince electors to begin acquiring large diamonds during their reign. Augustus continued such acquisitions. Upon visiting Versailles as a young man, he had encountered Louis XIV in his gala robes. Augustus was strongly impressed by this magnificent depiction of royal majesty and absolute monarchy. In contrast to the French model, his interest was not limited to diamonds alone. The Saxon-Polish ruler transferred his preference for colored precious stones to his jewels and ornaments.

The garnitures took their names from the predominant precious stones or the characteristic materials that were mounted in gold and silver. Additionally, all parts of these ensembles were decorated with diamonds in various different cuts. Of the nine garnitures mentioned in the 1719 inventory, seven have survived, albeit in heavily altered states. The most precious ensembles by far were the rose and brilliant cut diamond garnitures. Further groups included the agate, carnelian, emerald, ruby, and sapphire garnitures. After 1719 Augustus the Strong had a tortoise shell garniture made. His son, Augustus III, completed the unfinished topaz garniture. He also donated the official jewel ensemble of brilliant cut diamonds worn by his spouse to the national treasure. One ought to note that the wives of Saxon rulers customarily owned extensive jewel collections which were considered their personal belongings and therefore not part of the Green Vault.

The process of making a jewel garniture was intimately tied to the fortune of the princely collector. Among the difficulties was not only the acquisition of necessary funds, but also the need to find ways to purchase the desired stones via jewelers in Amsterdam, London, or Hamburg, or through court agents. Most of the material came to Europe either from Asia or from South America, where the mining methods were comparatively primitive. Therefore, the European markets only rarely had exceptionally large, pure, or pristine stones in stock. Their scarcity elevated their value considerably. Finally, adequate jewelers were needed in order to create mounts that were both fashionable and singular and would elevate the jewels to a unique level. Luckily, Augustus the Strong had access to the most outstanding jewelers of his time: both Johann Melchior Dinglinger and Heinrich Köhler worked for him.

Jewel garnitures had a specifically political relevance. During late-Baroque times, the rank of a ruler within the hierarchy of European power was also measured by virtue of the quality and quantity of his stately robes. In accordance with compulsory class distinctions prevalent in absolutist monarchies, the ruler was obliged to appear in public in appropriate outfits, i. e. diamond-studded clothes. This was how he manifested his authority and his affluence. Seen in the shifting reflections of candle-light, he who wore a jeweled garniture with gleaming diamond ornamentation was perceived as nearly supernatural. Augustus the Strong utilized this type of political ornament in order to manifest his own visions of royal majesty. The national treasure which was composed of precious stones satisfied his desire to represent his power. In addition, the stones were a strategic financial reserve which could be mortgaged in times of need.

All sizable European courts imitated the French fashion for jewels. However, nearly all of the jewel collections have vanished, falling victim to wars, money shortages, or changing tastes. Only a few remnants of historic collections of this type remain. One of them is in Portugal, where the king was able to exploit his own diamond mines after 1720 when Brazil was incorporated into the empire. The Green Vault is the only place where a coherent and historic collection of jewels has survived to this day. During the course of the 18th and 19th centuries, the jewels were repeatedly mortgaged but ultimately they were always repurchased. There were also phases of drastic modernization leading to significant alterations, although this was mostly restricted to the diamond garnitures. Since the early 19th century the jewels have remained unchanged under state ownership. This is how they have come down to us to this day as a particularly valuable part of our cultural heritage.

Circle of FRANÇOIS
GIRARDON *(1628–1715)*

Equestrian Statue of Augustus the Strong

PARIS, BEFORE 1715
BRONZE, WOODEN BASE WITH
MIRROR GLASS, PLINTH: MARBLE
WITH TWO GILT BRONZE
SHIELDS WITH COLOR ENAMELED
COATS OF ARMS OF POLAND-
LITHUANIA (IN THE HEART
SHIELD: THE COAT OF ARMS OF
THE ELECTORATE SAXONY),
CARTOUCHES ON THE CORNERS
(BEARDED MASKS) GILT BRONZE
H. 41³/8 IN. (STATUETTE),
102³/8 IN. (WITH BASE)
INV. NO. IX 67

Provenance: *First mentioned
in the inventory of the Bronze
Room in the Green Vault 1733.*

Augustus the Strong's
dealer, Baron Raymond
Leplat, commissioned
the prestigious equestrian
statue in Paris in 1715. The
bronze monument shows
Augustus on a striding horse.
The regent wears magnificent
clothes in the manner of
Roman emperors, and his head
is crowned by a laurel wreath.
The typical gesture of command in which the king has
lifted up his right hand confirms his position as military
commander and bringer of
peace. There were two bronze
plaques (now lost) placed along
the base. The reliefs paid
tribute to the king of Poland as
statesman and victorious
leader. On the one, Augustus
was shown greeting ambassa-
dors in Warsaw, while the
other one was dedicated to the
Battle of Kalisz. Both the original base and the respective

reliefs burned during the Dresden bombardments in 1945.
However, the royal rider, the
four figures of slaves, the two
coats of arms, and some of the
bronze embellishments from
the marble plinth's corners
remained unharmed. The
missing pedestal was reconstructed in 1986/87 in an
attempt to recreate its original
appearance. With regards
to the general type and also to
some details, the striking rendering of Augustus closely follows Girardon's 1699 life-size
rendition of King Louis XIV.

Lit.: *Sponsel/Haenel 1932,
p. 164 (with plate 62).—Syndram
1999, pp. 117f., 177.—Kappel
2003.*

JK

After ANTOINE
COYSEVOX *(1640–1720)*

Fame Astride Pegasus Mercury Astride Pegasus

ORIGINAL MARBLES 1701/02,
SMALL BRONZES BEFORE 1715
BRONZE
H. 24³/8 IN., 23⁷/8 IN.
INV. NO. IX 68, IX 86

Provenance: *First mentioned in
the Sculpture Inventory 1726.*

In 1715 Augustus the
Strong commissioned
Raymond Leplat to pur-
chase for him in Paris—among
other objects—two small
bronzes depicting Fame and
Mercury astride Pegasus.
Fame, goddess of glory, by
blowing into her trumpet, dis-
seminates the glory (of the
king) in the world. Mercury,

messenger of the gods, tames the rising horse of the muses. These bronze groups almost replicate two marble sculptures by Coysevox in the garden of the French Château of Marly, which were quite popular at the time. Our sculptures are not copies, though: in contrast to the marbles, the Herculean trophies at their feet are unassuming and simple. This is particularly interesting since in this very instance Coysevox's marbles allude to the source of Fame's and Mercury's glory. Allegorical depictions of the goddess of victory, Victoria, may be seen on the shields, as well as "Flanders offering France the royal crown." Thus, the trophies allude to Louis XIV's military successes, turning the marble groups into monuments of the French

king's triumphs. By excluding this reference, the Dresden version undermines a crucial part of the original message. It can be assumed that only a politically "neutral" version was in the long run unproblematic in the Saxon residence of Augustus the Strong.

Lit.: *Exh.-cat. Berlin 1995, pp. 572f. (cat. nos. 220f. with further lit.).*

AS

CAT. NO. 4.3

The Four Elements: Earth, Water, Air, Fire

FRANCE, BEFORE 1726
BRONZE
H. 15³/₈ IN., 15³/₈ IN.,
16¹/₂ IN., 14¹/₂ IN.
INV. NO. IX 104, IX 105,
IX 107, IX 106

Provenance: *First mentioned in the Sculpture Inventory 1726.*

It is uncertain when these statuettes were acquired, because a series of "The Four Seasons" is documented in both 1699 and 1723, either of which might well be "The Four Elements" in question here. Holzhausen, without providing any evidence, assigns the acquisition to the year 1723 and suggests a formal

proximity to the work of Antoine Coysevox. The latter is known to have copied an antique personification of Earth wearing a city-wall crown. This rather unusual motif recurs in the Dresden version of "Earth," but the attribution is disputed. List did not accept it and suggests an unidentified sculptor from the circle of the Louvre workshops as the creator.

Lit.: *Holzhausen 1939, p. 172.—List 1983, p. 183.*

AS

Cat. no. 4.4A and 4.4B

After a marble group by
FRANÇOIS GIRARDON
(1628–1715) and
THOMAS REGNAUDIN
(design Charles LeBrun)

The Bath of Apollo
FRANCE, BEFORE 1715
BRONZE
H. 22½ in., W. 31½ in.
INV. NO. IX 23

Workshop of
ANDRÉ-CHARLES
BOULLE (1642–1732)

Pedestal
BEFORE 1715
CONIFERS, BOULLE TECHNIQUE:
TORTOISESHELL AND BRASS; GILT
BRONZE
H. 47⅝ in., W. 30¾ in.,
D. 12¼ in.
INV. NO. IX 23

Provenance: *Both first mentioned in the Sculpture Inventory 1726.*

As evidenced by the surviving acquisition list of 1715, Augustus the Strong commissioned his agent, Baron Raymond Leplat, to buy this heavy bronze (which weighs in excess of 150 pounds) and its pedestal in Paris. This bronze group is a smaller repetition of the marble by Girardon and Regnaudin which is based on a design by LeBrun. The original was created between 1666 and 1675 and was initially intended for the so-called Thetis Grotto in the park of Versailles where it was placed in the central one of three conch shells. The piece in Versailles was flanked by two sun horses who were offered water

by Tritons. The latter were works by the brothers Marsy and Gilbert Guérin. A river god dominated the lunette above this group. The grotto itself exemplified the palace of Thetis, goddess of the sea, whose dwelling grounds were located under water. This was the place where Apollo, god of the sun, reposed from his hard labors during the night. Thetis herself, identified by a diadem, washes her visitor's hair and is thus closest to him. Apollo served as the counterpart to Louis XIV: Here his relaxation after the efforts of ruling are stressed. A similar image was evoked with a relief portraying Louis XIV crossing the Rhine River in 1672. In the original marble the image is located on the jug held by the kneeling Nymph, but this detail was omitted in the bronze.

The Thetis Grotto was demolished in 1684. All that is known about its original appearance is depicted in an engraving of 1676 by J. Lepautre. The reduced bronze version in the Green Vault is the only remaining sculptural rendering of "The Bath of Apollo" which offers the original composition that was rendered numerous times. However, the arrangement of the figures in marble group is much changed today.

Lit.: *Holzhausen 1939, fig. 1, pp. 167f.—Souchal 1981, pp. 25–28 (no. 17).—Klidis 2001, pp. 29–39.*

UW

Cat. no. 4.5

After FRANÇOIS
GIRARDON (1628–1715)

Pluto Abducts
Proserpina

ORIGINAL MARBLE 1677–99,
SMALL BRONZE PRESUMABLY
BETWEEN 1693 AND 1715
BRONZE
H. 41¾ IN.
INV. NO. IX 66

Provenance: *First mentioned in
the Sculpture Inventory 1726.*

The original marble of
"Pluto Abducts Pros-
erpina" was finsihed
in 1699. It belonged—along
with three other "raptus
groups"— to an ensemble in
the park at Versailles. Even
before the marble was completed small bronzes were
made after Girardon's model.
In 1693 one of these bronzes
came into the collection of
Louis XIV. Together with
"Boreas Abducts Oreithyia"
and two further bronzes, it was
prominently exhibited in the
Château of Versailles' "Salon
Ovale." The Dresden bronze,
formally closely related to the
one in Versailles, was also
conceived as a counterpart for
"The Rape of Oreithyia." By
1726 both groups are documented as being exhibited—as
a pair—in the Picture Gallery
of the Dresden Residential
Palace. The Sculpture Inventory of 1728 reveals just how
admired this group was—
which so closely follows
Bernini's "Abduction of Proserpina" and the "Abduction of
the Sabines" by Giambologna:
a total of five bronze replicas
of Girardon's raptus group are
recorded.

Lit.: *Exh.-cat. Berlin 1995,
pp. 576f. (cat. no. 223 with
further lit.).*

AS

Cat. no. 4.6

After ANSELM FLAMEN
(1647–1717) after a model by
GASPARD MARSY
(1624–1681)

The Abduction
of Oreithyia

ORIGINAL MARBLE 1684–87,
SMALL BRONZE BEFORE 1726
BRONZE
H. 43¾ IN.
INV. NO. IX 41

Provenance: *First mentioned in
the Sculpture Inventory 1726.*

The earliest Sculpture Inventory of 1726 already describes this piece as the pendant of "Pluto Abducts Proserpina" (cat. no. 4.5). Like the latter, it follows the marble model in the park at Versailles. Colbert was commissioned to develop—based on designs by Charles LeBrun—a sculpture program for the "Parterre d'eau." Starting in 1674 he began work on four "raptus groups" that were to personify the Four Elements. The anticipated groups were the abduction of Zeus's beautiful daughter Proserpina by Pluto, god of the underworld (Fire), "Saturn and Cybele" (Earth), "Neptune and Coronis" (Water), and "The Abduction of Oreithyia" (Air). After an unsuccessful attempt to win her heart, Boreas, god of the north wind, wrapped Oreithyia, a king's daughter, into a cloud and carried her away. All subjects originate from Ovid's *Metamorphoses*.

Lit.: *Exh.-cat. Berlin 1995, p. 574 (cat. no. 222 with further lit.).*

AS

CAT. NO. 4.7

The Abduction of the Sabine Women

FRANCE, EARLY 18TH CENTURY
BRONZE
H. 16¹/₈ IN.
INV. NO. IX 26

Provenance: *First mentioned in the Sculpture Inventory 1726.*

This bronze group exists in two different casts in the Green Vault. Its theme stems from early Roman times: in order to populate his newfounded city of Rome, Romulus invited his neighbors, the Sabines, to a party. As soon as they arrived, the male Romans grabbed their visitors' daughters and chased away their relatives.

This bronze could possibly be a pastiche. It might have been fabricated by a French dealer for the flourishing market and was possibly intended as a pendant for contemporary variants of Giambologna's "Nessus and Dejanira." The multitude of surviving casts underscores the popularity of this bronze among princely collectors in the 18th century, with this being the earliest dated version. Our "Abduction of the Sabine Women" was quite likely purchased in Paris in 1715 by Baron Raymond Leplat for the price of 148 thalers. Mounted on a wall console, this group was exhibited—along with its pendant—in the Bronze Room of the Green Vault. The two quite similar pieces faced each other, resulting in an effective variation and a symmetrical, decorative wall arrangement.

Lit.: *Holzhausen 1939, pp. 162 f.—Cf. also Wenley 2002, pp. 46–49.*

UW

CAT. NOS. 4.8A AND 4.8B

After MICHEL ANGUIER (1614–1686)

Amphitrite

MODEL 1652,
CAST BEFORE 1699
BRONZE
H. 14⁵/₈ IN.
INV. NO. IX 62

Provenance: *First mentioned in the Sculpture Inventory 1726.*

After LOUIS GARNIER (ca. 1639–1728)

Bacchus

MODEL AND CAST BEFORE 1699
BRONZE
H. 14⁵/₈ IN.
INV. NO. IX 38

Provenance: *First mentioned in the Sculpture Inventory 1726.*

In 1699 Raymond Leplat purchased two statuettes in Paris that are based on models by the French sculptors Garnier and Anguier. Anguier created the model for his "Amphitrite" in 1652 and based it on the famous antique "Flora Farnese." Garnier's

"Bacchus," too, is close to antique prototypes. This explains the original perception of these two sculptures as "antique" in the acquisition list. Augustus the Strong owned "Amphitrite" in two different sizes. While the larger version was intended as a pair for the figure of an "Apollo," the smaller one exhibited here was combined with "Bacchus," a juxtaposition also encountered in other collections. Originally, though, the water goddess belonged in a different context. In 1652 Anguier created seven antique deities: "Jupiter", "Juno", "Pluto", "Mars", "Neptune", "Ceres", and "Amphitrite"; each of them was given a specific emotional characteristic. As Anguier pointed out in a paper from 1676, Amphitrite was to be "of beautiful, elegant proportions," her skin color was intended to be "fresh, sensuous, clear, and transparent, and her face agreeable." For Anguier, the sea goddess represented "calmness."

Lit.: *Exh.-cat. Berlin 1995, pp. 568f. (cat. nos. 218f. with more lit.).*

AS

Cat. no. 4.9

GIOVANNI DA BOLOGNA
(*1529–1608*)

Flying Mercury
Before 1622
Bronze
H. 13³/₈ in.
Inv. no. IX 83

Provenance: *First mentioned in the Kunstkammer Inventory 1640.*

Mercury, messenger of the gods, is hastily flying past while he points upward with his index finger to indicate that he exe-

cutes the commands of Jupiter. With his "Flying Mercury," Giambologna created the epitome of the quick, agile, and intelligent god. His "Mercury" appears to defy the laws of gravity. Only the tip of one foot touches the ground, in this instance the little head of the wind deity Zephyr. In this radically conceived sculpture Giambologna appears to negate the static laws of the plastic arts, thereby entering new terrain for this genre. It is possible that the architect and art agent, Nosseni, from whose collection this statuette comes, purchased it in 1588 in Florence, while Giambologna was still alive.

Lit.: *Holzhausen 1933, p. 58.*

AS

Cat. nos. 4.10A and 4.10B

PETER WIBER
(*died 1641, master 1603*)

**Cups and Lids
(So-Called *Buckelpokale*)**
Nuremberg, ca. 1603–09
Hallmarks for Nuremberg and maker's marks PW for Peter Wiber
Silver gilt
H. 24³/₈ in., 22⁷/₈ in.
Inv. no. IV 297, IV 300

Provenance: *First mentioned in the Silver Inventory of the Green Vault 1723.*

In contrast to the impressive *Buckelpokal* of the Hamburg goldsmith Peter vom Lohe, the Nuremberg examples are distinguished by *Buckel* (bosses) that are joined by diagonal ridges. The cup, therefore, looks as if it is twisted. Wiber belonged to a group of Nuremberg goldsmiths who were inspired by Gothic shapes and reinterpreted them at the beginning of the 17th century. However,

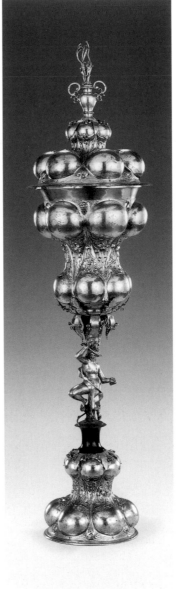

this cup and lid can be readily identified as Baroque creations: characteristic features include the individual shapes of the straps near the nodule and the lid's knob, the figure of the warrior on the lid, and the delicately cut silver foliage in the cup's lower portions. Drinking vessels of this type were worked in such a way that identical ones could always be slid into one another.

Lit.: *Rosenberg 1925–28, vol. III, p. 174 (nos. 4119f, g).— Sponsel 1928, p. 34, plate 14 .— Syndram 1997, p. 51 (nos. 70f.).*
UW

CAT. NO. 4.11

PETER VOM LOHE
(died 1687, master 1650)

Cup and Lid (So-Called *Hoher Buckelpokal*)

HAMBURG, INSCRIPTION WITH DATE SEPTEMBER 24, 1657
HALLMARKS FOR HAMBURG AND MAKER'S MARKS PL FOR PETER VOM LOHE
SILVER GILT, COLD ENAMEL
H. 34½ IN.
INV. NO. IV 186

Provenance: *First mentioned in the Silver Inventory of the Green Vault 1723.*

This impressive *Buckelpokal* follows a late Gothic model that Nuremberg goldsmiths

had to manufacture as their qualifying masterpiece. Well into the 18th century, drinking vessels of this type were a popular gift for public and private occasions. Here, the otherwise customary baluster-shaped shaft is replaced by a tree trunk painted in cold enamel. A female figure, the nymph Daphne, is portrayed in the process of being transformed into a laurel tree in order to escape the pursuit of Apollo. The height of this piece is more than two and a half feet, making it the largest *Buckelpokal* in the Green Vault. It was an official gift of the city of Wittenberg to Prince Elector Johann Georg II of Saxony, who played an important role as of *Reichsvikar* (Imperial Curate, i. e. someone who manages the power of the

regent, in this case the emperor, until the successor is crowned), a position he held for more than one year after the death of Emperor Ferdinand III in 1657.

Lit.: *Sponsel 1928, pp. 34f., plate 15.—Schliemann 1985, vol. II, p. 163 (no. 212/1).—Syndram 1997, p. 45 (no. 35).*
UW

CAT. NOS. 4.12A, 4.12B AND 4.12C

ABRAHAM TITTECKE
(died 1633, master 1587)

Two Goblets with Lids

NUREMBERG, BETWEEN 1588 AND 1590
HALLMARKS FOR NUREMBERG AND MAKER'S MARKS AT FOR ABRAHAM TITTECKE
SILVER GILT
H. 24 IN., 22⅝ IN
INV. NO. IV 121, IV 123

ABRAHAM TITTECKE and HANS ZEIGER *(master 1580)*

Goblet with Lid

NUREMBERG, BETWEEN 1588 AND 1590
HALLMARKS FOR NUREMBERG AND MAKER'S MARKS AT FOR ABRAHAM TITTECKE, MASTER MARKS ON BRIM OF LID HZ FOR HANS ZEIGER
SILVER GILT
H. 17¾ IN.
INV. NO. IV 153

Provenance: *All of them first mentioned in the inventory of the Electoral Chambers in the Stable Court 1591.*

Goblets with conical cups were widespread in South Germany in the last third of the 16th century. The edges of the depicted goblets are adorned with artfully chased scrollwork decoration. Depictions of animals before a landscape background

are rendered in three oval compartments, framed by bunches of fruit and floral motifs. The lids' knobs are embellished with silver figures of warriors in antique outfits. The goblets were kept in the Stables Building near the Dresden Residential Palace. By 1733 they were exhibited in the Silver-Gilt Room of the Green Vault. In 1766 they formed part of a total of 70 other parade vessels made of gilt silver which were exhibited in the Residential Palace and known as the *Schaubuffet*. In 1894 they decorated a festive dinner table in the palace's throne room.

Lit.: *Rosenberg 1925–28, vol. III, nos. 4051 (e,f), nos. 4018 (a,c).—Arnold 1994.—Münzberg 2002, pp. 40ff., 127–131.*
JK

Cat. no. 4.13

MEINRAD BAUCH
(1547–1623, master 1575)

Drinking Vessel in the Shape of a Jumping Stag

Nuremberg, early
17th century
Hallmarks for Nuremberg
and maker's marks MB for
Meinrad Bauch
Silver gilt, antlers: coral
H. 14⅝ in.
Inv. no. IV 13

Provenance: *First mentioned in the inventory of the Kunstkammer 1640.*

The collar of the vessel marks the spot where the animal's head may be removed. A plethora of such silver drinking vessels, which were primarily fabricated in 16th century Augsburg are known. Favorite motifs include exotic animals like lions and elephants, as well as typical domestic farm beasts like the ox, goat, and rooster. The boar and stag were among the most popular of animals in court hunts. Vessels such as this one were frequently used for decoration but also for drinking purposes and in connection with hunting ceremonies where they served as the "welcome" in festive toasts.

Lit.: *Rosenberg 1925–28, vol. III, no. 3993 (kf).—Sponsel 1928, plate 7.—Hernmarck 1978, p. 111, fig. 187.*
JK

BALTHASAR LAUCH
(1643–1694, master 1670)

Coin Tankard
LEIPZIG, 1687
HALLMARKS FOR LEIPZIG WITH
YEAR LETTER K (MIRROR IMAGE)
AND MAKER'S MARKS BL FOR
BALTHASAR LAUCH
SILVER GILT
H. 9 IN.
INV. NO. IV 351

the occasion of a rifle contest for young Prince Elector Johann Georg IV's confirmation in 1699. In addition, there are portraits of rulers on Saxon thalers, images of the dukes of Brunswick-Wolfenbüttel on so-called quarter thalers, and a gold coin commemorating the one hundredth anniversary of the "Augsburg Confession." The engraved coat of arms near the handle cites the year 1687 and refers to the original owner of the tankard, Baron

Provenance: *Received as a gift from a private collection to the Green Vault 1908.*

This gorgeous tankard is decorated with a total of 50 coins. The outside is embellished with ten square-shaped so-called *Taler-klippen* depicting the infant Hercules crushing serpents in his cradle—prizes awarded on

Hans Bastian von Zehmen (1629–1702). He served as court and chamber councilor under Duke Moritz von Sachsen-Zeitz (ruled 1657–81).

Lit.: *Sponsel 1928, p. 158, plate 4.—Schröder 1935, p. 129.—Syndram 1997, p. 52 (no. 77).*
UW

CAT. NO. 4.15

Tankard with Emerald Doublets
SOUTH GERMANY(?), CA. 1670
SILVER GILT, GOLD, ENAMEL,
PEARLS, ROCK CRYSTAL UNDER-
LAID WITH COLOR (SO-CALLED
"EMERALD DOUBLETS")
H. 6³/₈ IN.
INV. NO. IV 594A

Provenance: *First mentioned in the appendix of the Hall of Precious Objects Inventory 1725–33.*

One of the distinguishing features of this tankard is its noble elegance, which is even more appealing once one notices the contradiction between the simple, balanced shape of its body and the playful subtleties of its delicate adornments. Oddly enough, the applications are attached to the corpus by two fine silver wires over

four drill holes. Because of the small distance between the inset containing the beverage and the body of the vessel on the outside, the customary screw device did not work here. This may be evidence for the fact that the adornment was not originally intended. Another peculiarity is the fact that the backs of the appliqués are even decorated with painted enamel, which could be an indication that the pieces used here were prefabricated objects that could be employed in many different modes such as pieces of jewelry or to decorate state robes.

Lit.: *Sponsel 1925, p. 196, plate 61.—Syndram 1997, p. 52 (no. 79).*
UW

the Hall of Knights in Berlin's castle (today Museum of Decorative Arts Berlin). Apart from such commissions which involved various goldsmiths, individual pieces were manufactured for the trade. According to an entry in the 1723 Silver Inventory, Augustus the Strong purchased this unusual pair of beakers at the Leipzig fair in 1719. These objects are part of the important acquisitions of Augsburg silver by the Dresden court which included an extensive table service, multipart centerpieces, tazza, candlesticks, gueridons, sets of lavabos, and coolers.

Lit.: *Rosenberg 1922–28, vol. III, p. 111 (nos. 574n–o).— Sponsel 1928, p. 278, plate 64.— Syndram 1997, p. 203 (no. 4).*
UW

CAT. NO. 4.16

JOHANN LUDWIG I BILLER *(1656–1732, master 1684)*

Two Covered Beakers on Scroll-Shaped Feet

AUGSBURG, CA. 1710–12
HALLMARKS FOR AUGSBURG AND MAKER'S MARKS ILB FOR JOHANN LUDWIG I BILLER
SILVER GILT
H. 12³/₈ IN., 12¹/₄ IN.
INV. NO. IV 66, IV 67

Provenance: *First mentioned in the Silver Inventory of the Green Vault 1723.*

Biller was a member of one of the most distinguished dynasties of goldsmiths in Augsburg whose particular commissions included orders from Europe's leading princely courts. The high regard for the Billers is intricately tied to a spectacular commission by Prince Elector Frederick III of Brandenburg who procured from them the monumental silver buffet in

CAT. NO. 4.17

JOHANN ANDREAS THELOTT (1655–1734)

Basin with Bacchus Festival

AUGSBURG, DATED 1714
SILVER GILT
DIAM. 18¹/₂ IN.
SIGNED: J A/THELOT/1714
INV. NO. IV 5

Provenance: *Purchased in 1718 at the Leipzig fair.*

The matching jug—embossed with river gods and naiads—was melted down in 1772. It was Augsburg's chronicler of artisans, Paul von Stetten, who praised Thelott as early as 1779, calling him the "most famous artist specializing in the craft of embossing" and naming as one of his most distinguished works the set of basin and jug kept in the Green Vault. Thelott was indeed an astonishingly creative person who knew to apply his talents both as goldsmith and as copperplate engraver. At the same time he was capable of transforming the images he invented into three-dimensional objects that were embossed and chased masterpieces of goldsmithing. Contrary to custom, this basin is not marked; instead, it bears Thelott's signature—an act that manifests his self-confidence as an artist.

Lit.: *Exh.-cat. Munich 1994, vol. II, p. 392 (no. 94 with more lit.).—Seling 1994, p. 55 (no.1846*t).—Syndram 1997, pp. 210 (no. 1), 227 (plate 43).*
UW

CAT. NO. 4.18

DANIEL I SCHÄFFLER (1659–1727, master 1701)

Helmet-Shaped Ewer and Basin

AUGSBURG, CA. 1712–15
HALLMARKS FOR AUGSBURG AND MAKER'S MARKS DS FOR DANIEL I SCHÄFFLER
SILVER GILT
H. EWER 11³/₄ IN.,
DIAM. BASIN 22¹/₈ IN.
INV. NO. IV 155, IV 182

Provenance: *First mentioned in the Silver Inventory of the Green Vault 1723.*

This set is part of the extensive purchases Augustus the Strong made from Augsburg silver dealers at the Leipzig fair in 1718/19 (see cat. no. 4.17). The splendid, silver-gilt vessels were earmarked for exhibition in the Tower Room in the Dresden Residential Palace, which was transformed into a formal "buffet" in the fall of 1719 for the wedding of Prince Elector Frederick Augustus and the emperor's daughter, Maria Josepha. The objects epitomized the fashion of the day. Along with the older Wettin silver treasures, they were exhibited on innumerable consoles and pedestals, where they testified to the impressive affluence and royal splendor that prevailed at the Wettin Court. Only a few years later, most of these objects were the focal point in the two newly created Silver Rooms in Augustus the Strong's latest creation, the Green Vault, where they were once again exhibited as "buffet."

Lit.: *Graesse 1876/77, plate 84.—Exh.-cat. Munich 1994, vol. II, pp. 479f. (cat. no.131).*
UW

CAT. NO. 4.19

GEORG FRIEBEL (ca. 1656–1730, master 1695)

Two Chain Bottles

AUGSBURG, CA. 1712–15
HALLMARKS FOR AUGSBURG AND MAKER'S MARKS GF FOR GEORG FRIEBEL
SILVER GILT
H. 16³/₈ IN., 16³/₄ IN.
INV. NO. IV 258, IV 263

Provenance: *First mentioned in the Silver Inventory of the Green Vault 1723.*

In the 1723 Silver Inventory, all referenced objects are accompanied by a brief description with mention of their weight. In the case of the chain bottles it amounted to the equivalent of 18 marks (approximately 9 lbs.). The weight is also engraved into the bottom of the pieces. This is significant since the material value alone constituted a considerable fortune that could be turned into currency in times

DANIEL I SCHÄFFLER
(*1659–1727, master 1701*) and
GOTTLIEB MENZEL
(*1676–1757, master 1709*)

Set of Four Tazza

AUGSBURG, CA. 1712–15
HALLMARKS FOR AUGSBURG
AND MAKER'S MARKS DS FOR
DANIEL I SCHÄFFLER AND GM
FOR GOTTFRIED MENZEL
SILVER GILT
DIAM. 10⅝ IN.–11¼ IN.
INV. NO. IV 146, IV 148,
IV 286, IV 288

Provenance: *First mentioned
in the Silver Inventory of the
Green Vault 1723.*

These objects, called tazzas or *soucoupes*, were placed on the silver buffet, a stepped piece of furniture reminiscent of a modern sideboard. Located near the table, it played a crucial role in courtly ceremonies. A tazza is a plate on which servants offered visitors beverages or the napkin and the water of need. In this way, the silver treasure of the House of Wettin was substantially diminished in 1772: As a result of the Seven Years' War the rulers felt compelled to melt down a considerable portion of their pure silver and also large quantities of their silver-gilt objects. The chain bottles, intended to contain wine or mixtures of wine and water, were customarily kept in the wine coolers close to the table.

Lit.: *Graesse 1876/77, plate 73.—Exh.-cat. Munich 1994, vol. II, pp. 475f. (no. 128).— Syndram 1997, pp. 209f. (no. 3).*
UW

glass to clean one's hands. An advantage of these objects was that direct physical contact between servants and people of rank was avoided. The different variations of these silver objects reflect, in rather subtle ways, the status of the respective noble family. A gilt serving plate on a foot, for instance, was much more prestigious than a flat one made of silver and unembellished.

Lit.: *Exh.-cat. Warsaw 1997b, p. 186 (cat. no. V 73).—See also Seling 1980, pp. 293f. (no. 1951), 310f. (no. 2022).*

UW

CAT. NO. 4.21

JOHANN CHRISTOPH I TREFFLER (*ca. 1652–1723, presumably master 1680*)

Two Wine Coolers
AUGSBURG, CA. 1712–15
HALLMARKS FOR AUGSBURG AND MAKER'S MARKS ICT FOR JOHANN CHRISTOPH I TREFFLER
SILVER GILT
H. 8³/₈ IN., W. 9¹/₈ IN.;
H. 8³/₈ IN., W. 9¹/₂ IN.
INV. NO. IV 190, IV 191

Provenance: *First mentioned in the Silver Inventory of the Green Vault 1723.*

An integral part of the courtly table traditions, these wine coolers were filled with ice water. During the 17th century, large basins were customarily located beside the buffet, where they could each hold several bottles. "Wine fountains" or "water bladders"—vessels equipped with taps and stoppers—were placed higher up and enabled one to pour wine into the cooled bottles. The two coolers in the shape of buckets held individual bottles. Originating at the French court in the early 18th century, this general type of smaller cooler has survived to this day. The Augsburg goldsmith Treffler created flat lancet foliage and applied strapwork sparingly. The works of French contemporary goldsmiths served as a source of inspiration for the noble elegance of Treffler's decoration.

Lit.: *Exh.-cat. Munich 1994, vol. II, pp. 476ff. (cat. no. 129).— Exh.-cat. Warsaw 1997b, p. 186 (cat. no. V 72 (IV 190)).*

UW

CAT. NO. 4.22

Potsdam glass factory and Augsburg(?)

Tumbler with Ball Feet
CA. 1695–1700
GOLD RUBY GLASS, MOUNT: SILVER GILT
H. 5⁷/₈ IN.
INV. NO. 1968/1

Provenance: *First mentioned in the Accessions Inventory of the Green Vault 1968.*

This tumbler was not purchased for the Green Vault until 1968. Its shape is slightly conical, and it rests on ball feet which are soldered to a narrow foot ring. Its powerful dark red coloration and its meticulous state of preservation suggest that it is quite likely a product of the Potsdam glass factory of Johann Kunckel. Kunckel (1632/37–1703) had begun to work for the Brandenburg court in 1678. Until 1683 he was instrumental in inventing gold ruby glass. It appears highly probable that the vessel received its stable mounts—the height of the fashion for the time of their manufacture—in Augsburg. Comparable mounts may be observed in another gold ruby glass tumbler with lid, part of the same 1968 acquisition, which bears the mas-

ter mark of Tobias Baur from Augsburg.

Lit.: *Kerssenbrock-Krosigk 2001, p. 198 (no. 173), plate 5.*

JK

Cat. no. 4.23

Southern German glass factory and TOBIAS BAUR
(*ca. 1660–1735, master 1685*)

Teapot
Ca. 1695–1700
Hallmarks for Augsburg
and maker's marks TB for
Tobias Baur
Gold ruby glass, mount:
silver gilt
H. 4³/4 in. (with lid)
Inv. no. IV 209

Provenance: *First mentioned in the inventory of the Coats of Arms Room in the Green Vault 1733.*

Vessels of gold ruby glass were popular as containers for hot drinks. This is demonstrated by surviving teapots with mounts dating from the late-17th to the mid-18th centuries. It is, however, unlikely that they were ever put to practical use. More than anything else, these pots were collectors' items which sported a particular elegance. In the Green Vault's 1725 Inventory of Precious Objects, some 59 different gold ruby glass vessels are mentioned. In 1733 the holdings already numbered 83 vessels which were exhibited on tables and consoles in the Coats of Arms Room. In 1738 and 1746 three additional gold ruby glasses came into the treasury. A total of five pieces were destroyed in 1734/38. This loss was made up thanks to one new acquisition in 1927 plus three further ones in 1968 (cat. no. 4.15). This collection of gold ruby glass is one of the leading and most significant in the world.

Lit.: *Kerssenbrock-Krosigk 2001, p. 223 (cat. no. 277), plate 8.*

JK

Cat. nos. 4.24A and 4.24B

Southern German glass factory and TOBIAS BAUR
(*ca. 1660–1735, master 1685*)

Two Boxes with Lids
Ca. 1695–1700
Hallmarks for Augsburg
and maker's marks TB for
Tobias Baur
Gold ruby glass, mount:
silver gilt
H. 4⁷/8 in., 4³/4 in.
Inv. no. IV 138, IV 139

Provenance: *First mentioned in the inventory of the Coats of Arms Room in the Green Vault 1733.*

Although a number of glass factories are known to have existed in Munich, Freising, and Bayreuth during the last third of the 17th century, there is no evidence that any of them produced gold ruby glass. The abundance of surviving examples of gold ruby glass from this time make it highly probable that the manufacture of gold ruby glass was indeed practiced somewhere else at the same time in southern Germany. This is particularly likely as many of the extant objects are decorated with Augsburg mounts and are frequently adorned with exquisitely cut ornaments. Despite continued research, final proof of gold ruby glassworks in southern Germany has not been found. Unlike the gold ruby glasses from Brandenburg and Bohemia, the ones of supposed southern German origin

rarely exhibit flawless consistency in color. The flaws, however, do not diminish their compelling artistic value. Our two lidded boxes received their final shapes in the workshop of the Augsburg master Baur, who became known for his mounts, particularly those for vessels made of this precious and delicate material. The smaller box was used to keep sugar while the other one appears to have contained tea. They both belong to a tea service of which the pot (cat. no. 4.23) and two small cups with saucers are preserved in the Green Vault as well.

Lit.: *Kerssenbrock-Krosigk 2001, p. 240 (cat. nos. 362f.), plate 8.*
JK

CAT. NO. 4.25

GIOVANNI BATTISTA METELLINO
(active in Milan in the last third of the 17th century)

Goblet in the Shape of a Winged Dragon

MILAN, 1715/16
ROCK CRYSTAL, SILVER GILT, LAPIS LAZULI
H. 15³/₈ IN.
INV. NO. V 315

Provenance: *First mentioned in the Green Vault's Inventory of Precious Objects 1725.*

Metellino was the last important artist to master cutting rock crystal. His work continued the tradition of the workshops of famous stonecutters such as Miseroni and Saracchi. Metellino's rock crystal vessels are distinguished by their impressive size, their meticulous cut, their fully three-dimensional figures including dolphins or dragons, and their

mounts with extra embellishments made of lapis lazuli. The princely clients of Metellino included King Louis XIV of France and his son. Thanks to Augustus the Strong, the Green Vault owns the world's most important collection of this Milanese artist's oeuvre. The inventories reveal that he commissioned his first rock crystal dragon from Milan as early as 1715. Its high price (200 ducats) and the description might identify the piece as this one. The goblet's back shows a squatting dragon from the rear. The head with its wide open mouth is lifted beyond the rim of the vessel. Two wings lend the composition an idiosyncratic accent that is typical of Metellino's creations.

Lit.: *Weinholz 1967.—Syndram 1999, pp. 121f.—Exh.-cat. Vienna 2002, pp. 80–97, 217 (cat. no. 127).*

JK

CAT. NO. 4.26

GIOVANNI BATTISTA METELLINO
(active in Milan in the last third of the 17th century)

Splendid Bowl in the Shape of a Shell with Two Dolphins

MILAN, CA. 1720
ROCK CRYSTAL, SILVER GILT, LAPIS LAZULI
H. 8¹/₂ IN.
INV. NO. V 249

Provenance: *First mentioned in the Green Vault's Inventory of Precious Objects 1725.*

Each detail in this imaginatively created, stately dish identifies the maker as Metellino. In the case of our exquisite treasury piece, he once again proves himself as one of the leading masters of cutting rock crystal. The dish was cut in the shape of a shell which is decorated with occasional fine intaglio adorn-

ments. The foot is made up of two intimately intertwined dolphins. On either side of the vessel, the dolphins' tails are executed in elegant, vertical movements. The tail ends terminate in handles which are utterly decorative and hardly usable. Augustus the Strong purchased two other "dolphin vessels" from the estate of Metellino. His heirs initially offered them to Augustus using brush drawings as illustrations (dated June 12, 1724, preserved in the Dresden Collection of Drawings, Prints, and Photographs).

Lit.: *Weinholz 1967.—Syndram 1999, pp. 121 f. (with fig.).*

JK

CAT. NO. 4.27

Design: GIOVANNI BATTISTA FOGGINI *(1652–1725)*, execution: Galleria dei Lavori

Lidded Box

FLORENCE, BEGINNING 18TH CENTURY
DIVERSE HARDWOODS, EBONY VENEER, PLAQUES AS COMMESSI IN PIETRE DURE TECHNIQUE (SLATE, POLISHED BLACK LIMESTONE, AGATE IN DIFFERENT COLOR VARIETIES, LAPIS LAZULI), FRUIT (AGATE AND MARBLE IN DIFFERENT COLOR VARIETIES), GILT BRONZE, GILT COPPER, AND BRASS
H. 14 IN., W. 18 1/2 IN., L. 22 5/8 IN.
INV. NO. I 13

Provenance: *First mentioned in the inventory of the Fireplace Room in the Green Vault 1818.*

The Galleria dei Lavori in Florence was founded in 1588 by Ferdinando I Medici. A rigidly organized court workshop, it was established in the Uffizi and reached its Baroque culmination under the reign of Cosimo III (1670–1723). This lidded box is a typical product of the Galleria. What is most captivating about it is the luxurious combination of diverse materials. The execution of such objects lay in the hands of experienced masters of stone intarsia work (*commettitori di piano*) and cabinetmakers (*ebanisti*). The corners of the box are adorned by bronze "garlands" which are decorated by colored fruit made of varied pieces of agate. The latter were fabricated by specially trained stone polishers (*fruttista*). There is no doubt that Foggini, head of the Galleria since 1694, was responsible for the lidded box's design. His distinguished decorative style was formative for the Uffizi workshop.

Lit.: *Syndram 1999, p. 16. (with fig.).*

JK

CAT. NO. 4.28

Presumably PAUL HERRMANN *(1673–1732)* and JOHANN CHRISTOPH HÜBNER *(1665–1739)*

Female Bust

DRESDEN, BETWEEN 1725 AND 1730
BUST: AMETHYST AND SEGMENTS OF AMETHYST ON TUFF, GARMENT: GILT BRONZE
H. 21 7/8 IN.
INV. NO. V 592

Provenance: *First mentioned in the inventory of the Hall of Precious Objects in the Green Vault 1733.*

This bust was almost certainly designed by Herrmann, a Dresden court sculptor and restorer of antiques. It was possibly executed by Hübner, known to have collaborated on Johann Melchior Dinglinger's cabinet pieces. Thanks to his excellent stonecutting abilities, he had a special reputation, particularly regarding gemstones. The technical bravado of this bust is dumbfounding: custom made, polished pieces of amethyst are mounted on the perfectly sculpted upper neck and chest. The amethyst is adhered to the upper portions of the garment using a putty compound. The head is cut from one huge block of amethyst except for the right portion of the face. In order to render a bust of this size, exceptionally compact pieces of amethyst with densely structured crystals were

required. The appropriate minerals were quarried in 1721 in Schlottwitz in the Erzgebirge, a mountain range not far from Dresden.

Lit.: *Exh.-cat. Munich 1990, pp. 80f. (cat. no. 91).—Exh.-cat. Idar-Oberstein/Berlin/Dresden 1998, p. 172 (cat. no. 71).*

JK

Cat. no. 4.29

JOHANN MELCHIOR DINGLINGER *(1664–1731)*

Parts of the Sword Belt from the Sapphire Set (Buckle, Slide, and Tip)
DRESDEN, CA. 1700–10, ALTERED
SAPPHIRES, DIAMONDS, GOLD, SILVER
BUCKLE: H. 4⅞ IN., W. 2⅞ IN.; SLIDE: L. 5 IN.; TIP: H. 1¾ IN., W. 3¾ IN.
INV. NO. VIII 156A, VIII 149A, VIII 150A

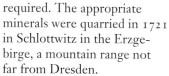

Provenance: *First mentioned in the Inventory of Royal Jewelry 1719.*

One of the cultural and historic rarities among the jewel sets in the Green Vault is the decoration of the sapphire set's great sword belt, which has survived in its entirety. In the earlier part of the 18th century, the small sword was carried on the left hip. Fastened to a broad band, it was suspended from the right shoulder. The largest buckle—equipped with slide and tips—was positioned in the center of the chest. The two pairs, consisting of smaller buckles with slide and tip mounts, were attached to the band which widened as it descended and terminated in two parts. One single embellished tip completed the richly decorated group of objects at the bottom. The ten parts that have come down to us belong to the oldest portions of the sapphire set. The elegant ornament consists of

dynamic, wavy striations and acanthus foliage. It was created shortly after 1700 and garnished with rose diamonds slightly later.

Lit.: *Arnold 2001, pp. 47–51.*
DS

Cat. no. 4.30

JOHANN MELCHIOR DINGLINGER *(1664–1731)*

Hat Brim (*Aigrette*) from the Agate Set
DRESDEN, BEFORE 1719
DIAMONDS, GOLD, SILVER GILT
H. 9⅛ IN., W. 3⅛ IN.
INV. NO. VIII 24

Provenance: *First mentioned in the Inventory of Royal Jewelry 1719.*

The only surviving elements of Augustus the Strong's once elaborate agate set are a stately small sword and this hat decoration (*aigrette*) which is incidentally

reminiscent of a turban ornament. In the early 18th century, two different types of princely hat decoration were common. The *agraffe* or *Krempe*, as preserved in the set with the Green Diamond, served as a decorative clasp, elegantly fastening the hat brim to the headpiece. The main function of the *aigrette* was to hold a plume of heron feathers. The *aigrette* of the agate set comes from the hand of Dinglinger, the most important jeweler of late-Baroque times. Here, the feathers are secured in a hidden case in the *Bukett*, located in the lower part of the brim.

Lit.: *Arnold 2001, pp. 29–31.*
DS

CAT. NO. 4.31

JOHANN MELCHIOR DINGLINGER (*1664–1731*)

Watch with Watch Chain and Two Sets from the Carnelian Set

DRESDEN, 1719
WATCH CASE SIGNED: MASSY LONDON
CARNELIAN AND OTHER COLORED PRECIOUS STONES, DIAMONDS, GOLD, SILVER, STEEL
DIAM. 2 1/8 IN., L. OF CHAIN 7 3/4 IN.
INV. NO. VIII 234

Provenance: *First mentioned in the Inventory of Royal Jewelry 1719.*

With its 127 surviving parts, this is the biggest remaining set from the times of Augustus the Strong. The watch case was made for the festivity of Saturn which concluded the grandiose wedding of Augustus's son in 1719. Engraved into the center of the face is the festival hall. With its decorations of precious stones, the back of the case conjures up the prior festivities with their references to planets Jupiter, Mars, Mercury, Saturn, and Venus as well as the Sun and the Moon. The alchemical symbols of the metals may be found on the surface of the watch case. It was the alchemists' belief that all terrestrial metals ultimately originated from the planets.

Lit.: *Arnold 2001, pp. 73f.— Syndram 1997, p. 286.*

DS

CAT. NO. 4.32

DANIEL GOUERS (*documented in Paris 1723/24–40*)

Snuff Box from the Ruby Set

PARIS, 1730/31
GOLD, RUBIES, BRILLIANT CUT DIAMONDS
W. 2 3/4 IN., L. 2 IN., H. 7/8 IN.
INV. NO. VIII 127

Provenance: *First mentioned in the Inventory of the Jewel Room 1733.*

The acquisition of this snuff box in Paris deviates from the regular purchase practices of jewelry sets for the Green Vault. Gouers, court smith for the French King Louis XV, must have produced it for the open market and not for a princely commissioner because it bears three hallmarks provided by the Parisian goldsmiths guild. Equally unusual are the French Rococo ornaments, which were just evolving at the time in Dresden, although this mode was already on the verge of being unfashionable in Paris. Because Augustus the Strong loved to give away golden snuff boxes as presents, the survival of this ravishing piece in the Green Vault is almost miraculous. The ruby set was once among the most elaborate sets of the Saxon-Polish elector kings. Most of the surviving parts originate from the reign of Augustus the Strong. Their color values, red and white, corresponded to the colors of the Polish coat of arms and thus lent the set a political symbolism that can hardly be overestimated.

Lit.: *Arnold 2001, p.134.*

DS

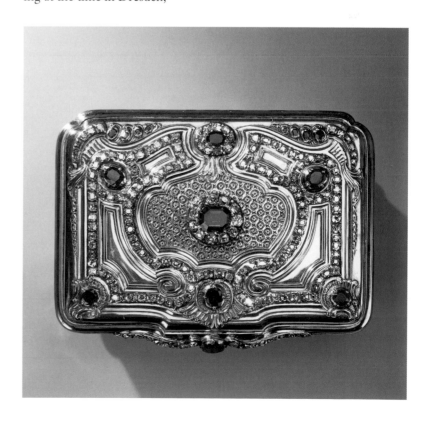

CAT. NO. 4.33

JEAN-JACQUES PALLARD
(1701–1776)

Golden Fleece with Brazilian Yellow Topazes

DRESDEN, 1755/56
TOPAZES, BRILLIANT CUT
DIAMONDS, GOLD, SILVER
H. 4¼ IN., W. 3⅛ IN.
INV. NO. VIII 5

Provenance: *First mentioned as a supplement to the Jewel Garniture Inventory 1750.*

This badge with yellow topazes from Brazil came to the Green Vault in 1756. It was the last "jewel fleece" which King Augustus III added to his set of jewelry. The three topazes are set with 369 diamonds. Together, they make up the elegant and dynamic "flaming iron of fire" from which the ram's fleece is suspended. The Order of the Knights of the Golden Fleece—founded by the Duke of Burgundy in 1430—was one of the oldest and most distinguished of all secular orders. At the same time it was the highest order of the imperial House of Hapsburg which inherited the title of sovereign of the order from Burgundy. In 1722, both Augustus the Strong and his son, later Augustus III, were admitted to the order as knights. The Saxon rulers got permission to produce jewels depicting the order's identifying badge for their personal use. However, upon a member's death, the emblem of the order had to be returned to the Master of the Order of the Golden Fleece Knights.

Lit.: *Arnold 2001, pp. 101–103.*
DS

CAT. NO. 4.34

CHRISTIAN AUGUSTUS
GLOBIG *(mentioned as court gold worker in Dresden since 1762, died 1798)*

Large Bodice Bow from the Jewelry of the Queens

DRESDEN, 1782
BRILLIANT CUT DIAMONDS,
SILVER, GOLD
H. 4⅞ IN., W. 8⅜ IN.
INV. NO. VIII 36

Provenance: *First mentioned in the Inventory of the Jewel Room 1817.*

Large decorative bodice bows were worn below the neck and belonged to the favorite accessories of court ladies until circa 1800. Prince Elector Frederick Augustus III commissioned this piece for his wife, Amalie Auguste, in 1782. Presumably made to celebrate the birth of their first child, this unusual object is abundantly studded with diamonds. They originally embellished coat and waistcoat buttons, as well as other objects associated with the brilliant cut diamond set. The bodice bow was designed as a volumetric object with ends that appear to dangle down from a gathered band. The cut diamond in its box-like setting—originally from the diamond set where it was used as a shirt button—forms the center of this object. The total weight of the bow, which is decorated with 51 large as well as 611 medium-size to small diamonds, amounts to roughly 614 ct. The comfort of wearing it simply as a piece of jewelry must be somewhat diminished by that fact that, together with its mount, the bow weighs 556 g (approx. one and a quarter pounds).

Lit.: *Arnold 2001, pp. 228f.— Holzhausen 1966, p. LXVIII.— Syndram 1997, pp. 258–261.*
DS

The Rose Diamond Set

Individual parts:

Badge of the Polish White Eagle Order (*Christian August and Augustus Gotthelf Globig, Dresden 1782–89*)

Star of the Polish White Eagle Order (*Jean-Jacques Pallard, Geneva 1753*)

Small sword with scabbard

Epaulette

Four hatbands for the hat brim (*agraffe*) (*Christian August and Augustus Gotthelf Globig, Dresden 1782–89*)

A pair of shoe buckles and two knee buckles (*workshop of Christian Augustus Globig, Dresden 1782–89*)

10 waistcoat buttons and 10 coat buttons (*Jean Jacques Pallard, Geneva 1753*)

Large diamond in boxlike setting
Inv. no. VIII 8.1–10, VIII 9.1–10, VIII 10–VIII 18

Provenance: *First mentioned in the Jewel Garniture Inventory 1750.*

Even before Augustus the Strong was crowned king of Poland in 1697, he owned a jewel set with rose cut diamonds, a type of cut known since the 14th century. Stones cut in this way appear particularly large, yet they do not sparkle as much as diamonds cut in other ways. The first rose diamond set which can be traced back to Augustus consists of the badge and the star of the Polish White Eagle Order, small sword and scabbard, hat brim with bands and buckles, shoe and knee buckles, coat and waistcoat buttons, as well as buttonhole mounts, two shirt buttons, a pair of spurs, a

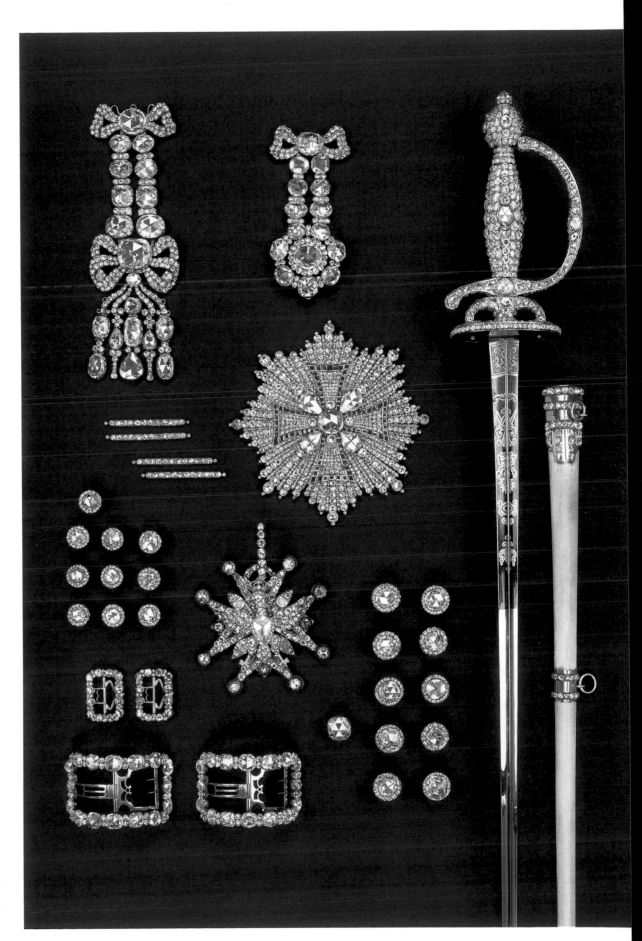

cane, and a snuff box. The stock of rose cut diamonds was continually altered, reset, and transformed into new pieces of jewelry according to the changing tastes of the later owners. Augustus III improved the inventory by replacing stones of inferior quality with superior ones. As a consequence, today's rose diamond set is smaller in quantity but of much higher quality than the one from the early 18th century. The epaulette is embellished with the heaviest of all the diamonds in the set: it weighs 31.518 ct. Almost all rose cut diamonds remaining today can be traced back to the set of Augustus the Strong.

Lit.: *Arnold 2001, pp. 174–191. —Tillander 1991, p. 210.— Exh.-cat. Essen 1986, p. 408.*

DS

FRANZ MICHAEL DIESPACH *(since 1763 in Dresden)*

Agraffe from the Brilliant Cut Diamond Set, contains "Dresden's Green Brilliant Cut Diamond"

DRESDEN AND PRAGUE, 1769 GREEN DIAMOND (41 CT), BRILLIANT CUT DIAMONDS, GOLD, SILVER
H. 5 1/2 IN., W. 2 IN.
INV. NO. VIII 30

Provenance: *First mentioned as a supplement to the Jewel Garniture Inventory 1750.*

The "Dresden Green Brilliant Cut Diamond" is the most valuable diamond of the entire jewel treasure in the Green Vault which it entered in 1742. Augustus III acquired it at the Leipzig fair. Like most other famous diamonds in the world, this unique, colossal, green diamond—the only one of its type ever found—is also shrouded in mystery. No one knows how it came from India to Dresden or how much it cost. Presumably, the price was approximately 400,000 thalers, an exorbitant sum in those days. Its unique coloration is owed to the fact that the stone came into contact with natural radioactivity. Augustus III ordered his "house diamond" to be mounted into a decorative badge of the Golden Fleece. This furnished him with one of the most splendid and magnificent orders any ruler of his day owned. In 1768 his grandson, Frederick Augustus III, commissioned the Dresden court jeweler Diespach to alter it radically: the framed diamond was incorporated into an extremely valuable *agraffe*. Now the focal point of a breathtakingly beautiful mount, it was surrounded by a huge brilliant cut diamond of 6.3 ct plus 411 additional medium- and small-sized brilliant cut diamonds.

Lit.: *Arnold 2001, pp. 195–205.—Exh.-cat. Munich 1990, p. 86.—Kane et al. 1990, pp. 248–266.*

DS

Unidentified Dresden sculptor (workshop of Permoser) and JOHANN HEINRICH KÖHLER *(1669–1736)*

Moor with Step Made of Domestic Precious Stones

DRESDEN, 1724
VARNISHED WOOD, STEP MADE OF SILVER ORE AND ADORNED WITH SAXON PRECIOUS STONES (CARNELIAN, AMETHYST, TOPAZ), GILT COPPER, BRASS, VARIOUS COLORED STONES (SOME FOILED)
H. 26 3/8 IN.
INV. NO. V 156

Provenance: *First mentioned in the Green Vault's Inventory of Precious Objects 1725.*

In his bill concerning the new design for the diamond garniture of Augustus the Strong, the Dresden court jeweler Köhler also mentions the delivery of a "Moor". The document is firmly dated to July 4, 1724, and specifies the related body ornaments and the feather crown. Köhler was also responsible for assembling the step, which was intended to demonstrate, at the highest level imaginable, the splendor and abundance of precious Saxon stones. It remains uncertain who carved the somewhat stiff figure. A likely place of origin appears to be Permoser's workshop. The statuette is roughly contemporary with the "Moor on an Emerald Step" (cat. no. 4.38) and was intended as its less elaborate pendant. The decoration of both figures is obviously inspired by a series of engravings by Theodore de Bry. Intended as illustrations for an account of French adventurers' attempts to settle in Florida (1564), the engravings were incorporated into de Bry's *Historia Americae* (1591).

Lit.: *Watzdorf 1962, pp. 209f.
—Nickel 1981.—Exh.-cat.
Dresden 2000a, pp. 248f.*
(cat. no. 146).

JK

Cat. no. 4.38

Sculpture:
BALTHASAR PERMOSER
(1651–1732),
jewel work:
JOHANN MELCHIOR
DINGLINGER *(1664–1731),*
varnish work:
MARTIN SCHNELL
(1675–before 1740),
tortoiseshell work:
WILHELM KRÜGER
(1680–1756)

**Moor on an
Emerald Step**

DRESDEN, 1724
SCULPTURE: VARNISHED PEAR
WOOD; EMERALD STEP: BROWN

IRON WITH EMERALDS, GILT
SILVER, EMERALDS, RUBIES,
SAPPHIRES, TOPAZES, GARNETS,
ALMADIN, VENEER OF TORTOISE-
SHELL FOR THE BOWL, PLINTH,
AND TREE TRUNK
H. FIGURE 25 1/8 IN.,
L. EMERALD STEP 9 3/4 IN.
INV. NO. VIII 303

Provenance: *First mentioned
in the Green Vault's Inventory of
Precious Objects 1725.*

In 1581 Prince Elector
Augustus received the gift
of a sumptuous emerald
step from Emperor Rudolph II
in Prague. It appears that the
emeralds were quarried in the
mine of Chivor-Somondoco
(Columbia). Augustus had
decreed that the stones were to
be kept forever in the possession of the electoral house.
Augustus the Strong remained
faithful to his ancestor's edict.

He commissioned a statue
to be made to complement the
step. The adornment of the
step was modified, however:
Jewelers mounted the initial
16 emeralds into a limonite
compound. The statue
was intended as the culmination point of the Green Vault's
Jewel Room where it was
exhibited by 1729 beside a
more modest pendant figure
(cat. no. 4.37). The Dresden
court sculptor Permoser created the imposing pear wood
figure with its radiant appearance. Its dark brown skin color
was produced by the Dresden
court varnisher Schnell. Thinly
applied varnish lends the skin
a subtle gleam through which
tattoos executed in dotted lines
may be seen. The tortoiseshell
applications for base, tree
trunk, and bowl, on which the
step rests, are attributed to
Krüger, a renowned amber and

ivory artist who was also active
in Dresden. The "Moor" may
be clearly identified as an
authentically dressed aborigi-
nal Floridian. The elaborate
outfit is not to be confounded
with inhabitants of the African
continent. The costumes of
the dark-skinned young male,
executed in the workshop of
the Dresden court jeweler
Dinglinger, are based on
engravings (see cat. no. 4.37).

Lit.: *Sponsel/Haenel 1932,
p. 132.—Nickel 1981.—Syndram
1999, pp. 32, 149.*

JK

The Royal Porcelain Collection

Ulrich Pietsch

The name of Prince Elector Frederick Augustus I and King Augustus II (1670–1733) is quite correctly associated with the first European hardpaste porcelain: this ruler's initiative enabled Johann Friedrich Böttger (1685–1719) to invent the luxury item in 1709. This event led to the founding of the first European porcelain manufactory in Dresden, initially in January of the year 1710. A few months later, the operations were moved to Meissen's Albrechtsburg in order to better protect the secret of the recipe from treason. The monopoly of production brought revenue to the state, and the king hoped that he could secure independence from Asian porcelain imports.

Less well known is the fact that the Saxon prince elector appears to have started collecting porcelain—which he was able to admire in the cabinets of numerous European princes while on his Grand Tour and on other travels—from China and Japan even before his coronation as Polish king, in 1697. Frederick Augustus I's father, Prince Elector Johann Georg IV (1668–1694), was also an avid admirer of these exotic, colorful works of art who had already begun his own porcelain collection. As a consequence, the scientist Ehrenfried Walther von Tschirnhaus (1651–1708) was led to speak of the Chinese as "Saxony's porcelain bloodsuckers" (*porzellanene Schröpfköpfe*) in reference to the astronomical costs entailed by the prince elector's collecting habit. Tschirnhaus attempted, albeit in vain, to limit the immense expenditures by reinventing hardpaste porcelain.[1]

"Dragoon Vase", China, Jingdezehn, Kangxi Period (1662–1722), porcelain, decorated in underglaze-blue, H. 40 1/2 in., Porcelain Collection

East Asian porcelain was indeed an expensive hobby, since the Chinese and the Japanese sold their "white gold" exclusively to Portuguese and Spanish sailors who imported it into Europe. Ultimately, the cunning traders of the United East India Company (V. O. C.), in the Netherlands, amassed a phenomenal fortune with their porcelain trade. The fascination with China, the dream of the Far East—as expressed in garden design, palace decoration, and finally the architecture of castles—was all brought to the attention of Augustus the Strong and stimulated his particularly strong passion as an art collector, especially of East Asian porcelain. It appears that he was one of the best customers of the V. O. C.: He commissioned his agent, Count Peter Robert von Lagnasco (1659–1732), to purchase whole series and entire sets of East Asian porcelain on his behalf and to ship it to Dresden.

Apart from his purchases, the Polish king also received any number of state gifts which added significantly to his collection. One of the legendary acquisitions was the spectacular trade between the "soldier king," Frederick William I of Prussia (1688–1740), and Augustus II. In the spring of 1717, 600 Saxon cavalrymen were presented to Prussia as a gift. In return, a total of 151 blue Chinese porcelain vessels—among them 18 monumental vases of the Kangxi period (1662–1722) and originating from the rich collections of the castles in Oranienburg and Charlottenburg near Berlin—were shipped to Dresden. The Saxon soldiers formed a so-called dragoon regiment which led to the monumental vases being referred to as "Dragoon Vases."

Unlike other princes, who furnished more or less elaborate porcelain cabinets, Augustus the Strong dedicated an entire castle, the Japanese Palace (*Japanisches Palais*), to appropriately exhibit his porcelain treasures. The palace began its existence as the Dutch Palace (*Holländisches Palais*), which the king had purchased in

Wall Arrangements

1. View into the Porcelain Collection's *Bogengalerie* in the *Zwinger*

The large central field is filled with a wall arrangement of Japanese Imari porcelain, while other arches contain Chinese blue-and-white porcelain of the Kangxi period (1662–1722).

2. Wall Arrangement in the Porcelain Collection's *Bogengalerie* in the *Zwinger*

The arched field contains Chinese blue-and-white porcelain of the Kangxi period, among them various centerpieces (*Aufsätze*) in different sizes.

3. Wall Arrangement in the Porcelain Collection's *Bogengalerie* in the *Zwinger*

The arrangement consists of Chinese porcelain of the Kangxi period painted in the palette of the *famille verte*.

Chinese and Japanese porcelain not only populates the vitrines of the *Bogengalerie* in the Dresden Porcelain Collection, it is also arranged on wall fields below the arches. This type of presentation goes back to the original furnishings of the Japanese Palace as a porcelain palace. Contemporary plans and descriptions help imagine the rooms' splendor which were also equipped with lacquer furniture, textile wall coverings, and soapstone carvings. For each space a specific color was reserved dominating the atmosphere. The porcelain—frequently arranged over fireplaces—was symmetrically organized on golden consoles adorned with red or black lacquer. During the new installation of the *Bogengalerie*, reopened in October 2002, the individual porcelain objects were mounted on consoles and arranged symmetrically and according to Baroque taste into the respective arched wall niches. Similar arrangements will be used for the exhibition in Jackson, Mississippi.

Illustration 1 shows the large arch, richly equipped with Japanese porcelain, opulently embellished in the Imari style with underglaze-blue, iron-red, and gold. The Dresden Collection is one of the most comprehensive and most important holdings of such porcelain in the world. Their preciously painted surfaces corresponded ideally to the Baroque's requirements for ostentatious representations. Particularly impressive is the gigantic *Aufsatz* that makes up the foundation and that consists of a five-piece garniture including covered jars and slender, beakerlike vases. Such garnitures served exclusively decorative purposes. The same is true of the huge bowls whose use was restricted to the demonstration of wealth and power.

Illustration 2 offers a view into the arched field with Chinese blue-and-white porcelain. The large *Aufsatz* with covered jars and vases, each of which measures well over three feet in height, and all of which belong to the famous "Dragoon Vases", will be exhibited in Jackson. Apart from the technical accomplishment of fabricating such monumental vessels, the brilliant and radiant cobalt-blue of the painting—originating from the period of Emperor Kangxi—is extraordinary.

The porcelain that may be seen in illustration 3 belongs to a Chinese style of porcelain decoration entitled *famille verte*, which is dominated by a palette of bright and transparent green tones applied in overglaze. The technique also originated during the Kangxi period. It appears that Augustus the Strong was particularly fond of this technique since the Dresden Collection contains numerous examples of *famille verte* porcelain of the highest quality. In the *Bogengalerie* arrangement, large vessels are presented above the fireplace; in it, a covered jar may be seen, as customary during the summer in Baroque times when the fireplace was not being used. Water dispensers are mounted on each side of the fireplace.

ES

CAT. NOS. 5.1A AND 5.1B

Double-Walled Teapot, Cup, and Saucer

CHINA, QING DYNASTY
(1644–1911), 1700–20
PORCELAIN, DECORATED IN
UNDERGLAZE-BLUE
TEAPOT: H. 6¹/₈ IN.;
CUP: H. 2 IN.
MARK (CUP AND SAUCER): FU
(HAPPINESS) IN RUNNING SCRIPT
INV. NO. P. O. 2667, P. O. 7353
(INVENTORY 1721: N=649 VVV)

What makes these pieces superb examples of craftsmanship is the openwork outer wall, as this type of ornamentation requires a high degree of patience and skill. In China it was called *linglong*, "devil's work." Like the outer wall the inner wall is decorated in underglaze-blue with flowers, which is only possible if both parts were made separately. The small cup is decorated with the same technique of openwork in a coin pattern, the symbol for wealth, and the shape of a chrysanthemum flower, the symbol of beauty. Cup and saucer are painted in cobalt-blue with flowers. The mark on the base of cup and saucer in the form of the Chinese character for happiness adds to the expression of preciousness and good luck this tea set represents.

ES

Three Mounted Pots and Five Cups and Saucers

China, Qing dynasty (1644–1911), 1700–20, mounts probably Dutch, 1700–20
Porcelain, decorated in underglaze-blue, the pots mounted
From left:
Mounted teapot, decorated with ladies in a garden and potted plants; Dutch gilt-metal mount, leaf-shapes, on top of the lid a little squirrel, on the spout a chicken
H. 3³/₄ in.
P. O. 2690 (Inventory 1721: N=167 vvv)
Mounted ewer, decorated with precious objects, the "Hundred Antiquities" (Chin. *baigu*); Dutch gilt-metal mount
H. 5³/₄ in.
P. O. 2643 (N=15 vvv)
Mounted teapot, decorated with precious objects, the "Hundred Antiquities;" Dutch gilt-metal mount, leaf-shapes, on the handle two birds, on the spout a little hare
H. 4³/₄ in.
P. O. 2688 (N=165 vvv)
Cup and saucer, decorated with flowering sprigs
H. cup 1³/₈ in.
P. O. 7417 (N=718 vvv)
Cup and saucer, decorated with landscapes and aquatic animals, in the center of the saucer with a crab
H. cup 1⁵/₈ in.
P. O. 7343 (N=629 vvv)
Cup and saucer, quatrefoil, decorated with ladies in a garden and flowers
H. cup 1³/₈ in.
P. O. 1712, P. O. 7451 (N=450 vvv)
Cup and saucer, decorated with fighting soldiers
H. cup 1⁵/₈ in.
P. O. 7432 (N=270 vvv)

Cup and saucer, decorated with landscapes, a gentleman sitting at the shore
H. cup 1¹/₈ in.
P. O. 7492 a/b (N=719 vvv)

The new popularity of hot drinks—tea, coffee, and chocolate—in the 17ᵗʰ century proved advantageous for sales of expensive Chinese porcelain. None of the previous customary drinking vessels were able to withstand the boiling hot liquid, keep it warm, and preserve the taste unchanged. By the beginning of the 18ᵗʰ century drinking tea had become a widespread habit all over Europe. As tea was still a luxury item, it was the beverage of the upper classes. Tea was served in small cups, and during a tea party several types of tea were served. In China and Japan, teacups did not have a saucer; the combination seems to have been developed for export. The exclusiveness of drinking tea shows in the elaborate silver and brass mounts of the small teapots, which were added in Holland. At the same time the mountings served a practical purpose: they prevented the lid from falling off the pot when tea was being poured.

ES

Mounted Teapot and Seven Small Cups

Japan, 1700–20
Porcelain, decorated in underglaze-blue, iron-red and gold
Teapot with Dutch gilt-metal mount, on the spout a little chicken
H. 3³/₈ in.
Inv. no. P. O. 4909
(Inventory 1721: N=17 +)
From left:
Cup, decorated with flowers and landscapes in heart-shaped reserves
H. 1³/₄ in.
Inv. no. P. O. 5363 (N=92+)
Cup, decorated with flowering prunus and chrysanthemum
H. 1³/₄ in.
Inv. no. P. O. 5232
Cup, decorated with reeds
H. 1⁵/₈ in.
Inv. no. P. O. 5118 (N=143 +)
Cup, decorated with prunus and chrysanthemum
H. 1¹/₂ in.
Inv. no. P. O. 5120 (N=93 +)
Cup, decorated with vases and flowers
H. 1³/₄ in.
Inv. no. P. O. 5049 (N=108 +)
Cup, decorated with flowers
H. 1⁵/₈ in.
Inv. no. P. O. 3826 (N=38 +)
Cup, decorated with landscapes and fishermen on a river
H. 1⁷/₈ in.
Inv. no. P. O. 5068 (N=139 +)

Porcelain painted in Imari style was the most fashionable exotic porcelain available, be it large garnitures or tiny teapots and cups. Imari teaware, like the choice presented here, was painted in a wide variety of charming decorations of flowers, animals, and figures.

ES

as a student of the sculptor Balthasar Permoser (1651–1732).

Lit.: *Asche 1970, pp. 82f.— Menzhausen 1982a, p. 302.— Menzhausen 1982b, pp. 86f.*

AL

CAT. NOS. 5.23A TO 5.23F

Teapot
MEISSEN, CA. 1710/15
FINE STONEWARE, SO-CALLED
BÖTTGER STONEWARE
H. 4 IN.
INV. NOS. P. E. 2441A, B
(INVENTORY 1721: N 55.R)

Sugar Box
MEISSEN, CA. 1710/15
FINE STONEWARE, SO-CALLED
BÖTTGER STONEWARE
H. $2^5/8$ IN., W. AT BOTTOM
$4^1/2$ x $3^1/2$ IN.

INV. NO. P. E. 1717
(INVENTORY 1779: 150.R.)

Tea Bowl
MEISSEN, CA. 1710/15
FINE STONEWARE, SO-CALLED
BÖTTGER STONEWARE
H. $1^3/4$ IN.
INV. NO. P. E. 1755
(OLD INVENTORY: N.15 (?) R)

Saucer
MEISSEN, CA. 1710/15
FINE STONEWARE, SO-CALLED
BÖTTGER STONEWARE
DIAM. $5^5/8$ IN.
INV. NO. P. E. 1739
(INVENTORY 1721: N.75.R.)

Tea Bowl
MEISSEN, CA. 1710/15
FINE STONEWARE, SO-CALLED
BÖTTGER STONEWARE
H. $1^3/4$ IN.
INV. NO. P. E. 1756
(OLD INVENTORY: N 15)

In an account about the Meissen Porcelain Manufactory written by Johann Melchior Steinbrück (1673–1723), inspector of the manufactory and Böttger's brother-in-law, mention is made of producing a chess game that Böttger had promised the king in 1713. Today, two of the figures illustrated here may be found in the Dresden Porcelain Collection as well as another one in Roman dress, made of white porcelain. Presumably, these are the only two designs ever made. With its skillful modeling and its rendering in Böttger stoneware, the figure appears very lively and could also have been conceived as a model for a large monument. It probably predates the white porcelain figure of Augustus the Strong and must be counted among the first creations in Böttger stoneware. The design was likely supplied by Kretschmar, who was active in Dresden prior to 1712, when he worked

Saucer

MEISSEN, CA. 1710/15
FINE STONEWARE, SO-CALLED
BÖTTGER STONEWARE
DIAM. 5³/₈ IN.
INV. NO. P. E. 2632
(INVENTORY 1721: N.75.R.)

The hot beverages tea, coffee, and chocolate conquered the European continent at approximately the same time Meissen porcelain was invented. The new material was an ideal match for modern drinking habits: neutral in taste, it was an inferior heat conductor.

The almost spherical teapot is artfully adorned with freely modeled, three-dimensional flowering branches floating over the polished surface. The thin-walled tea bowls and their saucer are distinguished by their extraordinary simplicity of shape and the renunciation of decoration, and they are characterized by their highly polished, meticulous surfaces. The octagonal sugar box reveals clearly that its model may have been a silver object. Different decoration techniques were applied for the embellishment. The preshaped edges were left matte while the other areas were finely polished, and the lid's pommel received a special extra sanding.

AL

CAT. NOS. 5.24A AND 5.24B

Bottle Vase

MEISSEN, CA. 1710/15
FINE STONEWARE, SO-CALLED
BÖTTGER STONEWARE
H. 14³/₄ IN.
INV. NO. P. E. 2435A, B
(INVENTORY 1721: N.38.R)

Bottle Vase

MEISSEN, CA. 1710/15
FINE STONEWARE, SO-CALLED
BÖTTGER STONEWARE
H. 14³/₄ IN.
INV. NO. P. E. 2429

The Dresden Court Goldsmith Johann Jacob Irminger (1635–1724), was appointed designer of Böttger stoneware in 1710/12 and later also designed porcelain. These vessels bear clear similarities with contemporary works of silver- and goldsmiths. Typical characteristics of Irminger's decoration—also called "Irminger's evidence"—is a strictly horizontal organization of the vessels marked by small rings, applied lancet-shaped leaves, or acanthus stalks. The foliage was pressed into molds and then "garnished" onto the porcelain. In most cases, a central spot on the vessel was left blank, or it was reserved for a decoration of a different type. This is where mascerons, female heads mostly sculpted in relief, or small relief flowers found their place. The play of the light is particularly attractive on the object's highly polished curves and the relief surfaces which are left matte.

AL

CAT. NO. 5.25

Pastry Tureen

MEISSEN, CA. 1710/15
FINE STONEWARE, SO-CALLED
BÖTTGER STONEWARE
H. 6³/₄ IN., DIAM. 8⁵/₈ IN.
INV. NO. P. E. 2339A, B
(REMAINS OF THE OLD INVENTORY NUMBER)

The simple, cylindrical shape of this tureen is ennobled through relief applications of acanthus leaves. Laterally mounted lion heads and the lid's delicately shaped pommel are reminders of the container's original function, although this object certainly never served as a pastry tureen: like almost all early stoneware, its function was exclusively of symbolic nature within the royal court.

AL

Böttger Porcelain

CAT. NOS. 5.26A TO 5.26C

Covered Vase

MEISSEN, CA. 1710/15
PORCELAIN
H. 14¹/₂ IN.
INV. NO. P. E. 2717A, B

Covered Bowl

MEISSEN, CA. 1710/15
PORCELAIN
H. 4¹/₂ IN.
INV. NO. P. E. 1825

Covered Beaker

MEISSEN, CA. 1710/15
PORCELAIN
H. 8⁵/₈ IN.
INV. NO. P. E. 2729A (CORPUS),
P. E. 907 (LID)

These vessels were also manufactured under the artistic supervision of Court Goldsmith Johann Jacob Irminger. The parallels in their design with similar objects made of Böttger stoneware is obvious. The freely applied, almost naturalistic vine scrolls populating the beaker's surface are particularly successful. Even in such minute details as the laterally attached mascerons, the excellence of the Meissen sculptors' accomplishments, derived from 18th century Saxon sculpture, is revealed. Some blemishes including firing cracks in the vessels document the extreme challenge the firing process posed, especially regarding larger pieces.

AL

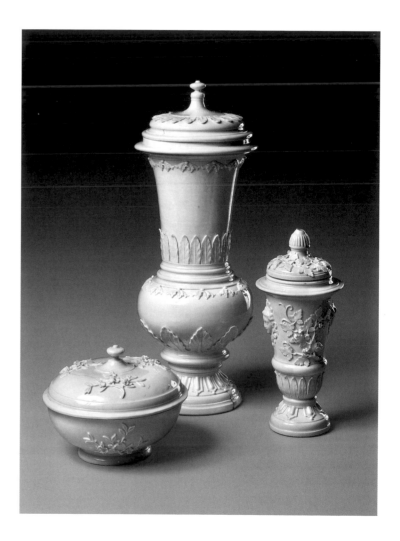

CAT. NOS. 5.30A TO 5.30C

Bowl

MEISSEN, CA. 1740
PORCELAIN
DIAM. 13 3/8 IN.
MANUFACTORY MARK: UNDER-
GLAZE-BLUE, CROSSED SWORDS
OFF CENTER NEAR EDGE; O OR
CIRCLE BETWEEN THE BLADES;
MOLD NUMBER: 22 AND 3
INV. NO. P. E. 2271

Provenance: *Purchased in
1890 with the Collection Carl
Spitzner, Dresden.*

Jug (Helmkanne)

MEISSEN, CA. 1710/15
PORCELAIN
H. 7 5/8 IN.
INV. NO. P. E. 2286

Small Pot

MEISSEN, CA. 1750/60
PORCELAIN
H. 6 IN.
MANUFACTORY MARK: UNDER-
GLAZE-BLUE, CROSSED SWORDS
WITH LINEAR POMMELS BELOW
AND NUMBER 8; CROSSED,
UNDERGLAZE-BLUE SWORDS
UNDER HANDLE, WITH LETTER B
INV. NO. P. E. 5598A, B

Provenance: *Purchased in
1890 with the Collection Carl
Spitzner, Dresden.*

Among the Indian pat-
terns, the onion pattern
is presumably the most
popular blue-on-white motif
on porcelain: it has come to
be almost synonymous with
Meissen porcelain. This
motif was inspired by Chinese
models of the Kangxi period
(1662–1722) and Japanese
porcelain from the Kakiemon
workshop in Arita. It appears
that in Meissen this decoration
was contemplated by 1728/30.
Such services were referred to
as "ordinarily painted in blue
and white," an indication for
an everyday kind of popular
and widespread blue painting.

The term "onion pattern"
(*Zwiebelmuster*) did not become
customary until the mid-19th
century and is the result of a
misunderstanding. The fruits
rendered on the plate rim—
pomegranate, peach, melon,
or pumpkin—were virtually all
unknown in Meissen. The
painters supposedly believed
that the fruits were actually

onions, something with which
they were familiar. Additionally, the shape of the original
fruits had been continuously
altered; through progressive
stylization, they were far removed from the prototypes.
The plants depicted in the center of the plate are collectively
called *shakiako* and may be
identified as bamboo, scrolls of
clematis, ominaeshi (*Feinslieb-
chen*), peonies, and lotus flowers. They are always seen in a
central arrangement, and they
are composed symmetrically.
The large flower is often identified as chrysanthemum or
aster. The entire composition is
surrounded by blooming stems.

In contrast to 20th and 21st
century customs, a certain liberty prevailed vis-à-vis variations of the decoration in the
18th century. By 1850 the
demand was so high that the
manufactory transferred the
pattern onto any conceivable
shape. By enriching the underglaze-blue adornment with
gold and smelt colors, it was
possible to further strengthen
the popularity of the *Zwiebelmuster*.

Lit.: *Exh.-cat. Dresden/Ham-
burg 1989, pp. 46ff., 228 (cat.
no. 179), 234 (cat. no. 193), 237
(cat. no. 202).—Miedtank 1991.*
AL

CAT. NOS. 5.31A TO 5.31C

Butter Dish

MEISSEN, CA. 1710/15
PORCELAIN
H. 2 5/8 IN., DIAM. 3 7/8 IN.
MANUFACTORY MARK: ON THE
INSIDE UNDERGLAZE-BLUE
SWORD MARK WITH WAVED QUIL-
LONS AND THE LETTER K OR L
INV. NO. P. E. 2245A, B
(INVENTORY 1779: N181W)

Tea Caddy

MEISSEN, CA. 1725/30
PORCELAIN
H. 3 7/8 IN.
MANUFACTORY MARK: UNDER-
GLAZE-BLUE, CROSSED SWORDS
INV. NO. P. E. 2249A, B
(INVENTORY 1779: N310W)

Tea Caddy

MEISSEN, CA. 1725/30
PORCELAIN
H. 4 IN.
MANUFACTORY MARK: UNDER-

GLAZE-BLUE, CROSSED SWORDS
INV. NO. P. E. 2251A, B
(INVENTORY 1779: N310W)

The underglaze-blue decoration is also based on East Asian motifs as its models. Indian flowers and descending birds are fantastic adaptations derived from Japanese Kakiemon porcelain adjusted to Meissen requirements. The term "Indian" is a far-reaching description encompassing any exotic subject matter. The painters were unaware of the symbolic meaning of the individual shapes.

Lit.: *Exh.-cat. Munich 1966, no. 527.—Bursche 1980, no. 146.—Exh.-cat. Dresden/ Hamburg 1989, pp. 157, (cat. no. 65), 162 (cat. nos. 80f.), 237 (cat. no. 202), 234 (cat. no. 193).*
AL

CAT. NOS. 5.32A AND 5.32B

Vase
MEISSEN, CA. 1710/15
PORCELAIN
H. 4⁵/₈ IN.
MANUFACTORY MARK: UNDER-
GLAZE-BLUE, CROSSED SWORDS
WITH LETTER K OR SMALL CROSS
INV. NO. P. E. 2259

Vase
MEISSEN, CA. 1740–45
PORCELAIN
H. 6³/₄ IN.
MANUFACTORY MARK: UNDER-
GLAZE-BLUE, CROSSED SWORDS
WITH DOT POMMELS AND
LETTER K; MOLD NUMBER: 20
INV. NO. P. E. 2258

Provenance: *Both purchased in 1890 with the Collection Carl Spitzner, Dresden.*

Both vessels are painted with peonies and lotus plants. The enormously detailed painting and the finely differentiated blue tonalities in this underglaze-blue decoration are remarkable. Since the blue glazed tended to run, there are frequent opacities and fuzzily contoured areas because clarity was difficult to attain. During the early period of Meissen's blue painting, the lack of crispness in the lines was considered a deficiency. It was not until later that the painterly quality of this blending of soft color tones was appreciated as a desirable aesthetic.

Lit.: *Exh.-cat. Dresden/Hamburg 1989, p. 213 (cat. no. 128).*
AL

CAT. NOS. 5.33A TO 5.33C

Tea Bowl and Saucer
MEISSEN, CA. 1735
PORCELAIN
TEA BOWL: H. 1⁵/₈ IN.;
SAUCER: DIAM. 4¹/₈ IN.

MANUFACTORY MARK: UNDER-
GLAZE-BLUE, CROSSED SWORDS
IN THE DOUBLE RING
INV. NO. P. E. 5638A, B

Provenance: *Purchased in 1890 with the Collection Carl Spitzner, Dresden.*

Beaker
MEISSEN, AFTER 1730(?)
PORCELAIN
H. 2⁵/₈ IN.
MANUFACTORY MARK: PSEUDO-
CHINESE CHARACTER
INV. NO. P. E. 5640

Beaker
MEISSEN, AFTER 1731(?)
PORCELAIN
H. 2¹/₂ IN.
MANUFACTORY MARK: PSEUDO-
CHINESE CHARACTER
INV. NO. P. E. 5641

The Ottomans cherished porcelain as desirous collectors' items and for their daily use. For their coffee ceremonies, they required vast quantities of small cups without handles, the so-called tea bowls (*Koppchen*), which until the invention of European hardpaste porcelain were obtained predominantly from China. However, opportunities now arose for the acquisition of inexpensive tea bowls and beakers from the manufactories in Vienna, Nymphenburg, and Ansbach, as well as the numerous manufactories in Thuringia, and naturally in Meissen. The Meissen manufactory received its first commission for over 24,000 tea bowls in 1732 and agreed to produce 43,200 pieces annually. The patrons desired quite specific, mostly underglaze-blue, pieces with chinoiserie decoration. They stipulated that the Meissen manufactory mark, the crossed swords, was not to be painted onto the vessels' bases. In order to lend a particularly Chinese air to the tea bowls, the manufactory employed a pseudo-Chinese manufactory mark under which the swords were sometimes hidden.

Lit.: *Exh.-cat. Dresden/ Hamburg 1989, pp. 170f. (cat. nos. 99f.), 214 (cat. no. 129).—Zimmermann 1911, p. 80 (ill. 3).—Just 1971.*
AL

CAT. NO. 5.34

Covered Box
MEISSEN, CA. 1730–35
PORCELAIN
H. 3¹/₈ IN., DIAM. 4¹/₂ × 3⁷/₈ IN.
MANUFACTORY MARK: UNDER-
GLAZE-BLUE, CROSSED SWORDS
INV. NO. P. E. 2244A, B

Lit.: *Bursche 1980, no. 130.— Exh.-cat. Dresden/Hamburg 1989, p. 157 (cat. no. 66).*
AL

Meissen Vases

It is likely that this ensemble was intended as a present to Louis Dauphin of France who later married Maria Josepha, daughter of the Saxon prince elector and Polish king. Four of the containers personify allegories of the elements, but the fifth one is the centerpiece. With its rendering of Flora distributing flowers from her basket, this vase symbolized the flowering of the French kingdom, whose glory is announced by the goddess Fame. The sun, with the head of Apollo above the relief portrait of the monarch, alludes to the realm of the Sun King Louis XIV. Below this, the Bourbon and the Navarre coats of arms may be spotted in cartouche frames. On the lid with its plastically modeled crown, two putti present a shield with the royal monogram. Apparently, Augustus III was so enthusiastic about this splendid creation that he ordered a second set to be fabricated for himself. The elements alluding to the French king were replaced by Augustus's portrait and his personal insignia, and the pieces were decorated all over with sculptural renderings of viburnum petals.

The style and spirit of the vessels referring to the elements are identical to that of the centerpiece. Earth is made identifiable for the spectator thanks to the depiction of a hunt, and the figure of the goddess of the hunt, Diana, crowns the lid. In contrast, Fire is depicted by the figure of Zeus seated on top of a mighty eagle from whence he throws bolts of lightning, as well as the relief of calvarymen firing canons seen on the body of the vase. The handles are made up of laterally mounted war trophies and the figure of the god of war, Mars, while a chained Turkish prisoner is captured at the bottom.

The elements Air and Water are represented through allegorical and mythological attachments on vase-like handled-jugs. Air—symbolized by a wind-filled piece of drapery—forms the handle, on the upper end of which two putti float through the air and play a bagpipe. Below this scene lies the winged Zephyr, god of the west wind. Resting on his stomach, he blows flowers into the air. Enthroned on a cloud above him is Juno, goddess of the air. The foot of the piece is embellished with feathers and surrounded by three little winged putti heads. With their puffed cheeks, they symbolize the other winds. The depiction of Water follows according to a similar scheme: The jug's spout mouth and its foot are decorated with shell reliefs and three dolphins. The handle is composed of a bundle of reeds; on its top, the child of a Triton is juxtaposed with the fish-tailed figure of a Nereid. On the vessel's shoulder, Neptune sits in a shell bowl drawn by little seahorses, whose relief—delineating a sail boat rocking on the waves—protrudes slightly from the vessel's body.

All containers have one presentation side; the back remains entirely blank. The shared characteristics of the ensemble lie primarily in the pathos-filled artistic language which is powerfully combined with a dynamic Baroque movement. The amorphous design of the vessels and their rich, sculptural decorative elements anticipate the dissolution of form typical of Rococo.

Lit.: *Berling 1900, p. 91.— Zimmermann 1926, pp. 172ff.— Albiker 1935, pp. 96f.—Gröger 1956.—Walcha 1973, p. 120.*

UP

CAT. NO. 5.35

Model by JOHANN JOACHIM KAENDLER (1706–1775)

Portrait Vase
MEISSEN, CA. 1740
PORCELAIN
H. (WITH LID) 34¼ IN.,
DIAM. 24⅜ IN.
INV. NO. P. E. 107

CAT. NOS. 5.36A TO 5.36D

JOHANN JOACHIM KAENDLER (1706–1775) and JOHANN GOTTFRIED EBERLEIN

Set of Parade Vessels
MEISSEN, 1740–42
PORCELAIN

Element Vase: Fire
H. 26¾ IN., DIAM. 15¾ IN.
INV. NO. P. E. 104

Element Vase: Water
BASE: 19. CENTURY.
H. 25¼ IN., DIAM. 15 IN.
INV. NO. P. E. 101

Element Vase: Air
H. 23⅝ IN., DIAM. 15 IN.
INV. NO. P. E. 7789s

Element Vase: Earth
H. 24⅜ IN., DIAM. 15¾ IN.
INV. NO. P. E. 3735

CAT. NO. 5.37

JOHANN JOACHIM
KAENDLER *(1706–1775)*

**Vase embellished with
Guelder Rose Petals
(so-called *Schneeball-
blütenvase*)**

MEISSEN, CA. 1750
PORCELAIN
H. 14 IN.
MANUFACTORY MARK: CROSSED
SWORDS IN UNDERGLAZE-BLUE
INV. NO. P. E. 420

Provenance: *Former Royal
Collection*

The artistic repertoire of 18th-century porcelain vessels from Meissen often reflects the Baroque preference for the inclusion of natural shapes. The resulting forms are not always the product of the designers' fantasy; rather, they frequently originate from Chinese prototypes kept in the porcelain collection founded by August the Strong. One such example was exe-

cuted by Kaendler around 1739: He embellished the surface of a coffee pot for Queen Maria Josepha, wife of King August III, with three-dimensional guelder rose petals comparable to the ones on a three-part vase of the Yongzheng period (1723–35) from Jingdezhen which he had apparently studied in the royal collection. This type of ornamentation became so popular that Kaendler eventually began to decorate vases with it, placing a bullfinch and a kingfisher between the petals which served to further enliven the surface. The first large size vases with guelder rose petal decoration were produced in 1742 for Louis XV of France.

*Lit.: Walcha 1973, ill. 100. –
Pietsch 1996, p. 50.*

UP

Cat. no. 5.38

Model by JOHANN
JOACHIM KAENDLER
(1706–1775)

**Equestrian Statue for
King Augustus III**

Meissen, 1753, later pull
19th century
Porcelain
H. (without pedestal)
21 1/8 in.
Inv. no. P. E.649

In 1751 Kaendler received a commission for a larger than life equestrian statue. After Kaendler had shaped the king's head in porcelain, his work was interrupted by the Seven Years War (1756–63) and was not resumed until after the end of the war as Augustus III died. In order to give his patron an idea of the planned statue Kaendler first created the porcelain model on a much smaller scale. The king holds the reins in his left hand and in his right hand a field marshall's staff. As a powerful ruler clad in the armor of a Roman emperor he rides roughshod over the figure below symbolizing Envy. The reliefs on the pedestal symbolize Saxony and Poland, while the river gods at the front are personifications of the Elbe and the Vistula. The rocks surrounding the pedestal are peopled with an abundance of figures which represent the virtues of the monarch in allegorical form. Fama writes the dedicatory inscription in a cartouche held by the crowned heraldic eagle of Poland. This later pull conveys an impression of the most daring of all porcelain projects ever envisioned in Meissen.

UP

Table Services
from Meissen

Ulrich Pietsch

With the creation of the Swan Service (*Schwanen-service*)—commissioned by Count Heinrich von Brühl (1700–1763) and comprised of more than 3,000 individual pieces—the evolution of Meissen table services reached its artistic zenith. Never before had a comparable service been created; this is true regarding its size and its overabundance of rich sculptural decoration. It is inconceivable that a table service could be created which would more perfectly coincide with the social, material, and artistic prerequisites of the time.

As Augustus III's cabinet minister, Count Brühl practically ruled the country since the king's interests leaned more towards the muses than towards politics. Brühl therefore needed a representative table service for receptions of foreign diplomats but also for the diverse festivities related to the court. As director of the Meissen Porcelain Manufactory, he was entitled to order as much porcelain as he felt he needed—free of charge. The only restriction was that his orders were not to impede the king's commissions.

The Swan Service was conceived by Johann Joachim Kaendler (1706–1775). Its themes are derived from elements related to acquatic flora and the fauna as well as from ancient mythological figures. The latter constitute the figural decoration, appearing as goddesses such as Venus, sea nymphs like Galatea, or as Nereids and Tritons. The vessel walls are designed like shells and embellished with swan and heron reliefs. The service is the chef d'oeuvre of Kaendler, who, for the longest time, clung to the pathos-laden, dynamic elements of the Baroque style. It epitomizes the perfection of all plastic expression imaginable in porcelain.

This development was preceded by the urge of Augustus the Strong for a table service. His service design was based on and accorded with the shapes and the decorative patterns of courtly table silver. Starting in 1730, the king ordered the first table services from his manufactory in Meissen. The earliest one expressly created for the Dresden court is the one with the "Yellow Lion," the beginnings of which date back to 1728. For their design, the Meissen painters used diverse elements derived from Japanese Kakiemon painting that they were able to study in the royal collection. Their chosen motifs—among them the lion and bamboo, around the trunk of which the feline is winding itself—personified elements pertaining to power and strength.

The service with yellow background and Indian flowers and birds in the reserves is roughly contemporary with the previously mentioned service. Like its predecessor, the painting follows Japanese prototypes, while the yellow background is an independent Meissen development. The principle to leave empty quatrefoil reserves for the decoration, on the other hand, is adopted from Chinese practices. Shortly afterward, the service with the red dragon followed. Its decoration was a direct copy from a Japanese model. It is evident that even then the Europeans were familiar with the East Asian ruler iconography, where the dragon is the symbol for the emperor and the phoenix that of the empress. The elongated, scaly beast and the bird of paradise are delineated twice on the plates, circling around one another. These images are embellished with symbols of happiness derived from Buddhist teachings. The "Red Dragon Service" was obviously the king's favorite: He decreed that this décor could only be applied to court porcelain; a rule respected by the Meissen Porcelain Manufactory until the revolution in 1918.

All these services were delivered directly to the Japanese Palace (*Japanisches Palais*) and not to the Royal

Court Silver Chamber (*Königliche Hofsilberkammer*) or the Court Housekeeping Chamber (*Hofwirtschaftskammer*) as the silver services were. Once in the Japanese Palace, they were intended to fulfill representative functions and to be admired by the king's visitors. Since they were brought into the "table room with the lion porcelain" (*Taffel Zimmer mit Porzellan der Loeben [Löwen]*)[1], the much more pragmatic intent was to actually use the service.

Another service was created in 1733. Included in it were monumental dishes and bowls, as well as smaller tureens. Its main decorative motif was a large coat of arms depicting the Saxon-Polish Union surrounded by Indian strewn flowers rendered in Kakiemon style. Since the table service was presented on a parade buffet during the festivities of King Augustus III's coronation, it later became known as the "Coronation Service."

The Saxon aristocracy followed the king's example. Court ministers, in particular, tried to glorify their elevated position within society even more by purchasing exquisite porcelain dishes. Count Alexander Joseph von Sulkowski's extensive table settings—ordered 1736—may have encouraged his rival, Count Brühl, to surpass him. Considering both the quantity of the individual pieces and their artistic quality, the Swan Service helped Count Brühl to achieve his goal quite easily.

Notes

1 Quoted from Sponsel 1900, p. 16.

Cat. no. 5.39: Service with the Yellow Lion

Service with the Yellow Lion

Tureen
MEISSEN
PORCELAIN, SMELT COLORS
H. 11 IN., DIAM. 9½ IN.
INV. NO. P. E 1251

Dish
MEISSEN
PORCELAIN, SMELT COLORS
H. 2¼ IN., DIAM. 13½ IN.
INV. NO. P. E. 1196

Provenance: *Royal Court
Confectionary Dresden.*

Dish
MEISSEN
PORCELAIN, SMELT COLORS
II. 1⅝ IN., DIAM. 8⅛ IN.
INV. NO. PE 1223F

Plate
MEISSEN
PORCELAIN, SMELT COLORS
H. 3½ IN., DIAM. 18⅛ IN.
INV. NO. PE 1223A

Coronation Service

Dish
MEISSEN, 1732–33
PORCELAIN
H. 3⅛ IN., DIAM. 17¾ IN.
MANUFACTORY MARK: CROSSED
SWORDS IN UNDERGLAZE-BLUE
INV. NO. P. E. 1279
(INVENTORY 1779: N.147.W.)

Provenance: *Former Royal
Collection (Japanese Palace).*

Cat. nos. 5.41A to 5.41C

Service with the Red Dragon

Dish
Meissen, ca. 1740
Porcelain, smelt colors,
gilding
H. 2¹⁄₂ in., diam. 16⁷⁄₈ in.
Inv. no. P. E. 5462

Provenance: *Former Royal
Collection.*

Dish
Meissen, ca. 1740
Porcelain, smelt colors,
gilding
H. 2³⁄₄ in., diam. 16³⁄₄ in.
Manufactory mark: crossed
swords in underglaze-blue
Inv. no. P. E. 7155

Provenance: *Royal Court
Confectionary Dresden.*

Bowl
Meissen, ca. 1740
Porcelain, smelt colors,
gilding
H. 1³⁄₄ in., diam. 11³⁄₄ in.
Inv. no. P. E. 1188f

Provenance: *Former Royal
Collection.*

CAT. NO. 5.42

Swan Service

Model by
JOHANN JOACHIM
KAENDLER (*1706–1775*)

Tureen
MEISSEN, 1738
PORCELAIN, SMELT COLORS,
GILDING
H. 19 IN.
MANUFACTORY MARK: CROSSED
SWORDS IN UNDERGLAZE-BLUE
INV. NO. P. E. 1449

Provenance: *Count Brühl,
Schloss Pförten.*

CAT. NOS. 5.43A TO 5.43C

So-called "Yellow
Hunting Service"

Tureen
MEISSEN, 1725–30
PORCELAIN, SMELT COLORS,
GILDING
H. 9¹/₂ IN., DIAM. 11³/₈ IN.
INV. NO. P. E. 1452
(INVENTORY 1779: N.148.W.)

Dish
MEISSEN, CA. 1728/30
PORCELAIN, SMELT COLORS,
GILDING
H. 2¹/₄ IN., DIAM. 12¹/₄ IN.
MANUFACTORY MARK: CROSSED
SWORDS IN UNDERGLAZE-BLUE
INV. NO. P. E. 7766
(INVENTORY 1779: N.148.W.)

Dish
MEISSEN, CA. 1735
PORCELAIN, SMELT COLORS,
GILDING
H. 2⁷/₈ IN., DIAM. 17³/₄ IN.
MANUFACTORY MARK: CROSSED
SWORDS IN UNDERGLAZE-BLUE
INV. NO. 1588
(INVENTORY 1779: N.148W)

Provenance: *All of them
Former Royal Collection
(Japanese Palace).*

Meissen
Animal Sculptures

Ulrich Pietsch

Augustus the Strong wished to have a large number of life-size animals in Meissen porcelain for the furnishing of his "porcelain castle," the Japanese Palace on the right bank of the Elbe River.

In the spring of 1731 the modeler Gottlieb Kirchner began to fashion the first examples of large-scale animal sculptures. In June Johann Joachim Kaendler, who soon became the outstanding master of European porcelain sculpture, was appointed to assist him. Working together, Kirchner (until 1733) and Kaendler created birds and mammals, sometimes after copperplate engravings but more frequently after living or stuffed models from the royal menagerie or the gallery of animals. Domesticated animals such as goats and sheep, cats, dogs, and cockerels, wild animals such as bears, wolves, foxes, and aurochs, and exotic animals such as elephants, rhinoceroses, lions, apes, casuaries, parrots, and vultures were all commissioned.

Each of the two modelers represented the animals according to his own style. Kaendler's works are distinguished by carefully observed characteristic features of the animals to capture a typical, sometimes exaggerated movement as a motif in a kind of snapshot. Kirchner mainly used engravings as models. He produced representations of animals with humanized facial expressions, which can be seen particularly clearly in the case of the pair of lions.

Never before had works of art of such monumental size been created in porcelain, which posed one of the greatest challenges to the Meissen manufactory. Initially, considerable problems arose frequently in the firing process causing distortions, firing cracks, and discoloration in the porcelain. Because of these impair-

ments they did not dare to decorate the larger pieces with enamels and expose them to the kiln a second time. The large-scale pieces were thus decorated in oils and coated with varnish which however darkened so much in the course of time that both the varnish and the paint were removed. Today, the Dresden Porcelain Collection still owns 90 large-scale animal sculptures out of several hundred originally.

Lit.: Albiker 1935.

Cat. no. 5.44

Cat. no. 5.45

Cat. no. 5.47

Cat. no. 5.46

CAT. NO. 5.44

Model by JOHANN
JOACHIM KAENDLER
(*1706–1775*)

Heron

MEISSEN, 1731
PORCELAIN
H. 31$\frac{1}{8}$ IN.
INV. NO. P. E. 684

Provenance: *Former Royal
Collection (Japanese Palace).*

CAT. NO. 5.45

Model by JOHANN
JOACHIM KAENDLER
(*1706–1775*)

Heron

MEISSEN, UNTIL DECEMBER
1731
PORCELAIN
H. 29$\frac{1}{8}$ IN.
INV. NO. P. E. 136

Provenance: *Former Royal
Collection (Japanese Palace).*

CAT. NO. 5.46

Model by JOHANN
JOACHIM KAENDLER
(*1706–1775*)

Eagle

MEISSEN, 1731
PORCELAIN
H. 35$\frac{5}{8}$ IN.
INV. NO. P. E. 143

Provenance: *Former Royal
Collection (Japanese Palace).*

CAT. NO. 5.47

Model by JOHANN
JOACHIM KAENDLER
(*1706–1775*)

Parrot

MEISSEN
PORCELAIN
H. 47$\frac{7}{8}$ IN.
INV. NO. P. E. 683
(INVENTORY 1779: N.174.W.)

Provenance: *Former Royal
Collection (Japanese Palace).*

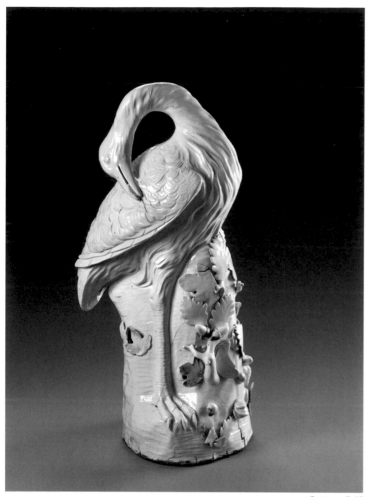

Cat. no. 5.48

Cat. no. 5.49

CAT. NO. 5.48

Model by GOTTLIEB
KIRCHNER
(1706–before 1768)

Trappe
MEISSEN
PORCELAIN
H. 32⅝ in.
INV. NO. P. E. 33

Provenance: *Former Royal
Collection (Japanese Palace).*

CAT. NO. 5.49

Model by JOHANN
JOACHIM KAENDLER
(1706–1775)

Peacock on a Trunk
MEISSEN
PORCELAIN
H 46⅝ in.
INV. NO. P. E. 53

Provenance: *Former Royal
Collection (Japanese Palace).*

Cat. no. 5.50

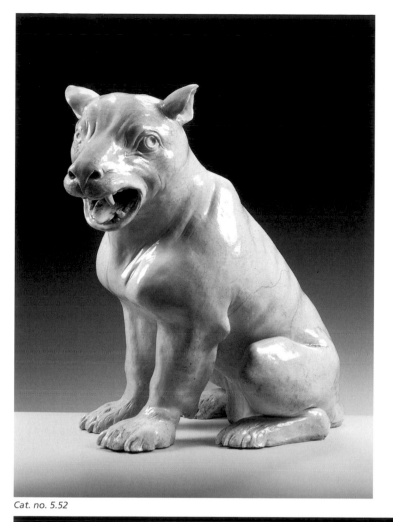

Cat. no. 5.52

Cat. no. 5.53

Cat. no. 5.51

Cat. no. 5.50

Model by GOTTLIEB KIRCHNER
(1706–before 1768)

Lion
Meissen
Porcelain
H. 20¹/₈ in.
Inv. no. P. E. 701

Provenance: *Former Royal Collection (Japanese Palace).*

Cat. no. 5.51

Model by GOTTLIEB KIRCHNER
(1706–before 1768)

Lioness
Meissen, before March 1733
Porcelain
H. 19⁵/₈ in.
Inv. no. P. E. 702

Provenance: *Former Royal Collection (Japanese Palace).*

Cat. no. 5.54

CAT. NO. 5.52

Model by GOTTLIEB
KIRCHNER
(*1706–before 1768*)

Leopard
MEISSEN, 1732–33
PORCELAIN
H. 28 IN.
INV. NO. P. E. 145

Provenance: *Former Royal
Collection (Japanese Palace).*

CAT. NO. 5.53

Model by GOTTLIEB
KIRCHNER
(*1706–before 1768*)

Lynx
MEISSEN, 1732–33
PORCELAIN
H. 24³/₈ IN.
INV. NO. P. E. 715

Provenance: *Former Royal
Collection (Japanese Palace).*

CAT. NO. 5.54

Monkey
MEISSEN
PORCELAIN
H. 9⁷/₈ IN.
INV. NO. P. E. 86

Provenance: *Former Royal
Collection (Japanese Palace).*

CAT. NO. 5.55

Model by GOTTLIEB
KIRCHNER
(*1706–before 1768*)

Chamois
MEISSEN, 1735
PORCELAIN
H. 20¹/₄ IN.
INV. NO. P. E. 691
(INVENTORY 1779: N.347.W.)

Provenance: *Former Royal
Collection (Japanese Palace).*

Cat. no. 5.55

CAT. NO. 5.56

Squirrel as a Teapot
MEISSEN, CA. 1737/38
PORCELAIN, SMELT COLORS,
GILDING
H. 5³/₈ IN.
INV. NO. P. E. 3904
(INVENTORY 1779: N.441.W.)

Provenance: *Former Royal
Collection (Japanese Palace).*

CAT. NO. 5.57

Monkey as a Teapot
MEISSEN, CA. 1735/40
PORCELAIN, SMELT COLORS
H. 7¹/₈ IN.
INV. NO. P. E. 3899

Provenance: *Purchased in
1919, Ball Company, Dresden*

CAT. NO. 5.58

Pug with a Puppy
MEISSEN, CA. 1741–45
PORCELAIN, SMELT COLORS
H. 7¹/₄ IN.
INV. NO. P. E. 3894

Provenance: *Exchange 1919,
Ball Company, Dresden.*

CAT. NO. 5.59

Pug
MEISSEN, CA. 1741–45
PORCELAIN, SMELT COLORS
H. 6⁷/₈ IN.
INV. NO. P. E. 3895

Provenance: *Exchange 1919,
Ball Company, Dresden.*

Cat. no. 5.56   Cat. no. 5.57

Cat. no. 5.58   Cat. no. 5.59

His Majesty's Might and Power

The King's State Apartments in the Dresden Residential Palace

André van der Goes

The common man, who cares but for outward appearances and is not given to reasoning, cannot really imagine what the majesty of the king means. However, by the impression of objects he can see and that touch his other senses, he beholds a clear understanding of his majesty's might and power.

(Rohr 1733, p. 2)

The year 1719 included a major event in the long reign of Augustus the Strong, when his son and successor, Frederick Augustus II, married the daughter of Emperor Charles VI of Hapsburg. Dresden became the scene of dazzling festivities and celebrations. A series of seven feasts with the planets as central theme, mythological reenactments, grandiose fireworks, balls, theatrical performances, and opera were held for nobles and commoners alike. Apart from all this public magnificence, however, the most important event was the official reception of the prince and his newly wedded wife, the Archduchess Maria Josepha of Hapsburg, by her royal parents-in-law in the Dresden Residential Palace. This marriage was important to the dynastic ambitions of Augustus. The rise from the rank of prince elector to the status of king was of enormous importance in the age of absolute monarchy, and dynastic allegiance to the Holy Roman Emperor himself indicated great expectations indeed.

The coach with the royal couple rolled through the gateway to the so-called English Stair, an immense building project begun in February 1717, that had been recently completed. The old medieval and renaissance castle in Dresden had been transformed into a splendid Baroque royal residence of truly European stature.[1]

Chair of State (1718/19) with two pilasters and a lambrequin (1709–15), see cat. nos. 6.4 f., pp. 221 f.

The second floor of the palace contained the string of galleries and chambers that made up the State Apartments. As a young man, Augustus had visited Versailles and was so impressed by the grandeur of Louis XIV's court that it influenced his own decisions during later building projects, leading his architect to tactfully inform the king that his ideas were slightly outdated. Although Augustus, like most European rulers, followed the example that had been set by the king of France, he did not adhere to French court etiquette. The courts of the princes and rulers of the Holy Roman Empire logically followed the Viennese standard for court ceremonies. Contrary to French court etiquette with its elaborate public ritual of the *lever* and *coucher* of the Sun King, the rising and retiring of the Hapsburg emperors was a more private matter. Consequently, the role of the State Bed Chamber (*Paradeschlafzimmer*) had a far less dominant position in the ceremonies and the plan of the State Apartments.[2] In Dresden the king did not sleep in the State Bed Chamber, using it for private audiences at most. When the archduchess arrived in Dresden, she was received by the king and queen on a private audience in the State Bed Chamber. Here, the royal family sat together in front of the State Bed while courtiers thronged the doorways. Two weeks later, on September 2, 1719, the official reception of the royal couple took place and they proceeded to the ultimate state room: the Audience Chamber (*Audienzgemach*) where the paraphernalia of majesty were shown.

Almost three hundred years later, the series of copper engravings that Raymond Leplat made of the official reception allow us to follow the prince elector and his wife on their way to the heart of the palace. Great halls and galleries, where the walls were decorated with mirrors and tapestries and the ceilings adorned with frescoes, led to the enfilade of state rooms where the decoration of each successive room displayed increasing splendor and magnificence. Royal guards and

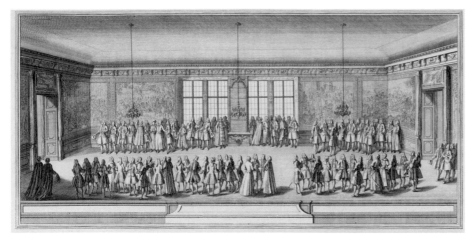

Chambre du Lit de l'Appartement de parade du Roy.
Où sa Majesté et la Reine ont reçu la première visite de la Princesse Royale après son arrivée
et entrée solemnelle, et réception dans la Ville et Château de Dresden le 13. Aoust 1719.

Top: R. Leplat, *The Stone Hall with the Landstände, on the Occasion of the Audience of the Bride,
Archduchess Maria Josepha of Hapsburg,* 1719, copperplate engraving, CDPP

Center: R. Leplat, *Offical Reception of the Archduchess by the King and the Queen in the Audience
Chamber,* 1719, copperplate engraving, CDPP

Bottom: R. Leplat, *Private Audience of the Archduchess and the Prince by the King and the Queen in
the State Bed Chamber,* 1719, copperplate engraving, CDPP

throngs of courtiers lined the couple's path: the Saxons dressed after the French fashion with men wearing large *allonge* wigs, while the Polish nobles had short hair and wore exotic long coats, with sabers dangling at their sides.

The first antechamber was decorated in chinoiserie style. The walls were hung with crimson velvet, bordered with vertical bands of silk embroidered with chinoiserie scenes. Tables, chairs and gueridons, carved in Chinese style and lacquered or japanned, lined the walls and displayed the elegant and exotic taste that was in vogue at the European courts. Large mirrors, crowned with elaborate bronze decorations made the rooms seem larger and reflected the movement of the parading court. The large double doors, "broken" doors as this novelty was called,[3] then led through the second antechamber, decorated with furnishings in the current European court style, to the Audience Chamber. In this, the most important chamber of the palace, the king and queen waited to welcome their daughter-in-law.

Here the palatial impression reached its climax in a display of Baroque splendor. The crimson velvet hangings were intersected by pilasters that had been ordered in Paris and were richly embroidered with gilt silver thread on gold brocade; a band with lambrequins ran directly under the molding.[4] The chair of state stood beneath a canopy, impressively and spectacularly carved, representing the majesty of the king. And it was here, where the light shone on the gilded ornaments of the architecture and textiles, that the regal might and power was symbolized and emphasized by the most dazzling representation of luxury in the form of gilt silver furniture. The silver tables flanked by gueridons and topped by mirrors, formed the so-called *ensembles*; near the hearth stood the huge gilt silver fire screen. Large clocks, of great importance in the absolutist order of the day, meticulously ticked the hours away, regulating the ceremonies of court life. The sequence of the galleries and chambers with their furnishings and decorations was, together with the strict court etiquette, the most perfect expression of the way in which relations between the king and his subjects were organized in this microcosm. Everyone had his part in this play and thus knew his place, at court and in society.

Augustus the Strong is the perfect example of a Baroque monarch. Able, ambitious, virile, modern, and open to new ideas that could develop the wealth of his country and support his struggle for absolutist power, he was always keen for grandeur where his authority could be manifest. His correspondence with Count August Christoph von Wackerbarth, who was responsible for the furnishing of the palace, survived and gives us the extremely rare opportunity to show the king at work, directing the decoration of the State Apartments. His prolonged stays in Poland forced him to correspond about the proceedings of the project. The letters give the appearance that Augustus was a monarch with a good eye for details, always retaining an overall view of the project; he even provided a sketch of the plan for the second floor of the palace where the State Apartments are located, considering the hangings in every room.[5] When discussing the kind of textiles that are to be used, the king referred to the common practice of changing the hangings according to the season, sometimes even four times a year: light damask or silk in spring and summer, velvet or tapestries in the cold season. It is remarkable that the king had the habit of arguing in a certain open way with his officials. He did not press his point, but discussed it later in another letter, wisely avoiding the use of his status. But he certainly had a keen eye in matters of art and discussed many different topics concerning building activities, lodgings for the guests, plans for great feasts, and so on.

Of great interest to us are the references to silver furniture. Augustus reserves the gilt silver for use in the palace and states that the white silver is to be used in the palace of the prince elector.[6] Later he remarks on the use of silver galloon in apartments where gilded ornaments are to be found at the same time. For greater uniformity, he suggests that the furniture in the rooms can be silvered; he recalls that he saw examples of this mixture in some house of the king of France.[7] There seems to have been a controversy on this topic between Augustus and his official, Count Wackerbarth. Apparently the count disapproved of the king's taste for silver furniture. Suggesting that it is more fashionable to display gilt silver, he seems to have written that white silver easily tarnishes, transforming the lustrous Audience Chamber into a place of mourning. Moreover one saves money if the silver is gilt, since white silver needs regular polishing. In this matter the king is quite stubborn. He argued against Wackerbarth's example, using the fashionable Prince Eugene (of Savoy) as an example; some years ago the prince stated that he preferred white silver since one could not tell the difference between gilt silver and gilt bronze. Saving money was no argument to Augustus: if gilt silver turned black, cleaning and regilding would cost a fortune. Last but not least, the king remarked almost indignantly, no one who had seen the apartments and galleries of Versailles with their gilt ornaments, could say in earnest that the tables, gueridons, chandeliers, tabourets, and vases, all made of white silver, looked like a *Castrum Doloris*, a splendid catafalque![8]

It is unknown who had the last word in this interesting controversy, it seems that Wackerbarth must have convinced the king somehow, since the silver furniture has been gilded. These imposing silver masterpieces, have been treasured by the successors of Augustus the Strong ever since their creation. It is a great miracle that they survived the disastrous Seven Years' War with Frederick the Great (1757–63), the French occupation under Napoleon's rule (1806–13), and finally, the devastating bombardments in 1945. In 2010 they will stand in their original place, in the reconstructed State Audience Chamber of the Dresden Residential Palace, where they will demonstrate the majesty, might, and power of the illustrious kings of Saxony.

Notes

[1] See Oelsner/Prinz 1992.
[2] See Graf 2002.
[3] See Rohr 1733, p.79.
[4] See Pisareva 2003.
[5] See SHStA Dresden, Geheimes Kabinett, letters exchanged between Augustus II and Wackerbarth, Loc. 2095, vol. 201, p.16 (October 15, 1718).
[6] See ibid., p.19 (October 22, 1718).
[7] See ibid., pp. 24–24B (November 4, 1718).
[8] See ibid., pp. 36–37B (December 10, 1718).

ALBRECHT BILLER
(1653–1720)

Pair of Tables

Augsburg, before 1719
Silver, cast, chased,
engraved, gilt; wooden
structure, iron joints
H. 31³/4 in., W. 47¹/4 in.,
D. 31³/4 in.
Table with representation
of the Four Elements
marked: a pinecone for Augs-
burg, AB for Albrecht
Biller; inscribed: No. 2
Table with representation
of the Four Seasons or the
Four Stages of Life marked:
a pinecone for Augsburg;
AB for Albrecht Biller;
inscribed: No. 1
Inv. no. 37 532, 37 533

Provenance: *1945 so-called
Schlossbergung, Dresden Residential Palace.*

Augustus the Strong
chose Albrecht Biller
from the principal
silversmiths in Augsburg to
deliver these tables. They
belonged to the sumptuous
furnishings that completed the
decoration of the Audience
Chamber in 1719. Each table
likely stood against a window
pier, with a large mirror
above and two flanking gueridons, thus forming impressive
ensembles. Their strong in-
wardly curved legs, decorated
with scrolls and female masks,
are crowned by tops worked
with great skill. Each tabletop
shows an intricate pattern,
consisting of bands, scrolling
foliage, and *mascerons*, surrounding an allegorical representation. The center of
one tabletop shows the Four
Elements, symbolized by two
putti; Neptune; Aeolus; and
Ceres or Venus, here sym-
bolizing fertility, with Mars at
her side. The second table is
decorated with four dancing

maidens, representing the Four
Seasons or the Four Stages of
Life, flanked on one side by
Chronos playing the lyre, on
the other side by a herm with
Janus. This last scene was
made after Jean Dughet's
engraving of Nicolas Poussin's
painting *Allegory on Human
Life* (1638–40).

Lit.: *Exh.-cat. Dresden 1973,
no. D1.—Exh.-cat. Munich
1994, no. 136.*

AG

JOHANNES LUDWIG I
BILLER *(1656–1732)*

Gueridon
(Candlestand)

Augsburg, before 1719
Silver, cast, chased,
engraved, gilt; fit on an
iron core
H. 49 in., diam. 15¹/8 in.
marked: a pinecone for
Augsburg, six-pointed star
over ILB for Johann
Ludwig I Biller
Inv. no. 37 464

Provenance: *1945 so-called
Schlossbergung, Dresden Residential Palace.*

Augustus the Strong
placed his orders for
the furniture that was
to show his magnitude and
wealth with craftsmen in Augsburg. In the 17th and 18th centuries, this city developed into
the most prominent center
for silver and gold production
in the Hapsburg Empire. The
Biller family belonged to the
foremost gold and silversmiths
and produced representative

silver furniture for the courts of the greatest monarchs in Central Europe. Although the 1720 and 1769 inventories of the royal palace in Dresden were not specific as to which pieces of furniture were in the various rooms, four gueridons of this type and the silver tables are mentioned in 1794 as standing in the Audience Chamber. By now rather outdated in France, the baluster-shaped support with its decoration of foliage and bands is typical of Augsburg in the first decades of the 18th century.

Lit.: *Exh.-cat. Dresden 1973, no. D3.—Exh.-cat. Munich 1994, no. 137.—Exh.-cat. Dresden 1996 c, no. 16.*

AG

Cat. no. 6.3

PETER RAHM
(ca. 1661–1737) and
JOHANN JAKOB II
PRIESTER *(1676–1762)*

Sconce

Augsburg, before 1719
Silver, chased, cast, engraved, gilt; mirror; fit on wood; the branches of inv. no. 45 085 are recent reproductions
H. 39¾ in., W. 27⅛ in., D. 15¾ in.
Marked: a pinecone for Augsburg, PR over a six-pointed star, II·P on the drip-pan
Inv. no. 46 776

Provenance: *1915 so-called Schlossbergung, Dresden Residential Palace.*

Of the six large sconces that the Augsburg silversmith Rahm apparently produced for the Audience Chamber, only two survived. Their forms, with strong, scrolling acanthus leaves forming the shape of the sconce, recall the decorative schemes shown in engravings by great advocates of the fashionable interior and the French or French-oriented court style, like Jean Le Pautre (1618–1682) and Daniel Marot (about 1663–1752). In contrast to the Billers, Rahm did not belong to an established Augsburg family or dynasty of silversmiths; he acquired a workshop by marrying his master's widow.

Lit.: *Seling 1994, nos. 1890a, 2023a.—Exh.-cat. Dresden 1996 c, no. 15.*

AG

Cat. no. 6.4

Two Pilasters and a Lambrequin (see fig. p. 216)

Paris, 1709–15
Wooden construction with textile covering; supporting tissue: linen; ground for embroidery: gold lamé-tissue; appliqué: metal thread
Pilasters: base H. 8½ in., W. 25¼ in.; shaft H. 118⅛ in., W. 21⅝ in.; capital H. 25¼ in., W. 27½ in.; total H. 132¼ in.; lambrequin: H. 12 in., L. 84⅝ in.
Inv. no. 47 992, 47993 (bases), 47 976, 47 977 (shafts), 47 986, 47 982 (capitals), 47 959 (lambrequin)

Provenance: *1915 so-called Schlossbergung, Dresden Residential Palace.*

These are two of the fourteen pilasters that once adorned the walls of the Audience Chamber. Running from the dado (plinth) up to the plasterwork of the ceiling, these so-called

"It Is Impossible for Our Imagination to Conceive of Anything More Beautiful."

The paintings in Augustus the Strong's Audience Chamber in the Dresden Residential Palace

Harald Marx

In all the spaces of the royal palace one sees such splendor of exquisite embellishments and paintings that it is impossible for our imagination to conceive of anything more beautiful; but the meticulous order and the accomplished arrangement of the above goes far beyond the sheer presence of all these marvelous items."[1] It was Johann Michael von Loen who, in his 1726 publication entitled *Discurs von der Bau-Kunst*, speaks so enthusiastically about the furnishings of the Dresden Residential Palace.

After a disastrous 1701 fire in the palace, Augustus the Strong (*August der Starke*) had been contemplating plans for extensive new construction, continually commissioning his architects with new designs. All of them remained unrealized until reconstruction of the destroyed portions began, in February 1717. In early 1718 the king decided to rebuild the entire floor dedicated to official functions and festivities. This task was brought to exemplary ends under Matthäus Daniel Pöppelmann, who was assisted by Raymond Leplat.[2] The work was completed, at the very latest, in September of 1719, when Prince Elector Frederick Augustus married Maria Josepha, eldest daughter of Emperor Joseph I.

"Female Representing Braveness and Strength," "Hercules" (details), reconstruction of the original ceiling painting by A. van der Linde, 2003

L. de Silvestre, The Ceiling Painting in the Audience Chamber, Dresden Residential Palace, 1719, destroyed on February 13, 1945, photograph from 1934

1 Audience Chamber, Residential Palace, photograph from ca. 1920

We know from old inventories and descriptions of the palace that most of the paintings for these newly created rooms were by Louis de Silvestre. They also included the picture on the ceiling in the Parade Bed Chamber (*Paradeschlafzimmer*), the picture on the ceiling and the supraports in the Audience Chamber (*Audienzgemach*). The latter was the most important

The History of the Dresden Armory

Heinz-Werner Lewerken

The Dresden Armory (*Rüstkammer*) is compiled from the possessions of the Saxon dukes, prince electors, and kings. Beside other comparable collections—such as the Hapsburg collections in Vienna, the holdings of the Spanish kings in Madrid and the Swedish kings in Stockholm, the royal English collections in the Tower of London (now Leeds), or the Russian czars' holdings in Moscow's Kremlin and St. Petersburg's Hermitage—the Dresden Armory holds a formidable position. Thanks to its holdings reaching back to the 15th century and due to its early inventories, it is considered the oldest of Dresden's princely collections still in existence. It unites circa 10,600 works of distinguished weapons makers, artists, and artisans from all over Europe, the Near East, and Asia.

As is true with other comparable princely collections, the exact year when the Dresden Armory was founded is unknown. Since the electoral vote was bestowed upon the Wettins in 1423, substantial collections of arms had accumulated and were kept in numerous fortresses and castles. In 1485 the House of Wettin was subdivided into two different territorial entities: Prince Elector Ernst founded the Ernestines, his brother Albrecht (ruled 1464/85–1500) chose Dresden as the main residence of the newly created Albertinian Dukedom of Saxony. Upon assuming power, Duke Georg the Bearded (*der Bärtige*, ruled 1500–39), founded an Armory (*Rüst- und Harnischkammer*) in the Dresden Residential Palace. Since that time there has been a continuous flow of accessions, mostly state weapons. The Armory, located on the ground floor of the elevated tower called *Hausmannsturm*, was held in high esteem and received its first administrator under Duke Georg in 1539.

In the year 1547, Moritz (ruled 1541/47–53) gained the Saxon electorship for the Albertinian branch of the House of Wettin. This event gave rise to his decision to double the size of the old castle in order to transform it into a satisfactory princely residence. The ensuing spacious four-winged structure with a stately interior courtyard—in which horse tournaments took place—was based on French and Italian prototypes. After the contestants were adequately equipped in the Electoral Armory they were able to proceed directly to the Castle Court (*Schlosshof*) for the games. The majority of arms and armor preserved in the Armory from the time of Moritz's reign document important historic events. These objects include the Electoral Sword of 1547 and the field armor Moritz wore during the occupation of Magdeburg in 1550/51.

While Moritz's fame is predominantly based on his talents as warrior and ruler, his successor and brother Augustus (ruled 1553–86) is remembered as the Saxon prince elector with distinguished business abilities: During his reign, the country underwent an enormous economic boom. In the Residential Palace, an affluent festival culture evolved, in which equestrian competitions and the hunt played major roles. Under Augustus, who also founded the *Kunstkammer* and the library, the inventory of the Armory multiplied tenfold, and new accessions mostly affected the department of tournaments. Among the additions were armor, helmets, and shields as well as precious rapiers and swords. The new works also included exquisite firearms, powder flasks, crossbows, riding equipment, and hunting utensils. It is likely that the prince elector was inspired and stimulated by the overabundance of the Vienna *Leibrüstkammer*, owned by his friend, the Hapsburg Emperor Maximilian II, as well as by Archduke Ferdinand of Tyrol, brother of the latter, with his impressively

Scale Armor, late 17th to early 18th century, see cat. no. 7.12, p. 244

arranged *Leib- und Heldenrüstkammer*. The first inventory of the scattered collections was authored in 1567 by Heinrich von Schönberg and Valerius Cracus; further inventories followed in 1568 and 1576.

After the death of Augustus in 1586, he was succeeded by his son Christian. In June of the same year Christian lay the foundation stone for the New Stable (*Neuer Stall*), future home to the electoral horses and the Armory. Numerous artists such as Giovanni Maria Nosseni and approximately 2,000 craftsmen participated in the construction of the building which was completed, for the most part, by 1588. The Armory's holdings were accommodated in a total of 32 spaces within the three-winged structure. Armor and Sleigh Chambers (*Waffen- und Schlittenkammern*) were located on the second floor along with four electoral suites. The rooms above the latter were exclusively used for the Armory. The Stables Building was connected with the Residential Palace via a roughly 300 feet long corridor above which an Ancestral Gallery (*Ahnengalerie*)

was housed. The Stables Building, parts of the palace, and the Chancellery Building (*Kanzleigebäude*) framed a spacious court in which tournaments and other festivities took place starting in 1589. A ramp enabled contestants to ride directly from the court to the Armory, where they would dress appropriately. Despite the fact that his reign lasted but five years, Christian I enriched the collection with numerous precious objects by domestic, South German, Italian, French, Spanish, and Flemish weapons makers and goldsmiths. Among the works were two Dresden suits of foot tournament armor fabricated in 1590 and made of solid silver. Further objects included rapiers, small swords, and daggers with silver-embellished hilts, an impressive number of suits of armor by the famous Augsburg armorer Anton Peffenhauser, as well as distinguished white arms.

1   A. Vogel, Dresden's New Stable, 1623, Armory

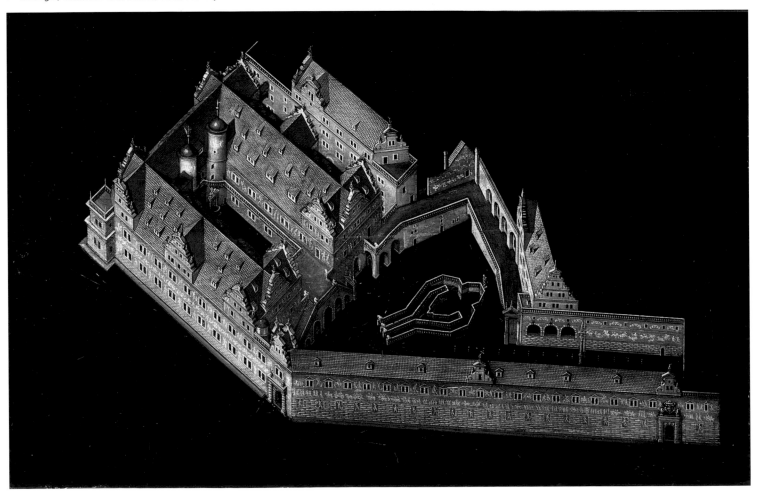

2   *Armory, permanent exhibition in the Semper Building, east wing*

Under the rule of Christian II, a fundamental inventory of the collection was undertaken between 1605 and 1606. On 1,602 handwritten pages, the inventory volume conveys a comprehensive image of the abundant arms and armor, weapons, riding equipment, vestments, sleighs, and vehicles. Christian II further completed the collection thanks to adding weapons, riding equipment, and invaluable suits of armor richly embellished with precious stones or other costly materials. Among the prestigious works are the turquoise and the emerald suits of the Dresden goldsmith Gabriel Gipfel, dated 1606/08, or the suit of parade armor and riding equipment decorated with precious stones. For the latter, Christian II commissioned the Prague goldsmith Johann Michael in 1611. In 1606 he acquired a suit of parade armor for man and horse by the Antwerp goldsmith Eliseus Libaerts that the Swedish king, Eric XIV, had commissioned in 1562–64. One of the definitive highlights of the Armory, this is one of the most gorgeous works of armor ever produced. The succeeding prince electors, Johann Georg I to IV, supplemented the collection with hunting weapons, hunting utensils, and Near Eastern weapons. Until the beginning of the 18th century, the Dresden Armory, along with the *Kunstkammer* and the Huge Hall (*Riesensaal*), was among the most famous attractions in the Residential Palace.

Brigandine

ITALIAN, MID-16TH CENTURY
IRON SCALES, COVERED WITH
PURPLE SILK VELVET; BRONZE
RIVETS; EMBOSSED LEATHER
MORIAN, BRASS RIVETS
22 LB. 3 OZ.
INV. NO. M 155

Provenance: *Inventory Turkish Chamber (Türkenkammer) 1674.*

Brigandines were particularly fashionable in 16th-century Italy, offering an alternative to the heavy and inflexible plate armor. Comparable to the Italian muscle cuirass, they evolved from close scrutiny of ancient Roman scale armor. The brigandine consists of iron scales riveted to textile or leather covers. The result is more reminiscent of a garment than armor. This brigandine originally belonged to Prince Elector Augustus. It consists of breast (with 17 rows of plain scales), back (13 rows), tassets (10 rows each), and collar elements with mail inside. Scales and velvet are joined by profiled bronze rivets. The tails are tied to the breast pieces. It appears that the helmet—equipped with braided leather chin straps attached to the cheek guards—did not originally belong to the brigandine.

Lit.: *Haenel 1923, p. 48, plate 24.*

HS

ELISEUS LIBAERTS

Parade Armor

Antwerp, ca. 1562
Iron, embossed, punched,
blackened, partially etched,
and gilt
56 lb. 3 oz.
Inv. no. M 106

Provenance: *Armory Inventory 1608, under Duke Johann Georg.*

Shortly after his coronation as king of Sweden, in 1560, Erik XIV proposed to Queen Elizabeth I of England. In order to emphasize his serious intentions, he commissioned the embellishment of numerous pieces of parade armor from the Antwerp goldsmith Libaerts. Two of the suits were confiscated by Danish troops upon their delivery to Stockholm and taken to Copenhagen instead. It was not until 1603 that Prince Elector Christian II purchased them for a total of 9,525 guilders. While he kept the golden "Hercules Armor" for himself, he gave this partially gilt and blackened suit (armor and saddle) to his younger brother, Johann Georg (I). The central motifs may be spotted on the breast and the back; they are the head of Medusa and Hercules with his club, respectively. Libaerts's point of departure for the composition was the so-called "Farnese Hercules," a Roman copy of a Greek original by the sculptor Lysippus, which was found in the Baths of Caracalla in Rome in 1546 and is now in Naples.

Lit.: *Ehrenthal 1899a, p. 58 (E 12).—Haenel 1923, p. 34, plate 17.—Schöbel 1973, p. 29 (no. 11).*

HS

ANTON PEFFENHAUSER
(ca. 1525–1603)

**Parade Armor for
Man and Horse**

Augsburg, before 1591
Iron, embossed, etched,
partially gilt, enamel
coats of arms
Inv. no. M 99

Provenance: *Armory Inventory
1606.*

Prince Elector Christian I (ruled 1586–91) and his wife, Sophia, purchased a total of 18 suits of armor from Peffenhauser—the most important Augsburg armorer at the time—in only five years. To the present day, this parade armor, along with its various exchange pieces and its four armored saddles, constitutes the most elaborate suit in the Dresden Armory. The quantity of related saddles is most extraordinary. The Saxon coat of arms with the abbreviated motto of the prince elector— FSV for *Fide Sed Vide* (trust but know whom you trust)— may be spotted on the chamfron, peytral, and crupper. The decoration of the suit consists of broad, etched stripes with trophies on a black punched ground framed by golden margins of braided bands with geometric design. Emerging from the etched stripes are flowering tendrils with lacy, spiraling foliage, decorative devices typical of Peffenhauser armor. When the prince elector was buried in 1591 this armor followed his sarcophagus in procession.

Lit.: *Haenel 1923, p. 24, plate 12.—Wozel 1979, p. 86 (no. 40).—Schuckelt 2002.*

HS

PETER VON SPEYER
THE YOUNGER
(*1580 established own workshop, 1606 head of the Dresden Chamber for Tilting Armor*)

Boy's Armor

Dresden, ca. 1590
Iron, embossed, blackened
22 lb. 8 oz.
Inv. no. M 88

Provenance: *Inventory
Old Armor Chamber
(Alte Harnischkammer) 1688.*

Equipping the prince electors with weapons and armor was necessary for their education as well as their function as members of the princely class. In 1590 Prince Elector Christian I commissioned Speyer the Younger to fabricate three suits of black boy's armor. Intended for his sons, Christian (II), Johann Georg (I), and Augustus (later administrator of Naumburg), they are preserved in the Dresden Armory, along with children's weapons, a saddle, and a chamfron for a pony. In addition to this suit, additional boy's armor of various sizes is preserved, including that belonging to the later Prince Elector Christian II. Thanks to the numerous pieces of his armor in the collection, Christian's physical development from a seven-year-old boy to a grown man can be reconstructed.

Lit.: *Ehrenthal 1899a, p. 47 (D 12).—Haenel 1923, p. 40, plate 20.—Schöbel 1973, p. 28 (no. 5b).*

HS

JACOB JÖRINGK
(armorer, worked for the Dresden Court 1650–69) and
CHRISTIAN HEROLD
(etcher and chaser, documented 1666–81)

Armor for Foot Combat Belonging to Duke Johann Georg (III) of Saxony

DRESDEN, 1666
IRON, EMBOSSED, ETCHED, SILVERED, AND PARTIALLY GILT
37 LB. 8 OZ.
INSCRIBED ON THE BREAST WITH THE CROWNED INITIALS IGAS (JOHANN GEORG (III) OF SAXONY/ANNA SOPHIA, ROYAL DANISH PRINCESS)
INV. NO. M 84

Provenance: Inventory Chamber for Tilting Armor (Pallienkammer) 1720.

CHRISTIAN HEROLD

Tournament Sword with Scabbard

DRESDEN, 1667
IRON BLADE: FORGED, ETCHED; IRON HILT: ETCHED, SILVERED, PARTIALLY GILT; WOODEN SCABBARD: COVERED WITH VELVET; IRON MOUNTS: EMBOSSED, ETCHED, SILVERED, PARTIALLY GILT
L. (TOTAL) 103 CM, BLADE 34½ IN., 3 LB.
INSCRIBED ON THE BLADE: ANNO 1667; ON THE SHELL GUARD (BOTTOM) AND ON THE CHAPE THE INTERTWINED INITIALS JG AND AS
INV. NO. VII 71

The richly decorated armor is among the last of its kind. Fabricated for Johann Georg (III), the future prince elector and father of Augustus the Strong, it was worn on the occasion of his marriage to Anna Sophia, daughter of King Frederick III of Denmark. This accounts for the intertwined initials that embellish the breastplate and parts of the sword. Interestingly, at least the sword blade was not made until the year after the wedding. The close family ties between the Saxon prince electors and the Danish royal house always gave rise to luxuriously staged festivities. A multitude of objects in Dresden's Armory derive from such celebratory events.

Lit.: *Ehrenthal 1899a, p. 50 (D 30).—Haenel 1923, p. 46, plate 23—Exh.-cat. Nuremberg 1998, p. 354 (cat. no. 241).*

HS

Cat. no. 7.6

Saxon Electoral Hat

Dresden, second half of the 17th century
Crimson silk velvet, ermine (supplemented with rabbit), leather, silk lining
Sidelength 8¹/4 in., circumference at the inner border 22⁷/8 in.
Inv. no. I 88

Provenance: *Armory, Inventory Electoral Clothing Chamber (Kurfürstliche Kleiderkammer) 1703.*

In 1423 King Sigismund bestowed upon the Wettins the Saxon office of prince elector. When the seven princes of the empire who elected the king of the Holy Roman Empire of the German Nation gathered for the Imperial Diet (*Reichstag*) or to elect the king, they put on special ceremonial vestments there—and only there—in the presence of the emperor. The crimson-colored silk velvet cloak with ermine trimmings reached down to the ankles. It was part of an outfit to which also the electoral hat belonged, and which only the prince electors were granted the privilege to wear. The hat, as part of the ceremonial vestments, attained an independent value as an insignia based on its general significance. As a consequence, it appears in the electoral Saxon coat of arms. Augustus the Strong never wore the electoral vestments because he always appointed representatives to the Imperial Diet who acted on his behalf. During funerary ceremonies for a prince elector, the electoral hat, the electoral sword, and the great seal were mounted beside the corpse and led the ensuing procession. The electoral insignia also appeared on Louis de Silvestre's state portrait of Augustus.

Lit.: *Bäumel 1997b, pp. 374f., 378f. (cat. no. 739/II 16, 740/II 18).*

JB

Cat. nos. 7.7A to 7.7C

JOHANN FRIEDRICH KLEMM

Crown, Scepter, and Orb

Dresden, 1697

Crown:
Signed with the maker's mark FK on the band and the Dresden view mark D
Silver, embossed, chased, gilt; 97 mounted stones as imitations of precious and semiprecious stones: yellow quartz, rock crystal, triplets of rock crystal with mastic
H. 9⁷/8 in., Diam. 7⁷/8 in., circumference 23¹/4 in
Inv. no. P 343

Scepter:
Wood, carved, red bolus, leaf gold; silver; gold, brass; rock crystal
L. 28⁷/8 in.
Inv. no. P 344

Orb:
Wood, red bolus, leaf gold; rock crystal, yellow quartz; brass, gold
H. 10¹/2 in.
Inv. no. P 345

Provenance: *Transferred to the Armory in 1697.*

Crown, scepter, and orb are free adaptations of the Polish insignia which were created on the occasion of Augustus the Strong's coronation as king of Poland. During the coronation ceremonies on October 5/15, 1697, in the cathedral of St. Stanislaus in Kraków, the original insignia of the Polish kingdom were used, and not this set. Because of the dispute over the election of the king—apart from the Saxon prince elector, the French candidate, Prince Conti, also claimed the victory for himself—Augustus did not have safe access to the Polish crown treasure. It is possible that Augustus kept the reproductions for the event that the originals would be denied to him. The replicated insignia could possibly have been used in the procession from the royal castle to the coronation in the cathedral. An eyewitness stated with regards to this event: "Also were crown, scepter, and orb carried in front of his [royal majesty] on a cushion made of red velvet." In this parade, the king was dressed as an emperor, in classical Roman costume. Augustus had this outfit, along with the replicated insignia, a wax portrait of his head, and a life-size figure mounted in the Dresden Armory. The pieces were presented as a "statua" in

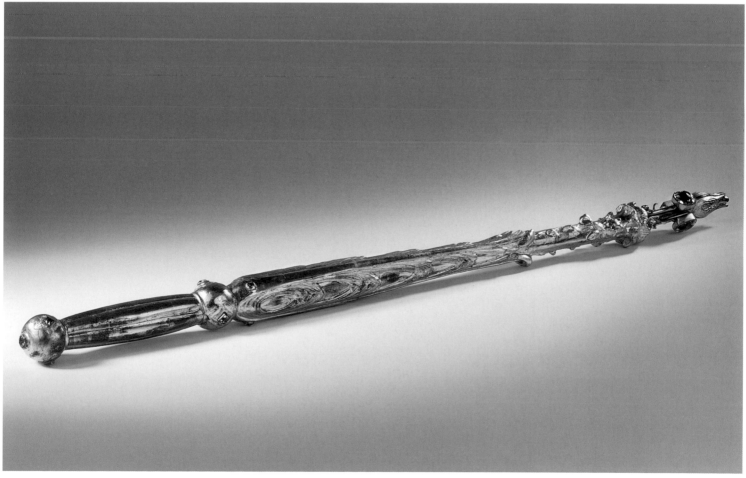

a closet whose interior was painted in imitation of the heavens.

Lit.: *Exh.-cat. Warsaw 1997a, p. 90 (cat. no. II 1).—Bäumel 1997a, pp. 124–133.—Exh.-cat. Dresden 1997b, pp. 380f. (cat. nos. 741–743).—Bäumel 1998/99.*

JB

Saber

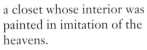

German, before 1688
Back-edged blade: bent,
partly etched, blued, gilt;
hilt: silver, cast, chased,
gilt; cameos; Scabbard:
wood, leather
Overall L. 34⅝ in.,
blade 28½ in., 1 lb. 10 oz.;
scabbard 29¾ in., 7 oz.
Inv. no. VI 448

Provenance: *Armory, Inventory Chamber for Tilting Armor (Pallienkammer) 1688 (Postscript ca. 1704).*

The saber with a pommel in the shape of an eagle's head and sumptuous stone embellishments, was once the property of Prince Elector Johann Georg II or Johann Georg III and apparently initially belonged to a classicizing Roman masquerade costume. Augustus the Strong selected this piece as an addition to his "Roman" ruler costume which he wore on the occasion of his coronation. The double meaning of the eagle as symbol of the ancient ruler and as heraldic motif in the coat-of-arms of the kingdom Poland was quite conducive to Augustus's intentions. In an illustration of his coronation, the former Polish king, Jan Sobieski, is also depicted holding a saber with an eagle's head.

Lit.: *Exh.-cat. Warsaw 1997, p. 90 (cat. no. II 1).—Exh.-cat. Dresden 1997b, p. 381 (cat. no. 747).—Bäumel 1998/99.*

JB

Cat. no. 7.9

State Dress

1697
Upper fabric: French
Elector's Personal Tailor
(*Leibschneider*) Simon
Rudolph(?), electoral
tailoring workshop, Dresden
Parts: coat, waistcoat,
breeches with sword belt,
stockings
Main fabric: *Gros de Tours*
with pattern weft of gold
thread (*glacé drap d'or*); silver
embroidery; main lining and
waistcoat: *Gros de Tours*, silk
salmon-red (*ponceau*); golden
passementrie buttons;
stockings: silver gilded
thread with silk core,
knitted, silver embroidery
Inv. no. I 25

Provenance: *Royal Wardrobe. Armory, Inventory Old Electoral Tailoring Workshop (Alte kurfürstliche Schneiderei) 1711 (Postscript 1733).*

Augustus the Strong wore this state dress on the occasion of the coronation banquet which took place September 5–15, 1697, in Kraków Castle on the Wawel. On the coronation day, the costume was embellished with the star of the royal Danish Elephant Order as well as a suit of buttons with diamond roses. It follows entirely the latest French court fashion of the day; its preciousness exceeds all other dresses previously in the possession of the Saxon prince electors. The frequently quoted royal splendor becomes literally tangible thanks to the "*glacé*" of the dress's golden cloth.

Lit.: *Bäumel 1997a, pp. 97–103, 133f.—Exh.-cat. Warsaw 1997a, p. 93 (cat. no. II 4).*

JB

Parade Riding Equipment

Presumably Saxon, 1694,
reworked and supplemented
1709, 1719, and 1733/34
Silk velvet, gold braid,
brass, silver, gold; rock
crystal, partly with red
mastic; facet cut; sun gems:
brass, gilt, red poured glass,
rock crystal
Inv. no. L 12

Provenance: *Armory, Inventory Fine Saddle Chamber (Gute Sattelkammer) 1697.*

This parade riding equipment is among the most important dynastic objects left by Augustus the Strong and Augustus III. Augustus the Strong carried it while riding his ermine-colored personal horse during his coronation procession on September 2/12, 1697, in Kraków. It was later appropriately exhibited in the Armory on a wooden horse "painted in the color of an ermine." In 1709 Augustus utilized this riding equipment—which was modified to incorporate two sun badges—for his appearance as the sun god, Apollo, during the procession of the gods through the Residential Palace and during a nocturnal riding at the ring in the so-called *Reithaus*. For the princely wedding in 1719 he carried this riding equipment when personifying the "chief of fire" during the Carousel of the Four Elements in the *Zwinger*. For this festivity, black silk velvet was substituted for the red silk velvet, and the sun badges from the horse's head and crupper were exchanged for larger ones with a fire-red face. Augustus III continued the tradition established by his father and used the riding equipment during his coronation in Kraków

1734. For this occasion, the black silk velvet was exchanged for blue silk velvet.

Lit.: *Bäumel 1997a,
pp. 91–95, 110–121.—Exh.-cat.
Dresden 2000a, pp. 210f.
(cat. nos. 111a/b).*

JB

Scale Armor

POLISH, LATE-17TH TO
EARLY-18TH CENTURIES
LEATHER, TRIMMED WITH STEEL
SCALES, ALL PARTS FRAMED WITH
GOLD TRIMMINGS, GILT MOUNTS,
LINEN LINING
36 LB. 1 OZ.
INV. NO. Y 19

Provenance: *Inventory Turkish
Chamber (Türkenkammer)
1716.*

The scale armor con-
sists of breast- and
back-plate, pauldrons,
hollow rim, and a heavy helmet
with cheek guards. The scales
of shiny iron are attached with
470 gilt brass rivets in the
shape of Maltese crosses; in

CAT. NO. 7.11

SAXON WORKSHOP

Parade Riding Equipment

1693–97
SILK VELVET CRIMSON; LEATHER;
IRON, BRASS, GOLD, SILVER;
DIAMONDS, RIVER PEARLS, MILK
OPAL, MOTHER-OF-PEARL, GOLD
ENAMEL, PAINTER ENAMEL; GOLD
TRIMMINGS, GOLD TASSELS
INV. NO. L 8

Provenance: *Armory, J. G.
von Thielau: "Beschreibung des
Einzuges [...] den 12. September
1697 in Cracau"—Inventory
Chamber with Pike Pages (Spießpagenkammer) 1716.*

This riding equip-
ment—richly adorned
with "Oriental" dia-
monds and pearls—is the
most precious group formerly
owned by the Saxon prince
electors. Johann Georg VI
commissioned it for a Turkish
procession during horse tournaments 1693. During conservation treatment in 1921–22,
661 diamonds, 532 pearls, and

113 pieces of mother-of-pearl
were counted. They are artfully arranged in a so-called
Oriental manner on the
rosettes decorating head, chest,
and back of the horse. Also belonging to this group is a rich
gold-embroidered red saddle
with diamonds and pearls, as
well as an extremely rich gold
and silver-embroidered Turkish saddle-cloth. During the
entry of Augustus the Strong
for his coronation in Kraków,
on September 2/12, 1697, this
riding equipment—along with
other appropriate stately pieces
of riding equipment and personal horses—were part of an
impressive parade. On October
6/16, 1697, while in Krakow,
Augustus wore a diamond-
studded Polish dress during a
procession in order to receive
homage being paid him.
His personal horse bore the
diamond riding equipment.

Lit.: *Bäumel 1997a, pp. 93,
134–146, fig. 52. Bäumel
1998b, pp. 142f., 147, 201–205,
210–213 (fig.).*

JB

addition, 14 small lion's heads may be seen. Cheek guards and an haute piece are attached to the scale helmet. In order to protect the face, a moveable nose piece is affixed to its front. The helmet is embellished with a plume holder and crowned by a gilt eagle with spread wings. Presumably, this scale armor was owned by the Polish Royal Crown Marshal, Prince Hieronymus Lubomirski, who gave it to Augustus the Strong. In the 17th century, the Polish aristocracy were believed to be descendents of the ancient Sarmatians, a nomadic people of horseriding archers who wore scale armor. Thought to originate in Iran, the Sarmatians were defeated by the Romans in the lower reaches of the Danube River. Polish scale armor of this type stands in the tradition of reinforcing the relationships between the East and West.

Lit.: *Quandt 1834, p. 143.— Reibisch no year, list 9, fig. 28.— Ehrenthal 1899, p. 187 (J 175).*
HS

Cat. no. 7.13

Military State Dress

Presumably 1709
Elector's Personal Tailor
(*Leibschneider*) Simon
Rudolph(?), electoral
tailoring workshop, Dresden
Parts: coat, waistcoat,
breeches, sword belt
Chamois leather off-white;
Gros de Tours, salmon-red
(*ponceau*); gold and silk
embroidery; golden
passementrie buttons
Inv. no. I 27/I 464

Provenance: *Royal Wardrobe. Armory, Inventory Old Electoral Tailoring Workshop (Alte kurfürstliche Schneiderei) 1711 (Postscript 1733).*

The use of leather in the upper material and the decoration with the star of an order identify this as one of Augustus the Strong's military state dresses. During the Nordic War in Poland, in 1702, the king carried a similar dress with him. It was captured by the Swedes and later regained, although incomplete and damaged. The newly made military state dress closely follows its model; it appears that the intention was to make it appear so close to the original that the previous defeat would be symbolically forgotten. On the upper left chest, the dress bears the star of the royal Danish Elephant Order which Augustus received in 1686. The fact that the dress does not bear the Polish Order of the White Eagle proves that it must come from the time when Augustus had temporarily lost the Polish crown in 1706. The victory of Czar Peter I against Charles XII in 1709 enabled Augustus to regain the Polish throne. The visit of King Frederick IV of Denmark in the same year and the ensuing meeting with King Frederick I of Prussia served to renew the alliance. Apparently, Augustus wore the new military state dress for the Three Kings Meeting (*Drei-Königs-Treffen*) in Berlin.

Lit.: *Bäumel 1998a.*
JB

Cat. no. 7.14

Military Sword

German, before 1733
Colichemarde-blade, hollow
cut, partly etched and gilt;
hilt: iron, polished;
gripbound: gilt silver wire;
portepee: silver, gold, white,
and olive green silk
Overall L. 43 1/4 in.,
blade 34 7/8 in.
Inv. no. XIV 3

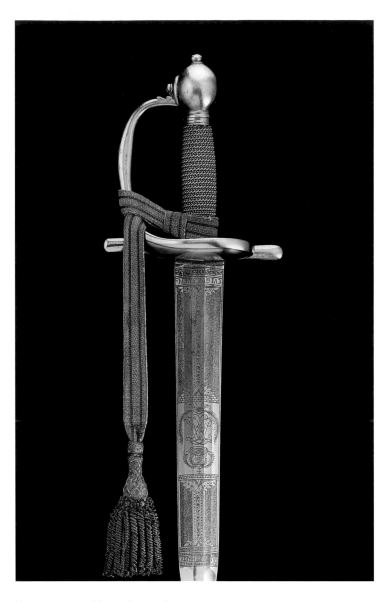

electorate Saxony, as well as the first letter for his royal Polish name, Augustus II.

Lit.: *Hilbert 1998, pp. 24f. (cat. nos. 3/4), 33 (fig.).— Exh.-cat. Warsaw 1997a, p. 266 (cat. no. VIII 14).—Exh.-cat. Dresden 1997b, p. 187 (cat. no. 270).*

JB

CAT. NO. 7.15

FRENCH WORKSHOP

Parade Saddle

PARIS(?), 1715
UPPER MATERIAL: CRIMSON SILK
VELVET; GOLD EMBROIDERY;
LEATHER, LINEN, TOW, WOOD,
IRON
L. 20⅝ IN., W. 26¾ IN.,
H. 21⅝ IN.
INV. NO. L 26

Provenance: *Armory, Inventory Small Chamber with Fine Saddles (Kleine Gute Sattelkammer) 1720.*

This parade saddle was a gift of Louis XIV of France for Augustus the Strong. It belongs to a group of six gold and silver embroidered saddles which Louis XIV sent to Dresden. The donation was preceded by the Saxon electoral prince's visit to Louis' court. The saddles were presented on six Spanish stallions, each saddle equipped with saddle blanket and two pistol holsters with holster covers. In the case of the exhibited saddle, the latter no longer exist. The elaborate relief embroidery executed on both sides entailed the use of much precious metal; this and the modernity of the design were truly top of the line. The pistol holsters each bore two pistols made by renowned French court rifle makers. Augustus was so impressed by the saddles and the pistols that he ordered more of them from Paris. The French saddles were used during a procession on the occasion of the prince

Provenance: *From the wardrobe of Augustus the Strong, after his death to the Armory; Inventory Electoral Chamber (Kurkammer) 1716 (Postscript 1733).*

Like its pendant, an infantry sword, this identically equipped cavalry sword stems from the personal possessions of Augustus the Strong. On its blade, the sword bears the crowned mirror monogram FAR (Fridericus Augustus Rex) and the motto ARTE ET MARTE/ CVIQUE SUUM/QUO FAS ET FATA/DUCUNT COURAGE AUEC/ESPRIT (In the arts as in war/everyone his own/wherever law and destiny guide you/courage with intelligence). The initials encompass the birth name of Augustus, Frederick Augustus, which he used when dealing with issues concerning the

elector's wedding in 1719, when a running at the ring was being held in the Stable Court.

Lit.: *Bäumel 1996, see also cat. no. 244, pp. 260f.*

JB

CAT. NO. 7.16

Horse Harness for a Parade Sleigh

VIENNA, 1719
SALMON-RED (*ponceau*) SILK VELVET, GOLD EMBROIDERY, GOLD FRINGES, GOLD TASSELS; WHITE AND RED OSTRICH FEATHERS; GOLD TRIMMINGS; BELLS: BRASS, GILT; CARDBOARD, LINEN, LEATHER; IRON, GILT INV. NO. L 15

Provenance: *Armory, Inventory Fine Saddle Chamber (Gute Sattelkammer) 1717 (specification from 1719).*

The horse harness belonged to the equipment of two of Augustus III's parade sleighs. He acquired them as electoral prince when he stayed in Vienna in 1718–19, where he went on a sleigh ride on February 8, 1718. He led the procession, consisting of 36 parade sleighs, together with Princess Domenica of Liechtenstein, in a Diana sleigh drawn by a horse with a blue and gold parade harness with bells. This red-gold horse harness is quite similar and belonged to the "entirely gilt" Cupid sleigh, referenced in the inventory, which the electoral prince had purchased upon his father's command for the imperial sleigh ride. It is this very horse harness which he employed in Vienna in 1719 when he immediately followed behind the emperor's sleigh, which carried his future wife, Archduchess

Maria Josepha. Both horse harnesses for parade sleighs were used in Dresden until 1751.

Lit.: *Mikosch 1998, pp. 85–88, 127–131.*

JB

CAT. NO. 7.17

State Dress

DRESDEN(?), 1719, ALTERED 1730
ELECTOR'S PERSONAL TAILOR (*Leibschneider*) SIMON RUDOLPH(?), ELECTORAL TAILORING WORKSHOP
MAIN FABRIC: FRENCH
PARTS: COAT, WAISTCOAT, BREECHES, SWORD BELT
GROS DE TOURS WITH PATTERN WEFT (*lancé*) OF GOLD THREAD (*glacé drap d'or*); GOLDEN EMBROIDERY; LAPEL COVERS, SLEEVE CUFFS AND MAIN LINING: WARP-FACED SILK VELVET, BLUE (*bleumerent*); GROS DE TOURS,

SILK SALMON-RED (*ponceau*); GOLDEN *passementrie* BUTTONS INV. NO. I 28

Provenance: *Royal Wardrobe. Armory, Inventory Old Electoral Tailoring Workshop (Alte kurfürstliche Schneiderei) 1711 (Postscript 1733).*

According to the "Wardrobe" list, Augustus the Strong wore his most precious outfits—if one bases this evaluation on a historical perspective—for the entry of the prince elector's bride, the emperor's daughter Maria Josepha, into Dresden in 1719. The king went on horseback to Blasewitz/Elbe to greet the couple who arrived on a golden parade ship. He returned to the Residential Palace with a small entourage in order to greet the couple again when they arrived with their own

large procession. The printed accounts of the festivities mention a purple-colored velvet dress with diamonds worn by the king during the entry. Augustus wore the golden dress once more during the so-called *Zeithainer Lager*, the large military display in the presence of King Frederick William I of Prussia in 1730. For the latter event, the dress was modified: silk velvet lapels were attached, lending this dress a military character.

Lit.: *Mikosch 1998, pp. 118–125, app. 3.6, pp. 29–40.*

JB

CAT. NO. 7.18

Partisans of the Royal Polish *Chevalier-Garde*

GERMAN, 1719
WAVED BLADE, ETCHED, PARTLY AND ENTIRELY GILT; TASSEL: BLUE AND WHITE SILK, SILVER SPUN YARN; SHAFT: WOOD
OVERALL L. 109/104^{3}/$_{8}$ IN.,
BLADE 20^{7}/$_{8}$ IN.
INV. NO. R 44/R 45

Provenance: *Armory, Inventory Chamber with Pike Pages (Spießpagenkammer) 1716 (Postscript 1719).*

The *Chevalier-Garde* was founded as a Polish elite guard on July 30, 1703. It performed its duty during the royal ceremonies. For the electoral prince's wedding in 1719, the guard was equipped with new red and yellow uniforms and with partisans. The blade of the partisans shows the personal union of Augustus the Strong as prince elector of Saxony and as Polish king in a symbolic depiction of the double eagle, the crossed swords, the royal crown, and the coat of arms. The partisan with the entirely gilt blade belonged to the four partisans "carried by the generals."

Lit.: *Exh.-cat. Warsaw 1997a, p. 269 (cat. no. VIII 22).— Exh.-cat. Dresden 1997b, p. 197 (cat. no. 300).*

JB

CAT. NO. 7.19

JOHANN JACOB IRMINGER *(1635?–1724)*

Kettledrum

DRESDEN, 1719
SILVER, EMBOSSED, CAST, CHASED, PARTIALLY GILT; SPANNING SCREWS: IRON BLANK; CALFSKIN
WITH MAKER'S MARK AND THE STAMP OF THE SILVER WEIGHT, THE SO-CALLED *Lotzeichen*
H. 17^{3}/$_{4}$ IN., DIAM. 24^{3}/$_{4}$ IN.,
34 LB. 3 OZ.
INV. NO. P 297

Provenance: *From the Court Silver Chamber (Hofsilberkammer); in 1973 moved from the Hunting Castle Moritzburg to the Armory.*

For the electoral prince's wedding in 1719, Augustus the Strong commissioned the goldsmith Irminger to fabricate "2 pairs of silver drums [and] 12 silver trumpets." The heavy silver works cost more than 3,450 thalers. The kettledrums bear the Saxon and the Polish-Lithuanian coats of arms, as well as the gem of the Polish Order of the White Eagle. According to his royal status, Augustus had four army drummers and twenty-four trumpeters perform on important dynastic festivities—this is twice the number ordinarily granted a prince elector according to the law defined in the Imperial Privileges (*Reichsprivileg*). During the so-called *Zeithainer Lager*, in 1730, the most extensive military parade Augustus ever undertook, the kettledrums were placed on a wagon drawn by four horses where they were played by an army drummer in Turkish dress.

Lit.: *Ô Byrn 1880, p. 149.— Exh.-cat. Dresden/Bonn 1995, pp. 322f. (cat. no. 398).—Bäumel 1997a, pp. 88–91.*

JB

CAT. NO. 7.20

JOHANN MELCHIOR DINGLINGER *(1664–1731)*

Invention Shield

DRESDEN, 1695
COPPER, EMBOSSED, GILT, PUNCHED, STUDDED WITH PASTE JEWELS, VELVET LINING
H. 19¼ IN., W. 14⅝ IN.
INV. NO. N 168

Provenance: *Inventory Fine Sleigh Chamber (Gute Schlitten-kammer) 1708.*

This shield's main decoration is an apple made of two hemispheres soldered together. The inscription reads A LA PLUS BELLE (To the most beautiful). The apple alludes to the mythological Judgment of Paris, in which the son of the Trojan king Priam was to choose between the goddesses Hera, Aphrodite, and Athena as to who was the most beautiful among them. He decided in favor of Aphrodite, who helped Paris kidnap Helen from Sparta, an event that led to the Trojan War. The shield was made for the great procession of the gods during carnival festivities in 1695. In the great procession for the Carousel of the Four Continents—honoring the visit of King Frederick IV of Denmark to Dresden, in 1709—this shield was carried by a "native American" in front of Duke Friedrich von Sachsen-Weißenfels, head of the "American continent." Finally, it was Augustus the Strong, chief of the Fire Quadrille in the Carousel of the Elements, who wore this shield during the wedding festivities of 1719.

Lit.: *Nickel 1983 (figs. 5, 9).— Exh.-cat. Warsaw 1997a, p. 348 (cat. no. XI 18).—Exh.-cat. Nuremberg 1998, p. 356 (cat. no. 244).*

HS

CAT. NO. 7.21

JOHANN MELCHIOR DINGLINGER (*1664–1731*)

Invention Mask—Sun Mask with the Likeness of Augustus the Strong

DRESDEN, 1709
COPPER, EMBOSSED COPPER AND GILT
H. 19¼ IN., 1 LB. 7 OZ.
INV. NO. N 171

Provenance: *Inventory Fine Sleigh Chamber (Gute Schlittenkammer) 1708.*

The embossed mask is made from copper sheets and bears the likeness of Augustus the Strong. Thanks to a double wreath of rays, it takes the shape of the sun. Tiny rivet holes along the inner wreath are evidence for the lining, now lost. Augustus wore this mask when personifying the god Apollo in a procession of gods which took place during a nocturnal running at the ring to honor King Frederick IV of Denmark (June 22, 1709). King Louis XIV of France was the first to equate the identity of the ruler with that of the god of light or the sun god. Augustus repeated his appearance as sun god in 1727: In the procession of gods, Augustus's Danish guest took on the role of the god of war, Mars. The Persian inscription on the medal struck to commemorate his 58th birthday praised his royal qualities, calling them "worthier than those of the sun."

Lit.: *Exh.-cat. Stockholm 1992, p. 212 (cat. no. 248).—Bäumel 1995, pp. 91f.—Exh.-cat. Dresden 2000a, p. 210 (cat. no. 110).*
HS

CAT. NO. 7.22

MARTIN SCHNELL (*ca. 1675–1740*)

Jousting Lance for Running at the Ring

DRESDEN, PRESUMABLY 1709 AND 1719
WOOD, LEAF GOLD, BRONZE, RED BOLUS, BLADE GILT, GOLD FRINGES; RED (*ponceau*) SILK VELVET
OVERALL L. 97¼ IN., BLADE 10⅝ IN., 3 LB. 12 OZ.
INV. NO. R 287

Provenance: *Armory, Inventory Electoral Chambers (Kurfürstliche Gemächer) 1688—Manual 1709.*

When the Danish king visited Dresden in 1709, Augustus the Strong organized a running at the ring for ladies. For this event, "two French jousting lances for running at the ring—in shining gold, one of them decorated with a red cloth, to be used by the king" were produced.

Lit.: *Bäumel 1998c, pp. 68f., ill. 4.—Exh.-cat. Dresden 2000a, p. 143 (cat. no. 53).*
JB

CAT. NOS. 7.23A AND 7.23B

Suit of Hunting Weapons

LEIPZIG, 1708
Hunting hanger:
DATED ON THE SHEATH MOUNT: 1708
PARTS: HUNTING HANGER, SCABBARD, ONE KNIFE, ONE FORK, ONE FILE
BACK-EDGED BLADE: AT THE DOUBLE-EDGED TIP, STAMP; HILT, HANDLES, AND MOUNTS: IRON, CUT, PUNCHED; FACINGS: DEER ANTLER; BONE INLAYS; SCABBARD: WOOD, LEATHER
OVERALL L. 32½ IN., BLADE 26⅝ IN., SCABBARD 29⅛ IN., 2 LB. 2 OZ.
INV. NO. X 439
Hunting trousse:
DATED ON THE SHEATH MOUNT: 1708
PARTS: CHOPPER, SHEATH, THREE KNIFES, ONE FORK, ONE FILE
CUTLASS: BACK-EDGED BLADE, STAMP; HILT, HANDLES, AND MOUNTS: IRON, CUT, PUNCHED; FACINGS: DEER ANTLER, BONE INLAYS; SHEATH: WOOD, LEATHER
OVERALL L. 20⅛ IN., BLADE 14 IN., SHEATH 15⅛ IN., 7 LB. 15 OZ.
INV. NO. X 410

Provenance: *Both Armory, Inventory Hunters' Chamber (Jägerkammer) 1821.*

The hunting hanger and the trousse are the masterpiece of a Leipzig hilt maker. In order to be accepted into the guild, each craftsman was obligated to prove not only his civic birth and proper apprentice-

ship, but he was also required to submit pieces fitting the specifications defined in the guild laws. Augustus the Strong purchased this solid suit which was suitable for the traditional German hunt on January 24, 1710. With reference to the hilt design with the heads of a lion and an eagle—and with the depiction of a lion killing a stag, prominently pictured on the sheath—it appears likely, that the hiltmaker anticipated a potentially princely client.

Lit.: *Ehrenthal 1899a, p. 213 (M 17).—Haenel/Watzdorf 1933, pp. 112f.—Schöbel 1976, cat. no. 21.*

JB

Cat. no. 7.24

BALTHASAR PERMOSER(?) *(1651–1732)* (handle)

Hunting Hanger

Before 1732
Blade: presumably Solingen; hiltmaker's work: Saxon, presumably Dresden
Handle: ivory, carved; hilt and mounts: brass, gilt; back-edged blade: steel, partly etched and gilt; sheath: wood, leather
Overall L. 30³/₄ in., blade 25¹/₄ in., handle 4⁵/₈ in., sheath 26⁵/₈ in.
Inv. no. X 366

Provenance: *Royal Wardrobe. Armory, Inventory Electoral Chamber (Kurkammer) 1716 (Postscript 1733).*

Augustus the Strong carried this delicate hunting hanger in his wardrobe until the end of his life, for personal use and as a revered souvenir. It was intended to be carried by the head of the hunt, whose privilege it was to ceremonially stab

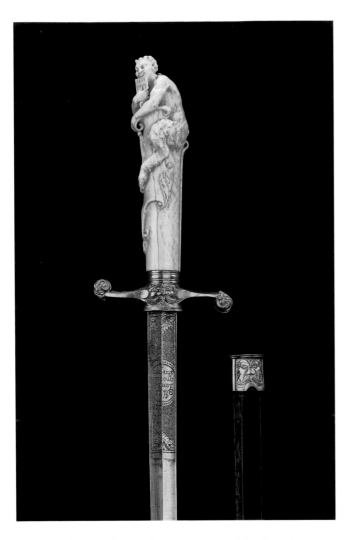

to death the already caught stag during a parforce hunt. The inscription on the blade refers to the original intent of this weapon which might otherwise be easily mistaken as a pure work of art: "Hoc langi morti ferrum" (This iron is intended for killing).

Permoser was particularly famous for his creatures derived from the myth of Bacchus which he rendered throughout his artistic career in various shapes, sizes, and materials including stone, ivory, and wood. Permoser also furnished figural ivory cutlery handles including renderings of Adam, Eve, and Venus. The Pan figure which Permoser created for this hunting hanger is distinguished by its expressive mimics and its direct reference to allegories concerning the ruler. In its specific expression, it is distinguished as an individual work of art; it is quite radically different from Permoser's Satyr herms in the *Zwinger*. The customary attrib-

ute of the Satyr is the goatskin; in this case, it has been stylized: it appears that a ram's skin is depicted, a direct reference to the golden fleece.

Lit.: *Exh.-cat. Dresden 2001a, pp. 76f. (cat. no. 29).*

JB

CAT. NO. 7.25

Hunting Trousse
BEFORE 1730
PARTS: CHOPPER, SHEATH, FOUR CUTLERY KNIFES, ONE FILE
CHOPPER: BACK-EDGED BLADE, PARTIALLY ETCHED AND GILT; HILT AND CUTLERY KNIVES'S HANDLES: BRASS, CAST, CHASED, GILT; SHEATH: LEATHER, MOUNT BRASS, EMBOSSED, SILVERED, GILT
CHOPPER: OVERALL L. 25 1/4 IN., BLADE 19 7/8 IN., 7 LB. 6 OZ.
INV. NO. X 503

Provenance: *Armory, Inventory Rifle Chamber (Büch-*

senkammer) in the Hunting Lodge (Jägerhaus) in Altendresden 1730.

The cutlass bears the crowned monogram AR (Augustus Rex) and the coat of arms of Augustus the Strong. As its main motif, the sheath sports a triumphant Diana; the cutlass's handle shows Acteon whom she punished with death: Acteon, transfigured into a stag, was attacked by his own dogs. The lively arrangement of the figures is also a reference to the parforce hunt, which achieved great importance at the Dresden court during Baroque times.

Lit.: *Ehrenthal 1899b, p. 15 (no. 122).—Exh.-cat. Warsaw 1997a, p. 372 (cat. no. XI 77).—Exh.-cat. Dresden 1997b, p. 369 (cat. no. 722).*

JB

CAT. NO. 7.26

ROYAL MEISSEN PORCELAIN MANUFACTORY (handle)

Hunting Hanger
PRESUMABLY 1753
BLADE INSCRIBED AND DATED: JULION 1753/VIVAT PANDUR
BACK-EDGED BLADE: AT THE DOUBLE-EDGED TIP, PARTIALLY ETCHED, BLUED, GILT, GOLD DAMASCENED; HILT AND MOUNTS: BRASS, GILT; HANDLE: PORCELAIN, WHITE, COLOR PAINT, GLAZED; SCABBARD: WOOD, LEATHER
OVERALL L. 23 5/8 IN., BLADE 18 1/2 IN., 14 OZ.
INV. NO. X 61

Provenance: *Purchased from a private collection in 1932.*

The embellishment of this hunting hanger epitomizes Rococo decoration. The handle is ornamented in the taste of China fashion: it displays, in

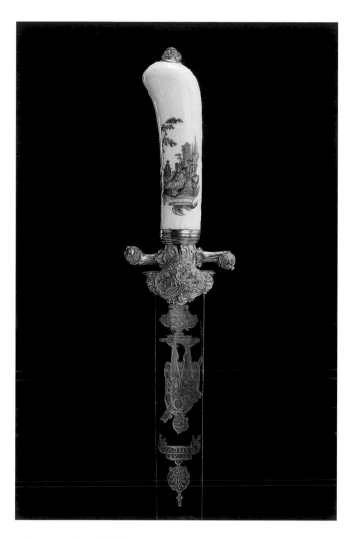

delicate colors, idyllic scenes. On its presentation side a reclining noble couple may be spotted who are located apart from a group of hunters below a ruin in the mountains. The design of the porcelain handles is based on the idea of the Baroque dining culture: like the dishes, the knife handles are made of porcelain. To furnish a hunting hanger with a porcelain handle corresponds to the ceremonial use of this weapon in the parforce hunt.

Lit.: *Exh.-cat. Munich 1990, pp. 108f. (cat. no. 148).*

JB

CAT. NOS. 7.27A AND 7.27B

JOHANN GOTTFRIED HAENISCH THE ELDER (1696–1778)

Sporting Crossbow and Bolt Case

DRESDEN, CA. 1750
SIGNED ON THE SPORTING

CROSSBOW'S BUTT PLATE: J G H
STEEL BOW BLANK; BIND STRING
OF HEMP, YELLOW WOOL
TASSELS; TILLER EBONY,
ENGRAVED BONE INLAYS
OVERALL L. 27³/₈ IN., W. 22 IN.,
4 LB. 14 OZ.
INV. NO. U 25
BOLT CASE INSCRIBED WITH
"W," "S," "No 124"
WOOD, VENEER, ROOT OF
WALNUT AND ROSEWOOD;
ENGRAVED BONE INLAYS;
SILK WITH SILVER EMBROIDERY;
ONE IRON KEY
OVERALL L. 14⁵/₈ IN.,
W. 8¹/₈ IN., 4 LB. 14 OZ.
INV. NO. U 204

The ebony column of the spring-bolt lock is richly decorated with engraved foliage, cartouches, and polished strips of bone. The cheek piece is embellished with an engraved cartouche with a monogram on its top. The sporting crossbow's cock is missing. The bolt case rests on four ball feet; its lid is decorated with pierced and en-

graved bone inlays. The central motif of the decoration is the king's crowned AR monogram. The lockable bolt case contains ten feather bolts to shoot at the target; they are distributed in two removable trays. The trays are subdivided into compartments containing utensils for shooting at the target. Among them are a small set of binoculars, a brass pencil, an ivory board subdivided into twelve sections to note hits, two little boxes with moveable lids for (charcoal) writing tools and a pair of scissors. All but one of the bolts are inscribed. Two of them bear the inscription "Her Royal Highness, the Electoral Princess." The inner side of the bolt case is decorated with a yellow piece of silk which is embroidered with the silver monogram AR under a crown.

The Stockmaker and Court Shooting Master (*Hofschützenmeister*) Haenisch the Elder originated from a Dresden family which had served

the electoral Saxon court almost without interruption since 1554. Haenisch worked together with his son who had the same name (1728–57). He was an excellent stockmaker as well and also held the office of electoral Saxon court master marksman. Numerous objects preserved in the Dresden Armory to this day were fabricated by this family. They include crossbows, sporting crossbows, and bolt cases of the highest quality. Sporting crossbows were used to shoot decoys or targets. Augustus the Strong and his son held numerous elaborate crossbow contests at Moritzburg Castle and in the park of Großsedlitz. These contests were among the most popular of all court amusements.

Lit.: *Ehrenthal 1900, p. 116.*
HWL

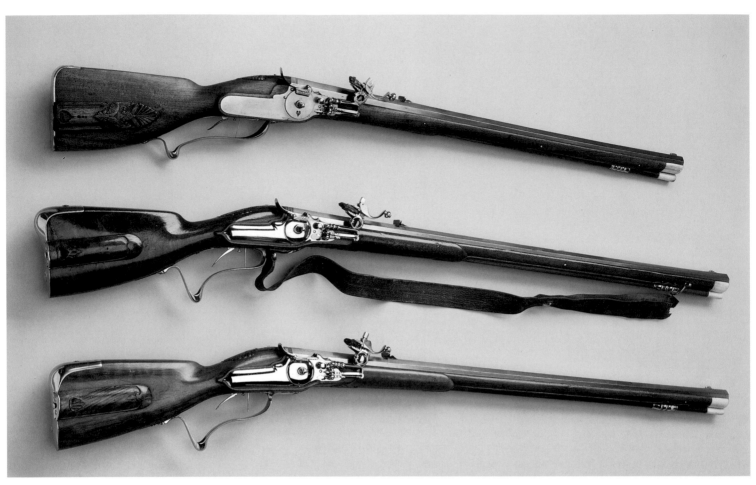

Wheel-Lock Rifles of the Hesse-Kassel Miller-Rifle Type

Wheel-lock rifles of the so-called Hesse-Kassel Miller-Rifle Type were particularly popular during the late-17th and early-18th centuries. In the case of wheel-lock weapons, sparks of pyrite are produced thanks to friction originating from the roughened surface of a steel disk. The sparks ignite the powder. Despite their simple appearance, these arms occupied a special place within Dresden's Royal Firearms Gallery (Gewehrgalerie). Their solid fabrication, reliability, and, most importantly, their accuracy are among the characteristics held in high esteem. External qualities of these weapons include an excellent barrel with 7 to 8 riflings and a turn of three-quarters, rounded lock parts, the idiosyncratic shape of the hollow-embossed trigger hilt, and the powerful, somewhat stout stock with a French butt neck rounded off toward the top. Further characteristics include a pearl border at the far end of the barrel, the unsurpassed polishing of the locks and the mounts, bone rosettes instead of the lock's counter plate, as well as the frontal end of the stock made of bone. These weapons—equipped with a hair trigger—are valued as hunting rifles or target guns. The Princely Hessian Court Rifle Maker, Hans (Johann) Jakob Lagemann from Vollmarshausen near Kassel—it appears that he also worked as miller—created this weapon type which was later copied by many masters. Of the approximately 80 "Hesse-Kassel Miller-Rifle Type" weapons kept in the Dresden Armory (Rüstkammer) today, the majority came to the Royal Firearms Gallery either as princely or as aristocratic gifts.

Lit.: Haenel 1905.

HWL

CAT. NO. 7.28

HANS JAKOB LAGEMANN *(1642–1713)*

Wheel-Lock Rifle

CA. 1690
BARREL SIGNED: HL; INSCRIBED ON THE APPENDIX OF THE BUTT PLATE: NO: 59 GR. VON KEYSERLING
IRON, POLISHED; WOOD, CARVED
OVERALL L. 42 1/8 IN., BARREL 28 IN., BORE 15 MM, 9 LB. 4 OZ.
INV. NO. G 719

Provenance: *Inventory Personal Royal Arms (Königliches Leibgewehr) 1740.*

In contrast to most guns of this type, the barrel is marked "HL," identifying this wheel-lock rifle as a work of the Princely Hessian Court Rifle Maker Lagemann.

HWL

Wheel-Lock Rifle

Ca. 1750
Inscribed on the butt plate:
No:61 Prem. Min. Gr.v.Brühl
Iron, polished; wood, carved
Overall L. 46⅛ in.,
barrel 31¼ in., bore 15 mm,
9 lb. 4 oz.
Inv. no. G 707

Provenance: *Inventory
Personal Royal Arms
(Königliches Leibgewehr) 1748.*

According to the inventory entry, this rifle was presented to Count Heinrich von Brühl in Pförten/Saxony in September 1750. *Schloss Pförten*, the primary residence of Count Brühl, served the Saxon court as a stopover en route to Warsaw and Dresden.

HWL

Wheel-Lock Rifle

Ca. 1730
Inscribed on the butt plate:
No:20 Obr.Lieut. Ponikau
Iron, polished; wood, carved
Overall L. 44⅝ in., barrel
29⅛ in., bore 15 mm, 4,650 g
Inv. no. G 681

Provenance: *Inventory Royal
Prince's Rifle Chamber
(Des Königlichen Prinzen
Büchsenkammer) 1730.*

Lit.: *Haenel 1905.*

HWL

JOHANN LEOPOLD MILOTTA
(active in Dresden 1733–60)

Pair of Wheel-Lock Rifles

Dresden, 1757
Barrels signed and marked:
MILOTTA A DRESDE;
maker's mark stamped in gold, locks signed:
MILOTTA A DRESDE
Iron, polished, carved and engraved; stock walnut, carved, bone inlays in white and green die, inlays of brass wire
Overall L. 46⅛ in., barrel 34½ in., bore 16 mm,
10 lb. 4 oz.
Inv. nos. G 449, G 450

Provenance: *Inventory
Personal Royal Arms (Königliches
Leibgewehr) 1765.*

Although Milotta was active as court rifle maker for a long time—in Dresden since 1735 and since 1738 in Warsaw—the Dresden Rifle Maker's Guild demanded that he fabricate two rifles with German locks as qualifying masterpieces. Milotta submitted this distinguished pair of target guns to the guild in 1757. According to the entry in the inventory, Count Heinrich von Brühl gave them to King Augustus III as a present in Warsaw. The locks of these weapons are richly adorned with finely engraved landscapes, figures, and hunting motifs, as well as foliage and ornaments.

Lit.: *Schaal 1975 a, no. 495 f.*
HWL

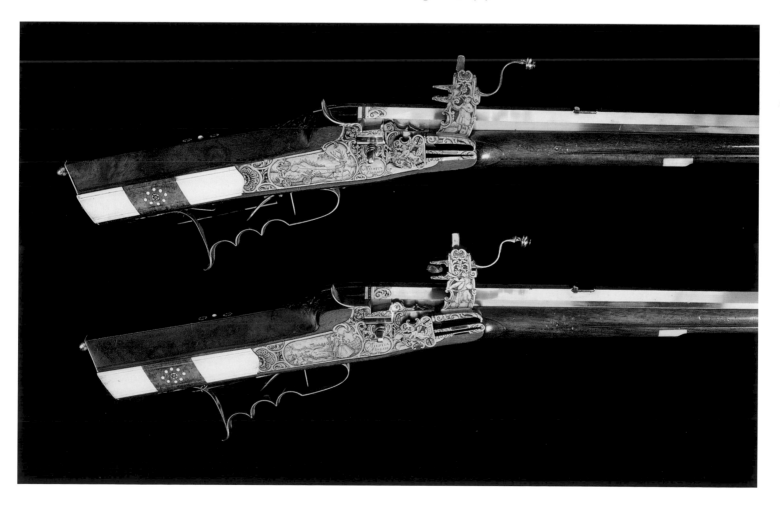

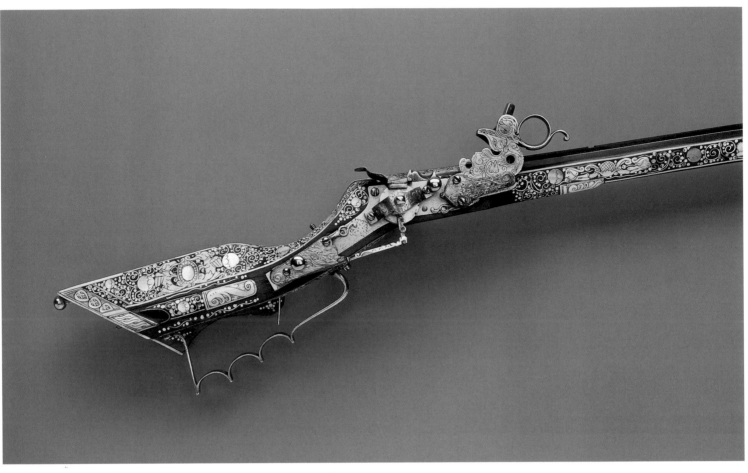

Tschinke

TESCHEN, EARLY 17TH CENTURY
SHINY STEEL, CARVED AND
PUNCHED, PARTIALLY GILT;
BRASS, ENGRAVED; STOCK PLUM
WOOD, ENGRAVED BONE AND
MOTHER-OF-PEARL INLAYS
OVERALL L. 46^{1}/8 IN., BARREL
39^{1}/8 IN., BORE 7 MM, 6 LB.
INV. NO. G 224

Towards the end of the 16th century, a special weapon, the *Tschinke*, became fashionable for bird hunt. Because of its moderate weight and its delicate stock it was preferred by women. Typical characteristics of this weapon—named after the place where it was first produced, Teschen in Silesia—are its small-bore barrel, the unusual lock construction, its extravagantly shaped stock, and its artistic decoration. One of the lock's specialities is the robust cock spring with wheel and chain located on the outside of the lock plate, which is a prerequisite to the introduction of the delicate stock. The stocks are mostly decorated with an overabundance of engraved inlays made of bone, mother-of-pearl, or brass. The finger-parted trigger and the negligible recoil assure a well-aimed shot. Many princely collections preserve *Tschinken*—which were favored for the hunt of bustard chicken, wood and black grouse until the end of the 17th century.

Lit.: *Ehrenthal 1900, pp. 21, 23 (no. 224, 226).—Schöbel 1976, p. 86, (no. 25).*

HWL

MASTER "HR"

Wheel-Lock Revolver with Four Shots

NUREMBERG, CA. 1600
LOCK SIGNED: "HR" OVER THE
SUN
SHINY STEEL, CYLINDER WITH
FOUR CHAMBERS; STOCK
WALNUT, ENGRAVED BONE
INLAYS
OVERALL L. 26^{3}/8 IN., BARREL
WITH CYLINDER 16^{1}/2 IN.,
CYLINDER 2^{3}/4 IN., BORE 9 MM,
3 LB. 5 OZ.
INV. NO. J 489

Since the introduction of firearms in the early-14th century, inventive rifle makers aimed for technical perfection. As a result, they produced hand firearms with multiple barrels for matchlock, wheel-lock, and flintlock. They were thus able to meet the demand for arms with multiple shots. Breech loaders, revolvers, and repeater arms count among further developments which impacted the future. Towards the late-16th century the first revolver arms for matchlock and wheel-lock emerged. A multitude of technically interesting pistols and rifles in the collections of the Dresden Armory testify to these impressive efforts, for which this wheel-lock revolver with four shots is a distinguished example. Its richly engraved and inlaid walnut stock reveals birds, flowers, and creatures derived from fables, placed in decorative tendrils and vines.

Lit.: *Heer 1979, p.1089*

HWL

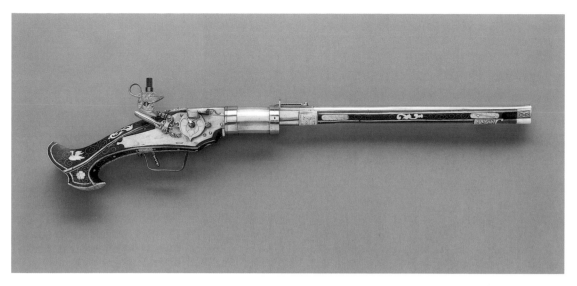

stock has a butt which points
downward; it is equipped with
a solid butt cap.

Lit.: *Hoff 1969, pp. 254–270.*
HWL

CAT. NO. 7.35

GEORG GESSLER
(1569–1616)

Wheel-Lock Pistol with Two Shots

DRESDEN, CA. 1610
BARREL SIGNED: GG
SHINY STEEL, ENGRAVED,
PARTIALLY PIERCED; LOCK PLATE
BLUED, BRASS, ENGRAVED AND
GILT; STOCK PEAR WOOD, BONE

CAT. NO. 7.34

MASTER "PD"

Wheel-Lock Revolver with Six Shots

NUREMBERG(?), CA. 1610
LOCK SIGNED: PD
SHINY STEEL, CYLINDER WITH
SIX CHAMBERS; STOCK WALNUT
OVERALL L. 24^{3}/$_{8}$ IN., BARREL
WITH CYLINDER 15^{1}/$_{8}$ IN.,
CYLINDER 2^{3}/$_{4}$ IN., BORE 9.5 MM,
3 LB. 7 OZ.
INV. NO. J 454

This weapon is the prototype for the modern cylinder revolver although the cylinder must still be operated by hand. It turns around an axle which is located in the butt and attached to the lower side of the barrel's back end. A spring screwed to the barrel's end grips one of the cylinder's six drill holes with its beak-shaped front end and thereby locks it (the spring is missing). The cylinder has six chambers to receive the powder and the bullet. The lock's cock with its exterior wheel is located behind the cylinder. Each of the chambers is equipped with a firing hole connected through a canal in the breech-plug plate with the priming pan's firing canal. Although six successive shots can be fired, the cock spring must be recocked after each shot, and powder must be placed into the priming pan. This diminishes the firing speed. The

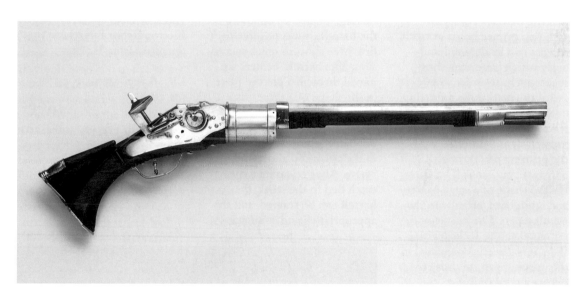

INLAYS PARTIALLY ENGRAVED
OVERALL L. 32^{1}/$_{4}$ IN., BARREL
22 IN., BORE 9 MM, 3 LB. 3 OZ.
INV. NO. J 363

Georg Geßler, born as the son of the rifle maker Elias Geßler in Strasbourg, came to Dresden in 1603. Thanks to the recommendation of the prince elector he was made a member of the Dresden Rifle Maker's Guild as early as 1606. He did not even have to produce a masterpiece. In the same year he was awarded the court office of Armory Servant (*Rüst-*

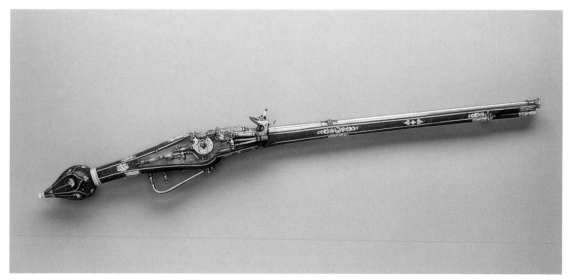

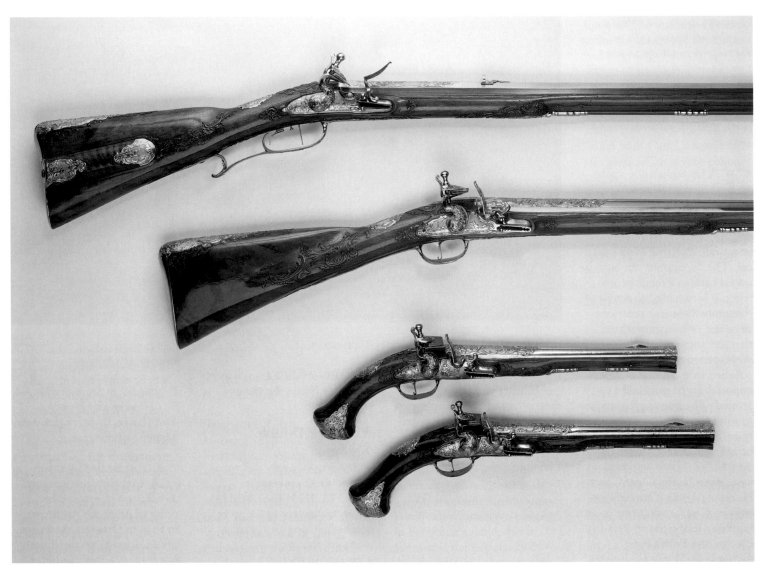

CAT. NOS. 7.47A TO 7.47D

JOHANN GOTTLIEB
KOLB (active in Suhl/
Thuringia 1730–57)

**Suit of Flintlock
Firearms (Rifle,
Shotgun, Pair of Pistols)**

SUHL, 1747
IRON, POLISHED, CARVED,
ENGRAVED, AND GILT; STOCKS
WALNUT, CARVED
RIFLE: OVERALL L. 42 1/2 IN.,
BARREL 27 1/2 IN., BORE 16 MM,
7 LB. 10 OZ.
SHOTGUN: OVERALL L. 54 IN.,
BARREL 39 1/8 IN., BORE 17 MM,
6 LB. 6 OZ.
PISTOLS: OVERALL L. 17 7/8 IN.,
BARREL 11 3/8 IN., BORE 15 MM,
2 LB. 2 OZ.

INV. NOS. G 896, G 866, J 694,
J 695

Provenance: *Inventory
Personal Royal Arms
(Königliches Leibgewehr) 1748.*

Suhl, long a center for
German rifle production,
fell under electoral Saxon
government in 1718. Firearms
produced by Kolb belong to
the artistically accomplished
works fabricated in Suhl in the
18th century. They are distinguished by their elegance, the
unsurpassed finesse and profi-
ciency of their iron cut and
gilding, and through the gracious sophistication of their
Rococo ornaments. The weapons are abundantly adorned

with *rocailles*, depictions of figures, and hunting scenes such
as hawking, bird, and red deer
hunts. The pistols, likewise
used for the parforce hunt, are
decorated with war trophies.
As can be inferred from the
inventory, the only year Kolb
delivered firearms to the Dresden court was in 1747.

Lit.: *Schaal 1979, pp. 69 ff.
(nos. 49–52).*

HWL

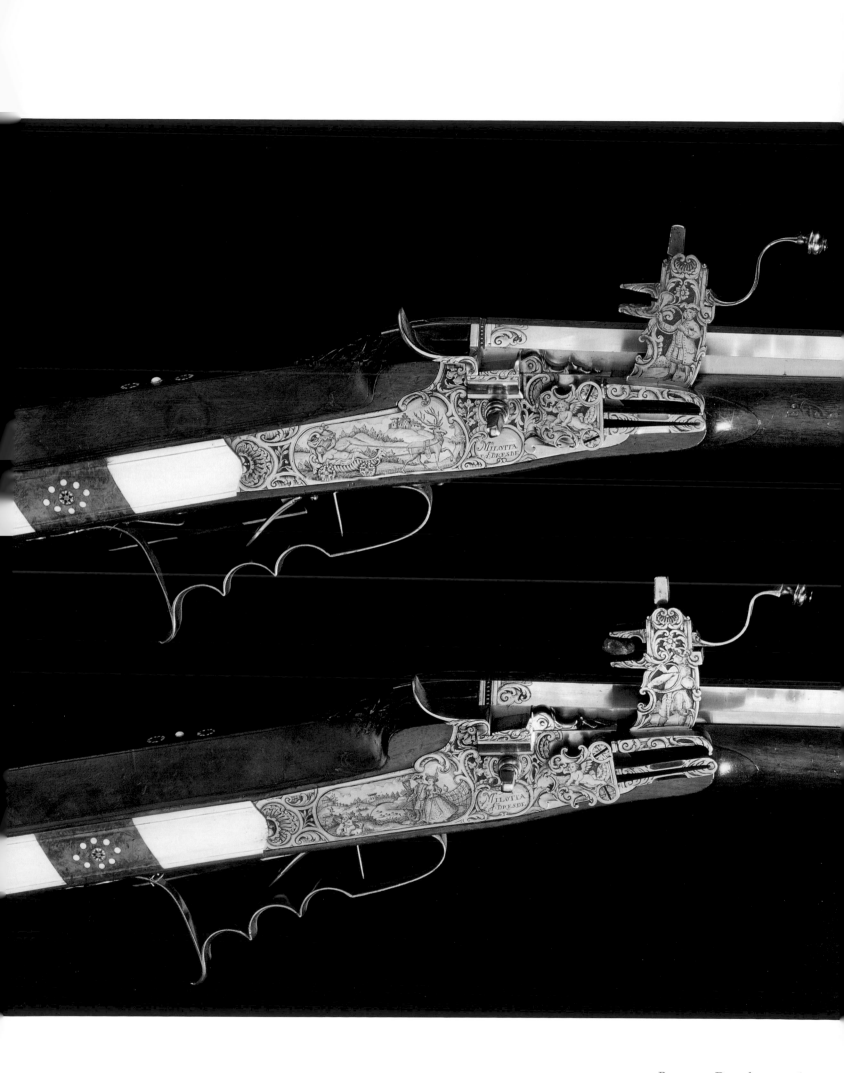

"Nothing Comparable to This Moritzburg Is to Be Found Anywhere."

THE HUNTING CASTLE MORITZBURG AND AUGUSTUS THE STRONG'S COLLECTION OF ANTLERS

Ralf Giermann

These flattering words about the Baroque Hunting Castle Moritzburg (*Jagdschloss Moritzburg*)—situated only a few miles away from the former residential city of Dresden—may be found in a Saxon chronicle of 1735. An unidentified, fictitious "foreign, high passenger" is supposed to have made this statement publicly, after he had studied and seen "in Italy many admirable things, in France many magnificent things, in Spain many unbelievable rarities."[1]

Duke (and later Prince Elector) Moritz of Saxony (1521–53) had a practical hunting lodge built in a wooded area rich in game as early as the mid-16th century. Starting in 1723, the late Baroque modification into a stately hunting and pleasure castle took place under the direction of Chief Building Master (*Oberlandbaumeister*) Matthäus Daniel Pöppelmann. The commissioner was Prince Elector/King Augustus the Strong (1670–1733), who supplied his own plans for the alterations.

The king dedicated the castle to Diana, goddess of the hunt, a figure derived from ancient mythology. He and many of his predecessors and successors had a great love of the hunt and related aspects of forestry and wildlife. Saxony offered plenty of wooded areas and abundant wildlife for them to indulge this passion. In Germany, the hunt was a privilege restricted to the higher echelons of the aristocracy—mostly the rulers—for centuries. For the longest time, the issue of the right to hunt was based not on laws of propriety

but rather the specific class structure (*Ständeverhältnisse*). Since the Middle Ages, as the high aristocracy grew more powerful, they had successively appropriated more privileges.

Rising in the middle of a lake, the castle rests on a foundation and is surrounded by a terrace (fig. 1). In terms of function and design, it is the zenith of an extensive ensemble of buildings and parks conceived by Augustus the Strong and located in the *Friedewald*. Major constituents included the park of the castle, a pheasant farm, a hunting ground with belvedere, as well as a system of aisles, numerous ponds, and canals. The king's death interrupted the work, and some parts remained forever unfinished.[2]

Today, Moritzburg Castle contains a *museum for baroque and court culture*. Among the many admired treasures are the Feather Room (*Federzimmer*) (Augustus the Strong's state bed with more than one million bird feathers woven into its bedcovers and baldachino), the largest holdings, worldwide, of ornamental and figural leather wall coverings, as well as an extraordinary collection of antlers assembled over numerous centuries by the Saxon rulers.[3]

The collection of antlers is located near the entrance and in three of the main floor's four halls. The most fascinating aspect is not so much the abundance, but the quality of the material and the way the trophies are presented. All of the antlers are mounted onto carved and painted, sometimes even gilt wooden deer heads, illustrating the immense importance attributed to every single trophy and demonstrating its uniqueness.

The setting of the Stone Hall (*Steinsaal*)—formerly the entry to the castle—recalls European aristocrats' passion, especially during Baroque times, for all things exotic. The walls are adorned with trophies of animals who had long since perished in the Saxon forests dur-

The famous Moritzburg stag with 66-point antlers

According to tradition, the Moritzburg antlers were found on the Crimean peninsula near the Black Sea. They were brought to Moritzburg by Czar Peter the Great as a present for Augustus the Strong. In the Hall of Monstrosities (*Monströsensaal*) monumental paintings on leather cover the walls with scenes derived from ancient mythology and depicting the goddess of the hunt, Diana.

ing Augustus the Strong's reign, among them reindeer and elk. The elk—certainly living on German soil until approximately 1,000 years ago—was later exterminated in the wild. The reindeer on the other hand—incidentally both male and female have antlers—is not known to have lived in German lands. There are numerous requests by German princes to the courts of Norway, Sweden, and Prussia between the 16th and 18th centuries asking for reindeer and elk for hunting purposes or simply to try to resettle them in German forests. However, in Saxony as elsewhere, such attempts remained unsuccessful under prince electors Christian I (1560–1591), Johann Georg I (1585–1656), and Augustus the Strong.

Most of the elk and reindeer antlers in the Moritzburg collection originate from the Saxon Hunting Castle Augustusburg, where the vast majority of the Wettin antler and horn collection—amounting to well over 2,000 items—was kept before Augustus the Strong modified Moritzburg. The trophy collection was begun under Prince Elector Augustus (1526–1586) during the second half of the 16th century. The bulk of the reindeer and elk antlers was a gift to Augustus from his brother in law, the king of Denmark, Frederick II (1534–1588).

The collection is complemented, in the Stone Hall, by fossilized antlers of a gigantic stag whose species became extinct approximately 8,000 years ago. Despite its shovel-shaped antlers, this stag was not related to the elk. The gigantic stag's extraordinary antlers could reach a span of up to 14 feet.[4] During the last ice age, this animal populated steppes and park landscapes as well as swampy and marshy areas in the northern world.

Decoratively arranged between the images are exclusively malformed red deer antlers. They are mounted onto dear heads which are entirely gilt and embellished with oak leaves. A greater glorification of zoological anomalies than this quintessentially Baroque one is barely conceivable. The ultimate step would have been to gild the trophies themselves.

How far the glorification of an individual trophy could go is demonstrated by the story of the famous "66-point antlers" from Moritzburg Castle (see p. 266). It appears that no other set of antlers has attained similar fame within the history of the European hunt. The uniqueness of the points numbering system was only established arbitrarily, yet its ultimate goal was the documentation of great hunting successes and the complimentary portrayal of the huntman's skill. Numerous depictions of the antlers immortalized the object. Among the items including depictions of this trophy were paintings, engravings, silver and gilt drinking vessels, a weather pane, and illustrations on a powder flask and on the hunting rifle with which the animal had been shot. The spot where the stag had been killed was memorialized by a 14-foot-high stone marker, erected in 1707. Prince Elector Frederick III of Brandenburg (1657–1713) was the 850-plus-pound stag's fortunate marksman in the year 1696.[5] His successor, King Frederick William I of Prussia (1688–1740), later gave the set of antlers to Augustus the Strong as a present to commemorate the recently inaugurated Moritzburg Castle.

There is only one other set of antlers in the collection for which a continuous provenance can be established. Captured by the collection's founder, Prince

2 The Festival Hall

Elector Augustus, it originates from 1585 and is thus the oldest known set. Supposedly, the prince elector had a special love for abnormally shaped antlers.

The most important and at the same time the most significant space in the castle is the Festival Hall (*Festsaal*). It reveals how the architecture and the organization of the antlers are deliberately arranged so they form a cohesive unit. Thanks to the deeply recessed window niches—an architectural necessity—the elaborately decorated stags' heads contrast with each other quite splendidly. Despite their vast number, it is still possible to survey them individually (fig. 2). The heads are decorated with vines and grapes. Grapes are a symbol of fertility and life; as the wine of life signify the promise of immortality.

Johann Christian Kirchner (1691–1732), one of the best-known Baroque sculptors in Saxony, and his studio were put in charge of the design and the execution of the deer heads. Not the least bit less accomplished than other works of Baroque sculpture, the Kirchner heads—as a student of the famous Permoser he also sculpted works for the *Zwinger*—adorn the walls of the Festival Hall and the Hall of Monstrosities. In addition, a plethora of vases and figures of children rendered in sandstone and mounted on the balustrade of the terrace and the drive to Moritzburg Castle are attributed to Kirchner.

The number of points on the antler's main beams was of major importance during Baroque times. This is why the number was listed—visible to everyone—on a gilt shield in the lower portion of the cartouches on which the heads rest. A total of seventy-one sets of antlers with a minimum of 24 points are displayed in the Festival Hall. The examples with the most points are exhibited on the lowest level, i.e., at eye level. The antlers were frequently blackened in order to further emphasize the glossy tips of the points, which appear to protrude as if they were made of ivory.

As in the preceding spaces, in this hall, too, only a very few pieces have a conclusive provenance. Most of them are, however, likely to originate from Saxon districts close to Augustusburg and other Wettin castles. Gifts are documented from Brandenburg/Prussia. Among them, along with the "66-point antlers," are four sets of antlers still bearing the letter "P" (for Prussia) under their points, which were presented in 1727.

Among the antlers kept in the Festival Hall is the world's heaviest red deer trophy.[6] Weighing in excess of 40 pounds,[7] it was evaluated by the commission Trophies and Exhibitions of the World Hunting Council (*Weltjagdrat*) with a total of 298.25 international points in 1991. Unfortunately, nothing is known about the provenance.

Notes

1 Iccander 1735, p.7.
2 For more information regarding Moritzburg as a cultural landscape see esp. Hartmann 1990, Schlechte 1984.
3 About the Feather Room cf. Giermann 2003; for the leather wallpaper, see Schulze 1997; Giermann 2000; for the collection of antlers, see Giermann 1993.
4 The span of the Moritzburg antlers is roughly seven feet.
5 Today, the weight of Central European red deer rarely exceeds 450 pounds.
6 Criteria for evaluation include mass of the antlers, length and circumference of the main beams, number of points, and color.
7 Today, the weight of European red deer antlers can reach circa 28 pounds. Weights beyond this are excessively rare; the average weight of such antlers is in the vicinity of 20 pounds.

CAT. NO. 8.1

JOHANN CHRISTIAN
KIRCHNER *(1691–1732)*,
workshop

**Stag's Head with
Cartouche and
Red Deer Antlers**

DRESDEN, CA. 1728–32
LINDEN WOOD, CARVED,
HILTED, GILT, CARTOUCHE
30³/₈ × 17³/₄ IN.
24-POINT ANTLERS (UNEVEN),
PROJECTION 59¹/₂ IN.,
MINIMUM AGE CA. 300 YEARS
STAATLICHE SCHLÖSSER,
BURGEN UND GÄRTEN SACHSEN,
SCHLOSS MORITZBURG:
INV. NO. 23/79.

A t the time of Augustus
the Strong, this was
regarded as a 28-point,
as is still indicated by the label
in the lower part of the cartouche. Since the criterion for
a point has been established
to measure at least 20 milli-
meters in length, in contemporary terms this is a 24-point.
The second heaviest trophy in
the Moritzburg Collection
with its weight of ca. 35
pounds, it is surpassed only by
the world's heaviest set of
antlers, also kept in Moritzburg.

Lit.: *Meyer 1883, plate X.—
Bösener 1972, pp. 131, 133.—
Giermann 1993, p. 28.*

RG

CAT. NO. 8.2

JOHANN CHRISTIAN
KIRCHNER *(1691–1732)*,
workshop

**Stag's Head with
Cartouche and
Red Deer Antlers**

DRESDEN, CA. 1728–32
LINDEN WOOD, CARVED,
HILTED, GILT, CARTOUCHE
29¹/₂ × 18¹/₈ IN.
26-POINT ANTLERS (UNEVEN),
PROJECTION 69¹/₄ IN.,
MINIMUM AGE CA. 300 YEARS
STAATLICHE SCHLÖSSER,
BURGEN UND GÄRTEN SACHSEN,
SCHLOSS MORITZBURG:
INV. NO. 9/79

T he structure of these
antlers is harmonious.
With a length of
51⁵/₈ in. and 52 in. respectively,
the length of its main beams is
the longest of all the Moritzburg antlers. It holds third
place in the overall evaluation,
weighing over 30 pounds,
which is unusually heavy. The
brown-black coloration is arti-
ficial.

Lit.: *Meyer 1883, plate XIII.—
Bösener 1972, pp. 129, 131.—
Giermann 1993, p. 28.*

RG

The *Histoire Métallique* of Augustus the Strong

Paul Arnold

The art of medal engraving played a leading role in the glorification of Saxon Prince Elector and Polish King Augustus the Strong (*August der Starke*).[1] Thanks to his support, medal engraving of the Baroque era reached its state of highest perfection under his rule. During his 39-year reign approximately 180 different medals and other medal-like commemorative coins were struck. They were either given away on festive occasions or could be purchased. A total of 20 medalists worked for Augustus. Six of them—Martin Heinrich Omeis, Heinrich Paul Groskurt, Oluf Wif, Johann Wilhelm Höckner, Georg Lorenz Kaufmann, and Albrecht Krieger—were simultaneously the engravers and die sinkers of his mints in Dresden and Leipzig. Of the medalists working for him outside Saxony, the following warrant special mention: Georg Hautsch, Philipp Heinrich Müller, Martin Heinrich Smeltzing, Georg Wilhelm Vestner, and Christian Wermuth of Gotha who had received his training at the Dresden Mint.

Augustus mandated that all designs for medals be approved by himself. This is how he created his own *Histoire Métallique* (Metal History) a standing chronicle of the history of his government. Ancient Roman coins served as Augustus's point of departure and prototype. Roman emperors used coins to propagate their political agendas, publicize noteworthy domestic and foreign events of their tenure, and their military successes. The first portrait medals in Italy, created as early as the 15th century, were based on the Roman imperial prototypes. With the invention of the screw press, in the second half of the 16th century, it became possible to strike medals in larger editions, enabling the evolution of commemorative event medals in the 17th century. Because of their practical format, medals were particularly designed to satisfy the sovereign's desire for fame and glory. Therefore, the art of medal engraving became widespread and popular in all larger mints.

Louis XIV, the Sun King, founded the Académie Royale des Médailles et des Inscriptions in Paris. Its mission was not just to create medals but also to publish in order to increase the king's glory. In 1702, the

G. Hautsch, Medal Commemorating the Election of Augustus the Strong to Polish King, silver, diameter 1.69 in., Coin Cabinet

Académie Royale published the lusciously printed book *Médailles sur les principaux événements du règne Louis Le Grand avec des explications historiques*. This was after Claude François Menestrier had published the *Histoire du Roy Louis Le Grand par les médailles, emblêmes, devises, jettons, inscriptions, armoiries et autre monumens publics* in 1693. The idea of the *Histoire Métallique* goes back to Bizot who had issued his *Histoire métallique de la republique d'Hollande* in 1687. In Saxony, the court historiographer Wilhelm Ernst Tentzel published the *Saxonia Numismatica* in 1705.

A multitude of people were involved in the fabrication and the publication of medals. At first, the inventors delivered their plans which often consisted of Latin inscriptions and quotations taken from ancient literature. Then, the court artists drew their designs for medals. They were subsequently engraved by the medalist into a die. Finally, the court historiographer published the medal designs with extensive descriptions.

The themes of Augustus the Strong's *Histoire Métallique* are multifaceted. They include the important events of his family, domestic, and foreign politics. By far the most significant family event in the *Histoire Métallique* is the 1719 marriage between Prince Elector Frederick Augustus and the oldest daughter of Emperor Joseph I, Archduchess Maria Josepha. The events and the personalities portrayed are often represented in allegorical ways. Augustus the Strong, for example, liked to be pictured as *Hercules Saxonicus* or as *Phoebus Apollo*, adding a certain theatrical notion to his depiction.

Attaining the Polish crown formed the Saxon-Polish Union's foundation for which Augustus was striving. It therefore plays an important role on the medals. The medal Georg Hautsch coined on the occasion of the Polish coronation in 1697 shows Augustus as *Hercules Saxonicus*. Over his armor, he wears the lion skin of Hercules, he leans on a club and steps on the Hydra. Standing in front of him is Polonia, offering him the Polish crown. In response, he answers her with words taken from Virgil's *Aeneid*: NEC ME LABOR ILLE GRAVABIT (Not even this trouble will be too hard for me).

Undoubtedly the most impressive testimony to the art of Saxon medal engraving is the portrait of Augustus the Strong created by Heinrich Paul Groskurt between 1705 and 1707 which he executed with a

sense of plasticity and spatial disposition (cat. no. 9.4). It met with the king's vision for the proper representation of his political plans and his ideas of how royal dignity was to be delineated. He, therefore, selected this image to be his official portrait, employing it for almost 30 years on his medals and coins.

Notes

1 Cf. Arnold 1985, Arnold 1995, Grund 2001.

Provenance: *Former Royal Coin Cabinet.*

The Polish Kaminiec Fortress—situated in the province of Podolia—was located near the former border with the Ottoman Empire. After the peace treaty of Karlowitz, in September 1699, the Turks were obliged to vacate the fortress.

Lit.: *Exh.-cat. Schallaburg 1984, no. I. 201.—Arnold 1985, p. 42 (no. 9).—Grund 1996, no. O 1699/01.*

RGr

CAT. NO. 9.1

MARTIN HEINRICH OMEIS *(1650–1703)*

Medal Commemorating the Election as King and the Coronation

1697
OBVERSE:
AUGUSTUS. II. D. G. REX. POLON.&.M. D. L. LAUREATE, ARMORED, AND DRAPED BUST FACING RIGHT. SIGNED ON THE ARM: MHO.
REVERSE:
SAC. ROM. IMP. ARCHIM. ETLECT. SAXON./ELECT. D.27.IUN. CORONAT. D. 15.SEPT. ANNO.1697. CROWNED SHIELD WITH POLISH-LITHUANIAN COAT OF ARMS, SURROUNDED BY PALM BRANCHES AND COVERED WITH THE CROWNED ELECTORAL AND DUCAL SAXON COAT OF ARMS.
EDGE: WREATH OF RUES
GOLD, DIAM. 1.74 IN., 2.46 OZ.
INV. NO. 3723

Provenance: *Former Royal Coin Cabinet.*

The date of the election and the coronation of Augustus the Strong as king of Poland are cited according to the Julian Calendar, which was still used in Saxony in 1697. It was not until February of the year 1700 that Saxony introduced the Gregorian Calendar which had been in use in Poland since the 16th century. According to the Gregorian Calendar, the election and the coronation occurred on June 17 and September 5, 1697, respectively.

Lit.: *Arnold 1985, p. 42 (no. 4.)—Exh.-cat. Essen 1986, no. 74.—Grund 1996, no. O 1697/02.*

PA

CAT. NO. 9.2

MARTIN HEINRICH OMEIS *(1650–1703)*

Medal Commemorating the Recovery of the Kaminiec-Fortress in Podolia

1699
OBVERSE:
D. G. FRID. AUGUST₉ POLONIARUM REX, SAX. DUX & ELECT.1699. ARMORED AND DRAPED BUST FACING RIGHT. SIGNED ON THE ARM: MHO.

REVERSE: IN THE FOREGROUND KNEELING FEMALE PERSONIFICATION OF KAMINIEC WITH MURAL CROWN AND SHIELD, ON IT THE SUN, TO THE LEFT AND TO THE RIGHT OF THIS 1699. IN THE BACKGROUND VIEW OF THE FORTRESS. TOP: GLORIOSE' RECUPERATUM. D.22.SEPT., BOTTOM: CAMINIEC IN PODOLIA. EDGE: ROSETTE DIVINO ANNVENTE NVMINE EX VOTO NON INIQVO NON INIVSTO FELICITER ET. THE CHRONOGRAM IN THE UNDERLINED ROMAN NUMERAL LETTERS ADDED IN THE EDGE INSCRIPTION GIVES THE YEAR OF THE RECOVERY 1699.
GOLD, DIAM. 1.73 IN., 2.45 OZ.
INV. NO. 3424

CAT. NO. 9.3

CHRISTIAN WERMUTH *(1661–1739)*

Medal Commemorating the Struggle to Regain the Polish Throne

1705
OBVERSE: D. G. AUGUST₉ II. REX. POL. M. D. L. S. R. I. A. M. D.EL. SAX. LAUREATE, ARMORED, AND DRAPED BUST FACING RIGHT. ON THE ARM: ANN. MDCCV.ÆT. XXXV./ELECT. XII/ET CORONAT. VIII. SIGNED TO THE RIGHT: C. W.

REVERSE: SVSTINENDO. HERCULES, WITH LION SKIN AND CLUB, CARRIES THE GLOBE WITH THE COUNTRIES POLAND, LITHUANIA, AND SAXONY. IN THE EXERGUE: MDCCIV/ C. WERMUTH. F. SILVER, DIAM. 28.7 IN., 8.19 OZ. INV. NO. 8841

Provenance: *Former Royal Coin Cabinet.*

Hercules carrying the globe symbolizes the struggle of Augustus the Strong, the *Hercules Saxonicus*, for the Polish crown, which he would temporarily lose to Stanislaw Leszczyński after the peace treaty of Altranstädt in 1706.

Lit.: *Exh.-cat. Essen 1986, no. 80.—Wohlfahrt 1992, no. 05019.—Arnold 1995, p. 37 (no. 617).*

PA

CAT. NO. 9.4

HEINRICH PAUL GROSKURT (*1675–1751*)

Medal Commemorating the Foundation of the Order of the White Eagle

N. D. (1705/06)
OBVERSE:
D. G. AVGVSTVS II. REX POLON. ELECT. SAXON. HEAD FACING RIGHT, SIGNED BELOW: H. P. GROSKVRT. REVERSE: RESTAVRATOR ORDINIS AQVILAE ALBAE. THE POLISH THRONE — RESTING ON A PANELED FLOOR — TERMINATES IN THE POLISH CROWN AND TWO EAGLES. HANGING FROM ITS BACK ARE THE BREAST STAR AND THE CROSS WITH THE SASH OF

THE ORDER OF THE WHITE EAGLE. THE MOTTO OF THE ORDER MAY BE SEEN ON THE BREAST STAR: PRO/FIDE/ REGE/ET LEGE. GOLD, DIAM. 2.55 IN., 6.10 OZ. INV. NO. 3641

Provenance: *Former Royal Coin Cabinet.*

The medal was also struck with a 1.73 in. diameter. The Order of the White Eagle had two mottos. As Master of the Order, the king wore the motto PRO FIDE LEGE ET GREGE (for fidelity, law, and people), while the knights' crosses were inscribed with the motto PRO FIDE, REGE ET LEGE (for fidelity, king, and law).

Lit.: *Exh.-cat. Schallaburg 1984, no. I. 205.—Arnold 1985,*

p. 45 (no. 19).—Exh.-cat. Warsaw 1997a, no. II. 25.

PA

CAT. NO. 9.5

HEINRICH PAUL GROSKURT (*1675–1751*)

Medal Commemorating the *Baubegnadigungsmandat*

1707
OBVERSE:
D. G. AVGVSTVS II. REX POLON. ELECT. SAXON. HEAD FACING RIGHT, SIGNED BELOW: H. P. GROSKVRT. REVERSE: PRAEMIA. AEDIFI-CANTIBVS. CONSTITVTA. A PUTTO SHOWS A SEATED MER-CURY, THE VERTICAL PROJECTION OF A BUILDING, RECEIVING A PURSE WITH MONEY IN RETURN. IN THE BACKGROUND A STREET

CONSTRUCTION MAY BE SEEN WITH SOME HOUSES STILL UNFINISHED. IN THE EXERGUE: EX AERARIO.OPT. PRINC./MDCCVII. SILVER, DIAM. 2.57 IN., 4.12 OZ. INV. NO. 2955

Provenance: *Former Royal Coin Cabinet.*

Augustus the Strong decreed the *Baubegnadigungsmandat* on April 24, 1706. This guaranteed all homeowners and those willing to build—given that their previous homes had been damaged either by fire or water—tax cuts. The goal was to contribute to new, homogenous facades and to beautify the streets of the residential city of Dresden.

Lit.: *Exh.-cat. Schallaburg*

(cat. no. 9.3). This medal emphasizes the king as supporter of the arts and of science in conjunction with the university's jubilee.

Lit.: *Exh.-cat. Schallaburg 1984, no. I. 207.—Arnold 1985, p. 44 (no. 12).—Exh.-cat. Essen 1986, no. 136.—Wohlfahrt 1992, no. 09035.*

PA

Cat. no. 9.7

HEINRICH PAUL GROSKURT (1675–1751)

Medal Commemorating the Recovery of the Polish Crown

N. d. (1714/17)
Obverse:
D. G. AVGVSTVS II. REX POLON. ELECT. SAXON. Head facing right, signed below: H. P. GROSKVRT. Reverse: PRO REGNI CVSTODIA. Royal Polish insignia and Saxon electoral swords.
Silver, Diam. 3.19 in., 8.35 oz.
Inv. no. 8849

Provenance: *Former Royal Coin Cabinet.*

F or the obverse of this jubilee medal, Christian Wermuth used the same die as for the 1705 medal commemorating Augustus the Strong as *Hercules Saxonicus*

1984, no. I. 206.—Arnold 1985, p. 45 (no. 14).

PA

Cat. no. 9.6

CHRISTIAN WERMUTH (1661–1739)

Medal Commemorating the 300th Anniversary of Leipzig University

1709
Obverse:
D. G. AUGUST9 II. REX POL. M. D. L. S. R. I. A. M. D.EL. SAX. Laureate, armored, and draped bust facing right. On the arm: ANN. MDCCV.ÆT. XXXV./ELECT. XII/ET CORONAT. VIII. Signed to the right: C. W.
Reverse: VTRIQVE INTENTA. A standing Minerva with owl-embellished helmet, spear, and shield,

and surrounded by the attributes of science, the arts, and war. In the exergue: MEMORIAE NATAL. III. ACAD. LIPS:./AN:MDC-CIX. IV. DEC. CEL. SACR./ CHRISTIAN WERMVTH. F. Silver, Diam. 2.83 in., 6.72 oz. Inv. no. 8839

Provenance: *Former Royal Coin Cabinet.*

Lit.: *Exh.-cat. Essen 1986,
no. 307.—Exh.-cat. Warsaw
1997b, VI, 48.*

PA

CAT. NO. 9.8

HEINRICH PAUL
GROSKURT (*1675–1751*)

Medal Commemorating the Recovery of the Polish Crown

N. D. (1714/17)
OBVERSE:
D. G. AVGVSTVS II. REX
POLON. ELECT. SAXON.
HEAD FACING RIGHT, SIGNED
BELOW: H. P. GROSKVRT.
REVERSE: ADVERSIS RESIS-
TENDVM PRVDENTIA.
HERCULES WITH LION SKIN AND
CLUB, FIGHTING THE HYDRA.
THE ENLARGED INITIALS IN THE
LEGEND REVEAL NAME AND
ROYAL TITLE OF AUGUSTUS THE
STRONG: ARP (AUGUSTUS REX
POLONIAE).
SILVER, DIAM. 3.19 IN., 8.19 OZ.
COIN CABINET, COLLECTION
HORN

Provenance: *Collection Horn.*

Groskurt based his
engravings of the
reverse dies for both
medals on designs by Dresden
painter Georg Christian Fritz-
sche (see Arnold 1985, fig. 17).
The medals belong to a series
of four which show the same
obverse and which were
struck in three different sizes.
Augustus the Strong selected
them himself from 17 designs.
In 1714 Groskurt received
the commission which he
delivered in 1717. It took such
a long time to produce them
because for the striking alone
he needed to engrave 15 dies.
On this medal, too, the depiction of Hercules slaying the
Hydra symbolizes Augustus's
struggle for the successful
recovery of Poland: By virtue
of his intelligence he was able
to resist his enemies (adversis
resistendum prudentia).

Lit.: *Exh.-cat. Schallaburg
1984, no. I. 204.—Exh.-cat.*

*Essen 1986, no. 88.—Arnold
1995, p. 38 (no. 8/9).*

PA

CAT. NO. 9.9

GEORG WILHELM
VESTNER (*1677–1740*)

Medal Commemorating the Pacification of Poland and the Return of Augustus the Strong to Saxony

1717
OBVERSE:
FRID. AVGVST. D. G. REX
POLON. ET EL. SAX.
LAUREATE, ARMORED, AND
DRAPED BUST FACING RIGHT.
SIGNED UNDER THE BUST: V.
REVERSE: POLONIA PACATA
REX REDVX. AUGUSTUS THE
STRONG, DEPICTED AS PHOEBUS
APOLLO, IS SURROUNDED BY

SUN'S RAYS AND IS SEATED
FRONTALLY IN A QUADRIGA
ABOVE THE CLOUDS. IN HIS
RIGHT HAND HE HOLDS A LAUREL
WREATH AND A PALM BRANCH IN
HIS LEFT HAND. IN THE EXER-
GUE: PLAVDENTE
SAXO=/NIA. D.12.APR. 1717
GOLD, DIAM. 1.72 IN., 1.47 OZ.
INV. NO. 3754

Provenance: *Former Royal
Coin Cabinet.*

On the Imperial Diet
of Pacification (*Pazi-
fikationsreichstag*) of
February 1, 1717, Augustus II
gained the acknowledgement
as king of Poland—even from
the supporters of his enemy,
Stanislaw Leszczyński. Afterwards he was able to return—
as "Phoebus Apollo in the sun
chariot"—to "Saxony who
happily anticipated" him (plau-
dente Saxonia).

Lit.: *Bernheimer 1984, II,
no. 127.—Arnold 1985, p. 48
(no. 22).—Exh.-cat. Essen 1986,
no. 89.*

PA

JOHANN WILHELM
HOECKNER (1671–1756)

**Medal Commemorating
the Laying of the
Foundation Stone of
Dresden's *Frauenkirche*
1726**

OBVERSE:
PERFICIETVR. OPVS:DIVI
NO. NVMINE. COEPTVM.
VIEW OF THE FRAUENKIRCHE.
SIGNED IN THE EXERGUE:
HOECKNER. FEC.
REVERSE:
D. O. M. S/AVGVSTO. AVSPI
CIO/POTENTISS. POLON.
REGIS/ET.
SERENISS. ELECT. SAXON/
FRIDERICI. AVGVSTI/AED
ES. A. B. VIRG.DICTA/
CRESCENTEM.SACRA.FRE
QVEN/TANTIVM
NVMERVM/VIX.AMPLIVS.
CAPTVRA/ET.VETVS-
TATE.FERME.COLLAPSA/P
RIMO.FABRICAE.OVAE.LAP
IDE/D.XXVI.AVGVST.MDC-
CXXVI/SOLLEMNI.RITV.IA
CTO/INSTAVRARI.EXTRVI
QVE/COEPTA/CVRANTE.C
IVIT.DRESD/SENATV
GOLD, DIAM. 2.16 IN., 3.07 OZ.
INV. NO. 3651

Provenance: *Former Royal
Coin Cabinet.*

On August 26, 1726, the foundation stone for Dresden's *Frauenkirche* was laid. The church was completed in 1734. The Dresden city council had commissioned the building, whose execution was in the hands of municipal master builder George Bähr. The medal reflects precisely his second design for this Protestant church. The final building deviated from this plan in many details.

Lit.: *Exh.-cat. Schallaburg 1984, no. I. 216.—Grund 1992, no. II. 5.—Exh.-cat. Warsaw 1997b, VI, 50.*

RGr

HEINRICH PAUL
GROSKURT (1675–1751)

**Medal Commemorating
the So-Called
*Zeithainer Lager***

1730
OBVERSE: D. G. AVGVSTVS·II
REX POLON. ELECT
SAXON. HEAD FACING RIGHT,
SIGNED BELOW:
H. P. GROSKVRT.
REVERSE: IN THE FOREGROUND
THE ENCAMPMENT WITH AN
ARMY ARRANGED IN TWO RANKS
AND THE PAVILION IN THE BACK-
GROUND; ABOVE: TROMBONE-
PLAYING FAME WITH THE
POLISH-LITHUANIAN AND
THE SAXON COATS OF ARMS.
IN THE EXERGUE: OTIA
MARTIS./MDCCXXX./
MENS. IUN.
SILVER, DIAM. 3.19 IN., 8.17 OZ.

COIN CABINET, COLLECTION
HORN

Provenance: *Collection Horn.*

The large maneuver of the electoral Saxon army took place near Zeithain and lasted from June 1 to 23, 1730. The entire army of 30,000 men participated in it. Among the several hundred observers was the Prussian King, Frederick William I, Augustus the Strong's ally in the Nordic War.

Lit.: *Exh.-cat. Schallaburg 1984, no. I. 218.—Exh.-cat. Essen 1986, no. 102.—Exh.-cat. Warsaw 1997a, no. VIII, 31.*

PA

CHRIST. R. P. E/FIL.
AVG. III. NEP. NAT.
XXIII. DEC. MDCCL.
GOLD, DIAM. 2.14 IN., 3.69 OZ.
INV. NO. 3626

Provenance: *Former Royal Coin Cabinet.*

Augustus III had this medal—presumably a unique object because it is made of gold—struck for the birth of his grandson Frederick Augustus III who reigned as Saxon prince elector from 1768 until 1827. In 1806 he proclaimed himself king of Saxony. Between 1807 and 1815 he was simultaneously duke of Warsaw in personal union.

Lit.: *Exh.-cat. Essen 1986, no.14.—Wiçek 1989, p.78, fig.107.—Exh.-cat. Warsaw 1997a, V, 54.*

PA

CAT. NO. 9.12

HEINRICH PAUL
GROSKURT (1675–1751)

Medal Commemorating the Coronation of Augustus III as Polish King

1734
OBVERSE:
D. G. AVGVSTUS III. REX.
POL. M. D. LITH. D. SAX.
EL. ARMORED AND DRAPED
BUST WITH BREAST STAR AND
SASH OF THE ORDER OF THE
WHITE EAGLE FACING RIGHT,
SIGNED BELOW:
H. P. GROSKVRT.
REVERSE: CONCORDIBVS
LIBERÆ GENTIS SVF-
FRAGIIS. THE BISHOP OF CRA-
COW CROWNS THE KING WHO IS
KNEELING IN FRONT OF THE
ALTAR. THE MAGNATES WHO ARE
PRESENT CARRY THE POLISH
CROWN JEWELS AND BANNERS.
IN THE EXERGUE: ELECT:V.
OCT:MDCCXXXIII/
CORONATVS XVII. IAN:/
MDCCXXXIV.
GOLD, DIAM. 2.18 IN., 3.06 OZ.
INV. NO. 3639

Provenance: *Former Royal Coin Cabinet.*

Augustus III was elected Polish king on October 5, 1733. This was after he had acknowledged the Pragmatic Sanction of Emperor Charles VI as well as the imperial title of the Tsarina Anna. He had also promised to refrain from seeking political influence—in favor of

Russia—in the Baltic areas of Livonia and Courland. However, France and Turkey continued their support for Stanislaw Leszczyński, who had been proclaimed Polish king by Count Potocki, head of the Catholic Church in Poland. A Russian army assisted Augustus III against Leszczyński. It was not until the end of the Polish war of succession that Augustus III gained support of the entire Polish nation.

Lit.: *Wiçek 1989, p.81.—Exh.-cat. Warsaw 1997a, no. II, 44.*

PA

CAT. NO. 9.13

FRIEDRICH WILHELM
DUBUT (1711–1779)

Medal Commemorating the Birth of Prince Elector Frederick Augustus III

1750
OBVERSE:
D. G. AVGVSTVS III. REX
POLON. ELECT. SAX. -
DRAPED BUST FACING RIGHT,
SIGNED BELOW: FR. G. DU
BUT F.
REVERSE: NOVVM DECVS
AVGVSTÆ DOMVS (STAR).
CERES, LEANING TO THE RIGHT,
IS HOLDING THE NEWBORN
PRINCE IN HER ARMS. IN FRONT
OF HER A SMALL GENIUS WITH A
LAUREL WREATH. ON THE FLOOR
LIES A CORNUCOPIA. SIGNED TO
THE LEFT ON THE GROUNDLINE:
F. G. D. B. IN THE EXERGUE:
RID. AVG. FRID.

CAT. NO. 9.14

JOHANN WILHELM
HOECKNER *(1671–1756)*

**Medal Commemorating
the Consecration
of Dresden's Catholic
Court**

1751
OBVERSE: DEO UNI ET
TRINO. VIEW OF THE CHURCH,
BELOW A SCALE (80 FOOT).
SIGNED IN THE SMALL EXERGUE:
HOECKNER. SC.
REVERSE: AVGVSTVS
III/POLON. REX
SAX. DVX/ET ELECTOR/
SACRIS CATHOLISCO
RITV/FACIENDIS/
ÆDEM HANC S. S. TRINI-
TATI/SACRAM/IACTO
ANNO MDCCXXXVIIII/
V. KAL. AVGVSTI/PRIMO
LAPIDE/SVA IMPENSA
ÆDIFICAVIT/ET SOLEMNI

RITV/CONSECRARI
FECIT/ANNO MDCCLI/III
KAL. IVLII
GOLD, DIAM. 2.15 IN., 2.46 OZ.
INV. NO. 3655

Provenance: *Former Royal
Coin Cabinet.*

The authorship of this
medal is not yet
entirely clear. It may
be a collaboration between
Hoeckner and his son, Karl
Wilhelm I (1720–1786).

Lit.: *Exh.-cat. Munich 1990,
no. 187.—Grund 1992, no. II.
10.—Exh.-cat. Warsaw 1997a,
no. XV, 31.*

RGr

CAT. NO. 9.15

PHILIPP FRIEDRICH
STOCKMAR
(lived in Dresden in 1768/69)

**Medal Commemorating
the Wedding between
Prince Elector Frede-
rick Augustus III and
Maria Amalia Augusta
of Pfalz-Zweibrücken**

1769
OBVERSE:
FRID:AUG:EL:SAX:-
AMAL:AUG:BIPONT: BOTH
HALF-LENGTH PORTRAITS FACE
EACH OTHER. ON THE EXERGUE:
P. F. STOCKMAR. IN THE
EXERGUE: D:XVII. IAN:/MDC-
CLXIX.
REVERSE: IN FRONT OF A GABLED
TEMPLE THE BRIDE AND
GROOM — DRESSED IN CLASSICAL
GARMENTS — OFFER EACH OTHER

THEIR HANDS OVER A BURNING
SACRIFICIAL ALTAR. BEHIND
IT IN THE CENTER A STANDING
HYMEN HOLDING A BRIDAL
TORCH. FORTUNE WITH A SHIP'S
RUDDER AND THE BOY PLUTO ON
THE LEFT AS WELL AS MINERVA
WITH A LONG STAFF ON THE
RIGHT PLACE WREATHS ON THE
NEWLYWEDS' HEADS.
GOLD, DIAM. 2.44 IN., 5.36 OZ.
INV. NO. 3743

Provenance: *Former Royal
Coin Cabinet.*

The image on the
reverse is a very early
example of Classicism.
It was inspired by classical
Roman reliefs of nuptial
scenes.

Lit.: *Baumgarten 1812/16, add.
32.—Schuler 1956, no. 135.—
Exh.-cat. Munich 1990, no. 200.*

RGr

The Imperial Curates of Augustus the Strong and His Son as Reflected in Coins

Wilhelm Hollstein

Prince Elector Frederick the Wise (*der Weise*, ruled 1486–1525) was the first Saxon ruler whose portrait appeared on small silver coins towards the end of the 15th century. Large silver coins had been minted in Saxony since the year 1500. They were to become instrumental in the introduction and the spread of the thaler as German currency. Thanks to their larger diameter they offered more surface space for images and legends. Self-confident as they were, the respective rulers had their own portraits depicted on the obverse of the thaler, while the reverse was reserved for their coats of arms. This is illustrated on coins portraying Frederick Augustus I (ruled 1694/97–1733)—later nicknamed "the Strong" (*der Starke*)—and his son, Frederick Augustus II (ruled 1733–63), who were prince electors of Saxony and kings of Poland. The coats of arms on the reverse are the electoral Saxon and the royal Polish ones. Until the German Empire was founded, in 1871, the above scheme remained intact. Since the mid-16th century, additional coins were issued on special occasions. Such commemorative coins served as instruments of self-promotion for the prince electors. Special events from the lives of Renaissance, Baroque, and Rococo princes were celebrated on them, including birth, marriage, accession to the throne, awards of honors, peace treaties, construction of palaces, and jubilees.[1] The so-called Imperial Curate coins (*Vikariatsmünzen*) belong to the commemorative coinage as well.[2]

In his Golden Bull of 1356, Emperor Charles IV decreed that upon an emperor's death and until the election of his successor two deputies were to take over the empire's government and were to continue certain duties of the emperor. These Imperial Curates (*Reichsvikare*) were selected from the circle of seven prince electors who elected the ruler. While the Count Palatine of the Rhine assumed the role of deputy in the Rhinelands and in Swabia, the prince elector of Saxony did the same in the areas where Saxon law applied.[3] Frederick the Wise was the first of the Saxon prince electors who appealed to his rights as Imperial Governor General (*Reichsgeneralstatthalter*). In 1507/08, when Emperor Maximilian I led a military campaign in Italy, he served as Imperial Curate for the first time and then again in 1519 upon the emperor's death. During the time between 1612 and the dissolution of the Holy Roman Empire of the German Nation, in 1806, there were a total of eight Saxon prince electors who served at the very top of the imperial hierarchy as Imperial Curates.

After Emperor Joseph I died on April 17, 1711—without a male heir and without appointing a successor—Prince Elector Frederick Augustus I, also king of Poland since 1697, assumed the post of Imperial Curate until King Charles VI had been elected, on October 12, 1711.[4] The power of his rule was extended to the areas where Saxon law applied, i. e., the Upper and Lower Saxon District, the eastern part of the Westphalian Imperial District, and the Kingdom of Bohemia. A ten ducat piece commemorates this Imperial Curate (cat. no. 9.18). Its die was engraved by Heinrich Paul Groskurt, medalist in the Dresden Mint. The captionless obverse depicts Augustus—astride a horse and sporting the royal Polish crown—superimposed over the coats of arms of Poland-Lithuania and Saxony. On the reverse his royal and electoral insignia are displayed on pedestals. He is REX (king of Poland), and ELECTOR (prince elector of Saxony). As VICARIUS POST MORTEM IOSEPHI IMPERAT(oris) (Imperial Curate after the death of Emperor Joseph) his superior position among the princes of the Holy Roman Empire is demonstrated.

A further medal to commemorate the Imperial Curate of Augustus the Strong was made by the Leipzig medallist Albrecht Krieger (cat. no. 9.19). On it, the continuity of the electoral status of the House of Saxony—which had been divided into the Albertinian and the Ernestine lines since 1485—is praised. On the obverse, Augustus, depicted among the prince electors of the Albertinian line (LINEA ALBERTINA), is singled out as he towers above his predecessors. He wears the Polish crown and is the REX POL(oniarum) & EL(ector) SAX(oniae) VICARIVS IMP(erii). The reverse is decorated with the portraits of the prince electors from the Ernestine line (LINEA ERNESTINA).

After the death of Emperor Charles VI, on October 20, 1740, the son of Augustus the Strong, Prince Elector Frederick Augustus II, assumed the role of Imperial Curate. He had strong ambitions to ascend to the imperial throne himself, since Charles VI had left no male heirs. In the end, the Saxon prince elector—in an alliance with France and Prussia—supported the election of the Bavarian Prince Elector, Charles Albert, as Emperor Charles VII (ruled 1742–45). A number of coins were minted between 1740 and 1742 in order to commemorate this Imperial Curate. The obverse of a twelve ducat piece of 1740 shows the portrait of Frederick Augustus II in armor (cat. no. 9.21). Moved into the center of the reverse is the imperial double eagle revealing the Polish-Lithuanian and the Saxon coats of arms on its chest. The legend expressly clarifies his present legal position: He is IN PROVINCIIS IVR(is) SAXON(ici) PROVISOR ET VICARIVS, Imperial Curate in the areas where Saxon law applies.

A ten ducat piece honoring the Imperial Curate was made in 1741 (cat. no. 9.22). While the legends of reverse and obverse correspond with the gold coin of 1740, the images vary. The obverse presents Augustus on horseback, a manner typical of coins commemorating the Imperial Curate since the beginning of the 17th century. The obverse reveals the imperial throne, which may be identified thanks to the double-headed eagle. Placed on it are—a reference to the throne's vacancy—the imperial insignia crown, scepter, and orb.

After the death of Emperor Charles VII, in 1745, Frederick Augustus II served a second term as Imperial Curate. For this occasion, the minting of the 1740-type (like cat-no. 9.21) was reissued using the year 1745. Before the dissolution of the Holy Roman Empire, in 1806, Prince Elector Frederick Augustus III (ruled 1763/68–1806/27) served twice as Imperial Curate: First after the death of Emperor Joseph II (ruled 1765–90) and then after the death of Emperor Leopold II (ruled 1790–92). Coins for the Imperial Curate bearing the double-headed eagle on the obverse were last minted in 1792.

Notes

1 For commemorative coins see Haupt 1978, pp. 165 f.
2 See Haupt 1978, pp. 167 f.; Arnold 1986.
3 For the Imperial Curate, see Hermkes 1955.
4 Arnold/Arnold 2004.

Cat. no. 9.16

Saxony, Prince Elector Frederick Augustus I (1694–1733)
Five ducats, 1694, Dresden Mint, mint master Johann Koch
Obverse: FRID. AUGUST. D G DVX. SAX. I. C. M. A. &. W.—Armored and draped bust facing right.
Reverse: SAC. ROM. IMP. ARCHIM. &. ELECT. (crossed arrows)—Crowned electoral and ducal Saxon coat of arms between palm branches and flowers. To the left and to the right of the electoral hat 16–94; under the coat of arms I. K.
Gold, Diam. 1.49 in., 0.61 oz.
Inv. no. 1668

Provenance: *Former Royal Coin Cabinet.*

Lit.: *Baumgarten 1812/16, no. 591.*

WiH

Cat. no. 9.17

Saxony, Prince Elector Frederick Augustus I (1694–1733)
Two thalers, 1698, Dresden Mint, mint master Johann Lorenz Holland
Obverse: (Orb) D. G. FRID. AUG. REX POL. DVX SAX. I. C. M. A. &. W.—Laureate, armored, and draped bust facing right.
Reverse: SAC. ROM. IMP. ARCHIM. ET. ELECT. (Hook)—Beneath the royal Polish crown on the left a shield with the Polish-Lithuanian coat of arms, on the right a shield with the complete electoral Saxon coat of arms, surrounded by two palm branches. To the left and to the right of the royal crown 16–98; beneath the shields I. L. H.
Silver, Diam. 1.8 in., 2.06 oz.
Inv. no. 9977

Provenance: *Former Royal Coin Cabinet.*

Lit.: *Schnee 1982, no. 990.*

WiH

Cat. no. 9.18

Saxony, Prince Elector Frederick Augustus I (1694–1733)

Ten ducats commemorating the Imperial Curate of 1711, Dresden Mint, mint master Johann Lorenz Holland, medalist Heinrich Paul Groskurt (died 1751)
Obverse: Frederick Augustus I in armor with the royal Polish crown, cloak, and badge of the Danish Elephant order, holding the commander's staff rides toward the right. Beneath the horse the Polish-Lithuanian and the Saxon coats of arms.
Reverse: Three pedestals, in the upper left the insignia of the Polish king, in the right the insignia of the Saxon electorate, at the bottom, surrounded by laurel branches, continuation of the legend: ET/VICARIUS/POST MORT:/IOSEPHI/IMPERAT: To the left and to the right of the lower pedestal signed and dated: MDCCXI./I. L. H. (HOOK)
Gold, Diam. 1.23 in., 1.22 oz.
Inv. no. 1809

Provenance: *Former Royal Coin Cabinet.*

Lit.: *Baumgarten 1812/16, no. 759.*

WiH

Cat. no. 9.19

ALBRECHT KRIEGER (died 1726)

Medal Commemorating Saxon's Imperial Curate of 1711

Obverse: LINEA ALBERTINA — Crowned, armored, and draped bust facing right, surrounded by busts of the eight Albertinian prince electors dressed in their electoral vestments, with names and dates: FRID: AVG: D. G. REX POL & EL. SAX./VICARIVS IMP. 1711./MAVRIT. NAT. 1521./MORT.1553. AVGVST./NAT. 1526/M. 1586 CHRIST. I/NAT. 1560/M. 1591. CHRIST. II./NAT. 1583./M. 1611. IOH GEORG. I./NAT. 1585./M. 1656. IOH GEORG. II NAT./1613. M. 1680. IOH GEORG III NAT/1647. M. 1691. AND IOH. GEORG. IV. NATVS 1668. M. 1694.
Reverse: LINEA ERNESTINA — Crowned and mantled cartouche with the electoral and ducal Saxon coats of arms of the Ernestine prince electors in their electoral vestments, with names and dates: FRID. I NAT 1367. (MUST READ 1370) M. 1428. FRID. II NAT./1412.

M. 1464. ERNESTVS NAT/1455. (MUST READ 1441) M 1476 (MUST READ 1486) FRID. III NAT./1463 M. 1525. IOHANNES NAT/1469 (MUST READ 1468) M. 1532. AND IOHANNES FRIDERICVS. NAT. 1503 MORT. 1554
Silver, Diam. 2.78 in., 5.14 oz.
Inv. no. 8848

Provenance: *Former Royal Coin Cabinet.*

Lit.: *Exh.-cat. Schallaburg 1984, no. I. 209.—Exh.-cat. Essen 1986, no. 9.—Exh.-cat. Warsaw 1997a, no. II. 20.*

WiH

Cat. no. 9.20

Saxony, Prince Elector Frederick Augustus II (1733–1763)

Two thalers, 1737, Dresden Mint, mint master Friedrich Wilhelm ô Feral
Obverse: (Rosette) D: G: FRID: AUGUST: REX POL: DVX SAX: I: C: M: A: & W:— Armored and draped bust facing right.
Reverse: SAC: ROM: IMP: ARCHIM: ET ELECT. 1737.— Beneath the royal Polish crown on the left

a shield of the Polish-Lithuanian coat of arms. To the right the shield with the complete electoral Saxon coat of arms. Between the shield the orb; beneath F. W. ô F.
Silver, Diam. 1.76 in., 2.06 oz.
Inv. no. 10652

Provenance: *Former Royal Coin Cabinet (from the von Teubern Collection).*

Lit.: *Schnee 1982, no. 1025.*

WiH

Cat. no. 9.21

Saxony, Prince Elector Frederick Augustus II (1733–1763)

Twelve ducats, 1740, Dresden Mint, mint master Friedrich Wilhelm ô Feral
Obverse: (Rosette) D. G. FRID: AUG: REX POL: DVX SAX: ARCHIMARESCHALL: ET ELECTOR — Armored and draped bust facing right, with the badge of the Golden Fleece Order and the breast star of the Order of the White Eagle.
Reverse: (Rosette) IN PROVINCIIS IVR: SAXON: PROVISOR ET VICARIVS 1740 — The imperial double

EAGLE, NIMBED, REVEALING ON ITS CHEST THE POLISH-LITHUANIAN AND THE SAXON COATS OF ARMS. SUSPENDED FROM THE COAT OF ARMS IS THE CROSS OF THE ORDER OF THE WHITE EAGLE WITH A SASH. OVER THE ROSETTE A HOOK. GOLD, DIAM. 1.81 IN., 1.47 OZ. INV. NO. 1917

Provenance: *Former Royal Coin Cabinet.*

Lit.: *Baumgarten 1812/16, no. 864.*

WiH

CAT. NO. 9.22

Saxony, Prince Elector Frederick Augustus II (1733–1763)

TEN DUCATS COMMEMORATING THE IMPERIAL CURATE OF 1741, DRESDEN MINT, MINT MASTER FRIEDRICH WILHELM ô FERAL, MEDALIST HEINRICH FRIEDRICH WERMUTH (1703–1744)

OBVERSE: (ROSETTE) D. G. FRID. AUG. REX POL. DUX SAX. ARCHIMARE-SCHALL. & ELECT.—FREDERICK AUGUST I, WITH LAUREL WREATH, IN ARMOR AND CLOAK, WITH BADGE OF THE GOLDEN FLEECE ORDER AND THE CROSS OF ORDER OF THE WHITE EAGLE, AS WELL AS ELECTORAL SWORD, RIDING TOWARD THE RIGHT.

REVERSE: (ROSETTE) IN PROVINCIIS IUR. SAXON. PROVISOR ET VICARIUS. 1741.—IMPERIAL THRONE WITH CROWN, SCEPTER, ORB, AND CROWNED IMPERIAL DOUBLE EAGLE OVER THE BACK. GOLD, DIAM. 1.70 IN., 1.23 OZ. INV. NO. 1920

Provenance: *Former Royal Coin Cabinet.*

Lit.: *Baumgarten 1812/16, no. 867.—Exh.-cat. Essen 1986, no. 104.—Exh.-cat. Warsaw 1997a, no. II. 47.*

WiH

Bibliography

Akinscha/Koslow 1995
K. Akinscha/G. Koslow: Beutekunst. Auf Schatzsuche in russischen Geheimdepots, Munich 1995

Albiker 1935
C. Albiker: Die Meissner Porzellantiere, Berlin 1935

Andrews 1967
K. Andrews: Two Newly Discovered Drawings by Tanzio da Varallo, in: Paragone 207 (1967), pp. 63f.

Aragon/Cocteau 1957
L. Aragon/J. Cocteau: Entretiens sur le Musée de Dresde, Paris 1957

Arndt 1967
K. Arndt: Studien zu Georg Petel, in: Jahrbuch der Berliner Museen 9 (1967), pp. 165–231

Arnold 1985
P. Arnold: Die Regierungsgeschichte des sächsischen Kurfürsten und polnischen Königs August des Starken (1694/1697–1733) im Spiegel der Medaillenkunst, in: Jahrbuch der Staatlichen Kunstsammlungen Dresden 17 (1985), pp. 41–50

Arnold 1986
P. Arnold: Die Münzen und Medaillen auf das sächsische Reichsvikariat, in: Mitteilungen der Österreichischen Numismatischen Gesellschaft XXVI/3 (1986), pp. 39–44

Arnold 1988
P. Arnold: Das Münzkabinett Dresden, in: Numismatische Hefte 44 (1988), pp. 5–12

Arnold 1994
U. Arnold: Augsburger Silber im Grünen Gewölbe und das Dresdner Silberbuffet, in: Exh.-cat. Munich 1994, vol. II, pp. 76–82

Arnold 1995
P. Arnold: Die histoire metallique, die eherne Regierungsgeschichte Augusts des Starken, in: Saxonia 1995, pp. 34–40

Arnold 2001
U. Arnold: Die Juwelen Augusts des Starken, Munich/Berlin 2001

Arnold 2003
P. Arnold: Das Münzkabinett Dresden im Georgenbau des Dresdner Schlosses, in: Dresdener Kunstblätter 4/2003, pp. 185–194

Arnold/Arnold 2004
P. Arnold/U. Arnold: ELECTOR – REX – VICARIUS. Die sächsischen Reichsvikariatsprägungen von 1711. Ein numismatischer Beitrag zur Verfassungsgeschichte des Alten Reiches, in: Festschrift Klüßendorf, to be publ. 2004

Asche 1961
S. Asche: Drei Bildhauerfamilien an der Elbe, Vienna/Wiesbaden 1961

Asche 1966
S. Asche: Balthasar Permoser und die Barockskulptur des Dresdner Zwingers, Frankfurt a. M. 1966

Asche 1970
S. Asche: Die Dresdner Bildhauer des frühen achtzehnten Jahrhunderts als Meister des Böttgersteinzeugs und des Böttgerporzellans, in: Keramos 49 (1970), pp. 82f.

Asche 1978
S. Asche: Balthasar Permoser. Leben und Werk, Berlin 1978

Aspris 1996
M. Y. Aspris: Statuarische Gruppen von Eros und Psyche, PhD thesis, Rheinische Friedrich-Wilhelms-Universität zu Bonn 1996

Ayers 2002
J. Ayers: Blanc de Chine. Divine Images in Porcelain, New York 2002

Bailyn 1967
B. Bailyn: The Ideological Origins of the American Revolution, Cambridge, Mass. 1967

Bailyn et al. 1992
B. Bailyn et al.: The Great Republic. A History of the American People, vol. I, Lexington, Mass. 1992

Balzer 1956
W. Balzer: Dresdner Galerie. 120 Meisterwerke des 15. bis 18. Jahrhunders, Leipzig 1956

Bauch 1926
K. Bauch: J. A. Backer. Rembrandtschüler aus Friesland, Berlin 1926

Bäumel 1995
J. Bäumel: Die Rüstkammer zu Dresden. Führer durch die Ausstellung im Semperbau, Munich/Berlin 1995

Bäumel 1996
J. Bäumel: Zum Beispiel Sachsen – die sächsischen Kurfürsten aus Sicht der Liselotte von der Pfalz, in: Sigrun Paas (ed.), Liselotte von der Pfalz. Madame am Hofe des Sonnenkönigs, exh.-cat., Heidelberger Schloss, Heidelberg 1996, pp. 219–226

Bäumel 1997a
J. Bäumel: Auf dem Weg zum Thron. Die Krönungsreise Augusts des Starken, Dresden 1997

Bäumel 1997b
J. Bäumel: Der Kurhut und das sächsische Kurschwert, in: Exh.-cat. Dresden 1997b, pp. 374f.

Bäumel 1998a
J. Bäumel: Zwei goldgestickte Lederkleider Augusts des Starken. Kunstwerk des Monats in der Rüstkammer, in: Dresdener Kunstblätter 6/1998, pp. 185–192

Bäumel 1998b
J. Bäumel: Der Weg des Kurfürsten Friedrich August I. von Sachsen/Königs August II. in Polen (1670–1733, Kurfürst seit 1694, König seit 1697) zum Throne […], PhD thesis, Humboldt-Universität Berlin 1998

Bäumel 1998c
J. Bäumel: Ringelstechlanzen zu Damenringrennen am Hof Augusts des Starken, in: Schwert in Frauenhand, exh.-cat., Deutsches Klingenmuseum Solingen, ed. by G. Frohnhaus/B. Grotkamp-Schepers/R. Philipp, Essen 1998, pp. 68f.

Bäumel 1998/99
J. Bäumel: Die polnische Krönungsfigur Augusts des Starken in der Dresdner Rüstkammer, in: Jahrbuch der Staatlichen Kunstsammlungen Dresden 1998/99, pp. 49–68

Baumgarten 1812/16
J. G. Baumgarten: Historisch-genealogisch-chronologisch-kritisches Verzeichniß aller bekannten ducatenförmigen Goldmünzen der albertinischen Hauptlinie des uralten sächsischen Hauses, Dresden 1812, supplement 1816

Beazley 1963
J. D. Beazley: Attic Red-Figure Vase-Painters, 2 vols., 2nd ed., Oxford 1963

Beger 1701
L. Beger: Thesauri Regii et Electoralis Brandenburgici Volumen Tertium: Continens Antiquorum Numismatum et Gemmarum, Quae Cimeliarchio Regio-Electorali Brandenburgico nuper accessere, Rariora: Ut & Supellectilem Antiquariam Uberrimam, id est Statuas, Thoraces, Clypeos, Imagines tam Deorum quam Regum & Illustrium: Item Vasa & Instrumenta varia, eaque inter fibulas, Lampades, Urnas: quorum pleracque cum Museo Belloriano, quaedam & aliunde coëmta sunt, Cölln an der Spree 1701

Bellonci/Garavaglia 1967
M. Bellonci/N. Garavaglia: L'opera completa di Mantegna, Milan 1967

Benati 1996
D. Benati: Un San Sebastiano di Annibale Carracci da Modena a Dresda, in: Nuovi studi, vol. 1, no. 1 (1996), pp. 103–114

Benisch 1954–57
O. Benisch: The Drawings of Rembrandt. A Critical and Chronological Catalogue, 6 vols., London 1954–57, 2nd ed. 1975

Berling 1900
K. Berling: Das Meissner Porzellan und seine Geschichte, Leipzig 1900

Bernheimer 1984
F. Bernheimer: Georg Wilhelm Vestner und Andreas Vestner: zwei Nürnberger Medailleure (Miscellanea Bavaria Monacensia 110), Munich 1984

Bösener 1972
R. Bösener: Die Geweihsammlung des Jagdschlosses Moritzburg bei Dresden, in: Sächsische Heimatblätter 3 (1972), pp. 121–134

Bowron 1979
E. P. Bowron: The Paintings of Benedetto Luti (1666–1724), Ann Arbor 1979

Brown 1986
J. Brown: Velázquez. Painter and Courtier, New Haven/London 1986

Bürger 2001
K. Bürger: Die Gemälde Philips Wouwermans in der Dresdener Gemäldegalerie Alte Meister, 2 vols., unpubl.

Bursche 1980
S. Bursche: Meissen. Steinzeug und Porzellan des 18. Jahrhunderts, Berlin 1980

Camesasca 1992
E. Camesasca: Mantegna, Milan 1992

Cassidy-Geiger 2003
M. Cassidy-Geiger: Of Elephants and Porcelain, in: The French Porcelain Society (ed.), French Porcelain of the Eighteenth Century. A Symposium in Honour of Geneviève le Duc (1930–1999), vol. I, London 2003, pp. 113–129

Cogo 1996
B. Cogo: Antonio Corradini. Scultore veneziano 1688–1752, Este 1996

Constable 1962
W. G. Constable: Canaletto. Giovanni Antonio Canal 1697–1768, Oxford 1962

Cox Rearick 1964
J. Cox Rearick: The Drawings of Pontormo, 2 vols., Cambridge, Mass. 1964

Czok 1989
K. Czok: August der Starke und Kursachsen, Leipzig/Munich 1989

De Bruyn 1988
J.-P. de Bruyn: Erasmus II Quellinus (1607–1678). De Schilderijen met Catalogue Raisonné, Freren 1988

De Bruyn et al. 1982–89
J.-P. Bruyn/B. Haak/S. Lewie/P. J. J. van Thiel/E. van de Wetering (eds.): A Corpus of Rembrandt Paintings, 3 vols., Dordrecht/Boston/Lancaster 1982–89

Delogu 1928
G. Delogu: G. B. Castiglione detto il Grechetto, Bologna 1928

Denckmahl 1719
Das Königliche Denckmahl, Welches Nach geschehener Vermählung [...] Friedrich Augusti, Mit [...] Maria Josepha, [...] In [...] Dreßden, [...] 1719. gestifftet worden, Frankfurt/Leipzig 1719

Der große Garten 2001
Der Große Garten zu Dresden. Gartenkunst in vier Jahrhunderten, ed. by the Sächsische Schlösserverwaltung, Dresden 2001

DiFederico 1977
F. R. DiFederico: Francesco Trevisani. Eighteenth-Century Painter in Rome. A Catalogue Raisonné, Washington 1977

Dippel 1977
H. Dippel: Germany and the American Revolution, 1770–1800. A Sociohistorical Investigation of Late Eighteenth-Century Political Thinking, transl. by B. A. Uhlendorf, Chapel Hill, NC 1977

Dresden 1979
Verzeichnis der Inventare der Staatlichen Kunstsammlungen Dresden 1568–1945, ed. by the State Art Collections Dresden, Dresden 1979

Dresdner Hefte 1995
Die Moritzburger Kulturlandschaft, Dresdner Hefte 42, Dresden 1995

Ehrenthal 1899a
M. von Ehrenthal: Führer durch das Königliche Historische Museum zu Dresden, 3rd ed., Dresden 1899

Ehrenthal 1899b
M. von Ehrenthal: Führer durch die Königliche Gewehr-Galerie zu Dresden, Dresden 1899

Ehrenthal 1900
M. von Ehrenthal: Führer durch die Königliche Gewehr-Galerie zu Dresden, Dresden 1900

Erbstein 1889
A. Erbstein: Beschreibung des Königlichen Historischen Museums und der Königlichen Gewehrgalerie, Dresden 1889

Exh.-cat. Amsterdam 2000
The Glory of the Golden Age. Dutch Art of the 17th Century. Painting, Sculpture and Decorative Art, Rijksmuseum Amsterdam, Zwolle 2000

Exh.-cat. Antwerp 1977
Peter Paul Rubens. Paintings, Oil Sketches, Drawings, Koninklijk Museum voor Schone Kunsten Antwerp, Antwerp 1977

Exh.-cat. Basel 1984
Tobias Stimmer 1539–1584. Spätrenaissance am Oberrhein, Kunstmuseum Basel, Basel 1984

Exh.-cat. Basel 1974
Lukas Cranach. Gemälde, Zeichnungen, Druckgraphik, Kunstmuseum Basel, ed. by D. Koepplin/T. Falk, 2 vols., Basel/Stuttgart 1974/76

Exh.-cat. Berlin 1983
Kunst der Reformationszeit, Staatliche Museen zu Berlin, Preußischer Kulturbesitz, Berlin 1983

Exh.-cat. Berlin 1995
Von allen Seiten schön. Bronzen der Renaissance und des Barock, Skulpturensammlung, Staatliche Museen zu Berlin, Preußischer Kulturbesitz, ed. by V. Krahn, Heidelberg 1995

Exh.-cat. Berlin 2002a
Nach der Flut. Meisterwerke der Dresdener Gemäldegalerie in Berlin, an exh. of the State Art Collections Dresden, Altes Museum, Staatliche Museen zu Berlin, Dresden/Leipzig 2002

Exh.-cat. Berlin 2002b
Nach der Flut. Die Dresdener Skulpturensammlung in Berlin, an exh. of the State Art Collections Dresden, Martin-Gropius-Bau Berlin, Leipzig 2002

Exh.-cat. Boston/Toledo 1993/94
The Age of Rubens, Museum of Fine Arts Boston/Toledo Museum of Art, Gent 1993

Exh.-cat. Brühl/Bonn/Jülich/Miel 2000
Der Riss im Himmel. Clemens August und seine Epoche, Schloss Augustusburg Brühl/Stadtmuseum Bonn/Museum Zitadelle Jülich/Schloss Miel, ed. by F. G. Zehnder/W. Schäfke, Cologne 2000

Exh.-cat. Brunswick 1993
Bilder vom alten Menschen in der niederländischen und deutschen Kunst 1550–1750, Herzog Anton Ulrich-Museum Brunswick, ed. by T. Döring et al., Brunswick 1993

Exh.-cat. Cleves 1965
Govert Flinck, der Kleefsche Apelles. 1616–1660, Städtisches Museum Haus Koekkoek Cleves, Cleves 1965

Exh.-cat. Cologne/Utrecht 1991/92
I Bamboccianti. Niederländische Malerrebellen im Rom des Barock, Wallraf-Richartz-Museum Cologne/Centraal Museum Utrecht, ed. by D. A. Levine/E. Mai, Milan 1991

Exh.-cat. Columbus 1999
Dresden in the Ages of Splendor and Enlightenment, an exh. of the Old Masters Picture Gallery, State Art Collections Dresden, Columbus Museum of Art, ed. by H. Marx/G. J. M. Weber, Columbus, Ohio 1999

Exh.-cat. Cremona 1994
Sofonisba Anguissola e le sue sorelle, Centro Culturale "Citta di Cremona", ed. by P. Buffa, Milan 1994

Exh.-cat. Dijon 2001
Dresde ou le reve des Princes. La Gerlie de peintures au XVIIIe siècle, Dijon 2001

Exh.-cat. Dresden 1963
Altdeutsche Zeichnungen, Collection of Prints and Drawings, State Art Collections Dresden, Dresden 1963

Exh.-cat. Dresden 1971
Deutsche Kunst der Dürer-Zeit, Albertinum, State Art Collections Dresden, Dresden 1971

Exh.-cat. Dresden 1973
Kunsthandwerk des 18 und 19. Jahrhunderts, Museum of Decorative Arts, State Art Collections Dresden, ed. by G. Haase-Messner/G. Reinheckel, Dresden 1973

Exh.-cat. Dresden 1978
Die Albertina und das Dresdner Kupferstich-Kabinett. Meisterzeichnungen aus zwei alten Sammlungen. Eine Ausstellung mit der Graphischen Sammlung Albertina Wien, Collection of Drawings, Prints, and Photographs, State Art Collections Dresden, Dresden 1978

Exh.-cat. Dresden 1992
Verborgene Schätze der Skulpturensammlung, Sculpture Collection, State Art Collections Dresden, Dresden 1992

Exh.-cat. Dresden 1993
F. Reichel: Die Porzellansammlung Augusts des Starken. Porzellankunst aus China. Die Rosa Familie, Porcelain Collection, State Art Collections Dresden, ed. by K.-P. Arnold, Dresden 1993

Exh.-cat. Dresden 1996a
Godfried Schalcken. Eine Neuerwerbung. Das Alter zwischen Allegorie und Charakterkopf, Old Masters Picture Gallery, State Art Collections Dresden, ed. by U. Neidhardt, Dresden 1996

Exh.-cat. Dresden 1996b
Johann Gregorius Höroldt (1696–1775) und die Meissener Porzellan-Malerei, Porcelain Collection, State Art Collections Dresden, ed. by U. Pietsch, Dresden 1996

Exh.-cat. Dresden 1996c
Meisterwerke des 18. und 19. Jahrhunderts, Museum of Decorative Arts, State Art Collections Dresden, Dresden 1996

Exh.-cat. Dresden 1997a
Van Eyck, Bruegel, Rembrandt. Niederländische Zeichnungen des 15. bis 17. Jahrhunderts aus dem Kupferstich-Kabinett Dresden, Collection of Drawings, Prints, and Photographs, State Art Collections Dresden, Dresden 1997

Exh.-cat. Dresden 1997b
Unter einer Krone. Kunst und Kultur der sächsisch-polnischen Union, State Art Collections Dresden, ed. by W. Schmidt, Leipzig 1997

Exh.-cat. Dresden 1998a
Zurück in Dresden. Eine Ausstellung ehemals vermisster Werke aus Dresdener Museen, State Art Collections Dresden, Dresden 1998

Exh.-cat. Dresden 1998b
Der himmelnde Blick. Zur Geschichte eines Bildmotivs von Raffael bis Rotari, Old Masters Picture Gallery, State Art Collections Dresden, ed. by A. Henning/G. J. M. Weber, Emsdetten 1998

Exh.-cat. Dresden 2000a
Eine gute Figur machen. Kostüm und Fest am Dresdner Hof, Collection of Drawings, Prints, and Photographs, State Art Collections Dresden, ed. by C. Schnitzer/P. Hölscher, Dresden 2000

Exh.-cat. Dresden 2000b
La famosissima Notte. Correggios Gemälde "Die Heilige Nacht" und seine Wirkungsgeschichte, Old Masters Picture Gallery, State Art Collections Dresden, ed. by B. Kloppenburg/G. J. M. Weber, Emsdetten/Dresden 2000

Exh.-cat. Dresden 2000c
Götter und Menschen. Antike Meisterwerke der Skulpturensammlung, Sculpture Collection, State Art Collections Dresden, ed. by K. Knoll, Dresden 2000

Exh.-cat. Dresden 2000d
Für Sachsen erworben. Schätze des Hauses Wettin, Dresden Residential Palace, ed. by the Kulturstiftung der Länder Berlin in cooperation with the State Art Collections Dresden, Berlin 2000 (Patrimonia 186)

Exh.-cat. Dresden 2001a
"Balthasar Permoser hats gemacht". Der Hofbildhauer in Sachsen, Sculpture Collection, State Art Collections Dresden, Dresden 2001

Exh.-cat. Dresden 2001b
Hauptsache Köpfe – Plastische Porträts von der Renaissance bis zur Gegenwart aus der Skulpturensammlung, Sculpture Collection, State Art Collections Dresden, Dresden 2001

Exh.-cat. Dresden 2001c
E. Ströber: "La maladie de porcelain …". East Asian Porcelain from the Collection of Augustus the Strong, Porcelain Collection, State Art Collections Dresden, Leipzig 2001

Exh.-cat. Dresden/Bonn 1995
Im Lichte des Halbmonds, State Art Collections Dresden/Kunst- und Ausstellungshalle der Bundesrepublik Deutschland Bonn, Leipzig 1995

Exh.-cat. Dresden/Hamburg 1989
Meissener Blaumalerei aus drei Jahrhunderten, Porcelain Collection, State Art Collections Dresden/Museum für Kunst und Gewerbe Hamburg, ed. by K.-P. Arnold/V. Diefenbach, Munich 1989

Exh.-cat. Essen 1986
Barock in Dresden 1694–1763, Villa Hügel Essen, ed. by U. Arnold/W. Schmidt, Leipzig 1986

Exh.-cat. Essen 1988
Prag um 1600. Kunst und Kultur am Hofe Rudolfs II., Villa Hügel Essen, Freren 1988

Exh.-cat. Ferrara 2002
Il Trionfo di Baccho. Capolavori della scuola ferrarese a Dresda. 1480–1620, Castello di Ferrara, Turin/London/Venice 2002

Exh.-cat. Genoa 1990
Il Genio di Giovanni Benedetto Castiglione. Il Grechetto, Accademia Ligustica di Belle Arti Genoa, Genoa 1990

Exh.-cat. Idar-Oberstein/Berlin/Dresden 1998
Deutsche Steinschneidekunst aus dem Grünen Gewölbe zu Dresden, an exh. of the Green Vault, State Art Collections Dresden, Deutsches Edelsteinmuseum Idar-Oberstein/Kunstgewerbemuseum der Staatlichen Museen zu Berlin/Dresden Residential Palace, ed. by J. Kappel, Dresden 1998

Exh.-cat. Kronach/Leipzig 1994
Lucas Cranach. Ein Maler-Unternehmer aus Franken, Festung Rosenberg Kronach/Museum der bildenden Künste Leipzig, ed. by C. Grimm/J. Erichsen/E. Brockhoff, Augsburg 1994

Exh.-cat. Leiden 2001
The Leiden Fijnschilders from Dresden, Stedelijk Museum de Lakenhal, Leiden 2001

Exh.-cat. London 1983
The Genius of Venice 1500–1600, Royal Academy of Arts London, London 1983

Exh.-cat. London 2002
Masterpieces from Dresden, Royal Academy of Arts London, London 2002

Exh.-cat. Madrid 1992
Ribera 1591–1652, Museo Nacional del Prado Madrid, ed. by A. E. Pérez Sánchez/N. Spinosa, Madrid 1992

Exh.-cat. Madrid 1999
Velázquez, Rubens y Van Dyck. Pintores cortesanos del siglo XVII, Museo Nacional del Prado Madrid, Madrid 1999

Exh.-cat. Mantua 1961
Andrea Mantegna, Palazzo Ducale Mantua, Venice 1961

Exh.-cat. Milan 2000
Tanzio da Varallo, Realismo fervore e contemplazione in un pittore del Seicento, Palazzo Reale Milan, ed. by M. B. Castellotti, Milan 2000

Exh.-cat. Modena 1998
Sovrane Passioni. Le raccolte d'arte della Ducale Galleria Estense, Galleria Estense, Palazzo dei Musei Modena, ed. by J. Bentini, Milan 1998

Exh.-cat. Munich 1966
Meissener Porzellan 1710–1810, Bayerisches Nationalmuseum Munich, Munich 1966

Exh.-cat. Munich 1990
Königliches Dresden. Höfische Kunst im 18. Jahrhundert, an exh. of the State Art Collections Dresden, Kunsthalle der Hypo-Kulturstiftung Munich, Munich 1990

Exh.-cat. Munich 1994
Silber und Gold. Augsburger Goldschmiedekunst für die Höfe Europas, Bayerisches Nationalmuseum Munich, 2 vols., ed. by R. Baumstark/H. Seling, Munich 1994

Exh.-cat. Munich 1995
Apoll schindet Marsyas. Über das Schreckliche in der Kunst. Adam Lenckhardts Elfenbeingruppe, Bayerisches Nationalmuseum Munich, ed. by R. Baumstark/P. Volk, Munich 1995

Exh.-cat. New York 1989
Canaletto, The Metropolitan Museum of Art New York, ed. by K. Baetjer/J. G. Links, New York 1989

Exh.-cat. New York 1992
Jusepe de Ribera. 1591–1652, The Metropolitan Museum of Art New York, ed. by A. E. Pérez Sánchez/N. Spinosa, New York 1992

Exh.-cat. New York/London 2001
Vermeer and the Delft School, The Metropolitan Museum of Art New York/The National Gallery London, New Haven/London 2001

Exh.-cat. Nuremberg 1998
Von teutscher Not zu höfischer Pracht. 1648–1701, Germanisches Nationalmuseum Nuremberg, Nuremberg 1998

Exh.-cat. Paris/New York 1995
The Renaissance in France, Paris Nationale Supérieure des Beaux-Art/The Metropolitan Museum of Art New York, ed. by E. Brugerolles, Cambridge, Mass. 1995

Exh.-cat. Philadelphia/Houston 2000
Art in Rome in the 18th Century, Museum of Art Philadelphia/Museum of Fine Arts Houston, ed. by E. P. Bowron/J. J. Rishel, Philadelphia 2000

Exh.-cat. Prague 1997
Rudolf II and Prague. The Court and the City, Kunstsammlungen der Burg Prag, ed. by E. Fucikova et al., Prague/London/Milan 1997

Exh.-cat. Rome 2000
L' Idea del Bello. Viaggi per Roma nel Seicento con Giovan Pietro Bellori, Palazzo degli Esposizioni Rome, 2 vols., Rome 2000

Exh.-cat. Rome 2002
L'Eredità Esterhàzy. Disegni italiani del seicento dal Museo di Belle Arti Budapest, Palazzo di Fontana di Trevi Rome, ed. by A. Czére, Budapest 2002

Exh.-cat. Saarbrücken 1997
Zeichnungen aus der Toskana. Das Zeitalter Michelangelos, Saarland Museum Saarbrücken, ed. by H.-G. Güse/A. Perrig, Munich/New York 1997

Exh.-cat. Schallaburg 1984
Barock und Klassik. Kunstzentren des 18. Jahrhunderts in der Deutschen Demokratischen Republik, Niederösterreichisches Landesmuseum Schallaburg, Vienna 1984

Exh.-cat. St. Marienstern 1998
Zeit und Ewigkeit. 128 Tage in St. Marienstern. Erste Sächsische Landesausstellung, Kloster St. Marienstern, ed. by J. Oexle et al., Halle 1998

Exh.-cat. Stockholm 1979
1700-tal. Tanke och form i rokokon, Nationalmuseet Stockholm, Stockholm 1979

Exh.-cat. Stockholm 1992
Riddarlek och Tornerspel. Sverige – Europe. Tournaments and the Dream of Chivalry. Sweden – Europe, Livrustkammaren Stockholm, Stockholm 1992

Exh.-cat. Venice 1994
Tintoretto. Ritratti, Gallerie dell'Accademia Venice, ed. by P. Rossi et al., Milan 1994

Exh.-cat. Versailles 1997
Louis de Silvestre – Un peintre français à la Cour de Dresde, Musée national des Châteaux de Versailles et de Trianon, Versailles 1997

Exh.-cat. Vienna 1978
Das Dresdner Kupferstich-Kabinett und die Albertina. Meisterzeichnungen aus zwei alten Sammlungen, Graphische Sammlung Albertina Vienna, Vienna 1978

Exh.-cat. Vienna 2002
Die Kunst des Steinschnitts. Prunkgefäße, Kameen und Commessi aus der Kunstkammer, Kunsthistorisches Museum Vienna, ed. by R. Distelberger, Milan 2002

Exh.-cat. Vienna/Essen 2002
Das flämische Stilleben, Palais Harrach Vienna/Villa Hügel Essen, Lingen/Vienna 2002

Exh.-cat. Warsaw 1997a
Pod jedna korona. Kultura i stuka w czasach unij polsko-saskiej, an exh. of the State Art Collections Dresden, Zamek Królewski w Warszawie, Warsaw 1997

Exh.-cat. Warsaw 1997b
Pod jedna korona. Królewski Zbiory Sztuki w Dreznie, an exh. of the State Art Collections Dresden, Muzeum Narodowe w Warszawie, Warsaw 1997

Exh.-cat. Washington/New York/San Francisco 1978/79
The Splendor of Dresden. Five Centuries of Art Collecting, National Gallery of Art Washington/The Metropolitan Museum of Art New York/The Fine Arts Museums of San Francisco, New Haven 1978/79

Ferrari/Scavizzi 1966
O. Ferrari/G. Scavizzi: Luca Giordano, 3 vols., Naples 1966

Feuchtmayr/Schädler 1973
K. Feuchtmayr/A. Schädler (eds.): Georg Petel 1601/02–1634, Berlin 1973

Friedländer/Rosenberg 1989
M. J. Friedländer/J. Rosenberg: Die Gemälde von Lucas Cranach, 2nd ed., Stuttgart 1989

Gemäldegalerie Dresden 1992
Gemäldegalerie Dresden. Alte Meister. Katalog der ausgestellten Werke, Dresden 1992

Giampaolo 1990
M. di Giampaolo: Correggio. Die Zeichnungen, Basel 1990

Giermann 1993
R. Giermann: Die Moritzburger Geweihsammlung, Dresden 1993

Giermann 2000
R. Giermann: Sehnsucht nach Arkadien. Die Monumentalmalereien Augusts des Starken im Schloss Moritzburg, Dresden 2000

Giermann 2003
R. Giermann: "Mehr zum Staat als zum Gebrauche". Das Federzimmer im Schloss Moritzburg, Dresden 2003

Goldberg et al. 1998
G. Goldberg/B. Heimberg/M. Schawe: Albrecht

Dürer. Die Gemälde der Alten Pinakothek, Heidelberg 1998

Graesse 1876/77
T. Graesse: Das Grüne Gewölbe zu Dresden, Berlin 1876/77

Gramaccini/Meier 2003
N. Gamaccini/H. J. Meier: Die Kunst der Interpretation. Französische Reproduktionsgraphik 1648–1792, Munich/Berlin 2003

Graf 2002
H. Graf: "… umb Ihro Majestät Zeit zu geben, sich stöllen zu khönnen" – Das europäische Hofzeremoniell des 17. und 18. Jahrhunderts exemplarisch dargestellt am Münchner Hof, in: Pracht und Zeremoniell – Die Möbel der Residenz München, exh.-cat., ed. by the Bayerische Verwaltung der Staatlichen Schlösser, Gärten und Seen, Munich 2002

Greindl 1956
E. Greindl: Les peintres flamands de nature morte au XVIIe siècle, Brussels 1956

Gröger 1956
H. Gröger: Johann Joachim Kaendler – Der Meister des Porzellans, Dresden 1956

Groß 2001
R. Groß: Geschichte Sachsens, Leipzig 2001

Grund 1992
R. Grund: Die Kunstlerfamilie Hoeckner, in: Jahrbuch der Staatlichen Kunstsammlungen Dresden 23 (1992), pp. 55–81

Grund 1996
R. Grund: Die Entwicklung der Medaillenkunst an der Münzstätte Dresden im 17. Jahrhundert, Gütersloh 1996

Grund 2001
R. Grund: Geschichte und Kultur Sachsens im Spiegel der Medaillenkunst vom Barock bis zum Klassizismus, in: Arbeits- und Forschungsberichte zur sächsischen Bodendenkmalpflege 43 (2001), pp. 193–211

Günther et al. 1998
R. Günther/M. Hänel/J. Puls et al.: Der Plauensche Grund. Das Saturnfest 1719, vol. 2, Städtische Sammlungen Freital (1998)

Haase 1983
G. Haase: Dresdener Möbel des 18. Jahrhunderts, Leipzig/Rosenheim 1983

Hadeln 1922
D. Freiherr von Hadeln: Zeichnungen des Giacomo Tintoretto, Berlin 1922

Haenel 1905
E. Haenel: Die Hessen-Casseler Müllerbüchsen und ihre Meister, in: Beiträge zur Geschichte der Handfeuerwaffen 1905 (Festschrift Thierbach), pp. 128–151

Haenel 1923
E. Haenel: Kostbare Waffen aus der Dresdner Rüstkammer, Leipzig 1923

Haenel/Watzdorf 1933
E. Haenel (ed.)/Erna von Watzdorf: August der Starke. Kunst und Kultur des Barock, Dresden 1933

Hartmann 1990
H.-G. Hartmann: Moritzburg. Schloss und Umgebung in Geschichte und Gegenwart, 2nd ed., Weimar 1990

Hase 1826
H. Hase: Verzeichnis der alten und neuen Bildwerke in Marmor und Bronze in den Sälen der Kgl. Antikensammlung zu Dresden, Dresden 1826

Haake 1927
P. Haake: August der Starke, Berlin/Leipzig 1927

Hairs 1985
M. L. Hairs: Les peintres flamands de fleurs au XVIIe siècle, 2 vols., Paris/Brussels 1985

Haupt 1978
W. Haupt: Sächsische Münzkunde, Berlin 1978

Haverkamp-Begemann 1973
E. Haverkamp-Begemann: Hercules Seghers. The Complete Etchings, The Hague 1973

Heckmann 1996
H. Heckmann: Baumeister des Barock und Rokoko in Sachsen, Berlin 1996

Heer 1979
E. Heer: Der Neue Stoeckel, vol. 2, Schwäbisch Hall 1979

Heineken 1753/57
C. H. von Heineken: Recueil d'estampes d'après les plus célèbres tableaux de la Galerie Royale de Dresde, Dresden 1753 (vol. 1), 1757 (vol. 2)

Hentschel 1973
W. Hentschel: Denkmale sächsischer Kunst. Die Verluste des Zweiten Weltkrieges, Berlin 1973

Heres 1980 (1983)
G. Heres: Der Zwinger als Museum, in: Jahrbuch der Staatlichen Kunstsammlungen Dresden 12 (1980 (1983)), pp. 119–133

Heres 1983
G. Heres: Zur Entstehungsgeschichte von Leplats Tafelwerk "Recueil des marbres antiques", in: Dresdner Kunstblätter 2/1983, pp. 39–42

Heres 1991
G. Heres: Dresdener Kunstsammlungen im 18. Jahrhundert, Leipzig 1991

Hermkes 1955
W. Hermkes: Das Reichsvikariat in Deutschland. Studien und Quellen zur Geschichte des deutschen Verfassungsrechtes, Karlsruhe 1955

Hernmarck 1978
C. Hernmarck: Die Kunst der europäischen Gold- und Silberschmiede von 1450 bis 1830, Munich 1978

Herrmann 1925
P. Herrmann: Verzeichnis der antiken Originalbildwerke der Staatlichen Skulpturensammlung zu Dresden, 2nd ed., Dresden 1925

Hettner 1881
H. Hettner: Die Bildwerke der Königlichen Antikensammlung zu Dresden, 4th ed., Dresden 1881

Hilbert 1998
K. Hilbert: Blankwaffen aus drei Jahrhunderten. Zeugnisse sächsischer Waffengeschichte, Berlin 1998

Hoff 1969
A. Hoff: Feuerwaffen, vol. 2, Brunswick 1969

Hoffmann 1982
K. Hoffmann: Johann Friedrich Böttger – Stationen seines Lebens, in: Sonnemann/Wächtler 1982, pp. 71–98

Hoffmeister 1999
D. Hoffmeister: Meissener Porzellan des 18. Jahrhunderts. Katalog der Sammlung Hoffmeister, 2 vols., Hamburg 1999

Holzhausen 1927
W. Holzhausen: Lage und Rekonstruktion der kurfürstlichen Kunstkammer im Schloß zu Dresden, in: Repertorium für Kunstwissenschaft 48 (1927), pp. 140–147

Holzhausen 1933
W. Holzhausen: Die Bronzen der kurfürstlich sächsischen Kunstkammer zu Dresden, in: Jahrbuch der Preußischen Kunstsammlungen 54 (1933), pp. 45–88

Holzhausen 1939
W. Holzhausen: Die Bronzen Augusts des Starken in Dresden, in: Jahrbuch der Preußischen Kunstsammlungen 60 (1939), pp. 157–186

Holzhausen 1966
W. Holzhausen: Prachtgefäße, Geschmeide, Kabinettstücke. Goldschmiedekunst in Dresden, Tübingen 1966

Hoos 1981
H. Hoos: Augsbürger Silbermöbel, 2 vols., PhD thesis, Johann Wolfgang Goethe-Universität Frankfurt a. M. 1981

Iccander 1735
Iccander (J. C. Crell): Kurzgefasstes Sächsisches Kern-Chronicon, vol. 3, Leipzig 1735

Impey 2002
O. Impey: Japanese Export Porcelain. Catalogue of the Collection of the Ashmolean Museum Oxford, Oxford 2002

Íñiguez 1981
D. A. Íñiguez: Murillo. Su vida, su arte, su obra, Madrid 1981

Jacoby 2000
J. Jacoby: Hans von Aachen 1552–1615, Munich/Berlin 2000

Jöchner 1997
C. Jöchner: Dresden, 1719: Planetenfeste, kulturelles Gedächtnis und die Öffnung der Stadt, in: Kunst als ästhetisches Ereignis. Marburger Jahrbuch für Kunstwissenschaft 24 (1997), pp. 249–270

Jöchner 2001
C. Jöchner: Die "schöne Ordnung" und der Hof. Geometrische Gartenkunst in Dresden und anderen deutschen Residenzen, Weimar 2001

Jörg 2003
C. J. A. Jörg: Fine & Curious. Japanese Export Porcelain in Dutch Collections, Amsterdam 2003

Just 1971
J. Just: Marken und Markierungen auf Meissner Porzellan ab 1775, in: Keramos 51 (1971), pp. 22–26, 113f. (supplement)

Justi 1888
C. Justi: Diego Velázquez und sein Jahrhundert, Bonn 1888

Kane et al. 1990
R. E. Kane/S. F. McClure/J. Menzhausen: The Legendary Dresden Green Diamond, in: Gems & Gemology, vol. 26, no. 4 (1990), pp. 248–266

Kappel 2003
J. Kappel: "(…) den König in Polen zu Pferde, von dem berühmten Krüger aus Danzig (…)", in: Patrimonia 207 (2003), ed. by Kulturstiftung der Länder (Berlin) in cooperation with Schlossmuseum Gotha, pp. 7–18

Kerssenbrock-Krosigk 2001
D. von Kerssenbrock-Krosigk: Rubinglas des ausgehenden 17. und 18. Jahrhunderts, Mainz 2001

Klidis 2001
A. Klidis: François Girardon. Bildhauer in königlichen Diensten 1663–1700, Weimar 2001

Knoll 1998
K. Knoll: Alltag und Mythos. Griechische Gefäße der Skulpturensammlung, Leipzig 1998

Knoll et al. 1993
K. Knoll/H. Protzmann/I. Raumschüssel/M. Raumschüssel: Die Antiken im Albertinum. Staatliche Kunstsammlungen Dresden. Skulpturensammlung, Mainz 1993

Koreny 1985
F. Koreny: Albrecht Dürer und die Tier- und Pflanzenstudien der Renaissance. Buch zur 306. Ausstellung der Graphischen Sammlung Albertina, Munich 1985

Kowalczyk 2001
B. A. Kowalczyk: Canaletto. Prima Maniera, Venice 2001

Kozakiewicz 1972
S. Kozakiewicz: Bernardo Bellotto, 2 vols., Recklinghausen 1972

Kraus 1949
M. Kraus: The Atlantic Civilization. Eighteenth-Century Origins, Ithaca, NY 1949

Kreisel 1970
H. Kreisel: Die Kunst des deutschen Möbels. Spätbarock und Rokoko, vol. II, Munich 1970

Kren 1980
T. J. Kren: Jan Miel (1599–1664). A Flemish Painter in Rome, 3 vols., Ann Arbor 1980

Larsen 1988
E. Larsen: The Paintings of Anthony van Dyck, vol. 2, Freren 1988

Lenk 1973
T. Lenk: Steinschloßfeuerwaffen, 2 vols., Hamburg/Berlin 1973

Leplat 1733
R. Leplat: Recueil des marbres antiques qui se trouvent dans la Galerie du Roy de Pologne à Dresden, Dresden 1733

Lewerken 1989
H.-W. Lewerken: Kombinationswaffen des 15.–19. Jahrhunderts, Berlin 1989

Lewerken 1997
H.-W. Lewerken: Królewska Galeria Broni w Dreźnie, in: Exh.-cat. Warsaw 1997b, pp. 213–215

Lezzi-Hafter 1976
A. Lezzi-Hafter: Der Schuwalow-Maler. Eine Kannenwerkstatt der Parthenonzeit, 2 vols., Mainz 1976

Lipsius 1798
J. G. Lipsius: Beschreibung der Churfürstlichen Antiken-Galerie in Dresden […], Dresden 1798

Liss 1983
P. Liss: Atlantic Empires. The Network of Trade and Revolution, 1713–1826, Baltimore, MD 1983

List 1938
C. List: Kleinbronzen Europas vom Mittelalter bis zur Gegenwart, Munich 1983

Loen 1726
J. M. von Loen: Sylvanders von Edel-Leben Zufällige Betrachtungen. Von der Glückseeligkeit der Tugend […] Darin: Discurs Von der Bau-Kunst, Bey Gelegenheit des Königlichen Oranien-Gartens zu Dreßden/ Auffgesetzt, Und Sr. Königl. Majestät von Pohlen dedicirt, Frankfurt a. M. 1726

Löffler 1981
F. Löffler: Das alte Dresden. Geschichte seiner Bauten, 6th ed., Leipzig 1981

López-Rey 1996
J. López-Rey: Velázquez. Catalogue Raisonné, Cologne 1996

Lowenthal 1997
A. W. Lowenthal: The Golden Age by Joachim Wtewael at The Metropolitan Museum of Art, in: Apollo, vol. CXLV, no. 420 (1997), pp. 49–52

Mahoney 1962
M. Mahoney: Some Graphic Link between the Young Albani and Annibale Carracci, in: The Burlington Magazine 1041 (1962), pp. 386–389

Mancigotti 1975
M. Mancigotti: Simone Cantarini, il Pesarese, Pesaro 1975

Marx 1975
H. Marx: Louis de Silvestre. Die Gemälde der Dresdner Gemäldegalerie, Dresden 1975

Marx 1976/77
H. Marx: Johann Samuel Mock und das "Campement bei Czerniaków" 1732, in: Jahrbuch der Staatlichen Kunstsammlungen Dresden 1976/77 (1978), pp. 53–87

Marx 1999
H. Marx: The Dresden Gemäldegalerie as Ecole

Marx 2000a
H. Marx: Das Entstehen der Sammlung spanischer Gemälde in der Dresdener Galerie, in: C. Rodieck (ed.), Dresden und Spanien. Akten des interdisziplinären Kolloquiums Dresden 1998, Frankfurt a. M. 2000, pp. 67–84

Marx 2000b
H. Marx: Staatspropaganda und Liebeswerben. Die Gemälde im Trohnsaal Augusts des Starken im Dresdner Residenzschloß, in: G. Lupfer/K. Rudert/P. Sigel (eds.), Bau/Kunst – Kunst/Bau. Festschrift zum 65. Geburtstag von Professor Jürgen Paul, Dresden 2000, pp. 192–211

Menzhausen 1982a
I. Menzhausen: Das rothe und das weisse Porcellain, in: Sonnemann/Wächtler 1982, pp. 143–315

Menzhausen 1982b
I. Menzhausen (ed.): Johann Melchior Steinbrück: Bericht über die Porzellanmanufaktur Meissen von den Anfängen bis zum Jahre 1717. Vol. 2: Kommentar, Transkription und Glossar zum Faksimile, Leipzig 1982

Menzhausen 1985
I. Menzhausen: Kurfürst Augusts Kunstkammer. Eine Analyse des Inventars von 1587, in: Jahrbuch der Staatlichen Kunstsammlungen Dresden 17 (1985), pp. 21–29

Menzhausen 1988
I. Menzhausen: Alt-Meißner Porzellan in Dresden, Berlin 1988

Meyer 1883
A. B. Meyer (ed.): Die Hirschgeweih-Sammlung im königlichen Schlosse zu Moritzburg bei Dresden, Dresden 1883

Miedtank 1991
L. Miedtank: Zwiebelmuster. Zur 300jährigen Geschichte des Dekors auf Porzellan, Fayence und Steingut, Leipzig 1991

Mielke 1996
H. Mielke: Pieter Bruegel. Die Zeichnungen, Turnhout 1996

Mikosch 1998
E. Mikosch: Court Dress and Ceremony in the Baroque Age. The Royal/Imperial Wedding of 1719 in Dresden: A Case Study, PhD thesis, New York University 1998

Milde 1990
K. Milde (ed.): Matthäus Daniel Pöppelmann 1662–1736 und die Architektur der Zeit Augusts des Starken, Dresden 1990

Moltke 1965
J. W. von Moltke: Govaert Flinck 1615–1660, Amsterdam 1965

Montagu 1989
J. Montagu: Roman Baroque Sculpture. The Industry of Art, New Haven/London 1989

Morrogh 1992
A. Morrogh: The Medici Chapel. The Designs for the Central Tomb, in: C. H. Smyrn (ed.), Michelangelo Drawings (Studies in History of Art 33), Washington 1992, pp. 143–163

Müllenmeister 1981
K. Müllenmeister: Meer und Land im Licht des 17. Jahrhunderts, vol. III, Bremen 1981

Müller 1927
W. Müller: Aus der Dresdner Skulpturensammlung. Antoine Coysevox, in: Der Kunstwanderer 9 (1927), pp. 457–461

Münzberg 2002
E. Münzberg: Die Kurfürstlichen Gemächer im Stallgebäude Dresden – ihre Rekonstruktion und Rolle im europäischen Kontext, MA thesis, Technische Universität Dresden 2002

Nickel 1981
H. Nickel: Über die graphischen Vorlagen des "Mohren mit der Smaragdstufe im Grünen Gewölbe zu Dresden", in: Dresdener Kunstblätter 1/1981, pp. 10–19

Nickel 1983
H. Nickel: Über einige Inventionsstücke zum Großen Aufzuge des Caroussell-Rennens der Vier Weltteile zu Dresden im Jahre 1709, in: Waffen- und Kostümkunde 25 (1983), pp. 81–94

Nicolson 1958
B. Nicolson: Hendrick Terbrugghen, The Hague 1958

Nicolson 1979
B. Nicolson: Caravaggism in Europe, 3 vols., Oxford 1979

Nollain 1835
F. Nollain: Die Königliche Gewehr-Gallerie in Dresden, Dresden 1835

Ô Byrn 1880
(F. A.) Ô Byrn: Die Hof-Silverkammer und die Hof-Kellerei zu Dresden, Dresden 1880

Oelsner/Prinz 1992
N. Oelsner/H. Prinz: Die Residenz Augusts des Starken, in: Das Dresdner Schloss. Monument sächsischer Geschichte und Kultur, ed. by the State Art Collections Dresden, Dresden 1992, pp. 96–108

Palmer 1959
R. R. Palmer: The Age of the Democratic Revolution. A Political History of Europe and America, 1760–1800, Princeton, NJ 1959

Pepper 1984
D. S. Pepper: Guido Reni, Oxford 1984

Pepper 1988
D. S. Pepper: Guido Reni, Novara 1988

Pérez Sánchez/Spinosa 1978
A. E. Pérez Sánchez/N. Spinosa: L'opera completa del Ribera, Milan 1978

Petropoulos 1999
J. Petropoulos: Kunstraub und Sammelwahn. Kunst und Politik im Dritten Reich, Berlin 1999

Petzet 2000
M. Petzet: Claude Perrault und die Architektur des Sonnenkönigs, Munich/Berlin 2000

Pfuhl 1923
E. Pfuhl: Malerei und Zeichnung der Griechen, vol. I, Munich 1923

Pietsch 1996
U. Pietsch: Meissener Porzellan und seine ostasiatischen Vorbilder, Leipzig 1996

Pietsch 1998
U. Pietsch: Porzellansammlung Dresden. Führer durch die ständige Ausstellung im Zwinger, Meissen 1998

Pignatti 1976
T. Pignatti: Veronese, 2 vols., Venice 1976

Pisareva 2003
V. Pisareva: Spätbarocke Wandbekleidungen am Dresdener Hof, in: Dresdener Kunstblätter 2/2003, pp. 92–100

Popham 1975
A. E. Popham: Correggio's Drawings, London 1975

Popp 1927
A. E. Popp: Unbeachtete Projekte Michelangelos, in: Münchner Jahrbuch der Bildenden Kunst 4 (1927), pp. 389–451

Posse 1929
H. Posse: Die Staatliche Gemäldegalerie zu Dresden. Vollständiges beschreibendes Verzeichnis der älteren Gemälde. Erste Abteilung: Die romanischen Länder, Dresden/Berlin 1929

Posse 1930
H. Posse: Katalog der Staatlichen Gemäldegalerie zu Dresden, Dresden 1930

Posse 1931
H. Posse: Die Briefe des Grafen Francesco Algarotti an den sächsischen Hof und seine Bilderkäufe für die Dresdener Gemäldegalerie 1743–1747, in: Jahrbuch der Preußischen Kunstsammlungen 52 (1931), pp. 1–37

Quandt 1834
Quandt: Andeutungen für Beschauer des historischen Museums, Dresden 1834

Reeckmann 2000
K. Reeckmann: Anfänge der Barockarchitektur in Sachsen, Cologne/Weimar/Vienna 2000

Reibisch (no year)
F. M. Reibisch: Eine Auswahl merkwürdiger Gegenstände aus der Königl. Sächsischen Rüstkammer, Dresden

Reichel 1980
F. Reichel: Altjapanisches Porzellan. Arita Porzellan in der Dresdner Sammlung, Leipzig 1980

Reznicek 1980
E. K. J. Reznicek: Jan Harmensz Muller as Draughtsman. Addenda, in: Master Drawings 18 (1980), pp. 115–141

Riccoboni 1952
A. Riccoboni: Sculture inedite di Antonio Corradini, in: Arte Veneta 21–24 (1952), pp. 151–161

Richter-Nickel 2002
S. Richter-Nickel: Aufstieg zur Residenzstadt von europäischem Rang (1648–1763), in: Dresdner Geschichtsverein (ed.), Dresden. Die Geschichte der Stadt. Von den Anfängen bis zur Gegenwart, Dresden 2002, pp. 57–100

Rizzi 1996
A. Rizzi: Bernardo Bellotto, Venice 1996

Robels 1967
H. Robels: Katalog ausgewählter Handzeichnungen und Aquarelle. Wallraf-Richartz-Museum, Cologne 1967

Rohr 1733
J. B. von Rohr: Einleitung zur Ceremoniel-Wissenschaft der grossen Herren, reprinted with an epilogue and comments by M. Schlechte, Leipzig 1990

Rosenberg 1922–28
M. Rosenberg: Der Goldschmiede Merkzeichen, 3rd, enlarged and illustrated ed., 4 vols., Frankfurt a. M. 1922–28

Rosenberg 1960
J. Rosenberg: Die Zeichnungen Lucas Cranachs d. Ä., Berlin 1960

Rossi 1973
P. Rossi: Jacopo Tintoretto. I Ritratti, Venice 1973

Safarik 1976
E. A. Safarik: Johann Anton Eismann, in: Saggi e memorie di storia dell'arte 10 (1976), pp. 63–78

Savelle 1948
M. Savelle: Seeds of Liberty. The Genesis of the American Mind, New York 1948

Saxonia 1995
Saxonia 1: August der Starke und seine Zeit, ed. by the Verein für Sächsische Landesgeschichte, Dresden 1995

Saxonia 1998
Saxonia 4/5: Sachsen und Polen zwischen 1697 und 1765, ed. by the Verein für sächsische Landesgeschichte, Dresden 1998

Schaal 1975a
D. Schaal: Katalog Dresdner Büchsenmacher 16.–18. Jahrhundert, Dresden 1975

Schaal 1975b
D. Schaal: Jagdgewehre. Historisches Museum Dresden, Dresden 1975

Schaal 1979
D. Schaal: Katalog Suhler Feuerwaffen 17.–18. Jahrhundert, Dresden 1979

Schaal 1986
D. Schaal: Die Gewehrgalerie, in: Exh.-cat. Essen 1986, pp. 260–262

Schaal 1996
D. Schaal: Französische Jagdwaffen am Dresdner Hof, in: Sigrun Paas (ed.), Liselotte von der Pfalz. Madame am Hofe des Sonnenkönigs, exh.-cat., Heidelberger Schloss, Heidelberg 1996, pp. 215–218

Schlechte 1984
M. Schlechte: Das barocke Architektur- und Landschaftsensemble Moritzburg. Die Umgestaltungsphase in der Regierungszeit Augusts des Starken, PhD thesis, Technische Universität Dresden 1984

Schlechte 1990a
M. Schlechte: Kunst der Repräsentation – repräsentative Kunst (Zeremoniell und Fest am Beispiel von Julius Bernhard von Rohrs "Einleitung zur Ceremoniel-Wissenschafft" und der Festlichkeiten am Dresdner Hof im Jahre 1719), 3 vols., PhD thesis, Technische Universität Dresden 1990

Schlechte 1990b
M. Schlechte: Das Saturnfest 1719, in: M. Bachmann/H. Marx/E. Wächtler (eds.): Der silberne Boden. Kunst und Bergbau in Sachsen, Leipzig 1990, pp. 219–229

Schlechte 1990c
M. Schlechte: Die Dresdner Planetenfeste. Zur Ikonographie einer königlichen Tafel im Jahr 1719, in: Kunst und Antiquitäten 60 (1990) 9, pp. 56–61

Schlechte 1993
M. Schlechte: Recueil des Dessins et Gravures representent les Solemnites du Mariages. Das Dresdner Fest von 1719 im Bild, in: P. Béhar (ed.): Image et Spectacle. Actes du XXXIIe Colloque International d'Etudes Humanistes du Centre d'Etudes Supérieures de la Renaissance, Amsterdam/Atlanta 1993, pp. 117–169

Schliemann 1985
E. Schliemann (ed.): Die Goldschmiede Hamburgs, Hamburg 1985

Schnee 1982
G. Schnee: Sächsische Taler 1500–1800 und Abschläge von Talerstempeln in Gold und Silber (Dukaten, Mehrfach-Taler, Halbtaler), Frankfurt a. M. 1982

Schnitzer 1998
C. Schnitzer: "Ritterhafte Damen". Höfische Frauenturniere der Frühen Neuzeit, in: G. Frohnhaus/B. Grotkamp-Schepers/R. Philipp (eds.): Schwert in Frauenhand. Weibliche Bewaffnung, Essen 1998, pp. 54–67

Schöbel 1973
J. Schöbel: Prunkwaffen. Waffen und Rüstungen aus dem Historischen Museum Dresden, Leipzig 1973

Schöbel 1976
J. Schöbel: Jagdwaffen und Jagdgerät des Historischen Museums zu Dresden, Dresden 1976

Schoen 2001
C. Schoen: Albrecht Dürer. Adam und Eva. Die Gemälde, ihre Geschichte und Rezeption bei Lucas Cranach d. Ä. und Hans Baldung Grien, Berlin 2001

Schröder 1935
A. Schröder: Leipziger Goldschmiede aus fünf Jahrhunderten (1350–1850), Leipzig 1935

Schuchardt 1851
C. Schuchardt: Lucas Cranach des Älteren Leben und Werke, Leipzig 1851

Schuckelt 2002
H. Schuckelt: Der Augsburger Plattner Anton Peffenhauser. Kunstwerk des Monats in der Dresdener Rüstkammer, in: Dresdener Kunstblätter 3/2002, pp. 108–113

Schuler 1956
H. Schuler: Die Münzen und Medaillen der Birkenfelder Linie des Hauses Wittelsbach vor Erlangung der Königswürde, in: J. Dahl/K. Lohmeyer (eds.), Das barocke Zweibrücken, Waldfischbach 1956, pp. 645–732

Schulze 1997
A. Schulze: Die Ledertapeten im Schloß Moritzburg, in: Landesamt für Denkmalpflege Sachsen (Hrsg.), Denkmalpflege in Sachsen 1894–1994, pt. 1, Weimar 1997, pp. 229–240

Schumacher 1989
B. Schumacher: Studien zu Werk und Wirkung Philips Wouwermans, Munich 1989

Schwarm-Tomisch 2002
E. Schwarm-Tomisch: "… wo hohe Potentaten ihr Plaisier finden können …" – Das Königlich Holländische Palais zu Altdresden bis zu seinem Umbau im Jahr 1727, in: Dresdener Kunstblätter 2/2002, pp. 56–66

Seelig 1977
L. Seelig: Das Bildnis in der Barockskulptur Norddeutschlands, in: Barockplastik in Norddeutschland, exh.-cat., Museum für Kunst und Gewerbe Hamburg, Mainz 1977, pp. 63–91

Seling 1980
H. Seling: Die Kunst der Augsburger Goldschmiede 1529–1868, vol. III, Munich 1980

Seling 1994
H. Seling: Die Kunst der Augsburger Goldschmiede 1529–1868, supplement to vol. III, Munich 1994

Seydewitz/Seydewitz 1957
R. Seydewitz/M. Seydewitz: Das Dresdner Galeriebuch. 400 Jahre Dresdener Gemäldegalerie, Dresden 1957

Slive 2001
S. Slive: Jacob van Ruisdael. A Complete Catalogue of his Paintings, Drawings and Etchings, New Haven/London 2001

Sonnemann/Wächtler 1982
R. Sonnemann/E. Wächtler (eds.): Johann Friedrich Böttger. Die Erfindung des europäischen Porzellans, Leipzig 1982

Souchal 1977
F. Souchal: French Sculptors of the 17th and 18th Centuries. The Reign of Louis XIV. Illustrated Catalogue, vol. 1, Oxford 1977

Souchal 1981
F. Souchal: French Sculptors of the 17th and 18th Centuries. The Reign of Louis XIV. Illustrated Catalogue, vol. 2, London 1981

Spear 1997
R. E. Spear: The "Divine" Guido. Religion, Sex, Money and Art in the World of Guido Reni, New Haven/London 1997

Sponsel 1900
J. L. Sponsel: Kabinettstücke der Meissener Porzellan-Manufaktur von Johann Joachim Kaendler, Leipzig 1900

Sponsel 1906
J. L. Sponsel: Fürstenbildnisse aus dem Haus Wettin, Dresden 1906

Sponsel 1925
J. L. Sponsel: Das Grüne Gewölbe zu Dresden, vol. I, Leipzig 1925

Sponsel 1928
J. L. Sponsel: Das Grüne Gewölbe zu Dresden, vol. II, Leipzig 1928

Sponsel/Haenel 1932
J. L. Sponsel/E. Haenel: Das Grüne Gewölbe zu Dresden, vol. IV, Leipzig 1932

Staszewski 1996
J. Staszewski: August der III. Kurfürst von Sachsen und König von Polen, Berlin 1996

Ströber 2002
E. Ströber: Porcelain and Laquer – Oriental Blue and White Porcelain with Laquer Decoration in the Dresden Collection, in: Transactions of the Oriental Ceramic Society 65 (2000–01), London 2002, pp. 159–166

Sumowski 1983
W. Sumowski: Gemälde der Rembrandt-Schüler, vol. I, Landau, Pfalz 1983

Syndram 1997
D. Syndram (ed.): Das Grüne Gewölbe zu Dresden. Führer durch seine Geschichte und seine Sammlungen, 2nd ed., Munich/Berlin 1997

Syndram 1999
D. Syndram: Die Schatzkammer Augusts des Starken. Von der Pretiosensammlung zum Grünen Gewölbe, Leipzig 1999

Tietze 1948
H. Tietze: Tintoretto. Gemälde und Zeichnungen, London 1948

Tillander 1991
H. Tillander: Der Diamant. Mythos, Magie und Wirklichkeit, Erlangen 1991

Toledano 1987
R. Toledano: Francesco de Giorgio Martini. Pittore e scultore, Milan 1987

Tolnay 1975–80
C. de Tolnay: Corpus dei disegni di Michelangelo, 4 vols., Novara 1975–80

Trommler/McVeigh 1985
F. Trommler/J. McVeigh (eds.): America and the Germans. An Assessment of a Three-Hundred-Year History, vol. I, Philadelphia, PA 1985

Van de Velde 1975
C. van de Velde: Frans Floris (1519–1570). Leven en Werken, Brussels 1975

Van Regteren Altena 1983
J. Q. van Regteren Altena: Jacques de Gheyn. Three Generations, 3 vols., The Hague/Boston/London 1983

Voss 1924
H. Voss: Die Malerei des Barock in Rom, Berlin 1924

Voss 1928
H. Voss: Die Malerei der Spätrenaissance in Florenz und Rom, vol. II, Berlin 1928

Vötsch 2002
J. Vötsch: Kaiser, Reich und Religion im Spiegel des Kunstkammerinventars von 1595, in: Dresdener Kunstblätter 6/2002, pp. 208–214

Walcha 1973
O. Walcha: Meißner Porzellan, Dresden 1973

Walther 1992
A. Walther (ed.): Gemäldegalerie Dresden. Alte Meister. Katalog der ausgestellten Werke, Dresden 1992

Ward 1982
R. B. Ward: Baccio Bandinelli as a Draughtsman, PhD thesis, University of London 1982

Watanabe-O'Kelly 1992
H. Watanabe-O'Kelly: Triumphall Shews. Tournaments at German-speaking Courts in their European Context 1560–1730, Berlin 1992

Watanabe-O'Kelly 2002
H. Watanabe-O'Kelly: Court Culture in Dresden. From Renaissance to Baroque, Basingstoke/New York 2002

Watzdorf 1962
E. von Watzdorf: Johann Melchior Dinglinger. Der Goldschmied des deutschen Barock, vol. I, Berlin 1962

Wazbinski 2000
Z. Wazbinski: Marcello Bacciarelli e il suo contributo alle collezioni reali di Dresda e di Varsavia, in: M. Seidel (ed.), L'Europa e l'arte italiana, Venice 2000, pp. 479–497

Weber 1985
S. Weber: Planetenfeste August des Starken. Zur Hochzeit des Kronprinzen 1719, Munich 1985

Weber 1999
G. J. M. Weber: The Gallery as Work of Art. The Installation of the Italian Paintings in 1754, in: Exh.-cat. Columbus 1999, pp. 183–197

Weck 1680
A. Weck: Der Chur-Fürstlichen Sächsischen weitberuffenen Residentz- und Haupt-Vestung Dresden Beschreibung und Vorstellung, Nuremberg 1680

Weigert 1932
R.-A. Weigert: Documents inédits sur Louis de Silvestre, suivis du catalogue de son oeuvre (Archives de l'art français, new series 17), Paris 1932

Weinholz 1967
G. Weinholz: Zu Bergkristallarbeiten von Giovanni Battista Metellino, in: Jahrbuch der Staatlichen Kunstsammlungen Dresden 6 (1967), pp. 131–138

Wegner 1939
M. Wegner: Die Herrscherbildnisse in antoninischer Zeit, Berlin 1939

Weniger 2002
M. Weniger: Die spanischen Gemälde, in: Exh.-cat. Berlin 2002, pp. 246–279

Wenley 2002
R. Wenley: French Bronzes in the Wallace Collection, London 2002

Wethey 1971
H. E. Wethey: The Paintings of Titian. Complete Edition. II. The Portraits, London 1971

Więcek 1989
A. Więcek: Dzieje sztuki medalierskiej w Polsce, Cracow 1989

Winkler 1936
F. Winkler: Die Zeichnungen Albrecht Dürers, vol. 4, Berlin 1936

Winkler 1942
F. Winkler: Die Zeichnungen Hans Süß von Kulmbachs und Hans Leonhard Schäufeleins, Berlin 1942

Winkler 1989
J. Winkler (ed.): Der Verkauf an Dresden. Dresden und Modena, aus der Geschichte zweier Galerien, Modena 1989

Winzinger 1979
F. Winzinger: Wolf Huber. Das Gesamtwerk, 2 vols., Munich/Zurich 1979

Woermann 1896–98
K. Woermann (ed.): Handzeichnungen alter Meister im königlichen Kupferstichkabinett zu Dresden, 10 portfolios, Munich 1896–98

Wohlfahrt 1992
C. Wohlfahrt: Christian Wermuth, ein deutscher Medailleur der Barockzeit, London 1992

Wozel 1979
H. Wozel: Turniere. Exponate aus dem Historischen Museum zu Dresden, Berlin 1979

Zanzotto 1996
F. Zanzotto: Per una storia del Gusto a Venezia tra sei e settecento, in: Saggi e memorie di storia dell'arte 20 (1996), pp. 279–313

Zimmer 1988
J. Zimmer: Joseph Heintz der Ältere. Zeichnungen und Dokumente, Munich/Berlin 1988

Zimmermann 1903
E. Zimmermann: Der Gold- und Silberklumpen Böttgers in der Königlichen Porzellansammlung, in: Dresdner Anzeiger, Sunday supplement, September 6, 1903

Zimmermann 1911
E. Zimmermann: Die Anfänge der Blaumalerei im Meissner Porzellan, in: Mitteilungen aus den Sächsischen Kunstsammlungen II (1911), pp. 72–81

Zimmermann 1926
E. Zimmermann: Meissner Porzellan, Leipzig 1926